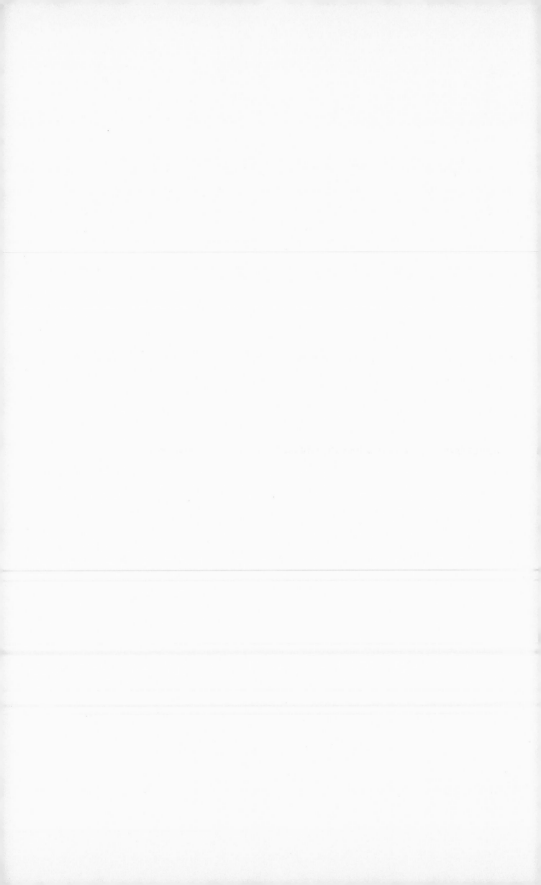

KARLSTADT AND THE ORIGINS OF THE EUCHARISTIC CONTROVERSY

TEACHING THE REFORMATION
Ministers and Their Message in Basel, 1529–1629
Amy Nelson Burnett

THE PASSIONS OF CHRIST IN HIGH-MEDIEVAL THOUGHT
An Essay on Christological Development
Kevin Madigan

GOD'S IRISHMEN
Theological Debates in Cromwellian Ireland
Crawford Gribben

REFORMING SAINTS
Saint's Lives and Their Authors in Germany, 1470–1530
David J. Collins

GREGORY OF NAZIANZUS ON THE TRINITY AND THE KNOWLEDGE OF GOD
In Your Light We Shall See Light
Christopher A. Beeley

THE JUDAIZING CALVIN
Sixteenth-Century Debates over the Messianic Psalms
G. Sujin Pak

THE DEATH OF SCRIPTURE AND THE RISE OF BIBLICAL STUDIES
Michael C. Legaspi

ARE YOU ALONE WISE?
Debates about Certainty in the Early Modern Church
Susan E. Schreiner

EMPIRE OF SOULS
Robert Bellarmine (1542–1621) and the Christian Commonwealth
Stefania Tutino

MARTIN BUCER'S DOCTRINE OF JUSTIFICATION
Reformation Theology and Early Modern Irenicism
Brian Lugioyo

CHRISTIAN GRACE AND PAGAN VIRTUE
The Theological Foundation of Ambrose's Ethics
J. Warren Smith

KARLSTADT AND THE ORIGINS OF THE EUCHARISTIC CONTROVERSY
A Study in the Circulation of Ideas
Amy Nelson Burnett

Karlstadt and the Origins of the Eucharistic Controversy

A STUDY IN THE CIRCULATION OF IDEAS

Amy Nelson Burnett

OXFORD UNIVERSITY PRESS

OXFORD
UNIVERSITY PRESS

Oxford University Press

Oxford University Press, Inc., publishes works that further
Oxford University's objective of excellence
in research, scholarship, and education.

Oxford   New York
Auckland   Cape Town   Dar es Salaam   Hong Kong   Karachi
Kuala Lumpur   Madrid   Melbourne   Mexico City   Nairobi
New Delhi   Shanghai   Taipei   Toronto

With offices in
Argentina   Austria   Brazil   Chile   Czech Republic   France   Greece
Guatemala   Hungary   Italy   Japan   Poland   Portugal   Singapore
South Korea   Switzerland   Thailand   Turkey   Ukraine   Vietnam

Published by Oxford University Press, Inc.
198 Madison Avenue, New York, New York 10016

www.oup.com

Oxford is a registered trademark of Oxford University Press

Library of Congress Cataloging-in-Publication Data
Burnett, Amy Nelson, 1957–
Karlstadt and the origins of the Eucharistic controversy : a study in the circulation
of ideas / Amy Nelson Burnett.
p.   cm.
Includes bibliographical references and index.
ISBN 978-0-19-975399-4
1. Lord's Supper—History of doctrines—16th century.   2. Karlstadt, Andreas Rudolff-Bodenstein von, ca.
1480–1541.   3. Luther, Martin, 1483–1546.   4. Reformation.   I. Title.
  BV825.3.B87 2011
  234.′163—dc22   2010012550

1 3 5 7 9 8 6 4 2

Printed in the United States of America
on acid-free paper

For Robert M. Kingdon, in grateful appreciation

Preface

THIS IS NOT the book I started out to write. I intended—and still hope—to write a more general account of the eucharistic controversy from its beginning through the signing of the Consensus Tigurinus in 1549. I thought that the period leading up to the outbreak of the controversy could easily be covered in one chapter, and I planned to devote only a few pages to Luther's conflict with Karlstadt.

Then I read Karlstadt's pamphlets on the Lord's Supper. I was surprised to discover the complexity of Karlstadt's eucharistic theology and intrigued by his ability to take ideas from a variety of sources and blend them into something that was both new and extremely controversial. The few pages I had originally planned to devote to Karlstadt grew to one chapter, then two, until I finally acknowledged the inevitable. If I, or anyone else, was to understand the controversy that broke out at the end of 1524, I would need to go into far more detail about the debate over the Eucharist in the early years of the Reformation, and Karlstadt would play a central role in the drama I was describing. Forty years ago, the English Reformation historian E. Gordon Rupp expressed the need for a monograph describing Karlstadt's contribution to the eucharistic controversy.[1] While this book is not devoted exclusively to Karlstadt, it supports Rupp's assertion that a full consideration of the Reformation debate over the Lord's Supper must take due account of Karlstadt's involvement in it.

The process of writing this book was made more enjoyable by the conversations I have had and the encouragement I have received from a number of sources. Fairly early on, Paul Rorem's suggestion that the time was ripe for a new book on Karlstadt confirmed what I had just begun to realize myself. Irene Dingel's invitation to speak to the Kulturwerkstatt at the Institut für Europäische Geschichte in Mainz enabled me to receive feedback on an early version of chapter 3 and to use the institute's resources for research on chapters 2 and 6. Chapter 2 benefited from the comments of the audience when I presented a shorter version of it at a meeting of the Sixteenth Century Society and Conference in Minneapolis. The opportunity to participate in a colloquium sponsored by the Institut für Schweizerische Reformationsgeschichte in Zurich also gave me the opportunity to spend a few precious days in libraries there and in Basel at a crucial time when I was doing the research for chapter 4. The finishing touches to the manuscript were applied in the stimulating intellectual environment of the Institute for Advanced Study in Princeton.

Even with the revolution in digital technology of the past decade, working on a project that requires access to pamphlets printed in the sixteenth century can still be a challenge for North Americans. Without the rapid and efficient help of the staff of Love Library's Interlibrary Loan Department, I would never have been able to write this book. I am indebted to the H. Henry Meeter Center for Calvin Studies at Calvin College in Grand Rapids, the Thrivent Reformation Research Library at Luther Seminary in Minneapolis, and the Folger Library in Washington, D.C., for access to their resources, whether through visits or Interlibrary Loan. Over the years I have made several trips to the Herzog August Bibliothek in Wolfenbüttel, where it is a genuine pleasure to work. A special thanks is due to John Thompson and to David Bundy and Nancy Gower of the David Allan Hubbard Library at Fuller Theological Seminary for helping me verify a citation as I was finishing the manuscript.

Closer to home, Steve Lahey has been a wonderful source of information on John Wyclif's eucharistic theology. Richard Muller has been tremendously supportive of this book since its inception, and Tim Wengert's input has been most helpful as I ventured away from the familiar ground of Switzerland and South Germany to look at developments in Wittenberg. As always, my husband, Steve, has been my constant discussion partner and critic, whether he was patiently listening to yet another monologue on eucharistic theology or reading the most recent draft of a chapter.

Last but certainly not least, I owe a great deal to my *Doktorvater*, Robert M. Kingdon. Throughout graduate school he provided me with the freedom to pursue my own intellectual interests while giving enough guidance to keep me focused on what was important. His direction so many years ago helped me develop the confidence necessary to begin research in an area that at least initially seemed quite distant from my earlier work. Bob has continued to take an active interest in my career, as he has for all of his former students. Too often we take such support for granted until it is too late to express our gratitude, and I am glad that I can dedicate this book to him as a small way of showing my thanks.

Epiphany, 2010

Contents

Abbreviations

Works by Andreas Karlstadt

Abuse   *Von dem widerchristlichen mißbrauch des hern brodt vnd kelch. Ob
            der glaub in das sacrament/sünde vergäbe/ vnd ob das sacrament
            eyn arrabo/oder pfand sey der sünde vergäbung. Außlegung deß xj.
            Capit. In der. j. Epistel Pauli zuo den Corinthiern von des hern
            abentmal.* Basel: Bebel, 1524.

Adoration   *Von anbettung und ererbietung der tzeychen des newen
            Testaments.* Wittenberg: Schirlentz, 1521.

Declaration *Erklerung wie Carlstat sein lere von dem hochwirdigen Sacrament
            vnd andere achtet vnd geacht haben wil.* Wittenberg: Rhau-
            Grunenberg, 1525.

Dialogue   *Dialogus oder ein gesprechbüchlin Von dem grewlichen vnnd
            abgöttischen mißbrauch/ des hochwirdigsten sacraments Jesu
            Christi.* Basel: Bebel, 1524.

Exegesis   *Auszlegung dieser wort Christi. Das ist meyn leyb/ welcher für
            euch gegeben würt. Das ist mein bluoth/ welches für euch vergossen
            würt. Luce am 22.* Basel: Bebel, 1524.

Explanation *Erklerung des x. Capitels Cor i. Das brot das wir brechen: Ist es nitt
            ein gemeinschaft des Leybs Christi.* Augsburg: Ulhart, 1525.

Forms	*Von beiden gestaldten der heylige Messze. Von Czeichen in gemein was sie wirken vnd dewten. Sie seind nit Behemen oder ketzer, die beide gestaldt nhemen sonder Ewangelische Christen.* Wittenberg: Shirlentz, 1521.
Masses	*Wider die alte vnd newe Papistische Messen.* Basel: Wolf, 1524.
Priesthood	*Von dem Priesterthum vnd opffer Christi.* Jena: Buchführer, 1523.
Prove	*Ob man mit heyliger schrifft erweysen müge/ das Christus mit leyb/ bluot vnd sele im Sacrament sey.* Basel: Wolff, 1524.
Recipients	*Von den Empfahern/ Zeychen/ vnd zusag des heyligenn Sacraments fleysch vnd bluts Christi.* Wittenberg: Schirlentz, 1521.
Sermon	*Predig zu Wittenberg von Empfahung des Hailigen Sacraments.* Wittenberg: Schirlentz, 1522.
Testament	*Von dem Newen vnd Alten Testament. Antwurt auff disen spruch: Der kelch das New Testament in meinem blut etc. Luce xxij. i. Corin. xj. . . . wie Carolstat widerrieft.* Augsburg: Ulhart, 1525.

Other Works

ABR	*Aktensammlung zur Geschichte der Basler Reformation in den Jahren 1519 bis Anfang 1534.* 6 vols. Edited by Emil Dürr and Paul Roth. Basel: Historische und antiquarische Gesellschaft, 1921–1950.
ASD	*Opera Omnia Desiderii Erasmi Roterodami.* Amsterdam: Elsevier, 1969–.
B&A	*Briefe und Akten zum Leben Oekolampads, zum vierhundertjährigen Jubiläum der Basler Reformation.* 2 vols. Edited by Ernst Staehelin. Quellen und Forschungen zur Reformationsgeschichte 10, 19. Leipzig: Heinsius, 1927–1934.
Barge, *Karlstadt*	Hermann Barge, *Andreas Bodenstein von Karlstadt.* 2 vols. Leipzig, 1905. Reprint, Niewkoop: de Graff, 1968.
BCorr	*Correspondance de Martin Bucer.* Martini Buceri Opera Omnia, Series III. Leiden: Brill, 1979–.
BDS	*Martin Bucers Deutsche Schriften.* Martini Buceri Opera Omnia, Series I. Edited by Robert Stupperich et al. Gütersloh 1960–.
BOL	*Martini Buceri Opera Latina.* Martini Buceri Opera Omnia, Series II. Leiden: Brill, 1982–.
Burnett, *Pamphlets*	*The Eucharistic Pamphlets of Andreas Bodenstein von Karlstadt.* Translated and edited by Amy Nelson Burnett. Early Modern Studies Series 6. Kirksville, Mo.: Truman State University Press, 2011.

Commentary	Ulrich Zwingli, *Commentary on True and False Religion*. Edited by Samuel Macauley Jackson. Durham, N.C.: Labyrinth, 1981.
CR	*Philippi Melanthonis Opera quae Supersunt Omnia*. Corpus Reformatorum 1–28. Halle, 1834–1860. Reprint, New York: Johnson, 1963.
CS	*Corpus Schwenckfeldianorum*. Leipzig: Breitkopf and Härtel, 1907–1961.
CWE	*Collected Works of Erasmus*. Toronto: University of Toronto Press, 1974–.
Furcha, *Carlstadt*	*The Essential Carlstadt: Fifteen Tracts by Andreas Bodenstein (Carlstadt) from Karlstadt*. Translated and edited by Edward J. Furcha. Scottdale: Herald, 1995.
HBBW	Heinrich Bullinger, *Werke*. Abteilung 2: *Heinrich Bullingers Briefwechel*. Zurich: Theologischer Verlag, 1973–.
HBTS	Heinrich Bullinger, *Werke*. Abteilung 3: *Theologische Schriften*. Zurich: Theologischer Verlag, 1983–.
Herminjard	Herminjard, A.-L., ed. *Correspondance des Réformateurs dans les pays de langue Française*. Geneva: H. Georg, 1866–1897. Reprint, Nieuwkoop: De Graaf, 1966.
Hertzsch, *Schriften*	*Karlstadts Schriften aus den Jahren* 1523–25. 2 vols. Edited by Erich Hertzsch. Halle: Niemeyer, 1956–1957.
HZW	*Huldrych Zwingli: Writings*. Edited by Edward J. Furcha and H. Wayne Pipkin. 2 vols. Allison Park, Pa.: Pickwick Publications, 1984.
Köhler MF	*Flugschriften des frühen 16. Jahrhunderts*. Edited by Hans-Joachim Köhler. Zug: IDC, 1978–1987 (microfiche series).
Köhler, *Zwingli und Luther*	Walther Köhler, *Zwingli und Luther: Ihre Streit über das Abendmahl nach seinen politischen und religiösen Beziehungen*. 2 vols. Quellen und Forschungen zur Reformationsgeschichte 6–7. Gütersloh: Bertelsmann, 1924–1953.
LB	*Desiderii Erasmi Roterodami Opera Omnia*. Edited by Jean Le Clerc. Leiden, 1703–1706. Reprint, London: Gregg, 1962.
LW	Martin Luther. *Luther's Works*. Edited by Jaroslav Pelikan and Helmut T. Lehmann. St. Louis, Mo.: Concordia, 1955–1986.
MBW	*Melanchthons Briefwechsel: Kritische und kommentierte Gesamtausgabe*. Edited by Heinz Scheible et al. Stuttgart-Bad Canstatt: Frommann-Holzboog, 1977–.

MPL   *Patrologiae cursus completus, Series Latina.* Edited by J. P. Migne. Paris, 1844–1864.

Müller, WB   Nicolaus Müller, "Die Wittenberger Bewegung 1521 und 1522. Die Vorgänge in und um Wittenberg während Luthers Wartburgaufenthalt." *Archiv für Reformationsgeschichte* 6 (1909): 161–226, 261–325, 385–469; 7 (1909): 185–224, 233–293, 353–412; and 8 (1910): 1–43.

Oberman, Forerunners   Heiko A. Oberman, *Forerunners of the Reformation: The Shape of Late Medieval Thought Illustrated by Key Documents.* Philadelphia: Fortress, 1981.

Osiander, GA   Andreas Osiander, *Gesamtausgabe.* Gütersloh: Gütersloher Verlagshaus Mohn, 1975–1997.

QGTS   *Quellen zur Geschichte der Täufer in der Schweiz.* Vol. 1, *Zürich.* Edited by Leonhard von Muralt and Walter Schmid. Zurich: Hirzel, 1952.

Sider, *Battle*   *Karlstadt's Battle with Luther: Documents in a Liberal-Radical Debate.* Edited by Ronald J. Sider. Philadelphia: Fortress, 1978.

Sider, *Karlstadt*   Ronald J. Sider, *Andreas Bodenstein von Karlstadt: The Development of His Thought, 1517–1525.* Studies in Medieval and Reformation Thought 11. Leiden: Brill, 1974.

Spruyt, *Hoen*   Bart Jan Spruyt, *Cornelius Henrici Hoen (Honius) and His Epistle on the Eucharist (1525).* Studies in Medieval and Reformation Traditions 119. Leiden: Brill, 2006.

VD16   *Verzeichnis der im deutschen Sprachbereich erschienenen Drucke des 16. Jahrhunderts.* http://www.vd16.de.

WA   Martin Luther, *Werke. Kritische Gesamtausgabe.* Weimar: Böhlaus Nachfolger, 1883–1986.

WA Br   Martin Luther, *Werke. Kritische Gesamtausgabe. Briefe.* Weimar: Böhlaus Nachfolger, 1883–1986.

Walch   *Dr. Martin Luthers Sämmtliche Schriften.* Edited by Johann Georg Walch. Halle, 1739–1753. Reprint, St. Louis, Mo.: Concordia, 1881–1910.

Z   Zwingli, Ulrich. *Huldreich Zwinglis sämtliche Werke.* Corpus Reformatorum 88–101. Leipzig/Zurich: Heinsius/TVZ, 1905–1991.

KARLSTADT AND THE ORIGINS OF THE EUCHARISTIC CONTROVERSY

Introduction

ON 22 AUGUST 1524, Andreas Bodenstein von Karlstadt met with Martin Luther to defend himself against the charges of sedition that Luther had raised in a sermon that morning. Their meeting, held at an inn in Jena, turned into a heated public confrontation. At the end, Luther gave Karlstadt a golden gulden and told him, "Take it and attack me boldly now. Attack me sharply!" Karlstadt in turn held up the coin, acknowledged that it was a sign authorizing him to write against Luther, and called on bystanders to serve as witnesses to this fact. He then bent the gulden, put it in his purse, and shook Luther's hand.[1]

In a very real sense, this ritualized exchange signaled the beginning of the eucharistic controversy. Karlstadt's attack on Luther would by no means be limited to his understanding of the sacrament, for, as both men acknowledged, the disagreements between them included other issues as well. Still, the agreement at Jena paved the way for Karlstadt to publish four pamphlets in which he argued that Christ was not present bodily in the Lord's Supper. These pamphlets provoked others to enter the debate, whether arguing for or against Christ's corporeal presence, and within a matter of months the evangelical movement had divided over the proper understanding of the sacrament.

To many modern students of the Reformation, the eucharistic controversy is one of its most puzzling developments. The positions championed by each side of the controversy seem not just impenetrable but pointless, while the polemic and the passions it evoked are unappealing and sometimes appalling. The eucharistic treatises of the major reformers are probably among the least read of their works, and the pamphlets of lesser-known figures are ignored altogether. The conflict as a whole is judged to be an unfortunate and unedifying episode in the history of the church, and the technicalities of the debate are avoided as much as possible. Yet the controversy concerning the Lord's Supper was one of the most significant developments of the sixteenth century, second only to the Reformation itself in its long-term consequences. It divided the evangelical movement at a time when it most needed to present a united front against its Roman opponents, and it led to the permanent establishment of two main theological traditions within Protestantism. Those who choose to ignore the eucharistic controversy, or to dismiss it as irrelevant, thereby overlook one of the defining issues of early modern Christianity.

There has long been a need for a detailed account of the eucharistic controversy in English.[2] This book is a first step in that direction. Although its chapters proceed in roughly chronological order, it is not a narrative account. Instead, each chapter focuses on a particular issue or development in order to answer questions related to the early Reformation understanding of the Lord's Supper. Each of them is a type of archaeological excavation that lays bare the layers of assumptions, attitudes, and ideas about the Lord's Supper.[3] Taken together they provide a foundation on which further studies of the eucharistic controversy may build.

I have chosen to concentrate on the background and development of the discussion of the Lord's Supper only through 1525. For obvious reasons, most studies of the eucharistic controversy are based on the plethora of publications and the strident polemics of the period from 1526 to 1529. These were the years when both Luther and Zwingli wrote their most important works on the Lord's Supper, and their differences have been described by other scholars.[4] In comparison, aside from the obligatory nod to Erasmus and the more specialized studies of both Luther and Zwingli during the early years of the Reformation, there has been little discussion of how evangelical criticisms of the mass may have paved the way for the very public break between Luther and Karlstadt and for the immediate response to their quarrel.

This early period is key, however, for an understanding of later developments. The debate over the sacrament that took place between 1518 and 1525 forms a crucial link between the late medieval understanding of the Eucharist and the popular piety that it encouraged before the Reformation, and the eucharistic theologies that emerged from the evangelical movement, whether Lutheran, Reformed, or Radical. During these early years most of the arguments later used either to defend or to reject Christ's corporeal presence in the Supper were formulated and introduced into the debate. The timing and development of the discussions about the

Lord's Supper are also important. In the same way that a historian describing a military or political campaign must take account of the dates of battles or speeches in order to trace the fortunes of war or shifts in public opinion, so a historian describing the course of the eucharistic controversy, especially in its early phase, must pay special attention to when, how, and why certain positions first entered into the debate.

As the book's title indicates, I have three goals in examining the public discussion of the Lord's Supper in the early years of the Reformation. The first is simply to explain the varying interpretations of the sacrament that developed within the early evangelical movement and that would become so hotly contested: What were the issues at stake in the early eucharistic controversy? Too often the controversy is presented only as a quarrel between Luther and Zwingli, without taking into account the views of others who contributed to the debate or distinguishing their positions from those of the two chief protagonists. I hope to give a more detailed picture of the range of the discussion about the Lord's Supper during these crucial years.

My second goal is to describe how those ideas were understood, modified, and passed along by those who participated in that discussion. I am interested not only in *what* was said but in *how, why,* and *when* it was said, in combining an elucidation of the theological arguments with an investigation into the historical developments. For this reason, I consider the contributions of lesser-known figures to be as important as those of the major reformers for understanding the background and outbreak of the eucharistic controversy, and I have embedded my discussion of individual works within the broader context of the circulation of ideas about the sacrament.[5]

Because I am interested in the public discussion of the Lord's Supper, I have relied particularly on the pamphlets that were printed in the early years of the Reformation. The study of Reformation pamphlets has grown exponentially since they first attracted serious scholarly attention in the 1970s. Examined quantitatively and qualitatively, and with regard to the background of their authors, their written and visual content, and the variety of genres used, Reformation pamphlets provide a window into the transmission and reception of evangelical ideas. Pamphlets were particularly important for spreading the new evangelical understanding of the sacrament, both before and after the outbreak of the eucharistic controversy. Biblical scholarship, contained in the Scripture commentaries and theological textbooks published in the early 1520s, was of course important for the development of evangelical eucharistic theology, but the pamphlets brought that theology out of the lecture hall and into the marketplaces and taverns of early modern Germany, explaining it to a broader audience and persuading the common man and woman to abandon traditional beliefs and practices concerning the mass.

My examination of the early Reformation discussion of the Eucharist is also shaped by an awareness of the role played by prior understandings and patterns of thought in shaping the reception of new ideas. Over the last generation, developments in cognitive psychology and learning theory have revolutionized the way we think about how people learn. Researchers are increasingly aware that the human mind is not a blank slate that accurately records new information as it is presented; rather, it constructs knowledge as new information comes in contact with established frameworks of thought. Existing knowledge is used to build new knowledge, and unfamiliar concepts may be modified so that they accord with previous understanding. The psychological approach to learning in the present has its counterpart in reception theory and studies of reading in the past. As Roger Chartier has argued, reading is a creative practice, and one cannot assume that readers understand a text in the same way that the author intended it.[6]

This observation has direct bearing on the early discussion of the Lord's Supper. All of those who contributed to the debate grew up in the medieval church and had an understanding of the sacrament shaped by late medieval theology and popular piety. To this framework many of them added the interests and insights of humanism, especially as propagated by Erasmus of Rotterdam. After the outbreak of the Reformation, Luther contributed to this mix with his attacks on the Roman church and his new understanding of the mass; others joined the discussion with their own pamphlets. For those who followed the debate, the result was not a seamless adoption of any one set of ideas but rather a synthesis of old with new that reflected the background and experiences of each individual. Even where old understandings were rejected, they continued to influence the new by shaping the way the larger debate was framed. Thus my concern throughout this book is not to determine whether a particular individual was a follower of Erasmus or of Luther or of Zwingli—a question that seems to dominate much of the older research—but rather to show how the contributors to the debate took ideas from a variety of sources and combined them with their preexisting understanding of the Eucharist to come up with something new.

My third goal is to reveal the central role played by Andreas Bodenstein von Karlstadt not simply as the one who sparked the eucharistic controversy but as one of the most important contributors to the discussion of the Lord's Supper both before and after that controversy began. In many accounts of the eucharistic controversy Karlstadt is depicted almost as a buffoon, whose sole argument against Christ's presence in the sacrament was that Christ pointed to himself rather than to the bread when he said, "This is my body." Karlstadt did indeed make this assertion, but it was neither his only nor his most important argument against Christ's bodily presence. In fact, his mature eucharistic theology was considerably more sophisticated than this caricature would lead one to believe. His mature position is also strikingly at odds with the understanding of the sacrament that he advocated three years earlier, as one of the leaders of the Wittenberg reform movement. This causes one to ask how and why Karlstadt's eucharistic theology evolved as it did, and it highlights the need to reexamine the interchanges between Karlstadt and Luther from the beginning of the Reformation through Karlstadt's last publications on the Lord's Supper in 1525.

This reexamination is all the more necessary because the evaluation of Karlstadt's relations with Luther has varied so greatly over time. Hermann Barge's two-volume biography of Karlstadt, published at the beginning of the twentieth century, was one of the first to challenge the negative view of Karlstadt that had simply been taken over from Luther by the reformer's theological heirs.[7] Barge's sympathetic portrayal of Karlstadt as the leader of a "lay Puritan movement" in Wittenberg sparked a strident response from Karl Müller and others, which in turn led Barge to publish a further defense of his interpretation of the Wittenberg movement.[8] This debate also prompted the publication of many of the archival documents used by Barge and Müller, which in turn made it possible for later scholars to advance new interpretations.[9]

A second wave of interest in Karlstadt that began in the 1960s and continued through the next decade resulted in several major studies that shed further light on Luther's troublesome colleague. These have stressed Karlstadt's importance as an agitator for liturgical reforms and as a pamphleteer criticizing the traditional understanding of the mass.[10] Those that have looked specifically at Karlstadt's writings on the sacrament, however, have tended to divorce theological analysis from historical context in a way that leaves one wondering how Karlstadt's thought was shaped by the events of the day.[11]

This study is intended to place Karlstadt firmly into his historical setting and to present him as one very significant voice among a host of others who helped shape the evangelical understanding of the sacrament in the early years of the Reformation. As chapter 1 demonstrates, Karlstadt's role in the Wittenberg movement of 1521–1522 set the stage for the later conflict with Luther that marked the public beginning of the eucharistic controversy. I have called it a prelude to that controversy, because although at that time there was no significant disagreement between Luther and Karlstadt concerning the Lord's Supper per se, their differences regarding the course of reform made clear some of the more fundamental issues that would eventually lead to the eucharistic controversy.

If chapter 1 is a prelude, then chapter 2 is the overture, because it introduces several of the themes that would recur in the discussion of the Lord's Supper. It focuses not on the major figures, whether Luther, Karlstadt, or Zwingli, but on the discussion of the mass carried out in popular pamphlets. Luther and Zwingli certainly helped shape that discussion, but they by no means controlled it. Studies of the pamphlets produced in such abundance after Luther's break with Rome have made us aware that what Luther said or wrote was not necessarily what people heard or remembered. By considering the many voices that contributed to the early criticism of the mass, we gain a better understanding of the concerns and commitments, the priorities and presuppositions, that influenced the direction the controversy would take once it began.

Chapter 3 returns to Karlstadt, this time to describe the development of his eucharistic theology as contained in the pamphlets he published in 1524–1525. That theology developed in dialogue with Luther and was shaped by ideas he drew from several others, ranging from Johannes Reuchlin to Ulrich Zwingli. Karlstadt's debate with Luther also helped determine the issues and the strategies used by both sides as disagreements concerning the Lord's Supper became apparent at the end of 1524.

Two prominent strains of thought that contributed to Karlstadt's understanding of the Lord's Supper and to the public discussion more generally were Erasmian humanism and late medieval heresy. Erasmus's influence on the Swiss reformers is well known, but the contribution of heretical ideas to the debate on the sacrament has not been closely studied. B. J. Spruyt's recent book on Cornelis Hoen is an important first step toward revealing the link between heretical criticisms of late medieval eucharistic piety and the outbreak of the eucharistic controversy.[12] I continue along this path in chapter 4 by showing how ideas from across the spectrum of Hussite teachings on the Eucharist were incorporated into the debate on the Lord's Supper.

With chapter 5, I consider the shaping of early Zwinglianism more generally. Although Zwingli and his colleagues repeatedly criticized Karlstadt and asserted the independent development of their thought, Karlstadt played a crucial role in the development of early Zwinglian eucharistic theology. This chapter shows how Zwingli's eucharistic theology was both deepened and broadened by the reformers of Basel and Strasbourg, in part by incorporating arguments against Christ's presence that had first been advanced by Karlstadt and Hoen.

The final chapter again steps back from the major figures in the eucharistic controversy to look at the debate as it developed in pamphlets published over the course of 1525. The conflict between Luther and his opponents over the proper understanding of the Lord's Supper was by no means as evenly balanced as it is usually presented. Those evangelicals who rejected Luther's position faced an uphill battle in making their own views public, and the positions they defended both in print and in private discussions reveal a good deal of variation despite their common rejection of Christ's corporeal presence.

The observant reader will note that in these chapters I rarely use the term "real presence" when discussing the sacrament. I have done this deliberately, in order to avoid ambiguity and to reflect the language of the debate itself. Although hallowed by long usage, "real presence" is imprecise as a description of a theological position. "Real" has both an epistemological sense, meaning true as opposed to false, and an ontological one, meaning essential or substantial as opposed to transitory or accidental (in the Aristotelian sense).[13] German scholars avoid this ambiguity by specifying "corporeal real presence" or "spiritual real presence." While I could have made the same distinction, I have chosen instead to apply Ockham's razor and eliminate the middle term, since it does not convey any additional meaning beyond that in the terms "corporeal presence" and "spiritual presence."

Avoiding the use of "real presence" also conforms more closely to the early debates over the Lord's Supper, since the term was not used during the period under consideration. The issue that separated Luther from Karlstadt, Zwingli, Oecolampadius, and their supporters at the outset of the controversy was whether Christ was present bodily (*leiblich, corporaliter*) in the elements of bread and wine. Up through 1525, there was no public discussion about whether and to what extent Christ might be present in any other way. While one might assert, on the basis of their later works, that many of Luther's early opponents actually held that Christ was spiritually present in the sacrament,[14] this was not an issue in the earliest published debates over the Lord's Supper, nor should this position be read back into the debate. Historians must judge the controversy on the basis of what was said, and not by what was left unsaid. By using the same terminology as the participants themselves, I hope to convey a sense of what they believed the central issue of the debate to be.

Although most of the arguments for and against Christ's corporeal presence had been expressed by the end of 1525, this does not mean that the eucharistic controversy had reached an impasse or would remain static. In fact, readers familiar with the controversy as it developed in the years after the Marburg Colloquy of 1529 may be struck by how different the terms of the debate were at the outbreak of the controversy. Nevertheless, the ideas that emerged through 1525 were the building blocks that would be used in the debate over the next decade, during the most active phase of the eucharistic controversy. In describing the emergence and diffusion of these ideas, this study makes clear the richness and the complexity of the debate over the sacrament during the early Reformation.

1

Prelude to the Eucharistic Controversy

LUTHER, KARLSTADT, AND THE WITTENBERG MOVEMENT

⟋⟍ ⎯⎯⎯

AS HE WAS returning to Saxony from the Diet of Worms in May 1521, Luther was "kidnapped" by a band of men acting on the orders of Elector Frederick the Wise. The reformer spent the next ten months in hiding at the Wartburg castle. During his absence, his colleagues in Wittenberg began the process of working out the practical consequences of Luther's evangelical teachings for worship and praxis. The "Wittenberg movement" gained momentum over the course of the fall, and by early 1522 Andreas Karlstadt had emerged as its leader. But the increasingly radical nature of the reforms led to growing divisions in the city and caused deep concern in the elector's court. Prompted by news of the unrest, Luther returned to Wittenberg in March and reestablished his leadership over the reform movement, endorsing some of the changes and rolling back others. Criticized for advocating the mandatory introduction of reforms before most people were ready for them, Karlstadt withdrew from the public eye and limited his activities to carrying out his lecturing responsibilities.

The story of the Wittenberg movement is a familiar one retold in general surveys and examined in greater detail in both biographies of the major figures and more specialized works on the early Reformation.[1] The issues debated during Luther's absence included the validity of monastic vows, the requirement of clerical celibacy, and the presence of images in churches, but the bulk of the discussions focused on the mass. Because of the central place that the mass held in late medieval theology and popular devotion, any changes made to it not only would have a dramatic impact within

Wittenberg but also would stir up controversy outside the city. This fact warrants yet another examination of the events that took place between September 1521 and March 1522, focusing specifically on the attempts to reform the mass during this period.

It is especially tempting to look at the Wittenberg movement for the roots of the later disagreement between Luther and Karlstadt on the Lord's Supper. An examination of the events does indeed yield important insights into Karlstadt's early eucharistic theology. It also hints at the origin of Karlstadt's later polemic against Luther as the "new pope," no different from the "old pope" in demanding acceptance of his authority. But the developments in Wittenberg do not reveal any major differences between Luther and Karlstadt on the sacrament. In fact, throughout 1521–1522 Karlstadt upheld the same understanding of the mass that Luther had formulated in 1520 and that was shared by other members of the reforming party. Instead, the developments in Wittenberg were important in a deeper way because they revealed the more fundamental theological differences that separated Luther and Karlstadt. Luther's response to Karlstadt in March 1522 demonstrated his ability to see past the specific issues being debated, whether or not he agreed with Karlstadt on them, and to point to their disagreements on these fundamental issues. Luther would follow the same strategy in 1524, with momentous consequences for the course of the eucharistic controversy. The Wittenberg movement can thus be seen as a prelude to the later debate over the Lord's Supper, not fully related to it but introducing themes that would be developed and elaborated upon in the future.

LUTHER AND KARLSTADT ON THE SACRAMENT, 1518–1521

In order to appreciate the debates concerning the mass in 1521 and 1522, it is necessary first to understand Luther's view of the mass as it was expressed in his earliest publications.[2] As Ronald Sider has pointed out, Karlstadt's earliest statements about the Eucharist, like his discussions of most other issues, were largely a repetition of Luther's ideas.[3] This is readily apparent from a comparison of the works of the two theologians published before October 1521.

Four of Luther's first five published works dealing with the mass began as sermons delivered during Holy Week, as lay men and women were preparing for the communion that church law required them to receive at Easter time.[4] In the fifth work, the 1520 treatise *On the Babylonian Captivity of the Church*, Luther's discussion of the mass was a more polemical restatement and development of ideas first expressed in the Maundy Thursday sermon of that year. All four of Luther's sermons directly addressed the question of worthy preparation for receiving the sacrament and were based on the epistle reading for Maundy Thursday, St. Paul's admonition to the Corinthians that they examine themselves so that they would not eat judgment upon themselves (1 Cor. 11:27–32). In these sermons Luther reacted against a current within late medieval preaching that defined worthy preparation as making a full sacramental confession of sins to a priest, combined with other ascetic exercises that would ensure the purity necessary to partake of Christ's body.[5] Against this emphasis on the Christian's own efforts, Luther argued that the most important preparation for communion was awareness of one's own sinfulness and trust in God's mercy. Faith in Christ's promise of forgiveness, rather than in the completeness of one's sacramental confession, was the necessary precondition for worthy reception.[6]

While the sermons of 1518 and 1519 were relatively traditional in their discussion of the sacrament, Luther's *Sermon on the New Testament, That Is, on the Holy Mass* of 1520 was more radical, for it combined a criticism of the understanding of the mass as a sacrifice with a redefinition of the sacrament as Christ's testament, confirming God's promise of forgiveness through the signs of bread and wine. Elaborating on his understanding of the sacrament as a sign, Luther described how in the Old Testament God first promised salvation and then confirmed that promise with a sign: that of the rainbow to Noah, of circumcision to Abraham, and of the sheep's fleece to Gideon. Like the seal added to a secular testament, so the signs of Christ's body and blood under the bread and wine gave recipients greater assurance of the promise of forgiveness.[7]

Luther repeated many of these arguments but sharpened them considerably in his treatise *On the Babylonian Captivity*. The bulk of the section on the mass was a restatement of the understanding of the mass as a testament established by Christ. The sacrament was the promise of forgiveness, confirmed by Christ's death and received by faith. Just as God added signs to his promises in the Old Testament as a memorial or remembrance, so Christ gave his own body and blood in the bread and wine as a sign of the forgiveness promised. Luther rejected the sacrifice of the mass in the strongest possible terms, for it turned the sacrament into a work done by man for God and so destroyed its character as a promise and a gift.[8]

Luther also criticized the refusal to allow the laity to receive communion in both kinds, and he condemned the church's claim to dictate acceptance of the doctrine of transubstantiation. Citing Pierre d'Ailly, he stated that it made more sense to believe that Christ's true body and blood coexisted with the substance of bread and wine, but it was absurd to argue about whether "bread" actually meant "the form or accidents of bread." Dismissing the Aristotelian categories of substance and accident as irrelevant, Luther argued that it was sufficient for the common people to believe that Christ's body and blood were truly contained in the sacrament.[9]

In his Maundy Thursday sermon of 1521, preached just days before his departure for Worms, Luther returned to the question of worthy preparation. He told his hearers again that faith made communicants pious and guarded them from future sin. Luther cited the centurion's words, "Lord, I am not worthy" (Matt. 8:8), which the priest spoke immediately before eating the consecrated host, and he emphasized that communicants should go beyond this prayer to acknowledge their faith in Christ's promise of forgiveness. The greater one's hunger and desire for such forgiveness, the more fit one was to receive the sacrament. In contrast, those who partook of the sacrament because they felt worthy, or who communicated out of custom or command rather than genuine desire, should instead abstain, as should those who lived in open sin. Luther saved his harshest criticism for those who said that only those who were truly pure were worthy of the sacrament, for they terrified and drove away the ones most in need of the sacrament's consolation.[10]

Karlstadt's first pamphlet to discuss the mass, *On the Recipients, Signs and Promise of the Holy Sacrament of Christ's Flesh and Blood*, picked up and enlarged upon these ideas expressed by Luther.[11] Published in June 1521, the pamphlet addressed two issues: whether sinners should abstain from communion, and which element of the sacrament, the promise or the sign, was more important. As archdeacon of the chapter of All Saints, Karlstadt was the regular preacher at the castle church, and the topic, contents, and style all suggest that at least the first part of his pamphlet originated as a sermon, probably delivered, like all of Luther's sermons on the sacrament, during Holy Week.[12]

In his dedication to Nicolaus Demuth, Karlstadt also referred to the centurion's words repeated just prior to communion, contrasting the centurion's sense of unworthiness before Christ with the joy expressed by Zacchaeus (Luke 19:6). While the centurion had received Christ only spiritually and had not brought Christ under his roof, Zacchaeus received Christ both spiritually and bodily by welcoming him into his house, thereby grasping the sign as well as Christ's word. In any case, what counted was not the centurion's confession of unworthiness but the faith that both he and Zachaeus demonstrated in Christ's word.

Karlstadt expanded on the importance of this faith in the first part of the pamphlet, in which he discussed what made one worthy to receive communion. Like Luther, Karlstadt rejected the conventional view that only those purified of sin through sacramental confession could communicate worthily. Citing Christ's words that the healthy did not need a physician, he argued that awareness of sin should drive one to the sacrament rather than cause one to abstain from it. Karlstadt went even further, presenting communion not as something that followed sacramental confession but rather as a replacement for it. He repeated the traditional analogy of sacramental confession with the healing that resulted from revealing one's physical illness to a physician, but he applied the analogy to the assurance of forgiveness received in the sacrament of the altar after revealing one's sins to Christ, not to the spiritual healing of priestly absolution.[13]

In the second part of the pamphlet Karlstadt discussed the relationship between promise and sign in the sacrament. He began with a clarification of terms: word, promise, covenant, and testament all meant the same thing. Christ instituted the sacrament through his word of promise, "given for you," and added the sign of bread. Karlstadt used John 3:14–15 to argue that just as the snake raised by Moses in the wilderness had been a sign of God's promise, so Christ on the cross was a sign that those who looked to him would be saved.[14] He then considered the purpose of signs more generally as things perceived by the senses. God established specific signs, such as the rainbow given to Noah, to confirm his promises. Those who saw the sign could take comfort and reject any doubt in the associated promise. The word or promise always came first, however. Thus those receiving Christ's body should use it to remind themselves that God had promised forgiveness. This brought Karlstadt back to the point he had made in his dedication: those who wanted to receive the sacrament worthily should not fear or doubt that Christ would fulfill his promise of forgiveness, and in fact they should rejoice in knowing that God would not desert them.

A comparison of Karlstadt's pamphlet with Luther's earlier sermons indicates some points on which the two differed. Although Karlstadt used the term "testament," the concept did not occupy the central place that it did at this time in Luther's understanding of the sacrament. Karlstadt placed more emphasis on, and greater separation between, the sign and thing signified than did Luther, reflecting the influence of a neoplatonic/Augustinian and Erasmian dualism that Luther did not share.[15] But in comparison to the similarities, these differences were still minor and seem to have gone unnoticed by contemporaries. Karlstadt sounded much like Luther due to his use of the word "testament," his pairing of promise and sign as well as his giving priority to the former, his emphasis on faith, his understanding that true worthiness consisted in recognition of one's sinfulness, and his rejection of traditional demands for the purity obtained through sacramental confession as the necessary prerequisite to communion. Propagated through Luther's and Karlstadt's published pamphlets, these common characteristics defined the approach to the mass identified with the evangelical movement as it spread outward from Wittenberg in 1521.[16]

Luther's excommunication and his outlawing at the Diet of Worms would dramatically change the situation in Wittenberg, however. With Luther in hiding from the spring of 1521, Karlstadt and his much younger colleague Philipp Melanchthon assumed leadership of the evangelical movement.[17] Within a very short time the reformers were faced with a major challenge: how to deal with rapidly developing pressures for concrete reforms of the mass to reflect the content of Luther's teaching.

THE WITTENBERG MOVEMENT, SEPTEMBER 1521–MARCH 1522

Despite the severity of his criticism of the sacrifice of the mass in *On the Babylonian Captivity*, Luther proposed only very modest reforms to the mass liturgy in that work. Priests should repeat Christ's words of institution in the vernacular as they elevated the consecrated elements, and they should invite others to commune with them when they celebrated the mass.[18] It would be left to others to put these reforms into practice.

The earliest movements in this direction were slow and hesitant. In July 1521, Karlstadt presided over a disputation in which it was argued that those who received both bread and wine "were not Bohemians but true Christians," and that it was better to abstain entirely than to receive communion under one kind only. The theses also criticized the ritual prescriptions intended to prevent desecration of the sacrament, stating that it was a lesser sin "to spill consecrated wine accidentally than to let it fall on an unbelieving heart."[19] Luther rejected Karlstadt's assertion that it was sin not to receive the sacrament in both kinds, arguing that one could not declare something to be sin without scriptural warrant. He agreed, however, that Christ's institution of both elements should be restored, and he wrote to his friends in Wittenberg that he would never again celebrate a private mass.[20] By the fall of 1521 there were some in Wittenberg who felt that these and other more far-reaching reforms were urgently necessary if the church was to conform to the teaching of the gospel.

The first real step toward liturgical reform involved communion in two kinds.[21] On the feast of St. Michael (29 September), Melanchthon and his students communicated in both kinds in the parish church. A week later the preacher at the Augustinian convent, Gabriel Zwilling, gave a sermon in which he argued that the sacrament of the altar was a sign given to confirm faith and not a sacrifice.[22] The Israelites were forbidden to adore the ark or their circumcised foreskins, both signs given under the old covenant. Likewise, Christians were not to adore the signs given to confirm their salvation, and such adoration was idolatry. Zwilling also condemned the traditional celebration of the mass and stated that it would be preferable to hear God's word preached first, and then to communicate under both forms. Going beyond Luther's renunciation of private masses, Zwilling announced that he would no longer give occasion for such idolatry by celebrating mass in the traditional way.[23]

The sermon touched off a storm of controversy in Wittenberg. Two days after it was preached, the university's theologians—Karlstadt, Melanchthon, Justus Jonas, and Johann Dölsch—summoned Zwilling to question him concerning its contents. They determined that, except for his rejection of the adoration of the sacrament, Zwilling's statements accorded with Scripture. Hoping to protect the Augustinians from the displeasure of their immediate superior, Melanchthon wrote to Wenceslaus Link in Nuremberg, the general vicar of the Augustinian order, and defended their desire to "restore the mass to its pristine usage" by distributing the bread to all present and by allowing communion under both forms.[24]

Informed of the disturbances, Elector Frederick the Wise authorized his adviser Gregor Brück to investigate rumors that the Augustinians were refusing to celebrate mass and to consult with representatives of the chapter and the university about the situation. In his report to the elector, Brück summarized Zwilling's sermon in three points. First, the sacrament should not be adored, for it was not instituted for this purpose; rather, it was meant for Christ's commemoration. Second, it was sin to celebrate the mass in its traditional form, for all who were present should receive communion under both forms—the position Karlstadt had defended in the disputation of the previous summer. Third, the monks could not be compelled against their consciences to celebrate private masses, for these did not meet the purpose of communion for which the sacrament was instituted. Because each of these points raised different problems, we must look at them individually.

Zwilling's most radical position was his contention that the sacrament was only a sign and therefore should not be adored. Unlike the other two points, his rejection of adoration was a new idea, not drawn directly from Luther's teaching or discussed earlier among the Wittenberg reformers. Ulrich Bubenheimer has suggested that Zwilling may have derived this view from the *Most Christian Letter* of the Dutch jurist Cornelis Hoen, which advocated a purely symbolic understanding of the sacrament.[25] According to a later account by the Reformed theologian Albert Hardenberg, Hinne Rode, the rector of the house of the Brethren of the Common Life in Utrecht, visited Wittenberg bearing a copy of this letter, and Bubenheimer's hypothesis would help pinpoint that visit more specifically as occurring in the late summer or early fall of 1521. Bubenheimer has pointed to parallels between Hoen's views and those attributed to Zwilling, particularly the linkage between rejection of Christ's corporeal presence and the claim that adoration of the sacrament was a form of idolatry. He has also suggested that the Dutch students staying in the Augustinian cloister at the time were advocates of Hoen's ideas. His conjecture is strengthened by possible allusions to Hoen's letter in Karlstadt's two pamphlets on the mass published in November.[26]

A summary of Hoen's letter helps make those parallels more clear. It opens with a comparison of the sacrament to the ring given by a husband to his wife as a pledge of his love. Like the bride, the recipient of the Eucharist should believe Christ was now his and should turn away from all other loves. Hoen condemned those who received the Eucharist without this faith, and he blamed the "Roman scholastics" for focusing instead on the consecration of the host, saying without scriptural proof that the bread had become Christ's body. Those who adored the consecrated bread were no different from heathens who worshiped wood or stone. Christ had warned his disciples against those who claimed, "here is the Christ," or "there is the Christ," (Matt. 24:23), and so one should not believe those who said Christ was in the bread. The disciples themselves had called it bread; in St. Paul's question, "the bread which we break, is it not a participation in the body of Christ?" (1 Cor 10:16), the word "is" should be interpreted as "signifies."[27] Hoen cited several other passages from Scripture where "is" had to be interpreted figuratively, including Christ's reference to John as Elijah (Matt. 11:14), Paul's statement that "the rock was Christ" (1 Cor. 10:4), and the interpretation of pharaoh's dream (Gen. 41:26–27). Thomas Aquinas rejected the view that Christ was in the bread as a sign sacramentally but not corporeally, but his position did not accord with Christ's warning not to believe those who claimed, "here is the Christ."[28]

Hoen distinguished between three kinds of spiritual bread: Christ who was eaten by faith, the manna eaten by the fathers in the desert, and the Eucharist. On the basis of John 6, he argued that Christ clearly distinguished between himself as the bread of life and the manna given to the Jews. The eucharistic bread had more in common with the manna, which signified Christ, than it did with the living bread that preserved one from death. Since those who received the Eucharist were not preserved from eternal death, the sacrament could not be Christ but instead only signified him. Moreover, Christ's command to "do this in remembrance of me" was more appropriately said by one who would be corporeally absent, rather than by one who would be present. Christ even saw his bodily presence as an obstacle, for he told his disciples that unless he went away the Paraclete could not come (John 16:7).[29]

Hoen rejected the scholastic interpretation of "do this" as authorizing priests to consecrate the bread, and he likewise scorned the argument that when the priest said, "this is my body," he spoke in Christ's place. Christ did not want the bread to be transubstantiated but rather intended to give himself through the bread, in the same way that ownership of land or a house was transferred by giving a staff or a key. It was necessary, therefore, to distinguish between the bread received by mouth and Christ received by faith. Christians who looked at the elevated bread and claimed to see God were no better than the children of Israel who made a golden calf and claimed to see the gods who had brought them out of Israel.[30]

Hoen criticized those who had neglected all of the words Christ had spoken as he instituted the Supper and focused only on the phrases "this is my body" and "this cup is the new testament in my blood." Christians were to listen to God's word alone, which included the command to "do this in remembrance of me." They were to avoid false teachers, whether they claimed to be Thomists, Scotists, Augustinians, or Franciscans, and they should not believe in his carnal presence, since Christ had told them that it was necessary that he go away.[31]

Hoen's letter raised several issues, most of which did not enter the public debate until the outbreak of the eucharistic controversy in late 1524. If Rode did bring the manuscript to Wittenberg, it is doubtful that copies were made so that its many subsidiary arguments could be studied more closely and discussed at greater length. But the letter's central argument against Christ's corporeal presence and its consequent rejection of adoration of the host made an impression, as can be seen by the immediate reaction to Zwilling's sermon. Wittenberg's theologians clearly believed that Zwilling had gone too far in condemning adoration, and they did what they could to suppress any criticisms of the practice. In a report to the elector on 20 October, they stated that Zwilling's words had been misunderstood, and that he had not attacked the adoration of the sacrament in his sermon.[32] The nature of Christ's presence in the bread and the adoration of the sacrament were also addressed in a disputation held on 17 October. In the theses he wrote for this disputation, Karlstadt asserted that the bread was the flesh of Christ and the true body of Christ.[33] His position was not, however, an endorsement of transubstantiation. He criticized the Parisian scholastics, "whose snotty noses are full of Aristotle and the 'little books on logic,'" and who taught that the bread ceased to exist at consecration. Echoing Luther's point in On the Babylonian Captivity, Karlstadt asserted that it was sufficient to say "the bread is the body" and "the wine is the blood," for no one should doubt the words of Scripture. Moreover, the identity of bread and body justified the practice of adoration: "I do not see why we ought not adore the bread, when we should and can adore Christ's body."[34]

Karlstadt also addressed the proper understanding of signs, since the criticism of adoration was based on the claim that the sacrament was only a sign. The signs of the Old Testament, which were not united with something that could be worshiped, should be distinguished from the bread and cup, which were united to Christ, who was properly to be worshiped. Karlstadt placed limits on this adoration, however, by reinterpreting the elevation of the consecrated elements. Where Luther saw the elevation as a gesture used to arouse faith in those present during mass, Karlstadt identified it with the motions made by the priests of the Old

Testament during the wave offerings and the heave offerings, an idea he took from Johannes Reuchlin's Hebrew lexicon. Since the mass was not a sacrifice, these gestures were not appropriate. He closed this portion of the disputation by restating a mediating position: adoration as such should not be condemned, but its abuses should be abolished.[35]

Melanchthon agreed with Karlstadt's position on adoration, and in a set of theses for a disputation held soon afterward he focused instead on the way in which the sacrament should be understood as a sign. The two signs of the New Testament, baptism and participation in the Lord's table, were given to remind and assure us of God's will, just as a painted cross reminded us of Christ's death. As signs given by God, the sacraments differed from signs made up by man because they not only reminded but assured us of God's promises. Melanchthon cited Gideon's fleece as one of the signs of the Old Testament that gave such assurance. These signs were not sacrifices, nor did they justify one in and of themselves, and God's promise was always more powerful than the sign associated with it.[36]

These discussions of the sacrament as a sign and the validity of its adoration were the context in which Karlstadt wrote his next two treatises on the mass. Although the two pamphlets clearly reflected Karlstadt's understanding of the sacrament, they are best understood as representing to the public the consensus of Wittenberg's theologians in the face of the challenge raised by Zwilling's sermon.[37] Karlstadt devoted the first work to *The Adoration and Veneration of the Signs of the New Testament*.[38] In his dedication to the Nuremberg artist Albrecht Dürer, he stated that he was publishing this pamphlet to counter the lies and rumors that the Wittenbergers believed that one should not honor the sacrament—Melanchthon's letter to Link had apparently not been the only report of the disturbances in Wittenberg to reach Nuremberg. Less obviously but just as important, Karlstadt responded to the points raised by Hoen's letter.

Karlstadt began his argument by asserting the primacy of faith: adoration was the fruit of faith, which united one with Christ. God has forbidden us to worship created beings, which raised the question of whether it was right to adore bread and wine. Karlstadt reminded his readers that the bread and wine had been instituted not so that they should be adored but rather to be consumed: Christ said that we should eat his flesh and drink his blood. This did not mean, though, that we should not show honor to the elements. Christ himself praised the woman who washed his feet with her tears, and in the Old Testament God punished those such as Korah, Dathan, and Abiram who did not show him honor. In fact, we are obligated to honor Christ, and St. Paul had criticized the Corinthians for not receiving the sacrament with the proper honor. Hoen had asserted that in 1 Corinthians 10:16 ("the bread that we break, is it not a participation in the body of Christ?"), Paul did not call the bread the body of Christ, and in this verse "is" should be interpreted as "signifies." Karlstadt argued instead that Paul wrote openly that the bread is the body of Christ, and for this reason it should be honored. Only blasphemers and the enemies of Paul and all of the prophets could assert that we should not honor the bread and wine that had become Christ's body and blood.[39]

Although Karlstadt did not refer to Hoen here, he was clearly rejecting the Dutchman's interpretation of the passage and the consequence that he drew, that the sacrament should not be adored. He was more scathing in his condemnation of the "puffed-up toad" who claimed that the Wittenbergers "want to call Christ down from heaven in order to trample on him." Karlstadt mocked this charge and referred his readers to his forthcoming pamphlet *On Both Forms of the Holy Mass*, where he proved that the bread and the wine were Christ's body and blood.[40]

As he had done in his disputation theses, so in his pamphlet Karlstadt was careful to distinguish his understanding of the consecrated elements from the Catholic dogma of transubstantiation. Just as he believed that Christ is true God and man, so he believed that the bread in the priest's hands remained bread baked by a baker but was at the same time the body of Christ. Though natural man might find these statements unbelievable, to those with faith both assertions were easy to believe.[41] Karlstadt rejected the claim of "the papists" that "the form of the bread is the body of Christ," stating that there was no Scripture to support this view. The Gospels stated simply that the bread was the body and the wine was the blood of Christ. The bread was worshiped not as a created thing but because it had become Christ's body. Christians were to direct their eyes and their faith to Christ, seeking help from the living bread come down from heaven (John 6:51). Those who separated the bread from the body of Christ and could not believe that the bread and wine were Christ's body and blood ("from which," Karlstadt added, "may God preserve me") were indeed correct in not worshiping the sacrament, for to do so would be to make a created thing into an idol—the position Hoen held in his letter. But this was clearly a matter of faith: "Each person must consider whether or not he believes in Christ. Only after he gives credence to the words of Christ can he truly honor bread and wine, in that they have become body and blood of Christ, as I have described above."[42] For Karlstadt, as it would be for Luther, the crucial issue was the literal understanding of Christ's words of institution.

Karlstadt then turned to the use of the word "sign," recognizing that some were offended that this term was applied to the sacrament. The bread and wine were not simple signs like the rainbow or Gideon's fleece, but they actually became the things they signified, the body and blood of Christ.[43] Furthermore, as signs they pointed not to Christ's body and blood but to God's promises given to silence our doubts. Again Karlstadt used Christ's reference to the snake raised by Moses in the wilderness to argue that Christ on the cross was also a sign to whom one must look for salvation. If Christ could be called a sign, then surely no Christian could be offended by calling bread and wine signs. Karlstadt closed his pamphlet by repeating that no one said that the created substance of bread and wine should be worshiped. But in adoring the sacrament one looked not to what one saw but to the invisible body and blood of Christ. Those who regarded the bread of the sacrament in the same way as any other bread were like the Picards and those whom St. Paul criticized for dishonoring the body of Christ. Ultimately, each person must be guided in what he or she believed about the sacrament by what Scripture said.[44]

Karlstadt's second pamphlet, *On Both Forms in the Holy Mass*, was an amplification and expansion of ideas discussed only briefly in his pamphlet on adoration.[45] It is both lengthier and more technical in its discussion of the Eucharist, and its tone is more polemical. While the first pamphlet was directed against those who rejected the adoration of the consecrated elements and against the symbolic understanding of the sacrament that underlay it, the second pamphlet was more concerned with refuting the Catholic doctrine of transubstantiation and condemning the practice of communion under one form.

The pamphlet was divided into three unequal parts. The dedication and introduction laid the foundation by stressing that all teaching about the mass must be based on God's word rather than custom. The first part of the pamphlet proper then discussed the relationship between the elements and Christ's body and blood. Here Karlstadt presented an evangelical defense of the doctrine of remanence, the belief that the substance of the bread remained along with the substance of Christ's body after priestly consecration, in contrast to the position that Luther had taken in *On the Babylonian Captivity*.[46] There Luther had granted that this doctrine was more plausible than transubstantiation, but he then rejected entirely the use of Aristotelian concepts to explain what one received in the sacrament and stated that one should simply adhere to Christ's words "this is my body."[47] Karlstadt also rejected the traditional terminology, basing his argument on the words of institution: "Christ didn't say, 'The form (*Gestalt*) of bread is my body,' but rather, 'The bread that I have taken in my hands and blessed, broken and given to you, that is my body.'"[48] But he used the Aristotelian concepts to argue for the coexistence of bread and body in the host. There was a fundamental difference between bread, or its underlying substance (*Wesen*) or ground, and the form of bread, which was something changeable that was attached to or predicated of the bread, for instance, whether it was sweet, white, or round. Christ told his disciples, "take bread and eat, this is my body," referring to bread made by a baker. Karlstadt contrasted this bread with Christ's body, the living bread from heaven, which was true food and which was joined with the bread in the sacrament. Again he drew the analogy with

Christology: Christ was God, yet he retained his human nature. Nor was it impossible for one thing to have two substances:

> So it is no less possible for God that with one little word he makes two substances into one thing and allows each to retain its own essence; namely, through the word God makes the bread the body of Christ and the wine the blood of Christ, so that one thing is made of the bread and the flesh of Christ. . . . And so I also say that bread and flesh are two natures, but the consecrated bread is the body of Christ. The natural bread is heavenly bread, the lifeless bread is living bread, and the baker's bread is God's bread.[49]

Once he had dealt with objections raised by the defenders of transubstantiation, Karlstadt turned to what he considered the more important part of his pamphlet, the evangelical mass as promise and sign. This second, longer section was itself divided into two parts, the first treating of signs in Scripture generally and the second looking more specifically at the signs of bread and wine in the sacrament. In it Karlstadt used the theological vocabulary, scriptural justification, and illustrative analogies common to the Wittenberg theologians to discuss the sacrament, but he developed them in a direction that the others would not necessarily follow. He cited the Old Testament to show that God confirmed his promises by giving signs: the rainbow to Noah, circumcision to Abraham, and the fleece to Gideon. The purpose of the sign was to help God's people remember those promises whenever they felt doubt. The signs themselves could not save one, since no external thing made a person righteous, but they were instead reminders of God's faithfulness, like the seals placed on letters. Moreover, each sign had its own particular promise. One could not apply the promise associated with one sign, such as the rainbow, to another sign, such as the snake raised in the wilderness.[50]

Applying this general understanding of signs to the sacrament, Karlstadt pointed to the promises associated with the bread and wine. Each element had its own specific promise: the wine signified forgiveness of sins, while the bread signified resurrection and victory over death.[51] Karlstadt used the existence of these two distinct promises with associated signs to defend communion in both kinds. He rejected concomitance, the doctrine that one received both the body and blood under the one form of bread, and he pointed out that Christ commanded all those who ate the bread to drink out of the cup as well. As a consequence, it was not only a sin for priests to divide the sacrament and communicate in only one kind; it was also a sin for the laity to receive communion under one form.[52]

Karlstadt condemned other abuses associated with the sacrament as well. It was wrong for the church to focus more on ritual purity than on inner disposition.

It was far worse for the pope to compel people to receive the sacrament without a genuine understanding of its meaning than to risk desecration due to the accidental spilling of consecrated wine. The laity too were guilty of placing their confidence in the external signs, seeking forgiveness in the bread and not moving beyond it to the heavenly flesh of Christ. Christ himself had said that the flesh was of no use (John 6:63). Forgiveness came through faith, and the signs functioned to assure recipients of the promised forgiveness.[53]

From a theological perspective, the two chief parts of Karlstadt's pamphlet coexisted uneasily. Karlstadt's dualistic emphasis on sign and promise provided no convincing reason that Christ's body and blood should be present in the elements, and his reference to the signs of the Old Testament, which were entirely symbolic, subtly undermined the belief that the signs of the sacrament were anything more than symbols. Karlstadt's defense of remanence was based entirely on his literal understanding of the words of institution, which in turn was a specific application of his insistence that all doctrine must have firm scriptural foundation.[54] The consequences of this double commitment to a spiritualist dualism and the literal understanding of Scripture would become clear in Karlstadt's eucharistic pamphlets of 1524–1525.

Taken as a whole, Karlstadt's defense of the evangelical mass was a fair representation of what was being taught by all of the members of the reform party in Wittenberg in the fall of 1521. His emphasis differed in some ways from Luther's previously published works, but these differences were not yet striking, and they were endorsed by the other Wittenberg theologians. Where Luther had focused on the sacrament as a testament and rejected the sacrifice of the mass as a form of good work, Karlstadt was more concerned with explaining the nature of the elements as signs—a concern that is also reflected in the first edition of Melanchthon's *Loci Communes*, which was being published at precisely the same time that Karlstadt was writing his pamphlets.[55] Karlstadt had begun to work out his defense of communion in both kinds the previous summer and had expressed similar positions in his disputation theses from mid-October. He argued more strongly than his colleagues that the two signs of the sacrament represented two different promises, and some supported his belief that it was better to abstain from communion entirely rather than to receive it in only one form. In their description of the evangelical mass as sign and promise, and in their support for adoration of the host and Christ's corporeal presence in the sacrament, as well as in their rejection of transubstantiation, the Wittenberg reformers remained united.

There were, however, other reasons for disagreement within the reforming party. To examine these reasons, it is necessary to go back to the second and third issues raised by Zwilling's sermon mentioned in Brück's letter to the elector, a criticism of the abuses associated with the traditional mass, along with the insistence that both bread and wine must be given to all present, and the rejection of private masses. The united action of Wittenberg's theologians may have ended discussion over the question of Christ's bodily presence in the elements and the adoration of the sacrament, but the remaining two issues would cause unrest within the Augustinian convent and throughout Wittenberg through the rest of 1521. The reports and complaints sent to the elector over the course of the fall reveal both the complexities associated with practical liturgical reform and the multiple sources of division, even among the proponents of the evangelical movement.

The issue of private masses was initially the most explosive because Luther's understanding of the sacrament left little justification for them. Within a few days of Zwilling's sermon, his fellow Augustinians declared that they would no longer celebrate mass in its traditional form. Their decision was supported by the university commission appointed to investigate the disturbances in October. As the commission told the elector, the mass was not an offering or a good work, nor could a priest say mass on behalf of others. Its purpose was communion, in which the laity received the sure signs that reminded them of their forgiveness. For this reason, the priest must not communicate alone but must offer the sacrament to others who were present. The commission also pointed to the burdening of consciences that resulted from the priests' obligations to say endowed masses. Rather than endorsing these abuses, the Augustinians had followed Zwilling's lead and decided that they would no longer celebrate private masses.[56]

These arguments did not persuade everyone, however. Against the complete rejection of private masses, the conservative reformer Johann Dölsch argued that because the mass was "a fruitful and sure medicine against all concerns, sins, faults and failings," individual priests should not be forbidden to celebrate mass, even when there were no other communicants.[57] The Catholic canons went even further, defending the benefit of masses said for the dead and justifying the practice of paying priests to celebrate mass.[58] As their arguments made clear, theological arguments were not the only factor that had to be considered with regard to the abolition of private masses, for the income from endowed masses was essential for the maintenance of the Augustinian monastery as well as the city's other ecclesiastical institutions.[59] Legal and financial concerns thus played as much of a role in the debate over private masses as did theological arguments. Moreover, the reformers themselves disagreed on tactical grounds, with Melanchthon supporting the immediate abolition of all private masses and Karlstadt arguing that it was necessary first to seek some form of public consent for such a major step.[60] As a consequence, the recommendation endorsed by the commission in October and repeated in December was a compromise: priests could be neither required nor forbidden to celebrate the mass privately.[61]

By December, however, the commission's recommendation had become a moot point. In both the Augustinian convent and the parish church, private masses were voluntarily suspended and only one mass was said each weekday, although there were complaints that a few Augustinians who desired to celebrate private masses were being pressured by the rest not to do so. Faced with the threat of popular violence, the Franciscan friars also celebrated only one mass a day. Only the canons of All Saints were able to celebrate several daily masses, because they were under the elector's protection.[62]

A second issue on which the reform party was initially united was the extension of the chalice to the laity. The reformers were well aware that advocacy of communion in both kinds automatically led to suspicions of Hussite heresy, which was associated not only with doctrinal dissent and schism but with political and social revolution as well. Most Wittenbergers and the more general public may not have known what the Hussites believed, but they did know that the Hussites demanded the chalice for the laity. The reformers therefore undertook to dispel any association with heresy. In his letter to Link, Melanchthon asserted that the Wittenbergers were not Bohemians, and Karlstadt proclaimed in the full title of *On Both Forms* that "they are not Bohemians or heretics who receive both forms, but evangelical Christians." In their October report, the commission told the elector that he should not heed accusations that he was a Bohemian or heretic, "for all who wanted to do something for God's word must endure such scorn, dishonor and shame."[63]

The reforming party seems to have been little influenced by Karlstadt's argument that communion must be received in both kinds because each element signified a different promise. Instead, they cited another of his arguments, that Christ commanded communion in both kinds when he told all of his disciples to drink from the chalice.[64] By early December they also cited history to defend their position: at least through the time of Cyprian, it had been the practice for all present to receive both the bread and the wine, and this was still the practice in the Orthodox churches.[65]

Their advocacy of communion in both kinds generated more radical actions over the next few months. On All Saints' Day, the chaplain in the parish church administered communion in both kinds to all present. By the end of November, both Justas Jonas and the scholasticus of All Saints were refusing to celebrate mass unless communion was distributed to all in both kinds.[66] This development led to divisions among the reform party itself. Dölsch, its most conservative member, asserted that communion under only one form had been practiced for more than a thousand years and may even have been instituted by the apostles or their disciples. He therefore could not agree that it was sin to receive the sacrament under only one form, although he granted that those who did believe this should be allowed to receive both bread and wine. The Catholic canons were even more outspoken in their opposition, arguing that it would be best to retain the traditional practice to avoid disturbances. Not only had the Councils of Constance and Basel decided that communion in both kinds was unnecessary, but references in the New Testament to bread and not the cup could be interpreted to support communion in one kind. In sum, the issue of communion in both kinds proved as divisive as the debate over the abolition of private masses.[67]

The extent and type of liturgical reform provided yet another bone of contention. Zwilling had argued that the mass should not be celebrated unless it included a sermon to explain the meaning of the sacrament to those present. There was initially little discussion of specific changes to either the wording or the language of the mass, other than a general desire to return to the form instituted by Christ and practiced by the apostles. The evangelical Augustinians were the first to experiment with a new form of worship, in which a sermon was preached and the celebrant placed both the bread and the chalice in the hands of communicants. As pressures for change mounted over the course of the fall, attention increasingly focused on the canon of the mass. The reformers pointed to differences between the Roman and the Ambrosian rites to argue that the form of the canon used in Wittenberg was neither ancient nor universally accepted, an argument questioned by Dölsch and rejected by the Catholic canons.[68]

Underlying all of these disagreements about liturgical reform were two fundamental questions. The first concerned the tension between what the reformers understood as God's command to eliminate abuses from the mass and the public offense that would be caused by changes to existing practices. Conservatives charged that the small group of reformers was causing scandal by attacking practices hallowed by long practice. The reformers retorted that the conservatives were the troublemakers, no different from the Pharisees who had opposed Christ. The reforming party was by no means united, though, in its view of where to draw the line between obedience to God and forbearance for the sake of the weak. Throughout the fall, Karlstadt proved to be more moderate than Melanchthon in advocating the introduction of reforms.[69]

The second issue concerned who had the authority to determine if and when any reforms were introduced. The opponents of reform claimed that only the church, whether through the ecclesiastical superiors of the regular and secular clergy in Wittenberg, as contained in the advice of other university faculties, or represented in a general church council, could authorize the types of changes advocated by the reformers. Supporters of reform rejected this claim, but there was still disagreement over whether the Augustinians constituted their own congregation and so could institute changes within their convent as they saw fit, or if various levels of secular authority, whether embodied in the whole citizenry of Wittenberg, the town council, or the elector, bore final responsibility for approving any innovations.[70]

The question of authority grew even more acute as the attacks on traditional worship changed from words to actions. In early December a crowd of students and citizens threw stones at priests singing the morning office in the parish church and later threatened with knives those saying mass in the church.[71] Two weeks later the citizens of Wittenberg presented the town council with six articles in which they demanded the free preaching of the gospel, the abolition of compulsory private masses and of all votive masses and masses for the dead, and communion in both kinds for all those who desired it.[72] In the face of this unrest, the elector decreed on 19 December that there should be no more innovations. The traditional usages were to be retained until agreement had been reached through preaching, lecturing, writing, and disputations.[73]

The news of the elector's decision reached Wittenberg at a critical moment. Like Jonas and Luther himself, Karlstadt had resolved sometime during the fall not to celebrate mass in the traditional way. His fellow canons had said mass for him on the days when he was required by the chapter's statutes to do so. But their forbearance came to an end after Karlstadt preached a sermon attacking the mass, and they decided that they would no longer substitute for him. In response, Karlstadt announced in a sermon that when he celebrated the mass on the feast of Christ's circumcision (New Year's Day), which as archdeacon of the chapter he was required to do, he would celebrate it in an evangelical way, without donning the required vestments, prefacing the mass with a short sermon, speaking simply the words of consecration, omitting the rest of the canon and the associated gestures, and distributing the sacrament in both kinds to all who desired it.[74]

In the event, Karlstadt did not wait until New Year's Day. On Christmas Eve, an unruly mob entered the parish church during the vespers service and threatened the clergy, mocked their chanting with bawdy songs, and broke the lamps. They then proceeded to the castle church, where they interrupted the service with curses. These disruptions moved Karlstadt to take action. On Christmas Day Karlstadt preached a sermon on the evangelical mass in the castle church. His sermon took up the same theme as his first publication on the mass: the question of worthy reception of the sacrament. After condemning the traditional view that worthiness consisted in ascetic exercises and full sacramental confession, he gave his own definition. Only unbelief, which dishonored God, made one unfit to receive the sacrament. Christ instituted the sacrament for sinners, and faith in God's promise of forgiveness was the only necessary preparation. Christians should take to heart the assurance of a joyful resurrection signified by the bread and of full forgiveness signified by the chalice. Karlstadt told those who had not confessed that they should approach the sacrament in joyful confidence, knowing that their faith made them righteous.[75]

Karlstadt's next step was completely unexpected.[76] After finishing his sermon, he crossed over to the altar and began to celebrate an evangelical mass in the way he had said he would, without the prescribed vestments and placing not only the consecrated bread but also the cup in the hands of lay recipients so that they could eat and drink themselves.[77] Two of the recipients were so affected by this new form of distribution that they dropped the host, to the consternation of those around them. The Catholic canons immediately reported Karlstadt's innovations to the elector, noting with horror that many of the recipients had neither confessed nor fasted—and some had even drunk brandy—before receiving the sacrament.[78]

From this point on the speed of reform accelerated.[79] Karlstadt repeated his evangelical mass a week later, this time in the parish church, with the consent of the parish priest, and again on the following Sunday (5 January) and on Epiphany. According to one contemporary account, more than a thousand people received communion in both kinds at these services. Karlstadt continued to preach to a full church, and even those who rarely or never attended sermons now did not miss any of them. There was talk of replacing the morning office with a service in which German Psalms and portions of the Bible were read and explained. The innovations were not limited to liturgical reform. On the day after Christmas, Karlstadt became engaged to a poor young noblewoman from a nearby village, in the presence of not only Melanchthon but "two wagons full of learned men"; other priests, including Justus Jonas, planned to follow his example.[80] Several Augustinians, among them Gabriel Zwilling, had already left the monastery in October. Zwilling was now preaching incendiary sermons against the mass in Eilenburg, and on New Year's Day he also distributed communion in both kinds. As the final ingredient in this heady brew of reform and rebellion, three men, the so-called Zwickau prophets, arrived in Wittenberg two days after Christmas, proclaiming the imminent arrival of one whose spirit surpassed that of Luther, predicting great changes to the world in the coming years, and casting doubt on the value of infant baptism.[81]

With the shift from discussion to deeds, the Wittenberg movement needed a visible leader. The obvious candidate was Karlstadt. Not only had his actions on Christmas Day placed him in the spotlight, but as the preacher in the castle church, he was the only member of the reforming party with regular access to a pulpit.[82] Although he had apparently refrained from preaching through most of the fall, he returned to the pulpit in December. He was joined by Zwilling, who returned to Wittenberg in mid-January. Their next goal was the removal of images from the parish church.[83] Through the month of January, Karlstadt, Melanchthon, and other university faculty met with the town council to draft provisions prescribing the form of the evangelical mass and regulating begging. The result was a church order adopted on 24 January. The new evangelical mass authorized in the ordinance followed the form introduced by Karlstadt on Christmas Day. There were few changes up through the Sanctus, which was followed by a sermon. The mass liturgy proper, however, was simplified: the priest spoke the words of consecration aloud in German, reminded the people that those who felt burdened by their sins were welcome to receive the sacrament, and then distributed communion in both kinds. Communicants could receive the bread and take the chalice in their own hands, and, although the ordinance did not specify this, later discussion implies that the elevation of the consecrated elements was omitted.[84]

But events in Wittenberg had gone too far for the elector. Both Karlstadt and Zwilling were warned to moderate their preaching so as not to cause further divisions, to which Karlstadt responded that he was only preaching what was contained in Scripture.[85] In mid-February the electoral counselor Hugold von Einsiedeln met with Christian Beyer, who had just become Wittenberg's mayor, and with representatives of the university and the chapter, to remind the latter that the elector had decreed that no innovations were to be introduced to the mass. The reforming party defended the liturgical changes, pointing out the need to speak the words of consecration in German so that the congregation could understand the power of the sacrament. They also argued that although it might be desirable to return to the traditional mass, the liturgical changes had too much popular support for this to be done without causing further unrest. The best solution was to ensure uniformity in the celebration of the evangelical mass throughout the city. The meeting resulted in a compromise proposal regarding liturgical reform: the mass would be celebrated daily, but the canon would be omitted, and instead the words of consecration would be spoken in German. The elevation would be retained "as a sign to the people," and all who desired to receive the sacrament could communicate, but they would be given the elements by the priest rather than taking them in their own hands.[86]

This compromise proved unacceptable to the elector, who saw it as a contravention of his order not to introduce any liturgical innovations. In addition, the elector was facing pressure from the imperial government to prevent any changes to traditional worship. Most significant, however, was his concern over the divisions that had arisen within the reform movement.[87] The disagreements between the university's theologians, who advocated reforms, and the majority of the canons, who opposed them, had long been apparent. By mid-February, though, the reform party was also showing signs of disunity. The criticism of Karlstadt's and Zwilling's preaching seems to have caused Melanchthon to assume a more cautious position regarding the introduction of reforms: in mid-February he drew up a list of theses on images and communion in one kind, in which he acknowledged that both might be tolerated in case of necessity, in order to avoid public scandal.[88] Beyer also had reservations about the removal of all images from the parish church.[89] By the middle of January Luther was also receiving reports that caused him to think about at least moving closer to Wittenberg; a month later he informed the elector that he had decided to return to the city.[90]

Luther arrived in Wittenberg on 6 March, and beginning on the following Sunday (Invocavit) he preached a series of sermons in which he gave his judgment on the reform movement at a whole. In these Invocavit sermons he addressed not only specific liturgical changes—celebrating the mass without vestments, distributing communion in both kinds, and allowing the laity to receive the elements with their own hands—but also the purpose and benefits of the sacrament more generally. Almost immediately afterward he began work on a pamphlet On Receiving Both Kinds in the Sacrament, which was published in mid-April; his Maundy Thursday sermon that year concerned communion in both kinds as well.[91]

In the Invocavit sermons, Luther endorsed the virtual end of private masses in Wittenberg. God opposed these because they were performed as a sacrifice and a meritorious work, and so it was necessary that they be abolished. Nevertheless, he criticized the manner of their abolition, for it had been done in a disorderly way, under threat of violence, and had therefore caused scandal to some.[92] Luther had even less sympathy for the way that the practical liturgical reforms had been justified. Karlstadt and Zwilling had condemned traditional practices, such as communion in one kind, as being opposed to Scripture and defended others, such as taking the consecrated host in one's hand, as commanded by Scripture. While Luther agreed about rejecting "papal laws," he argued that it was no improvement to make new practices mandatory, for these practices did not make one a good Christian. It was more important to preach the word and to leave the new practices voluntary, so that the weak were not driven away by them.[93]

Luther expanded on this thought in his pamphlet On Receiving Both Kinds, where he discussed liturgical change as a specific application of the principle of Christian liberty. It was true that the laity should receive both bread and wine and that neither vestments nor expensive communion vessels were necessary, but if these reforms injured the consciences of other Christians, they should be postponed. Until there were enough trained preachers to help people understand the proper celebration of the mass, it was necessary to proceed slowly, preserving the old rituals but eliminating as much as possible any wording that supported the idea of the mass as a sacrifice and preaching about Christ's promise in the words of institution. The first and most essential reform was to eliminate the requirement of annual communion, so that people would partake of the sacrament only from their own desire. Only as people came to a fuller understanding of the gospel could other necessary reforms be introduced. In the meantime, Luther endorsed some of the practices already introduced in Wittenberg. Priests celebrating the mass, for instance, could omit the words in the canon and the prayers that referred to the mass as a sacrifice without the laity's realizing it and so taking offense. In his sermon the priest should emphasize the significance of the words "my body given and blood shed for you." If both elements were offered, they could be received, but it was not wrong to communicate if only the host was offered.[94]

In accordance with his principle that preaching was the first and most necessary step, Luther repeated his understanding of the sacrament in both his Invocavit sermons and his Maundy Thursday sermon. The word of promise was more important than the signs, and internal reception of Christ through faith more important than external reception of bread and wine. Faith and awareness of one's own need made one worthy to receive the sacrament, which confirmed Christ's promise of forgiveness.[95]

Karlstadt did not readily accept Luther's arguments. In April he tried to publish a pamphlet ostensibly criticizing the Catholic mass but which could also be turned against Luther's arguments. In it Karlstadt rejected the word "mass" as misleading and unscriptural, preferring to call it the Lord's Supper, as St. Paul did. It was true that the form of the Supper was an external thing, but it was possible to sin regarding external things, and so Karlstadt described what he understood as the proper administration of the sacrament. It was not sufficient to explain the words of consecration in the sermon, nor should those words be spoken silently, but the priest should also speak them to the individuals receiving communion. The elevation should be eliminated, since Christ did not elevate the elements, and elevation was associated with sacrifice. Both elements should be distributed, and if one was omitted, it would be preferable to omit the bread rather than the wine. Because Christ said, "take, eat," the elements should be placed directly in the hands of the communicants.[96]

The pamphlet came to the attention of the university before the printing was finished, and the faculty refused to let it be published for fear of causing further unrest. With this final attempt to defend the innovations of the previous four months, Karlstadt's active involvement in the Wittenberg movement came to an end. Although he remained in the city for another year, he was not allowed to publish anything, nor was he permitted to preach.[97] As a consequence there are very few traces of either his theological development or his activities during this time.

INTERMISSION: THE SITUATION IN 1522

The end of the Wittenberg movement serves as a good place to assess the significance of developments for Karlstadt's relationship with Luther and their implications for the later eucharistic controversy. The two central issues were those that had overshadowed the Wittenberg movement from its beginning, but in each case with a twist. The first concerned Karlstadt's emphasis on the need for practical reforms in accordance with divine law, to which Luther responded with his understanding of Christian freedom. In this debate, the sacrament played only a secondary though still important role. The second concerned the question of who had the authority to institute practical reforms.

Eucharistic theology per se was not an issue of contention between Luther and Karlstadt, for through April 1522 they agreed in their understanding of the Lord's Supper. With regard to both the definition of the sacrament as promise and sign and its purpose—to assure sinners of forgiveness—Karlstadt still held to Luther's views. Likewise, there is no indication that Karlstadt had abandoned his belief in Christ's corporeal presence in the elements or rejected the adoration of the sacrament. The issues that divided the two men concerned not theology but practice. Even here, though, the disagreements were to some extent those of degree rather than of principle. Both of them opposed the celebration of private masses and supported the laity's right to receive communion in both kinds. Karlstadt's desire to gain public support before abolishing the private mass placed him closer to Luther's concern for bearing with the weak than was Melanchthon's more radical support for the immediate elimination of such masses. Where Karlstadt differed from Luther was on the absolute necessity of communion in both kinds. Already in the summer of 1521 Karlstadt insisted that Christians should receive both bread and wine or they should abstain entirely from communion, a position that Luther rejected because he believed that this placed too much emphasis on an external act.

But what initially seemed to be small disagreement regarding the proper observance of an external rite would eventually be revealed as the most important disagreement between the two reformers. All other differences between Luther and Karlstadt concerning the mass, as well as other questions such as the removal of images from the churches, were subsumed by this larger issue, which can be summed up as whether one should give priority to divine law or to Christian freedom.[98] For Karlstadt, the external forms of worship, including the celebration of the mass, had to reflect the message of the gospel. What contradicted that message must be eliminated, and the practices instituted by Christ must be restored. Thus the liturgy should be in the vernacular, the people should be able to take the elements in their hands physically, and the laity should receive the cup in accordance with Christ's commands, "take, eat" and "drink of it, all of you." Additions that distracted from Christ's institution, such as special vestments, utensils, and gestures, or that propagated the false belief that the mass was a sacrifice, such as the elevation of the consecrated elements, should be abolished.

Luther, however, believed that such a focus on externals distracted from rather than enhanced the message of the gospel. He made clear in his preaching and in his pamphlet *On Receiving Both Kinds* that it was far more important for people to understand the essence of the gospel than for the outer forms of worship to correspond to that gospel. The issue dividing Karlstadt and Luther therefore was not simply a question of timing and whether one should delay necessary reforms for the sake of the weak. Instead, as would become clear from Luther's later treatises against Karlstadt, it was a more fundamental disagreement on the relationship between external actions and internal disposition, particularly because that disagreement had significant implications for the doctrine of justification by faith. For Luther, justification by faith came first and foremost, and it was encouraged by preaching rather than by external ceremonies. Indeed, insistence on any external ceremonies endangered the principle of justification by faith alone, for it opened the door to reliance on works. For Karlstadt, however, external ceremonies had to conform to what was preached, both amplifying and confirming the message of the gospel and reflecting the form of worship that God had commanded in Scripture. First emerging in Wittenberg in the spring of 1522, this fundamental disagreement would only become more obvious in Luther's attacks on Karlstadt at the turn of 1524/25. It would also color Luther's understanding of Karlstadt's later pamphlets on the Lord's Supper, and it would form one of the issues that divided the parties in the eucharistic controversy.[99]

The second and related issue concerned that of authority, but the matter went beyond who had the right to authorize reforms to the larger question of who had the authority to judge doctrine. Luther and Karlstadt disagreed openly on the importance of external ceremonies and the interpretation of Christian freedom. This forced their supporters to ask which one was right. In Wittenberg, at least, there was no question in most people's minds that the answer was Luther. The reformer felt obligated by his calling as pastor and professor to take responsibility for the evangelical movement as it was developing in the city and the university community. The Wittenbergers too looked to Luther as the one capable of making authoritative decisions about belief and practice. Melanchthon felt that only Luther could correctly judge the Zwickau prophets, while the town council appealed to him to return as unrest in the city increased over the course of February.[100] Once Luther was back in Wittenberg, the reforming party accepted the arguments that Luther presented in his Invocavit sermons. Only Karlstadt persisted in his opposition, and he was forbidden both to preach and to publish ideas that might diverge from those of Luther. Karlstadt's frequent references to Luther as the "new pope" in his later writings on the Lord's Supper reflect the authoritative position Luther held among his followers, as well as Karlstadt's resentment that he was not regarded as having equal authority. For his part, Luther regarded Karlstadt's independence not simply as a challenge to his own authority but as evidence of his "insane lust for glory and praise."[101]

Luther's personal presence in Wittenberg mended the cracks that had appeared in the evangelical movement and reestablished the consensus that had existed earlier, but it also indicated a latent weakness in that movement. In other cities where the evangelical movement began to fragment over the type and timing of practical reform or over the understanding of the sacraments, whether the Lord's Supper or baptism, the question of authority was not so easily settled. In both Zurich and Strasbourg, for instance, the pastors remained united in their preaching, but significant radical movements developed in both cities whose adherents eventually withdrew from the official church. In Augsburg, where the pastors would divide on the issue of the Lord's Supper, there was no authority able to restore unity. And on the larger scene, the authority of reformers in other cities who did not see eye-to-eye with Luther on all matters—whether Ulrich Zwingli in Zurich, Johann Oecolampadius in Basel, or Wolfgang Capito and Martin Bucer in Strasbourg—could override the authority emanating from distant Wittenberg. Luther's reputation was not able to maintain a broader doctrinal consensus as preachers and pastors not only in Wittenberg but throughout Germany began to draw their own conclusions from his fundamental principles of sola Scriptura and sole fide. This too would have consequences for the outbreak of the eucharistic controversy.

Finally, there is the question of what, if any, continuities exist between the views on the sacrament expressed in Karlstadt's works from 1521–1522 and his later eucharistic treatises. These early works can be characterized as having three distinctive features. First, the Old Testament, especially the Pentateuch, played a prominent role in Karlstadt's understanding of the Lord's Supper. In the years preceding the outbreak of the Reformation, Karlstadt had devoted his energies to the study of Hebrew, and the fruit of that study was reflected in his earliest publications as a reformer, including those on the Lord's Supper.[102] This fascination with the Old Testament, especially as it was interpreted typologically in the epistle to the Hebrews, would be of decisive importance for Karlstadt's understanding of the parallels between the sacrificial system of the Israelites, Christ's sacrificial death on the cross, and the sacrament instituted in remembrance of that sacrifice.

Second, and just as significant for Karlstadt's understanding of the Old Testament, was a neoplatonic/Augustinian and Erasmian dualism that on the one hand sharply differentiated between external and internal and on the other hand understood the New Testament as that which fulfilled what was figured in the Old. Karlstadt's intensive study of Augustine over the course of 1517 and 1518 resulted in an understanding of the relation between law and spirit that differed from that of Luther and that would eventually lead him in a different direction theologically.[103] In this development, Karlstadt would also be influenced by Erasmus's spiritualizing interpretation of the epistle to the Hebrews. Both aspects of this dualism would have a prominent place in his later understanding of the Lord's Supper.

Last but not least, Karlstadt based his belief in Christ's bodily presence in the sacrament entirely on his literal interpretation of Christ's words "this is my body." Although he rejected the doctrine of transubstantiation, his defense of the adoration of the consecrated host reveals an unquestioning acceptance of the traditional belief that Christ was present bodily in the elements. If (and when) he could be persuaded that a literal understanding of those words did not require such a belief, he had no other theological justification to argue for that presence, and in fact his denigration of externals would incline him toward a purely symbolic understanding of the sacrament.

As we will see, all of these features would play a significant role in Karlstadt's later eucharistic theology. But before we examine that theology, we must first look at developments outside Wittenberg to see how others responded to Luther's reinterpretation of the mass.

2

From Pastoral Care to Polemic

THE EVOLUTION OF EARLY EVANGELICAL VIEWS OF THE MASS

⌒————————————————————————————————————

"ABOMINATION" AND "BLASPHEMY" are harsh words even to a secular twenty-first-century audience. They were even more offensive to a sixteenth-century one, especially when they were applied to the most holy ceremony of the late medieval church, the mass, in which the priest transformed the bread and wine into the very body and blood of Christ, to be offered to God for the sins of both living and dead. Nevertheless, by 1524 they were frequently used in evangelical pamphlets on the mass. How did polemics so quickly come to dominate the discussion of the sacrament?

The answer to this question can be found through a closer examination of these early evangelical pamphlets. In comparison to the eucharistic controversy that broke out at the end of 1524, the earlier evangelical discussion of the mass is not well studied. Scholars have scrutinized the publications of Luther and Zwingli for indications of their later positions on the Lord's Supper and examined the early works of other reformers to identify the influence of the two chief protagonists of the later controversy. But the pamphlets of lesser-known individuals have been virtually ignored, and other influences on their thought have been minimized or unrecognized.[1] As a consequence, the changing concerns of these pamphleteers and the importance of the pamphlets themselves in preparing the way for the eucharistic controversy have been overlooked.

This scholarly neglect is unfortunate for another reason, because the early pamphlets on the mass offer an illuminating case study of the reception and spread of evangelical ideas more generally. An examination of pamphlets published between

1518 and 1524 devoted to the mass reveals an important shift in the discussion of the mass as it moved outward from Wittenberg. In the first phase of this movement, Luther's ideas were picked up by other pamphleteers and reinterpreted within a framework influenced equally by late medieval preaching and by Erasmian humanism. A second phase began in 1523, when a number of new authors, including Ulrich Zwingli, joined the debate. Zwingli's criticism of the sacrifice of the mass moved the discussion away from the pastoral concerns that had characterized the early years of the Reformation to a more polemical attack on both the theology of the mass and the liturgical prescriptions for its celebration. If the earliest pamphleteers repeated Luther's evangelical understanding of the sacrament, those who wrote in 1524 demonstrated the equal impact of the Zurich Reformation.

This chapter will focus on how Luther's reformatory ideas were received and then passed on to others, highlighting differences in evangelical views of the mass between the Wittenberg circle and the reformers of South Germany and Switzerland that would contribute to the outbreak of the eucharistic controversy at the end of 1524. Before we look at the pamphlets themselves, however, let us begin with an overview of early evangelical publications on the mass.

THE PUBLICATION HISTORY OF PAMPHLETS ON THE MASS

Between 1518 and 1524, no fewer than 386 pamphlets were published that dealt with the sacrament of the altar.[2] Table 2.1 classifies these pamphlets by confession. Perhaps what is most striking about these numbers is Luther's obvious dominance as the author of pamphlets on the sacrament, a reflection of his dominance of pamphlet publication as a whole during this period.[3] The Eucharist was an important topic for Luther. His pamphlets concerning the mass constituted roughly 20 percent of the total number of works he published before 1525, ranging from a low of only 12 percent of the first editions printed in 1521 to a high of 35 percent in 1524.[4]

Luther not only published more than anyone else on the mass; in the early years of the Reformation, he also set the agenda for the discussion of the sacrament. In the three years immediately following the posting of the Ninety-five Theses, he was virtually the only person to publish anything specifically on the mass. Almost all of his pamphlets were sermons originally preached during Holy Week, as the laity prepared to receive their obligatory annual communion. The earliest of these was his *Sermon on Worthy Preparation for the Sacrament of the Eucharist*, which appeared in six Latin and three German editions in 1518.[5] It proved to be wildly popular, going through seventeen more editions in the next two years.[6] Luther's 1519 *Sermon on the Venerable Sacrament* was almost as popular. Published in two German editions the

TABLE 2.1

Pamphlets on the Mass, 1518–1524

	LUTHER		OTHER EVANGELICALS		CATHOLICS		TOTAL		NUMBER OF AUTHORS
	Titles[1]	Imprints	Titles	Imprints	Titles	Imprints	Titles	Imprints	
1518	3	9	0	0	1	1	4	10	2
1519	4	17	0	0	0	0	4	17	1
1520	6	42	0	0	2	3	8	45	3
1521	2	7	8	17	3	3	13	27	· 8
1522	7	36	10	32	7	13	24	81	13 + 1 anon.
1523	12	55	12	27	8	10	32	92	12 + 3
1524	13	29	30	72	6	13	49	114	26 + 2
Total	47	195	60	148	27	43	134	386	36 + 6

1. German and Latin versions of the same work are counted as separate titles because they were intended for different audiences.

year it was preached, the sermon went through nine editions in 1520, three more in 1523, and a final imprint in 1525; it was also published in Latin translation in 1524.[7]

Luther's Maundy Thursday sermon for 1520, *On the New Testament, That Is, on the Holy Mass*, was printed twelve times that year and four more times over the next four years, either alone or with other sermons by Luther.[8] In 1520 Luther also published his first discussion of the mass that was not in sermon form. His treatise *On the Babylonian Captivity of the Church* went through twelve editions, divided equally between the original Latin and the German translation.[9] Luther's treatise was at least in part a response to the *Tractate on Communion in Both Kinds* by the Leipzig Franciscan Augustin Alvedt. Alvedt's fellow Franciscan Thomas Murner appealed to a more popular audience by publishing an attack in German on several of Luther's works, including his *Sermon on the New Testament*.[10]

Luther's publications on the mass slowed while he was in hiding at the Wartburg. His Maundy Thursday sermon, preached a few days before he left for the Diet of Worms, was printed six times.[11] His only other work on the mass from this period, written in October and published at the beginning of 1522, was a polemical piece urging the abolition of private masses.[12]

The slack was taken up by Luther's colleagues in Wittenberg, the most important of whom was Andreas Bodenstein von Karlstadt. Over the course of 1521, Karlstadt published three vernacular pamphlets on the mass, the first addressing the proper preparation for receiving the sacrament, the second on the adoration of the consecrated host, and the third on communion in both kinds, all of which went through several editions. His Christmas sermon of 1521, preached immediately before he distributed communion in both kinds to the congregation, was published four times in 1522.[13] Because Karlstadt's understanding of the mass was at this time essentially the same as Luther's, his pamphlets served to reinforce rather than to compete with those of Luther. The early Wittenberg understanding of the mass was further propagated through a set of disputation theses on the mass and five imprints of the memorandum written by a university commission to Elector Frederick the Wise defending the decision of the city's Augustinians to suspend celebration of private masses.[14]

The remaining evangelical pamphlets on the mass from this period were published in Augsburg. Johann Oecolampadius's 1521 Corpus Christi sermon, preached to his fellow monks in the monastery at Altomünster, was published twice in its original Latin and once in German translation.[15] Urbanus Rhegius, who had succeeded Oecolampadius as the cathedral preacher in Augsburg, published his Corpus Christi sermon for 1521 as well.[16] A short pamphlet by Georg Fener from Weil also went through four editions, provoking a response from the Swiss priest Johann Manberger.[17] Last but not least, the Catholic Johann Eckart reprinted Luther's *Sermon on the New Testament* with his own critical response following each section.[18]

After his return from the Wartburg in 1522, Luther again took up the issue of the sacrament. His Maundy Thursday sermon, *The Chief Article of the Eternal and New Testament of the Venerable Sacrament*, went through fifteen editions, and his pamphlet *On Receiving Both Kinds in the Sacrament* was printed thirteen times before 1525.[19] The only other works to meet with such popular demand were Luther's pamphlet *On the Adoration of the Sacrament* and his *Formula Missae et Communionis*, each of which went through fifteen editions in 1523–1524.[20] During this same two-year period, Luther's response to Henry VIII was published in seven imprints in both Latin and German, his Invocavit sermons of 1522 went through six imprints, and his 1523 Maundy Thursday sermon was published seven times; his remaining sermons on the sacrament went through only three or four imprints.[21]

By this time other writers had entered the discussion of the mass. On the Catholic side, Murner was joined by Kaspar Schatzgeyer, Johann Cochlaeus, and King Henry VIII of England in 1522 and by Hieronymus Emser and John Fisher the following year.[22] As the controversy surrounding the mass spread to South Germany, the Augsburg preacher Mathias Kretz and the bishop of Constance, Hugo von Hohenlandenberg, entered the fray as well.[23]

Most of the evangelical newcomers to the public debate over the mass came from South Germany and Switzerland. In contrast to Luther, few of them published more than one pamphlet on the sacrament, and most of their pamphlets were not printed more than once. Virtually all of the pamphleteers were clergy, and the only author who could be seen as representative of "the common man" was the Strasbourg gardener Clemens Ziegler.[24] A few of the authors, most notably Ulrich Zwingli and Martin Bucer, were or would become leading reformers with influence far beyond their own cities, while others, such as Andreas Osiander in Nuremberg and Kaspar Kantz and Theobald Billican in Nördlingen, were responsible for introducing evangelical reforms into their home churches. Some of the authors were far less influential, but their works are significant as testimony to the popular impact of Luther's understanding of the sacrament and as evidence of the way the public debate on the mass evolved.[25]

This overview of evangelical publications on the mass is instructive for understanding Luther's role in the spread of a new understanding of the sacrament. On the one hand, Luther's dominance of the debate up through 1522 guaranteed that his views would be foundational for other evangelical authors. The sheer quantity of Luther's pamphlets tends to support Berndt Moeller's contention that the earliest stage of the Reformation was shaped decisively by the Wittenberg reformer.[26] On the other hand, the simple diffusion of ideas does not guarantee that they are correctly understood, and only an examination of the earliest works on the mass by other authors can determine how Luther's ideas were received. Moreover, from 1522 Luther's voice began to be obscured by the increasing number of pamphlets devoted to the mass. The Wittenberger was still the most popular authority on the sacrament, but his publications were bound to have less influence on the public debate, not only because there was more competition from other authors, but also because his newer works on the sacrament were not reprinted as frequently as his earliest pamphlets. And while the other early pamphlets on the mass attested to Luther's influence, they also helped spread slightly divergent views that would hasten the end of any early consensus around Luther regarding the mass.

THE FOUNDATIONS OF THE EVANGELICAL UNDERSTANDING OF THE MASS

What did Luther say about the mass? His earliest pamphlets on the subject—those published in 1518 and 1519—were fairly traditional. Reflecting their origin as Holy Week sermons, they dealt with how Christians should prepare to receive communion worthily. Both of these sermons emphasized the need for faith and humility, rather than trust in one's own ability to prepare sufficiently, as the best preparation for the sacrament. A secondary theme was that those who received Christ's body in the sacrament were also obliged to show love and mutual support for fellow members of Christ's mystical body, the church.[27]

Only in 1520 did Luther publicly adopt an understanding of the sacrament that put him at odds with the church's teaching. In his *Sermon on the New Testament*, and at more length in *On the Babylonian Captivity of the Church*, Luther rejected the understanding of the mass as a sacrifice. He described it instead as a testament in which Christ bequeathed forgiveness to his heirs, accompanied with the signs of his body and blood under the forms of bread and wine. Luther criticized the church for turning a sacrament that should strengthen and assure consciences into a good work through which men claimed to offer something to God. He also called the church's refusal to allow the laity to receive the wine "wicked and despotic," and he expressed his wish that the words of institution should be spoken in German, rather than Latin, so that others could hear and understand the central promise of the sacrament.[28]

In his sermons of the next few years, Luther repeated many of the themes already expressed in his earliest publications. In the sacrament Christ gave his promise, expressed in the words of institution, and the signs of his body and blood, which acted as the seal or assurance of that promise.[29] Intellectual assent to these words was not enough, however; recipients were also to apply Christ's words "given/shed for you" personally. In the sacrament Christians received all the benefits of Christ and were united with one another.[30] Luther asserted that Christ's words in John 6 had nothing to do with the sacrament of the altar, but in his Corpus Christi sermon published in 1523 he stressed the spiritual manducation of Christ's body as the precondition for sacramental communion: to eat and drink the flesh and blood of the son of God was nothing other than to believe that his flesh and blood were given for me, and it did not suffice only to receive the sacrament externally.[31] In the wake of the disturbances in Wittenberg during his absence, he held back from introducing mandatory liturgical reforms until he deemed his audience properly understood the sacrament and was ready for such changes. Only at the end of 1523 did he publish an evangelical liturgy—still in Latin—that could serve as a model for other evangelical churches.[32]

Outside of Wittenberg, the discussions of the mass proceeded somewhat differently, reflecting greater continuity with a strain of late medieval preaching on the sacrament that Luther largely ignored or even reacted against. This was the notion of spiritual communion, the mystical union between the believer and Christ that could take place without sacramental communion or the physical reception of the consecrated host. St. Paul's warning against unworthy reception (1 Cor. 11:27–30) had been given new significance by the late medieval emphasis on the presence of Christ's body in the consecrated host. Only through the most rigorous preparation, which included not only a complete sacramental confession but also ascetic practices such as fasting and prayer, was an individual worthy to receive the body of Christ.[33] This insistence on purity is what Luther criticized when he emphasized that the precondition for worthy reception was faith, not one's own actions. As a way to avoid the dangers of unworthy reception, late medieval theologians and preachers extolled the value of spiritual communion, which brought the benefits of sacramental communion but avoided the dangers associated with unworthy reception.[34]

Although believers could experience spiritual communion at any place or time, preachers associated it particularly with ocular communion, which occurred when an individual observed the consecration of the host and the priest's communion in the mass. Just as in sacramental communion one received the body and blood of Christ under the forms of bread and wine, so in ocular communion one received the body and blood of Christ, but through the eyes and with the spirit rather than with the mouth. Late medieval devotional books contained prayers to be said at consecration, elevation, or the priest's communion during the mass that acknowledged the laity's desire to receive Christ's body and blood spiritually as the priest did so physically.[35]

The alternative of ocular communion was closely linked with the doctrine of transubstantiation in another way. Just as late medieval preachers made belief in Christ's presence in the bread and wine one of the necessary preconditions for worthy reception of the sacrament physically, so they emphasized that those who communed spiritually or with their eyes should also believe that Christ's body and blood were present in the consecrated elements.[36] It was on this point that the most influential advocate of spiritual communion, Erasmus, diverged from the tradition of late medieval preaching.

Erasmus's understanding of the sacrament incorporated elements of medieval scholastic doctrine, but on several points the Dutch humanist questioned and even seemed to go beyond the boundaries set by scholastic teaching.[37] Thus he accepted Christ's presence in the sacrament, but he expressed his doubts about the doctrine of transubstantiation, preferring to say that Christ was present in the sacrament in an ineffable way. Although he did not reject the sacrifice of the mass, he stated that there was no direct support for it in the creeds of the early church, and in his paraphrase of Hebrews 10:11–14 he stressed that Christ's sacrifice was unique and need not be repeated.[38] Because he believed that the sacrament should be administered in the way it had been instituted by Christ, he opposed withholding the chalice from the laity. He also raised questions about the actual words used by Christ at the Last Supper with his disciples, which his opponents interpreted as an attack on the consecratory power of the words of institution.[39] In response to his critics, however, Erasmus consistently stated his willingness to accept the authority of the church on these and other matters. He thus never crossed over the line to outright opposition to the church.

In any case, Erasmus regarded the actual physical reception of the elements and the performance of the rite itself as far less important than the spiritual communion with Christ that the sacrament represented. Erasmus's understanding of the sacrament reflected his neoplatonic/Augustinian dualism, expressed perhaps most strongly in his *Enchiridion*, where he urged his readers to move from the material world to a higher spiritual reality. Drawing on the Augustinian tradition, Erasmus urged his readers to take to heart the spiritual meaning of the mass, which was union with Christ and with the church. Erasmus used Christ's words in John 6:63 ("it is the spirit that gives life, the flesh is of no avail") to argue that Christ had scorned the eating of his flesh and drinking of his blood unless they were received spiritually. Indeed, he implied that receiving sacramental communion without the proper spiritual understanding could be dangerous.[40]

Just as Erasmus stressed Christ's role as teacher and example rather than his death as expiation for sin, so he emphasized the psychological and ethical aspects of communion rather than seeing the mass chiefly as a repetition or representation of Christ's sacrifice on the cross.[41] Communion entailed commemoration of Christ's death and the mortification of the flesh, the imitation of Christ, and the love of neighbor.[42] These mystical and ethical aspects led Erasmus to place considerable emphasis on the proper disposition for worthy reception of the sacrament. Only the pure should approach the altar, for the unworthy fell under God's judgment. Sacramental communion represented and symbolized the fellowship of believers with each other as well as with Christ, and so those who participated in it should be at peace and in unity with their fellow Christians. Indeed, the realization of such fellowship was the chief reason that those already advanced in piety should participate in the external ritual of receiving the sacrament.[43]

Erasmus's emphasis on the subjective value of the sacrament tended to obscure the fact that he also recognized its objective value. Although he used the word "symbol" for the bread and the wine, he did not believe the bread and wine were only empty signs of Christ's body and blood. In the sacrament Christ bestowed his love to participants, which was the basis of unity among Christians. This objective element could easily be overlooked by Erasmus's readers, however, for it led quite naturally back to the ethical consequences of communion. Erasmus was more concerned with what individual Christians were to do as a result of their participation than he was with what either Christ or the priest did in or through the sacrament.[44]

Erasmus did not state his views on the Eucharist in any systematic way but rather scattered them throughout his *Annotations on the New Testament* and his paraphrases of individual books of the New Testament.[45] As a consequence, his primary audience was composed of men who were already committed to the careful study of the biblical text, and especially those who knew Greek. This was a much different group from the broader popular audience, literate only in the vernacular, who read Luther's sermons on the mass, but it included many of those who would write their own pamphlets on the sacrament. The earliest evangelical pamphlets published in south Germany concerning the mass reflected a blending of the three streams of thought coming from Luther, Erasmus, and late medieval preaching.

PHASE ONE: THE DIFFUSION OF LUTHER'S UNDERSTANDING OF THE MASS

Luther's new understanding of the mass appeared very quickly in evangelical pamphlets published outside of Wittenberg. One of the earliest, *A Useful Sermon . . . on the True Evangelical Mass*, by the Ulm preacher Johann Diepold, was a summary and simplification of Luther's 1520 *Sermon on the New Testament*.[46] The pamphlet proved to be quite popular, for it was reprinted eight times, including once in Low German, over the next year. Like Luther, Diepold described the evangelical mass as Christ's testament and promise of grace and mercy, confirmed by Christ's death. Faith made one worthy to approach the table, and those who recognized themselves to be sinners could approach the sacrament confident they would receive the spiritual goods promised to them. Paul's command to examine oneself did not mean one must confess all one's sins to a priest, and preachers who held up such a confession and other ascetic exercises as the proper preparation to receive the sacrament only produced despair and fear.

Diepold differed from Luther, though, in de-emphasizing the physical reception of the sacrament. He stated that Christ made us confident and assured of his grace and mercy, the forgiveness of sin and salvation, through the sacrament of his body and blood, but he tied this confidence to the elevation of the consecrated host, "as if the priest were telling the people, 'O dear Christians, look at this sign, the con-firmation, the assurance, the pledge, the letter and seal of your testament, that is, the grace and mercy of God and of eternal salvation.'"[47] In fact, he implied that spiritual communion was more beneficial than sacramental communion: "A person can receive the sacrament every day through faith, for spiritual communion with faith in Christ's promise is useful, and the physical reception of the sacrament without faith is useless, it is only a dreamed-up thing and a mockery."[48] He also assured those who had been excommunicated or had committed a public sin that as long as they recognized their sins, repented, and desired grace, they could receive the sacrament spiritually as often as they wished, and they should not be concerned that they could not receive the sacrament physically, even if they were on their deathbed.[49] This understanding of spiritual communion was not original with Diepold; the Dominican Johann Herolt had expressed a similar view in his popular sermon collection when he stated that those who prepared for the sacrament but were denied access by a priest and so abstained out of obedience could still commune spiritually.[50]

The same ideas occur with greater polemical force in Jakob Strauss's 1522 pamphlet, *A Comforting, Reasonable Teaching on the Word of St. Paul, "Each One Should Examine Himself."* In the first section of the pamphlet, Strauss condemned the preachers who taught that only those who had confessed all their mortal sins were worthy to receive the sacrament.[51] In the second section he presented the evangelical understanding of communion, emphasizing the sufficiency of faith that Christ's death had obtained forgiveness. The self-examination prescribed by Paul to ensure worthy communion consisted of three elements: the undoubted belief that Christ's body and blood were present in the sacrament, the knowledge that Christ gave himself for sinners, and the firm faith that one was freed from sin by Christ alone. Recognizing God's forgiveness in Christ, sinners could approach the Lord's table with joy, trusting in God's mercy.[52] In the final section, Strauss gave some advice to those who were prevented by their priest from receiving sacramental communion. They were to remember that Christ's body and blood could be consumed spiritually by Christians at all times and places. Thus it was sufficient to acknowledge in prayer that Christ's body and blood were present in the bread and wine, to believe that Christ had died for them and was present in the sacrament to confirm his promise of forgiveness, and to acknowledge that Christ gave himself to all who ate and drank in true faith.[53]

Strauss's advice must have struck a chord, for it was reprinted frequently over the next few years. The entire pamphlet went through six editions in 1522, and the second and third sections were published in 1524 with the title *A Lovely and Dear Instruction for Considering and Receiving the Precious, Most Holy Body of Christ and Receiving His Rosy Blood.*[54] Martin Reinhart, the Jena pastor who became one of Karlstadt's strongest supporters, also published an edition of the last section of Strauss's work as *Instruction How a Pious Christian Should Act During the Papist Mass*, which went through seven editions in 1524.[55] Portions of the pamphlet were also included in an anonymous broadsheet entitled *A Christian Confession* from 1524.[56]

Johann Bugenhagen also took up the question of the relationship between sacramental and spiritual communion in his 1524 pamphlet *On the Evangelical Mass . . . and How One Should Hear Mass and Receive the Venerable Sacrament.*[57] Bugenhagen opened his pamphlet with Luther's definition of the mass as Christ's testament, but he immediately tied this to the faith that constituted spiritual communion:

> If you want to hear mass rightly, then consider that here is one food and drink, and so you must eat and drink or your hearing of the mass is nothing. Take the words of the mass to yourself and consider rightly in faith that you

should not doubt that what Christ has promised you will happen, and in faith in that same word receive the venerable sacrament as a sure, holy sign under which such promise happens to you, through which your heart is shown to believe in the word. This is to go spiritually and bodily to God's table.[58]

The significance of spiritual communion was underlined by the inclusion in the pamphlet of a letter Bugenhagen had written to Georg Spalatin concerning whether a Christian should receive the sacrament in one kind only. Bugenhagen acknowledged that where Christians were given a choice, whether one received only the host or drank from the cup as well was a matter of Christian freedom. But in Catholic areas where Christians were offered only the host, it was better to abstain from communion than to receive it in only one form, thereby confirming "the godless" and condemning those who insisted on receiving both elements. For these Christians, as well as for those who were not allowed to commune, Bugenhagen gave some advice on how to hear mass. They should take the words of Christ's testament to heart, since if they believed the words and signs, they obtained the inheritance promised them and received the sacrament spiritually. The pamphlet also included a prayer for individual Christians to pray after the consecration that confessed the presence of Christ's body and blood in the bread and wine, acknowledged that Christ had assumed that body and blood to save Adam and all of his descendants, repeated the promise contained in the words of institution, and asked to be spiritually fed with that body and blood.[59]

Other early eucharistic pamphlets reflect a greater blending of Luther's ideas with those of Erasmus. Urbanus Rhegius published not only his Corpus Christi sermon of 1521 but two other pamphlets as well, an instruction for those wanting to receive communion from 1522 and a sermon preached on the octave of Corpus Christi in 1523.[60] In all three works Rhegius followed Luther in describing the sacrament as a testament in which Christ promised forgiveness along with his body and blood, the signs and seals of that forgiveness. Genuine contrition, the desire to reform, and faith in Christ were the best preparation to receive the sacrament, and those who believed Christ's words of forgiveness would surely obtain pardon, consolation, and assurance against the attacks of Satan. Worthy reception of the sacrament also brought union with Christ and with other Christians as members of his spiritual body.[61] Although Luther had also discussed this union with Christ and other believers in his sermons, Rhegius here echoed Erasmus's concern with the mystical and ethical aspects of communion. The sacrament was rightly called a *synaxis* or assembly, and those who came together were to serve and to help their neighbors. Participation in the sacrament also testified to fraternal unity among Christians, wherever they might be: "What Christians pray in Hungary, Austria, England, Scotland, France, Spain, Italy, Germany, and everywhere is for your help and consolation."[62]

Rhegius picked up on another Erasmian theme when he warned his hearers to avoid philosophical speculation about Christ's presence. Misguided preaching of such godless sophistry confused the simple and led them into despair. For Christians, the discussion of the timing, manner, and shape of Christ's body in the form of bread was irrelevant.[63] He also sounded more like a late medieval preacher than like Luther in acknowledging the value of spiritual communion as a substitute for sacramental communion. His *Instruction* contained two brief prayers to be said "when you want to receive the sacrament on Maundy Thursday or at any other time in the year," but it also included a prayer appropriate for those who would not themselves communicate, to be spoken at the elevation of the host, asking God "to let happen in me what the most worthy sacrament signifies, that I am united with you in genuine true love."[64] Although he devoted considerable space in his 1523 sermon to the question of how to prepare to receive the sacrament, he almost unconsciously relativized physical reception by holding up spiritual reception alone as its equivalent: "You may believe God's promise that Christ died for your sins, rose for your justification, and that this is the same body through which he worked our salvation, and so desire it as food for your soul and so go to God's table spiritually or receive the most worthy sacrament physically as a pledge of salvation."[65]

Johann Oecolampadius's Corpus Christi sermon was the most Erasmian of these early pamphlets in its discussion of the sacrament, and it contained little that could be traced directly to Luther. Oecolampadius divided his sermon into three points: the proper use of the "sacramental symbols" of bread and wine, the adoration due the sacrament, and the believer's incorporation into the mystical body of Christ.[66] Like Rhegius, he told his hearers that it did not matter how Christ was present in the sacrament or how the bread became Christ's body; it was sufficient simply to believe that the true body and true blood were present under the bread and wine. The bread not only signified but also was the body of Christ. Christians were not to focus on the visible elements, however, but instead should consider the invisible food that nourished the soul.[67] Citing Augustine's "believe, and you have eaten," Oecolampadius explained that one truly ate when one believed in "Jesus, the son of God and the savior of the world." In fact, sacramental communion was less important than spiritual communion, but the latter was "richer" when joined with the former, where Christ was supernaturally present.[68] Just as important as spiritual fellowship with Christ was the love that Christians were to show to their neighbors as fellow members of Christ's mystical body. This entailed not only living at peace with each other but also using one's wealth to meet their physical needs. The best evidence of worthy preparation for receiving the sacrament was the love one showed to one's neighbors after such reception.[69]

Taken as a whole, these pamphlets demonstrate that while Luther's ideas shaped the emerging debate over the mass, they were picked up and interpreted within an existing understanding of the sacrament that differed somewhat from Luther's. All of these works regarded spiritual communion as a valid alternative for sacramental communion, a view shared both by late medieval preachers and by Erasmus. Where the late medieval and Erasmian traditions differed was on the importance of confessing Christ's bodily presence in the consecrated elements, and these early evangelical pamphlets reflected this difference. Strauss taught that belief in that presence was a necessary part of communion, whether sacramental or spiritual, but Rhegius and Oecolampadius minimized the importance of this belief and deliberately discouraged speculation about the manner of that presence. Since Luther did not explicitly discuss Christ's presence until his 1523 pamphlet *On the Adoration of the Sacrament*, this difference among his followers seemed at the time to be more a matter of emphasis than genuine disagreement.

PHASE TWO: THE POLEMICAL TURN

Another factor that distinguished the debate over the mass in South Germany from the view emanating from Wittenberg was the argumentation used against the sacrifice of the mass. Luther had condemned this doctrine in *On the Babylonian Captivity* because it turned the mass into a good work and so contradicted his fundamental understanding of justification by faith alone.[70] He elaborated on this view in his 1522 pamphlet *On the Misuse of the Mass*, where he drew a sharp contrast between a sacrifice and a promise: "A sacrifice is a work in which we present and give to God something of our own. The promise, however, is God's word, which gives to man the grace and mercy of God."[71] One could not offer anything to God to merit forgiveness; thus it was wrong to claim that the mass was an offering made by priests on behalf of themselves and others.[72]

Ulrich Zwingli proposed a much more direct argument against the sacrifice of the mass in the articles he drew up for the first Zurich disputation in January 1523. There he rejected the church's claim to repeat Christ's sacrifice with the argument, taken from Hebrews 10:12–14, that Christ had offered himself as a sacrifice once and for all on the cross.[73] In his *Exposition of the 67 Articles* published six months later he expanded on this argument, pointing out that a sacrifice required a death, but

Scripture said that Christ died once and for all and so could not be sacrificed again. Indeed, the claim that Christ needed to be offered daily was "a belittling and a degrading" of Christ's perfect sacrifice.[74] Zwingli expressly agreed with Luther that the mass could be called a testament, but he preferred to call it a remembrance, thereby distinguishing it more clearly from Christ's unique sacrifice on the cross.[75] He also put far more emphasis than did Luther on the spiritual communion that he equated with faith, based on his understanding of John 6.[76] Finally, he questioned the use of the words "sacrament" and "mass," preferring instead to call it the Eucharist or "Christ's body and blood."[77]

Luther was obviously familiar with the passage in the epistle to the Hebrews that was the basis of Zwingli's criticism of the mass, but he did not use it the same way. In *On the Misuse of the Mass* he cited Christ's unique sacrifice not against the mass per se but to support his assertion that Christians had only one priest, Christ himself. Christ offered himself once, and he wanted that sacrifice to be remembered, but one could no more make a new sacrifice out of this remembrance than one could cause Christ to be born again by remembering his birth.[78] Luther cited Hebrews only in passing in the section of the pamphlet devoted more specifically to arguing against the sacrifice of the mass, and in fact he would not use the passage to oppose the repetition of Christ's sacrifice in works aimed at the general public until his pamphlet *On the Abomination of the Secret Mass*, published in early 1525.[79] The difference between Luther and Zwingli concerning the sacrifice of the mass was obscured, however, by the fact that in German the word *Opfer* was used for both "offering," as Luther interpreted the mass, and "sacrifice," which was the interpretation Zwingli preferred.[80] Readers could easily see that both reformers rejected the sacrifice of the mass without paying much attention to the differing theological justifications for that rejection.

Zwingli's argument against the mass was repeated in other official or quasi-official publications emanating from Zurich, such as the acts of the second disputation held in October 1523 and the city's response to the bishop of Constance. Zwingli's colleague Leo Jud also used it in a polemical pamphlet published at the end of 1524.[81] His ideas also proved to be immensely popular among South German reformers. To begin with, they combined the familiar emphasis on spiritual communion with the heightened neoplatonic/Augustinian and Erasmian dualism of flesh and spirit that many of these humanist-reformers shared. Zwingli's attack on the sacrificial nature of the mass was also clearer, more direct, and potentially more explosive than Luther's. Those who followed Zwingli's argumentation had what they believed was a direct mandate to preach against a doctrine that was contrary to the clear text of Scripture. Rather than using the doctrine of justification by faith alone to criticize the mass, all they had to do was quote Hebrews 10:11–14: "Christ offered for all time a single sacrifice for sins . . . [and] by a single offering he has perfected for all time those who are sanctified." To a lay audience being taught by the reformers that the word of God was the sole source of authority, such a direct citation of Scripture was a powerful weapon against Catholic apologists who defended the belief that Christ was sacrificed anew in the mass.[82]

Zwingli's argument against the repetition of Christ's unique sacrifice therefore spread quickly. Andreas Karlstadt, for instance, made Christ's unique sacrifice the central argument of his pamphlet *On the Priesthood and Sacrifice of Christ*, published at the end of 1523.[83] Martin Bucer combined Luther's understanding of the mass as a testament with a rejection of the mass as a repetition of Christ's sacrifice in his unpublished defense of Luther's teaching written in the fall of 1523, and he gave the argument against the repeated sacrifice a prominent place in his justification of the liturgical changes introduced in Strasbourg published at the end of the following year.[84] The Nördlingen pastor Theobald Billican and the Augsburg Carmelite preacher Johann Landsperger also rejected the repetition of Christ's sacrifice in pamphlets on the mass published in 1524.[85] Nor was this argumentation restricted only to those who would later adopt Zwingli's understanding of the Eucharist. Andreas Osiander and his fellow pastors in Nuremberg defended the abolition of the mass by appealing to Christ's unique sacrifice in their defense of liturgical changes published in the summer of 1524, and Johannes Brenz incorporated it into his own arguments against the mass.[86] All of these authors helped publicize further Zwingli's argument that Catholic teaching on the sacrifice of the mass contradicted the clear words of Scripture.

These works illustrate another major development in the published debate concerning the mass. Criticism of the mass as an unscriptural or even antiscriptural repetition of Christ's sacrifice shifted the debate away from the more pastoral emphasis in the early works of Luther and others who had written primarily to teach their audience how to prepare for communion, whether sacramental or spiritual. The polemical intent now predominated, at least in part in response to the slowly growing number of Catholic publications defending the traditional understanding of the sacrifice of the mass.[87] The pamphlets published in 1524 were chiefly concerned with warning their hearers against the "abomination" represented by Catholic teaching, even going to the point of telling them to avoid attending the mass altogether. Karlstadt equated those who claimed to sacrifice Christ with Christ's murderers.[88] Billican was equally harsh in his rejection of the sacrifice of the mass: whether said for the living or the dead, the mass was a mockery that nullified Christ's salvation and aroused God's wrath.[89] The polemic reached its greatest extent in Andreas Keller's *Declaration of What Kind of Blasphemy the Papist Mass Is*. Keller argued that it was both blasphemy and an abomination to claim to offer Christ to the Father in the mass. Likewise, it was an anti-Christian blasphemy to say that sins were forgiven by paying a priest to say mass on one's behalf. Those who elevated the bread and chalice as a sign of sacrifice were crucifying Christ anew, thereby denying his passion.[90]

One consequence of the sharpened polemic against the mass was greater pressure for liturgical reform. The later pamphlets insisted on the need to replace the "blasphemy" contained in the canon of the mass with a more scriptural under-standing of the Lord's Supper. Responding to this perceived need, printers began turning out German liturgies for the evangelical mass in significant quantities. Even before Luther published his *Formula Missae* at the end of 1523, there were seven editions of a liturgy attributed to Johann Oecolampadius.[91] The following year saw eight editions of a German mass liturgy first published in 1522 by the Nördlingen reformer Kaspar Kantz.[92] Portions of this liturgy circulated in a pamphlet bearing Johann Bugenhagen's name, although Bugenhagen denied any involvement in the pamphlet's publication.[93] Printers in Strasbourg also published two different versions of a German mass in the fall of 1524.[94] In fact, more than one-third of the evangelical pamphlets concerned with the mass published in 1524 contained either an evangelical mass liturgy or a description of evangelical worship.[95] Obviously, a number of factors contributed to the pressure for practical liturgical reform in the cities of South Germany, but the reformers' vehement preaching against the "blasphemy" of Christ's repeated sacrifice contained in the canon of the mass was one of those factors.

What are the implications of this debate over the mass for the outbreak of the eucharistic controversy? Three aspects of early Reformation preaching and pub-lishing on the mass are relevant to the disagreements over the sacrament that arose at the end of 1524. First, the fault line that would divide Luther and Zwingli on the issue of Christ's presence was already apparent in the earliest pamphlets of the South Germans, revealed by the differing responses to a common element of late medieval preaching on the sacrament, the need to believe that the consecrated elements were Christ's body and blood. Strauss's pamphlet demonstrates that at least some early evangelical preachers regarded belief in Christ's corporeal presence as a necessary part of worthy preparation to receive the sacrament and, by extension, an integral part of the Christian faith. It should come as no surprise that Strauss was one of the earliest reformers to attack Zwingli publicly for his rejection of Christ's corporeal presence.[96]

Those more indebted to Erasmus downplayed the importance of Christ's corporeal presence. Of course, as the example of Erasmus proves, avoiding discussion of

Christ's bodily presence in the sacrament was not the same as denying it completely. Nevertheless, those who were most concerned with spiritual communion were predisposed to cross the line from minimizing the importance of Christ's corporeal presence to denying it altogether. Of the earliest pamphleteers, Erasmus's influence was strongest in the preaching of Oecolampadius, who was both the oldest and the best educated of these authors, who had the closest personal ties with the Dutch humanist, and who would become one of the leading advocates of an understanding of the Lord's Supper at odds with Luther's.

Second, the common emphasis on spiritual communion in late medieval preaching and in Erasmus's writings tended to obscure the differences concerning the nature of Christ's presence among the early evangelical pamphleteers. All of the early pamphleteers stressed faith in Christ's promise of forgiveness and fellowship with other believers, and for many of them John 6 played a central role in their understanding of the Eucharist. Luther himself discussed the importance of spiritual communion, and his readers may have overlooked or ignored his assertion that John 6 had nothing to do with the sacrament.[97] Furthermore, because Luther clearly disagreed with the late medieval understanding of how to prepare to receive the sacrament worthily, and because he did not discuss Christ's corporeal presence in his earliest and most frequently reprinted works, the more Erasmian-minded of the early reformers were not aware that they diverged from the Wittenberger on this point. Zwingli, for instance, did not read Luther's defense of Christ's corporeal presence in On the Adoration of the Sacrament until after he had written the letter to Matthaeus Alber in which he rejected that presence.[98]

Finally, there was an important shift of emphasis away from the objective aspect of the sacrament, understood as God's gift and the assurance of troubled consciences, in the earlier, more pastoral pamphlets toward a greater focus on the subjective aspect, especially its importance as a form of public worship, in the later, more polemical works. In the pamphlets of the South Germans, the sacrament was presented as a means for individuals to exercise their faith and to remember (in the sense of meditate on) Christ's passion and death. Because the words of the canon of the mass contradicted the clear teaching of Scripture, the canon was to be eliminated and a German liturgy introduced that would assist the congregation in its remembrance of Christ's Last Supper and his unique sacrifice on the cross. The emphasis was thus on the subjective value of the sacrament, composed of both the internal disposition and the external actions of individual Christians. Luther and his colleagues in Wittenberg, however, continued to emphasize the objective nature of the sacrament as a testament, a gift given by God and confirmed by the visible signs of bread and wine. God, not the individual Christian, was the chief actor.[99] This difference hints at the later disagreement between Luther and Zwingli over the central understanding of the sacrament as a means of grace or as a public testimony of faith and commitment to the church.

These divergent tendencies can be seen already in the South German pamphlets published in 1521, and they would only become more obvious in the following years. The catalyst that brought these divergences into the open was Andreas Karlstadt, who published several vernacular pamphlets rejecting Christ's bodily presence in the sacrament in October 1524. The controversy that resulted would take the public debate over the sacrament in a new direction, but the views of the mass expressed in these early evangelical pamphlets helped prepare the way for later developments.

3

"This Is the Body Given for You"

THE DEVELOPMENT OF KARLSTADT'S EUCHARISTIC THEOLOGY

⌀ ——————————————————————————————————

THE PUBLIC DEBATES in Wittenberg over the mass, like other more radical reform efforts, effectively came to an end in the spring of 1522, as Luther reestablished control over the evangelical movement. Karlstadt no longer agreed with the consensus in Wittenberg concerning Luther's teaching, and in the summer of 1523 he left to assume the position of parish pastor in the small city of Orlamünde, roughly twenty-five kilometers south of Jena. The two reformers would continue to diverge in their understanding of the sacrament and how it should be celebrated, but the extent of their differences would not become clear to the general public until the fall of 1524, when Karlstadt published several pamphlets on the theology and administration of the Lord's Supper.

In an appendix to his 1904 bibliography of Karlstadt's works, Hermann Barge argued that Karlstadt wrote all of these pamphlets in the aftermath of his confrontation with Luther in August 1524 and then sent them to Basel with his brother-in-law Gerhard Westerburg, who oversaw their publication in late October and November. Barge concluded that Luther did not see any of Karlstadt's pamphlets before he received copies of the Basel imprints from Strasbourg's pastors in mid-December, and he dismissed as irrelevant any attempt to determine the order in which the individual treatises were written.[1]

Barge's careful reconstruction of the printing history of these pamphlets has distorted studies of Karlstadt's eucharistic theology in two ways. First, it has focused attention on the five Basel pamphlets that concerned the Lord's Supper, to the neglect of pamphlets on the sacrament that were published both before and after the end of 1524. Second, it has discouraged efforts to place the writing of the pamphlets—as opposed to their publication—in chronological order.[2] The result has been a failure to appreciate fully the development of Karlstadt's eucharistic thought.

A careful analysis of Karlstadt's Basel pamphlets, together with those published both earlier and later, allows us to place them more precisely within the context of his activities in Orlamünde and his growing estrangement from Luther. Over the first half of 1524, Karlstadt reiterated his insistence on the immediate implementation of changes to worship that were more far-reaching than Luther allowed in Wittenberg. More important, however, his eucharistic theology was transformed as he studied the relevant Scripture texts in the light of new publications by Luther and others. As a result of these studies, he rejected the belief in Christ's corporeal presence in the sacrament, but not until his decisive break with Luther in August was he able to publish the two pamphlets in which he had worked out this new understanding of the sacrament, as well as two additional pamphlets written after his meeting with Luther. Luther's two-part response to these pamphlets, *Against the Heavenly Prophets*, provoked Karlstadt to write two final pamphlets that both summarized and sharpened the positions expressed in his earlier works.

THE ROAD TO CONFLICT

In the wake of his virtual demotion in Wittenberg in the spring of 1522, Karlstadt's publishing activity dropped off sharply. In contrast to the seventeen pamphlets he published between July 1521 and April 1522, he published only four pamphlets over the next year and a half, three of them written before he moved to Orlamünde. These pamphlets reflect Karlstadt's deepening interest in German mysticism, which would in turn have an impact on his eucharistic theology.[3]

Aside from a sermon preached on the feast of St. Michael, Karlstadt published nothing during his first several months in Orlamünde. Only at the end of 1523, after the printer Michael Buchführer moved to Jena, did Karlstadt have access to a press eager to publish his works. Buchführer printed five of Karlstadt's pamphlets in rapid succession over the course of December and January. When Luther became aware of these pamphlets, however, he asked the electoral counselor Gregor Brück to see that Karlstadt was not permitted to publish anything, or at the very least to ensure that his pamphlets would be censored before being printed. Luther's request was not necessarily motivated by animosity toward Karlstadt; as he pointed out to Brück, he wanted Karlstadt to be subject to the same standards of censorship as the rest of the university faculty.[4] In practice, however, this meant that Karlstadt's pamphlets could be printed only if they conformed to what was taught at Wittenberg. As a consequence, Karlstadt was able to publish only two more pamphlets before his expulsion from Saxony in September; both of these had been written a year earlier and were printed outside of Saxony.[5]

This printing history demonstrates that there was no direct connection between composition and publication of Karlstadt's pamphlets. The same disjunction between composition and publication characterizes the pamphlets published in Basel, and so the order of their composition must be determined by looking not at the date of their publication but at the format, content, and intended audiences. They fall into two groups. The first group dealt with the timing and extent of practical reforms, not only with changes to the mass liturgy but also with the removal of images from churches. Karlstadt's pamphlets in this group repeated the principles that he had defended in Wittenberg from early 1522 and so continued his earlier disagreement with Luther. The second group of pamphlets concerned Christ's corporeal presence in the elements of bread and wine, a question first raised by Cornelis Hoen's letter and then taken up by Luther in a pamphlet addressed to the Bohemian Brethren. With regard to both theology and praxis, then, Karlstadt's understanding of the Lord's Supper must be placed against the background of developments in Wittenberg.

Although the Wittenberg reformers had acted quickly to suppress any questions about Christ's corporeal presence when they first emerged in October 1521, the issue did not disappear. Contact with representatives of the Bohemian Brethren over the summer of 1522 made Luther aware that there were some who rejected Christ's corporeal presence in the sacrament.[6] At some point he had also read Hoen's letter, for in his pamphlet *On the Adoration of the Sacrament*, written for the Bohemian Brethren and published in the spring of 1523, he rejected one of the most important arguments that Hoen had used in his letter, the equation of "is" with "signifies" in Christ's words of institution. Luther argued that this equivalence undermined Scripture, for it could be used to argue that "Mary signifies a virgin and the mother of God" or that "Christ signifies God and man." He also discussed passages that might seem to support the equivalence of "is" and "signifies" more directly. Chief among them was 1 Corinthians 10:4, "The rock was Christ." This statement, Luther asserted, meant not that the rock signified Christ but that Christ was the spiritual rock. He concluded that every word in Scripture must be allowed its natural meaning unless faith compelled a different interpretation.[7]

Luther made clear that his rejection of a symbolic interpretation of the sacrament did not automatically lead to the error of transubstantiation. Instead, he taught that "real bread and wine are truly present along with the body and blood of Christ." More pernicious was the Roman teaching that the sacrament was a sacrifice and good work. The sacrament was instead a gift to be received by each individual through faith. Last but not least, Luther criticized the understanding of the essence, or *res*, of the sacrament as union with the church as Christ's body. Luther argued that this understanding confused Christ's natural body with his spiritual body, the church, and was based on a false interpretation of 1 Corinthians 10:16, one that could not be reconciled with Christ's words "this is my body given for you."[8]

At the same time that Luther was rejecting a symbolic understanding of the sacrament, Karlstadt was moving closer to such an understanding. His pamphlet *On the Priesthood and Sacrifice of Christ*, published in the final days of 1523, was a refutation of the sacrifice of the mass.[9] Volkmar Joestel has suggested that Luther influenced the ideas in the pamphlet, pointing particularly to Karlstadt's contrast between the external anointing and tonsure of priests and the internal anointing of those whom God has called.[10] Far more important for Karlstadt's argumentation concerning the sacrament, though, was the influence of both Erasmus and Ulrich Zwingli.

In his paraphrase of Hebrews 9–10 published in early 1521, Erasmus emphasized Christ's single offering on the cross, although he did not mention the sacrifice of the mass. Instead, he contrasted the repeated sacrifice of dumb animals whose blood gave only carnal holiness with the one sacrifice of Christ whose blood cleansed consciences.[11] Zwingli went a step further in his *Exposition of the 67 Articles*, published in the summer of 1523. There he argued that Christ's sacrifice on the cross was unique and perfect and therefore could not be repeated in the mass.[12] For this reason he rejected the word "mass," which he believed was derived from the Hebrew word for an offering or sacrifice. He also argued that although the church fathers had called the mass a sacrifice, they could not prove this from God's word. Although Zwingli agreed with Luther that the mass could be called a testament, he preferred to call it a remembrance (*Wiedergedächtnis*), and he emphasized the importance of the spiritual eating, which was faith, described in John 6.[13]

These same elements reappear in Karlstadt's pamphlet, but with some important modifications and amplifications. Karlstadt argued that Christ's sacrifice on the cross was both unique and final, although he approached that sacrifice in terms of what was figured in the sacrifices of the Old Testament rather than from Christ's position as eternal mediator in heaven.[14] He also asserted that these sacrifices, in which the priest offered an innocent and unreasoning animal to God as atonement for sin, pointed forward to Christ's innocent, reasoning, and obedient suffering and death. Just as individual animals could die only once, so Christ could be sacrificed only once, and therefore no priest could sacrifice Christ repeatedly. It was blasphemy to claim that Christ's sacrifice on the cross was insufficient. Moreover, since in a sacrifice a living animal must die, those who claimed to sacrifice Christ in the mass became his murderers. Christ's death was the perfect sacrifice that he himself presented to God, and so he could no longer be sacrificed by a priest.[15]

Karlstadt also agreed with Zwingli in rejecting the word "mass" and in dismissing the authority of the church fathers who wrote about the mass as a sacrifice.[16] And like the Zurich reformer, he emphasized that the Supper was a memorial meal, arguing that "the bread and blood of the Lord" were eaten in heartfelt remembrance, just as one remembered a brother who had died for him.[17] This "heartfelt remembrance" had the same connotation as Zwingli's *Wiedergedächtnis*, since both terms went beyond simple recall to include inner reflection and meditation.[18]

Although there are similarities between Karlstadt's earlier use of promise and sign and his new emphasis on figure and fulfillment, there was also an important difference. In this pamphlet Karlstadt made no mention of either promise or testament in connection to the sacrament, and there was nothing to indicate that God gave something through the sacrament. If anything, the emphasis on Christ's fulfillment on the cross of what was figured by the Old Testament sacrifices implied that there was nothing more to give, since Christ's suffering and death were complete.

Karlstadt did not openly adopt a symbolic view of the sacrament in his treatise, but he was certainly close to doing so.[19] In this respect, his silence was more significant than his clear statements. In contrast to his earlier works on the mass, he said very little about the elements, and he never referred to them as Christ's body and blood.[20] More pointedly, he condemned priests for wanting to attribute the cleansing achieved by Christ's blood to bread made by a baker or wine from a winepress. Alluding to John 6:32–33, he distinguished between the heavenly bread that came down from heaven, which was Christ, and the bread and wine that grew upward as the fruit of the earth.[21]

Karlstadt's attention was not focused entirely on theology, however. The publication of Luther's *Formula Missae et Communionis* in December 1523 provoked a restatement of the need for more radical reform of the mass than what had been introduced in Wittenberg. The *Formula Missae* was written for Nicolaus Hausmann, the pastor of Zwickau who had asked Luther for guidance in reforming the mass.[22] Luther's new liturgy was extremely conservative, retaining the Latin language and making allowance only for a German sermon. It made few changes to the first part of the service beyond the elimination of sequences, antiphons, and other medieval accretions. The modifications to the communion service proper were more significant, for Luther rejected the prayers that made up the canon, and he eliminated the phrases from the canon's account of the sacrament's institution that were not found in the synoptic Gospels or in 1 Corinthians 11. But he retained the elevation of the host, a gesture that Karlstadt had tried to eliminate two years earlier, and although he allowed for communion in both kinds for those who wished to receive it, he did not make it mandatory.[23]

Karlstadt's reaction to Luther's *Formula Missae* might be inferred from the views expressed in his censored pamphlet from 1522; it is confirmed by his pamphlet *Against the Old and New Papist Masses*. This work was one of the tracts published in Basel in the fall of 1524, but its contents suggest that it was written in the first few months of that year. It was clearly a response to Luther's *Formula Missae*, written as a letter responding to a friend's questions about the reform of the mass.[24]

The chief arguments of the pamphlet are similar to those made in Karlstadt's suppressed pamphlet of April 1522, given a strongly polemical edge. As the pamphlet's title implied, Karlstadt saw little difference between the papist mass and the liturgy advocated by Luther and "the poor bishop of Zwickau." Karlstadt argued that the service must be in German, so that people could listen to and judge whether what was said accorded with God's word. He was particularly critical of anything that encouraged people to believe that the mass was a sacrifice. Repeating the argument he had advanced both in the censored pamphlet and in *On the Priesthood*, he asserted that the word "mass" should be abandoned, because its Hebrew etymology meant a voluntary offering. He also condemned the elevation of the host because it implied a sacrifice, in the same way that the gestures of the Old Testament wave and heave offerings denoted that they were sacrifices.

Karlstadt obliquely expressed his reservations about Christ's presence in the sacrament by referring to Christians "who called Christ in the sacrament—or the sacrament in which Christ is supposed to be—a mass." The bread and wine were not an offering but a Supper, or food to be eaten in Christ's remembrance. He did not describe how that Supper was to be celebrated, however, but instead referred his reader to the scriptural accounts of its institution, which were easy to understand. One should simply follow the procedure that Christ had established, rather than trying to improve it with all kinds of additions and embellishments. It would be best, he concluded, to let the mass fall away completely and to replace it with a celebration of the Lord's Supper in accordance with Christ's institution.[25]

There are only a few sources that might indicate when and how Karlstadt acted on his own advice and introduced practical changes to worship in Orlamünde. The earliest of these dates from the spring of 1524, when Luther reported to a friend that he had heard "monstrous things" about Karlstadt. These "monstrous things" may have included the removal of images, as well as the liturgical changes he had long advocated, such as singing the Psalms in German and mandatory communion in both kinds.[26] In early April, Karlstadt was summoned back to Wittenberg and pressured to give up his position in Orlamünde. In June Luther expressed his hope to Duke John Frederick that the situation in Orlamünde would improve once Karlstadt had left. These cryptic references imply that Luther was concerned chiefly with the same issue that had occupied him on his return from the Wartburg, that of defending Christian liberty against Karlstadt's demand for immediate and specific practical reforms.[27]

By midsummer, however, the situation in Thuringia had become even more tense, with radicals threatening to use violence to bring about the necessary reforms. In early July Luther complained to a friend about the emergence of "prophets and sects" encouraged by Satan, and he mentioned Karlstadt as one of those who seemed to reduce Christ to a mere example and "who destroyed all of the sacraments."[28] This draws our attention back to Karlstadt's rejection of Christ's corporeal presence.

Karlstadt's new understanding of the sacrament was first expressed in two treatises, *Whether One Can Prove from Holy Scripture That Christ Is in the Sacrament*, and *Exegesis of Christ's Words, "This is my Body."* In these works he proposed a new, literal exegesis of the words of institution that opposed that of "the two-fold papists"— both the Catholics and Luther—who taught Christ's corporeal presence in the elements. One can see the development in Karlstadt's thinking in these two pamphlets, as he combined exegetical strategies and interpretations learned from Erasmus with arguments against Christ's presence first advanced by Cornelis Hoen.

Whether One Can Prove was the more cautiously written of the two, for in its opening lines Karlstadt claimed to be presenting only the hypothetical answers of "our opponents" to seven arguments used to justify Christ's bodily presence in the bread and wine. Within a few pages, however, it becomes clear that Karlstadt found the arguments of these unnamed opponents more compelling than those used to defend Christ's corporeal presence. He began with a consideration of 1 Corinthians 10:16 ("The cup of blessing which we bless, is it not a participation in the blood of Christ? The bread which we break, is it not a participation in the body of Christ?"), used to justify both the power of the words of consecration and the participation or fellowship of Christ's blood in the cup. Karlstadt granted that "the cup of blessing" was a special cup, but one could not therefore assume that it held Christ's blood. To bless was not to consecrate, and there was no Scripture to prove that Christ's words had the power to transform the elements. If the apostles could not heal the deaf or expel demons even when Christ explicitly gave them the authority to do so, how could priests know that by speaking the words of consecration they brought Christ's body into the elements, when they had no express command to do so?[29] Karlstadt also defended the interpretation of 1 Corinthians 10:16 that Luther had rejected in *On the Adoration of the Sacrament*. He asserted that the fellowship of Christ's body and blood mentioned in the verse had nothing to do with Christ's natural body but was instead the spiritual association created among all those who shared the bread and wine in remembrance of Christ's death on the cross. This understanding was confirmed by the contrast Paul made between participating in the Lord's table and in the table of demons (1 Cor. 10:18–21).[30]

Karlstadt next addressed the proper understanding of Luke 22:20, "the cup of the new testament in my blood." Repeating a point that Erasmus had made in his annotations on the institution accounts, he noted that Christ did not speak the words concerning the cup until after the disciples had drunk from it. Therefore, he concluded, the disciples had received only wine. Furthermore, although the apostles had written much about Christ's life, teachings, death, resurrection, and ascension, none of them had said that Christ's body and blood were in the bread and wine. Christ shed his blood on the cross, not in the cup, and he had instituted the Supper as a memorial of that death, not to bring his body and blood into the elements.[31]

Karlstadt also argued that the Greek word *eucharistia* could not be understood as supporting a transformation of the elements. The act of blessing or giving thanks did not bring Christ's body into food; if it did, Christ would have transformed the loaves and fishes into his body when he fed the 5,000, and the one leper who was healed would also have produced Christ's body and blood because he gave thanks.[32] He used the same strategy of reductio ad absurdum to support the argument that Christ was not talking about the sacrament when he described himself as the bread of life in John 6. Like Hoen, he pointed out that if this were true, all who ate the sacrament would live forever—which was manifestly not the case. He listed a string of similar logical absurdities, ranging from making the sacrament necessary for salvation to exalting a soulless created thing—the bread—to higher than the angels and saints, which all pointed to the conclusion that Christ's body was not in the sacrament. As Zwingli would do, he cited John 6:63 to prove that eating the sacrament with the mouth was of no use; what was important was faith in the crucified Christ.[33]

Using an argument first advanced by Hoen, Karlstadt asserted that the miracles performed by Christ's disciples were public and testified to Christ, but the miracle that priests allegedly performed in the sacrament was hidden and did not benefit anyone's soul.[34] Not only were miracles public, but the entirety of Christ's life, death, and resurrection was public in the sense that it was foretold by the prophets. There was, however, no mention in Scripture either of Christ's hidden presence in the sacrament or of an intermediate state between the humility of his earthly life and the glory after his resurrection that described his mode of existence in the sacrament.[35] Faith in Christ's promises could indeed do all things, but there was no promise that Christ would bring his body into the bread. His statement "this is my body given for you" was fulfilled at the crucifixion; it was no longer a promise and so could not be used to prove that Christ was in the sacrament.[36]

Karlstadt defended his understanding of the sacrament as a memorial from the charge that this reduced its significance. St. Paul's insistence on worthy reception proved that one must have an "ardent remembrance" of Christ's blood shed for the forgiveness of one's own sins, and those who understood Paul rightly would therefore not treat the sacrament lightly. Karlstadt challenged the view that unworthy reception was the refusal to believe that Christ's body and blood were contained under the consecrated elements. Instead, he argued, Paul's purpose in describing the Last Supper was to show the Corinthians that they should remember and be thankful for Christ's passion whenever they ate and drank.[37]

Running through the pamphlet like a red thread is Karlstadt's understanding of the cross as fulfillment of what had been figured in the Mosaic sacrifices and foretold by the prophets. This, together with his recognition that the accounts of Christ's Last Supper stated that the meal was to be celebrated in remembrance, led him to suggest a new understanding of Christ's words of institution. He pointed out that Christ had not said, "This *bread* is my body," but rather, "Take, eat. This is my body, which will be given for you. Do this in remembrance of me." There was a change of subject between the first clause, "take, eat," which referred to the bread, and the second clause, which referred to Christ's physical body. The caesura between these two clauses could be supported by punctuation, for the first phrase ended with a period, and the second phrase began with a capital letter. It was also justified by the rules of Greek grammar, for in Greek the word "bread" (*artos*) was masculine, while "this" (*touto*) was neuter and so must refer to "body." In the same way that John the Baptist said, "This is the lamb who will take away the sins of the world," the words of institution should be understood as, "this is my body that will be given for you." The final command to "do this in remembrance of me" then referred back to Christ's first command to "take and eat" the bread which he gave to the disciples.[38]

Karlstadt would repeat his new understanding of the words of institution in the *Exegesis of Christ's Words, "This is my Body."* In this pamphlet he took a much bolder stance, declaring at the outset that Christ's words could not be used to justify his bodily presence in the bread and wine. Karlstadt then repeated the criticism of transubstantiation that he had advanced three years earlier. The papists did not take the words of institution literally because they stated that Christ's body was *in* or *under* the bread, rather than saying his body *was* the bread. In fact, he argued, it was patently self-contradictory to claim that Christ was both the bread and in the bread, just as one could not say both "the wine is the vase" and "the wine is in the vase."[39] But instead of arguing that two substances could coexist, as he had done in 1521, Karlstadt summarized his new understanding of the words of institution. "This is my body" should be understood together with the phrase that followed it, "given for you." With this entire phrase Christ demonstrated that his body, which would be given on the cross, was the sacrifice figured in Moses and the prophets.[40]

Karlstadt then turned this new understanding of Christ's words against claims that Christ's body and blood were contained in the elements. He argued that it was not only perverse but even heretical to apply the phrase "given for you" to the bread rather than to Christ's body, for this was equivalent to saying that the body of the Messiah to be given for us was bread baked from flour. The prophets all spoke of the suffering and death of Christ's natural body, but they said nothing about his body becoming bread. If Christ's body did indeed become bread, then it was the bread that would suffer on the cross and be given for sin, an obvious absurdity. When Christ said, "I give you my body," he meant the same as "I give my body for you," just as when he told his disciples that "the bread that I give is my flesh, which I will give for the life of the world" (John 6:51).[41]

Karlstadt also argued that Christ intended to give his body *after* the supper, and not in the meal itself. Christ could not redeem us in the sacrament because he did not die in it, but instead died on the cross. Again, Karlstadt pushed the traditional interpretation to the point of absurdity: Christ obviously did not shed his blood when he spoke the words to his disciples. Instead, his words pointed to the future shedding of his blood and were spoken as a promise that would be fulfilled. Scripture contained other examples where the present tense was used to express future events, and in this case Christ used the present tense to show that he was prepared to suffer and die.[42]

Last but certainly not least, Karlstadt used John 6 against the belief that Christ gave his flesh and blood as food in the sacrament. Although Zwingli had discussed John 6 in relation to the sacrament in his *Exposition of the 67 Articles*,[43] Karlstadt's use of the passage was different, and closer to that of Hoen's *Most Christian Letter*. Like Hoen, Karlstadt now argued that the sacramental bread, like the manna given to the Israelites, was earthly bread and so could not give life, and he contrasted it with Christ as the life-giving bread that came down from heaven.[44]

Karlstadt recognized that one of the strongest objections that might be raised against his view was the understanding of St. Paul's words about unworthy eating and discerning the Lord's body (1 Cor. 11:27–29), which late medieval preachers typically interpreted as requiring belief in Christ's corporeal presence.[45] He repeated his position that "discerning the body" meant the remembrance and serious consideration of Christ's death. St. Paul had warned the Corinthians against unworthy eating because God required that all he ordained be used in the way he had established it. Thus the Lord's bread could be misused, even if it was only bread. Communicants were to examine themselves to make sure they demonstrated the mutual love and fellowship that was figured by their sharing of the external bread.[46]

In these two pamphlets, then, Karlstadt presented both a theological and a philological argument against Christ's corporeal presence in the sacrament. Of the two, the theological argument was the more fundamental. It grew out of Karlstadt's understanding of the relationship between Old Testament sacrifice and Christ's sacrificial death, which functioned as the foundational hermeneutical principle for understanding Christ's words "this is my body." Like the sacrifices of the Old Testament, Christ's Last Supper with his disciples figured or looked forward to Christ's death on the cross. After the crucifixion, the celebration of the Supper caused participants to look back to that death, and so it functioned as a figure of what was past rather than of what was to come. This figural interpretation of the Old Testament sacrificial system served as the matrix from which Karlstadt developed his philological argument, which explained Christ's words of institution on the basis of grammar and punctuation. It therefore held a key position within Karlstadt's eucharistic theology analogous to Zwingli's understanding of John 6:63 or Luther's understanding of the incarnation.[47]

Karlstadt's rejection of Christ's corporeal presence forced him to develop a new justification for the sacrament's reception. The sacrament had no objective value, whereby communicants received something from God. Instead, its purpose was subjective, to evoke remembrance of and thanksgiving for Christ's death. Karlstadt thus opposed Luther's emphasis on the sacrament's power to console and strengthen consciences, a position that would come out more clearly in his subsequent pamphlets.

The thoroughness with which Karlstadt presented his new understanding of the Lord's Supper and the relatively calm tone of the discussion in these two pamphlets suggest that, like *Against the Old and New Papist Masses*, both pamphlets were written while Karlstadt's situation in Orlamünde was still relatively secure and he had time to develop his argumentation.[48] In this respect they differ significantly from all of the remaining eucharistic pamphlets, which were written in haste after Karlstadt's public break with Luther and his personal situation had become uncertain.

THE BATTLE IS JOINED

In mid-August Luther undertook a preaching tour through Thuringia at the request of the duke, in hopes that he could counter the growing unrest there. In a sermon preached in Jena on 22 August at which Karlstadt was present, Luther denounced the radicals, claiming that the "Allstedtisch spirits"—Thomas Müntzer and his followers—had "removed, uprooted and completely negated baptism and the sacrament [of the altar]."⁴⁹ This reference to the sacrament convinced Karlstadt that Luther included him among the "rebellious murdering spirits," since, as Karlstadt acknowledged, "no one since the apostles has written and taught about the manner, meaning, and ground [of the sacrament] as I have."⁵⁰

When the two men met later that day, Luther seemed surprised that Karlstadt felt he had been personally attacked—although he regarded Karlstadt's protests as a virtual admission of guilt. Luther's reaction indicates that he was concerned not with Karlstadt's understanding of the Supper but rather with the more general overturning of the sacraments that he saw in the radicals' emphasis on mystical experience and inner revelation, combined with their insistence on the reform of externals despite the potential harm to those weak in faith. This, Luther would argue five months later in the second part of his treatise *Against the Heavenly Prophets*, reversed the order instituted by God, whereby the external means of word and sacraments were channels through which God gave inner faith.⁵¹ The fact that Luther's remarks in his Jena sermon were explicitly directed against Müntzer supports this interpretation. Unlike Karlstadt, Müntzer did not reject Christ's corporeal presence in the sacrament, but he shared with Karlstadt the same neoplatonic and spiritualist downgrading of externals and an emphasis on inner experience derived from German mysticism.⁵²

At the end of their meeting, Luther gave Karlstadt a golden gulden as token of his permission to write against him. This public act signified the end of the policy of censorship and was the stimulus to the composition of two more pamphlets on the Lord's Supper. The *Dialogue . . . on the Horrible and Idolatrous Misuse of the Most Holy Sacrament* and *On the Anti-Christian Abuse of the Lord's Bread and Cup* are distinguished from Karlstadt's earlier works by the less sophisticated nature of their theological arguments and by their more polemical tone. In the opening lines of the *Dialogue* Karlstadt stated that the pamphlet was intended specifically for the common men and women who had been misled by the authority and the teachings of the so-called scholars. The knowledge of the truth would free them from false trust in externals and the mistaken belief in the power of the consecrated host.⁵³ Throughout the pamphlet Karlstadt kept the presentation of his ideas simple, and he frequently used interjections and brief rapid exchanges of few words to give the sense of genuine argument. He also used sarcasm, insults, name-calling, distortion, and deliberate exaggeration to spice up the exchange between the interlocutors, which only added to the negative tone of the pamphlet.⁵⁴

The *Dialogue* began as a conversation between Gemser, who upheld the traditional belief in Christ's corporeal presence in the elements, and Victus, who expressed his doubts about that belief.⁵⁵ They were soon joined by Peter, a self-confident layman who raised many of the same objections to Christ's corporeal presence that

Karlstadt had made in his earlier pamphlets. Victus then dropped out of the conversation, which continued between Peter and Gemser. It may be that Karlstadt decided that Victus seemed too learned, and so Peter was introduced to replace him.[56]

Like Zwingli's *Exposition of the 67 Articles*, the *Dialogue* opened with Victus's questioning the use of the word "sacrament." Gemser cited Augustine's definition of a sacrament used by Peter Lombard as "a sign of a sacred thing" as well as its classical definition as a military oath, but Victus dismissed both definitions because the word itself was not biblical and because he refused to recognize the church's right to name things.[57] The two men then turned to a discussion of transubstantiation, with Gemser defending the traditional view that Christ's body, with all of its parts and just as it was born of Mary and hung on the cross, was present in the consecrated host. Victus reacted to this position with frank skepticism, using the argument Karlstadt had advanced in his other works that there was no Scripture to support the belief that Christ was in or under the form of bread. When Gemser cited "this is my body" as the scriptural justification for Christ's corporeal presence, Victus responded with the interpretation of the words of institution introduced in *Whether One Can Prove*, pointing out that the phrases "take, eat," and "this is my body" were separated by their punctuation and raising questions about the original Greek. Gemser was forced to admit that the wording caused problems because "this" (*touto*) was neuter, while "bread" (*artos*) was masculine. Peter, who had overheard this discussion of the original Greek, now entered the debate to endorse this interpretation, adding that he had always thought that "Christ pointed to his body when he said, 'this is my body which is given for you.'"[58]

Significantly, Karlstadt presented here only his philological argument and did not introduce his theological argument based on the figural interpretation of the Old Testament sacrifices. In fact, by having Peter the layman suggest that Christ pointed to his body, Karlstadt replaced the metaphorical pointing of the Law and prophets with a physical gesture that obscured the underlying theological framework. Karlstadt may have introduced the idea here simply as a way to relate his interpretation to older heretical views that circulated among the common people.[59]

Peter now took over as Gemser's discussion partner. The arguments he used against Gemser are those Karlstadt had made in *Whether One Can Prove* to refute those who upheld Christ's corporeal presence in the sacrament. He cited the logical absurdities that resulted from accepting the corporeal presence, such as believing that the bread suffered or was given for us; he mocked the idea that Christ came into the elements secretly; he rejected the claim that the sacrament assured recipients of forgiveness; he argued that Christ did not give the apostles the authority to put his body into the bread; and he asserted that the words of consecration, benediction, or thanksgiving did not have the power to effect such a transformation. Christ's statement that one must eat his flesh and drink his blood in order to have life (John 6:53) had to be understood in light of his later assertion that the flesh is of no avail (John 6:63).[60]

Karlstadt did not limit Peter's discussion to a mere repetition of his own arguments, but he also cited the scriptural passages advanced by Hoen to combat the doctrine of transubstantiation. Thus he argued that because Christ told his disciples that the Paraclete would not come unless he departed (John 16:7), we could not receive his body naturally. He also used Christ's ascension and the existence of his glorified body in heaven to refute the belief that Christ was present in every consecrated host, and he repeated Christ's warning against those who said, "Christ is here, Christ is there" (Matt. 24:23).[61]

At the end of the *Dialogue*, Karlstadt told his readers that they could find the sacrament discussed in regular prose rather than in dialogue form in several of his other works. In addition to *Whether One Can Prove, Exegesis of Christ's Words*, and *Against the Old and New Papist Masses*, he gave three more titles: "the explanation of 1 Cor. 11; that the sacrament is not a sign; . . . and that faith in the promise and sacrament . . . does not forgive sins." Rather than individual pamphlets, these are actually three sections of *On the Anti-Christian Abuse of the Lord's Bread and Cup*. It is likely that Karlstadt intended to write three separate treatises but did not have the time to do so and so combined the three topics into the one pamphlet.[62]

Karlstadt clearly intended the *Anti-Christian Abuse* to be the opening volley in his public campaign against Luther.[63] He began by acknowledging the errors in his earlier pamphlets on the sacrament and asserted that he would now confess the truth, "whether it cost me life or death."[64] He then presented his interpretation of the Lord's Supper in the form of an analysis of the Pauline account of the institution of the Lord's Supper and of unworthy eating (1 Cor. 11:23–29). Karlstadt did not repeat the philological argument against Christ's presence in *Abuse* but gave instead a truncated version of the theological argument he had developed in his earlier pamphlets. Through the words of institution, Christ told his disciples that his body and blood would be given for them, as prophesied in the Old Testament:

> For this reason Christ spoke clearly, "Eat the bread, for this body is the body which is given for you, and this is my blood which is shed for you." As if he wanted to say . . . "Moses and the prophets wrote for you and all men about a body that would be given, which would be the seed of a woman and would crush the serpent's head, which would also stretch out his hand to the tree of life. 'My body' or 'this my body' is the same as that about which they prophesied, which would be given for the world. Therefore you should eat my bread in remembrance

of me." Christ said the same, or wanted to say the same, about his blood. "Moses and the prophets wrote about blood that would make a new testament and would be shed for sins. Realize that my blood is the same blood that will be shed for you for the forgiveness of sins."[65]

The essence of the sacrament was neither forgiveness of sins nor the assurance of that forgiveness, but rather remembrance of Christ's suffering and death, which took place as Moses and the prophets had foretold. As in his earlier pamphlets, Karlstadt consistently modified the word "remembrance" with adjectives such as "ardent" or "passionate." This remembrance was more than simply recalling Christ's death but entailed an internal, experiential realization of that death's meaning for the believer, and it brought about a Christlike transformation, bestowing the power to do or endure whatever God willed. Any remembrance that did not meet these criteria fell short of what was intended when Moses and the prophets prophesied about Christ's body and blood being given as a sacrifice for sin.[66]

Karlstadt wrote these two pamphlets in the wake of his confrontation with Luther. He then gave the manuscripts for all five of his eucharistic pamphlets on the sacrament, as well as three others that did not concern the sacrament, to his brother-in-law Gerhard Westerburg, who traveled to Basel to have the pamphlets published. After Karlstadt was banished from Saxony at the end of September, he joined Westerburg in Basel. He arrived there in time to add a new, polemical conclusion to the original text of the *Exegesis*, accusing Luther of engineering his expulsion from Saxony "unheard and unvanquished"—a phrase he had also used in two letters written to his parishioners in Orlamünde after his departure. He also summarized his arguments against Christ's presence in the sacrament, criticized the "idolaters" who caused others to worship pure bread, and attacked Luther for relying on his reputation rather than on sound argumentation to oppose Karlstadt's teachings.[67] Once the pamphlets were printed, he returned to central Germany, stopping in Strasbourg and Heidelberg on his way to meet his family at the borders of Saxony. By the end of the year he was living incognito in Rothenburg ob der Tauber, where he stayed until driven out by the turmoil of the Peasants' War.[68]

Karlstadt's brief visit to Strasbourg in October, as well as the circulation of his pamphlets there, aggravated divisions that had already begun to emerge within that city's evangelical movement.[69] As the divisions grew more serious, Strasbourg's pastors wrote to their colleagues in several other cities to ask for their judgment of Karlstadt's most persuasive arguments. Along with their letter to Luther they included five of Karlstadt's pamphlets: the *Dialogue, Against the Old and New Papist Masses, Exegesis of Christ's Words, Whether We Should Go Slowly,* and *The Reasons Why Andreas Karlstadt Was Expelled from Saxony*.[70] All five pamphlets included more or less open attacks on Luther, and four of them dealt in one form or another with the issues so central to the Wittenberg reformer: the proper relationship between the core of the faith and nonessentials, between internal and external, between divine law and Christian liberty, and even between the spiritual and secular kingdoms—in short, the whole complex of ideas that Luther would label as *Schwärmerei*, or "fanaticism."[71] Only two of the pamphlets explicitly rejected Christ's corporeal presence in the sacrament, and one of these was the theologically unsophisticated but highly polemical *Dialogue*. For this reason, it is not surprising that Luther's immediate published response, an *Open Letter to the Strasbourgers*, said little about Karlstadt's eucharistic theology and concentrated instead on the underlying issue: the centrality of justification by faith and the defense of Christian liberty.[72]

This understanding would also shape Luther's refutation of Karlstadt's understanding of the sacrament in *Against the Heavenly Prophets*, published in two parts at the turn of the year. The book combined polemic with pastoral concern, invective with serious theological argument. As had been the case in the Invocavit sermons of 1522, Luther responded not to the immediate questions concerning the sacrament but instead addressed the deeper theological issue that separated him from Karlstadt, in this case the proper ordering of the relationship between external and internal. This ordering included giving the essentials of the evangelical gospel priority and then showing how the contents of the gospel message were transmitted and appropriated through the external means of word and sacrament. In comparison to this fundamental issue, Karlstadt's understanding of the Lord's Supper played a subsidiary role. Luther addressed it in the second part of the book in order to counter what he saw as the many and manifest errors in that understanding, but those errors were derived from the more fundamental error that Karlstadt made in inverting the relationship between external and internal.

Luther's antagonism toward Karlstadt is clear from the opening lines of *Against the Heavenly Prophets*, in which he stated that Karlstadt "has deserted us . . . and become our worst enemy" and referred to him as "the Satan who here pretends to vindicate the sacrament . . . who seeks to destroy [the whole doctrine of the gospel] with cunning interpretation of Scripture."[73] Part I of the work was directed entirely against the two types of practical reform that Karlstadt most strongly advocated, the removal of images and the replacement of the mass with the evangelical Lord's Supper. The section concerning the mass was a direct response to the three criticisms of the Wittenbergers that Karlstadt had raised in *Against the Old and New Papist Masses*. Luther rejected Karlstadt's etymology of "mass" from the Hebrew but said that even if the etymology were correct, it was an infringement on Christian freedom to insist that the word not be used.[74] He used the same argument to defend the elevation of the host, which was an external action that had no connection with the wave and heave offerings of the Old Testament. The Wittenbergers were free to retain it if they wished, for its use did not imply that they believed that the mass was a sacrifice. Luther even went so far as to assert that in response to Karlstadt's rejection of the word "mass" and of elevation, Christians must use the word and retain the elevation as a sign of their Christian freedom.[75] Luther justified his hesitancy in producing a German mass with the difficulty of combining texts and music in a way that reflected the natural character of the vernacular. It was, however, sufficient if communicants understood and took to heart Christ's words of institution, which could be explained in the sermon, and so the Latin mass was not inherently wrong.[76]

In Part II Luther responded to Karlstadt's *Dialogue*, but he prefaced that response with a discussion of the proper relationship between external and internal—yet another indication that Luther saw this as the fundamental difference separating him and Karlstadt.[77] Again Luther began his attack by criticizing Karlstadt's concern with terminology—this time, his rejection of the word "sacrament" at the beginning of the *Dialogue*.[78] He then took up the question of Christ's corporeal presence in the sacrament. On this issue, he accused Karlstadt of reading his own errors into Scripture rather than allowing Scripture to shape his understanding.[79] He rejected Karlstadt's interpretation of the words of institution, arguing that there was no scriptural justification for Karlstadt's separation of the clauses "take, eat," and "this is my body given for you." He dismissed as absurd Karlstadt's use of capital letters and punctuation to defend this separation, pointing to the fact that punctuation was determined by printers, and one could not base one's faith on how a printer decided to set the text.[80] He heaped even more scorn on Karlstadt's use of the Greek *touto*. To claim that "this" must refer to "body" rather than to "bread" simply demonstrated Karlstadt's ignorance of both Greek and German.[81]

Luther did not restrict his defense of Christ's corporeal presence to his interpretation of the words of institution. He also cited 1 Corinthians 10:16 as a "thunderbolt on the head of Dr. Karlstadt and his whole party." St. Paul spoke here of the external fellowship of those who ate physically of Christ's body, distributed in the broken bread, not of the spiritual fellowship of Christ's suffering.[82] Karlstadt's understanding of eating and drinking unworthily came under attack as well. Luther argued that there was a difference between eating unworthily and remembering unworthily, and to identify the two was a use of allegory that ignored the primary, literal meaning of the text.[83]

Luther devoted the remainder of the book to refuting the arguments against Christ's corporeal presence that Karlstadt had put in Peter's mouth in the *Dialogue*. One could not use John 6:63 against that presence, for the verse did not pertain to the sacrament. Christ was talking not about his own flesh but about flesh as the "carnal mind," or as understanding spiritual words in a carnal way.[84] Luther also reacted strongly against Karlstadt's emphasis on knowledge and remembrance, which turned these acts into works.[85] To explain his assertion that the sacrament brought peace to troubled consciences, Luther distinguished between how Christ won forgiveness through his death on the cross at one point in time and how individuals appropriated that forgiveness at all times through their faith. Knowledge and remembrance, no matter how ardent they might be, pertained to the onetime event; only faith allowed individuals to apply that forgiveness to themselves. That faith in turn rested on the promise contained in word and sacrament.[86]

Luther's attack on Karlstadt's eucharistic theology was shaped by his limited exposure to it. As he himself admitted, he had not seen or read all of Karlstadt's "poisonous books,"[87] and in fact, he probably did not read at least one of the books that were sent to him. Although he responded at length to *Against the . . . Papist Masses* and the *Dialogue* in *Against the Heavenly Prophets*, his only references to the *Exegesis of Christ's Words* were a few allusions to "the two-fold papists," an epithet that was part of the pamphlet's lengthy title. His dependence on the *Dialogue* meant that he saw only the most popular and polemical form of Karlstadt's theology, and this in turn influenced the form and content of *Against the Heavenly Prophets*. Luther aimed his work at the same broad audience, and he not only resorted to the same polemical techniques— sarcasm, insults, name-calling, distortion, and deliberate exaggeration—that Karlstadt had used, but he used them to a much greater extent. To these techniques he added demonization, for he believed that in their fundamental confusion of external and internal, Karlstadt and the other "heavenly prophets" were inspired by Satan himself.

Karlstadt received a copy of the second part of *Against the Heavenly Prophets* a month after the work was published, and he immediately began a response. He originally planned to answer Luther in fifteen different pamphlets, but he was able to publish only two works on the Supper. His *Explanation of 1 Corinthians 10:16* contained his interpretation of the verse that Luther had regarded as a "thunderbolt" against Karlstadt, while *On the New and Old Testament* gave his interpretation of Christ's words concerning the cup (Luke 22:20; 1 Cor. 11:25).[88] The two pamphlets together were Karlstadt's most detailed defense of his understanding of the Lord's Supper as he derived it from the key scriptural texts related to the sacrament. Reflecting their rapid composition and polemical context, the pamphlets are repetitious, sometimes disjointed, and full of ad hominem remarks.[89] Despite these failings, though, they are significant as expositions of Karlstadt's mature eucharistic theology. Both pamphlets demonstrate how important the opposition between external and internal had become for his understanding of the sacrament, as Karlstadt drew out the consequences of the presuppositions and emphases of his earlier works. This opposition was expressed in two ways: in the contrast between corporeal and spiritual derived from John 6, and in the contrast between the sacrifices of the Old Testament and Christ's one sacrifice in the New Testament.

The *Explanation* was primarily a response to *Against the Heavenly Prophets*, but since Luther had repeated positions in that work that were first stated in *On the Adoration of the Sacrament*, Karlstadt's arguments were aimed against the earlier pamphlet as well. In the *Explanation* Karlstadt approached 1 Corinthians 10:16 within the context of St. Paul's preceding statement that Christ was the spiritual rock from which the fathers drank (1 Cor. 10:4). Karlstadt further developed the idea of Christ as spiritual food and drink with reference to John 6. The only way one ate and drank Christ was through faith, or through the "glorious, ardent, hearty and loving knowledge" that Karlstadt used as a synonym for faith. If the fathers ate spiritually, and if Christ fed his followers spiritually, it was of no use to eat Christ physically in the bread and wine.[90]

Karlstadt acknowledged that St. Paul was writing about external bread in 1 Corinthians 10:16, but he rejected Luther's argument that the bread distributed and shared among Christians was Christ's physical body. Instead, the sharing of bread established the fellowship of Christ's spiritual body. One could no more argue that Christ's body was in the bread on the basis of this passage than one could say that the giver of a gift was in the gift.[91] Although Karlstadt had argued that the words of institution were to be taken literally and had proposed his own way of avoiding any identification of the bread with the body of Christ, he adopted Hoen's equation of "is" and "signifies" to explain 1 Corinthians 10:16 and, like Hoen, he drew parallels to other scriptural metaphors: God was not naturally a fortress or a wall, and Christ was not a natural vine or lamb. Paul's words meant that Christians were "a figured and signified bread." If this was true of those who participated in Christ's body and blood, it was even more true of Christ's body, which therefore could not be in the natural bread.[92]

Karlstadt argued that the fellowship of Christ's body and blood was established not through eating Christ's body and drinking his blood, but rather through baptism and through knowledge of Christ or loving faith. This fellowship must exist before one received the bread and cup, and in fact faith was sufficient for fellowship with Christ. Such fellowship also had ethical consequences, for those who shared it separated themselves from all that hindered faith and love of neighbor. Following St. Augustine, Karlstadt asserted that eating was believing, and it was impossible for one to eat and drink Christ's body and blood and not live. For the same reason, evil and unbelieving persons, such as Judas, could not eat and drink Christ's body and blood.[93]

Karlstadt closed the pamphlet by emphasizing again the strict separation of physical and spiritual. The soul was neither fed nor assured nor strengthened by bodily eating. Scripture spoke only about spiritual eating, not about physical eating. One could not eat Christ's flesh and blood with the mouth, for Christ had been taken from the earth and would remain in heaven until his final return.[94]

The same separation of physical and spiritual characterized Karlstadt's pamphlet *On the New and Old Testament*, here expressed in terms of the contrast between the sacrifices associated with each testament. Karlstadt asserted that the wording of the institution narratives in Luke 22 and 1 Corinthians 11 concerning the cup could not support the claim that the cup contained Christ's blood. Christ's own words proved that the cup did not contain blood, for he spoke those words only after the disciples had drunk from it. No matter how one turned around the words in the phrase "the cup is the new testament in my blood," it could not be proved that Christ's blood was bodily in the cup.[95]

The occurrence of the word "testament" led Karlstadt to a comparison of the old and new testaments. Here he drew on the arguments first expressed in *On the Priesthood* to explain the relationship between Christ's body and blood and the Lord's Supper, now even more strongly reflecting the neoplatonic/Augustinian dualism that characterized Erasmus's paraphrase of Hebrews 8–10. Thus Karlstadt contrasted the sacrifices of the old testament, which cleansed only the external bodies touched by the sprinkled blood, with the new testament in which Christ as the high priest sprinkled us spiritually with his blood through the Holy Spirit.[96]

On the basis of this distinction, Karlstadt turned against Luther the charge that Luther had made against him: that he had confused the proper relationship between external and internal. By insisting on the physical drinking of Christ's blood, the "new pope" destroyed the spiritual drink and sprinkling of the new testament. Karlstadt compared Luther to Moses: just as Moses physically sprinkled the altar and its vessels with blood, so Luther took water and wine, called it blood, and gave it to the people to drink physically. Only Christ's blood shed on the cross corresponded to what was figured in the Old Testament. That blood had to be received spiritually, and those who received blood physically received it only as a physical drink and not for forgiveness of sins. Though he called it the blood of the new testament, Luther made the cup into the blood of the old testament when he said it must be received physically.[97]

Karlstadt identified the spiritual eating of Christ's flesh from John 6 with Christ's sprinkling believers with his blood as described in Hebrews 9. This in turn allowed him to criticize the role Luther and his followers gave to the priests who administered the sacrament. Despite all that Luther had written against the sacrifice of the mass, he retained "the roots of priestly error" by saying even godless priests could be mediators of Christ's blood. Against this view Karlstadt argued that all who had been sprinkled with Christ's blood were priests who offered their bodies in service to God.[98] Karlstadt also rejected the distinction Luther made between Christ's death on the cross as obtaining forgiveness and the sacrament as a means of distributing that forgiveness to individual believers. John 6 proved that Christ's blood could only be drunk spiritually and not bodily, and believers drank from the cup in remembrance of Christ's shed blood.[99]

None of the arguments that Karlstadt used here were new. The importance of the two pamphlets lay rather in the depth and the detail with which he laid out the basic principles underlying his eucharistic theology. The most important of these was a spiritualist dualism so strong that it could not allow for any overlap between external and internal. Corporeal and spiritual were oppositional, not complementary, categories. As applied to the Lord's Supper, the former could not assist or mediate the latter. External things might prepare, teach, or remind, but they did not convey or bestow anything.[100]

This spiritualist dualism also underlay Karlstadt's understanding of the Old Testament's relation to the New. The Old Testament had played a prominent role in shaping Karlstadt's eucharistic theology from the very beginning. Like Luther, he saw there a pattern of promise and sign that was repeated in the sacrament. His understanding of signs was shaped by St. Augustine, which not only reinforced his dualism but eventually led him to a deeper appreciation of the way the Old Testament could be interpreted figurally.[101] Karlstadt's figural interpretation differed from simple allegory by creating a stronger connection, one of foreshadowing and fulfillment, between the historical events and acts of the Old Testament and those of the New. But because the fulfillment came on the cross, all that preceded that event was itself a figure, including the bread and wine of the Last Supper.

The two pamphlets also make quite clear the fundamental differences between Luther and Karlstadt on the interpretation of the Scripture passages pertaining to the sacrament. Each felt that his interpretation of the texts being debated was the correct one and accused the other of misreading the text and lacking other scriptural support for his interpretation. The words of institution, "this is my body," were the chief bone of contention, but the two men disagreed on other key verses as well. Whether 1 Corinthians 10:4 should be understood as "the rock signified Christ" or as "Christ was the spiritual rock," whether 1 Corinthians 10:16 referred to Christ's natural body or his mystical body, whether John 6:63 applied to Christ's flesh or the fleshly nature, how one was to interpret "the cup of the new testament in my blood" (Luke 22:20; 1 Cor. 11:25) or to define worthy eating and discerning Christ's body (1 Cor. 11:27–29): all of these were controversial issues of exegesis that would continue to be debated through the course of the eucharistic controversy. Without the possibility of a higher authority able either to reconcile or to decide between the competing interpretations, this division was inevitable because the exegetical disagreements remained even after Karlstadt withdrew from the public debate.

Just as important as these exegetical differences was the underlying disagreement concerning the relationship between matter and spirit, reflecting Karlstadt's spiritualist orientation.[102] Luther was keenly aware of this disagreement, and it led him to present his differences with Karlstadt in much the same way that he had in his Invocavit sermons of 1522. He shifted the center of the debate away from the immediate question being debated, in this case whether or not Christ was bodily present in the sacrament, to the fundamental issue underlying the debate, that of the ability of material things to bear spiritual significance. This was the heart of the controversy for Luther, and it meant that all who shared Karlstadt's neoplatonic/Augustinian and Erasmian dualism would inevitably become Luther's opponents, regardless of the differences among them in their own understandings of the sacrament.

Luther's authority within the evangelical movement and the widespread diffusion of *Against the Heavenly Prophets* virtually guaranteed that his framework for understanding the debate would become the accepted one throughout northern and central Germany.[103] This in turn would make it much harder for those who advocated a spiritualist understanding to gain an audience as the eucharistic controversy began to spread. From the perspective of Luther and his followers, it did not matter that the Swiss, South German, or Silesian reformers did not agree with Karlstadt's exegesis of Christ's words instituting the sacrament. By advocating the same dualist metaphysics that separated external from internal, they had placed themselves on the wrong side of the debate. In this sense, then, Karlstadt's 1524 pamphlets and Luther's response in *Against the Heavenly Prophets* were the opening volley in the theological war that would eventually be institutionalized by the division of the evangelical movement into the Lutheran and Reformed churches.

After the heated polemics between Luther and Karlstadt, the end of their dispute seems almost anticlimactic. Already in December Karlstadt had written to Luther, asking him to intercede with the elector on his behalf. The elector refused Karlstadt's request for a safe conduct, as he did a second plea in March.[104] Driven out of one city after another, threatened by the violence of the Peasants' War, and concerned for the well-being of his family, Karlstadt tried one last time. In June he wrote to Luther again, and at Luther's request, he wrote a pamphlet in which he defended himself against the accusation that he had been involved in the peasant unrest. The apology satisfied Luther, who allowed Karlstadt to live with him in secret while he sought the elector's pardon. A precondition for such a pardon was the retraction of his published views on the Lord's Supper. The result was the *Declaration of How Karlstadt Regards His Teaching about the Venerable Sacrament*, which was finished toward the end of July.[105]

The *Declaration* was not the full recantation Luther hoped for. Instead, Karlstadt claimed that he had advanced his views only as hypotheses. No one was to regard them as certain proof that Christ was not corporeally present in the sacrament, and Karlstadt was himself open to "Christian instruction" on the matter. He said that he had not originally intended to publish his ideas, but a good friend had asked him to do so. He had published the pamphlets in the belief that their contents were "good and godly," but all teachings were to be tested against the clear text of God's word. He had thought to base his teaching on Scripture, but where he had misused Scripture that teaching should not be accepted.[106]

In the preface he wrote for the pamphlet, Luther endorsed this revisionist version of the debate, pointing out that most of Karlstadt's pamphlets had titles implying that the contents were suggestions rather than articles of faith, and that in their prefaces Karlstadt had repeatedly stated that he was open to further instruction. Luther acknowledged that he himself was guilty of overlooking the tentative nature of the titles and assuming that the pamphlets' contents represented Karlstadt's firm convictions, and so it was necessary that the latter publish this explanation. For his part, Luther highlighted the Christian obligation to help those who were wavering or questioning in matters of faith. Karlstadt was one of those who had not yet sunk in his obstinacy but was swimming toward the shore. Luther, however, had no corresponding reservations about his own reading of Scripture. It was obvious to him that "because Karlstadt, Zwingli, and all others who discuss this article speak from their own imagination and questions, as they themselves confess, it is certain that they do not yet have the Spirit in this article, and that they speak from human darkness and not from the Spirit." His own faith, however, was based on the "sure truth" as it was clearly revealed in Scripture.[107]

The *Declaration* served as Karlstadt's final public statement concerning the Lord's Supper. It was by no means an unequivocal surrender to Luther. Karlstadt's admonition to his readers that they should not consider his pamphlets as divine truth but should instead compare them with and judge them according to Scripture was certainly intended to apply to Luther's writings as well.[108] Nevertheless, when combined with Luther's preface emphasizing his own certainty concerning the truth of his views, the pamphlet subordinated Karlstadt's teaching authority to that of Luther. Moreover, as a condition for permission to return to Saxony, Karlstadt agreed not to discuss, write about, or publish on theological matters. As he himself later testified, he laid aside his books and spent the next few years trying to support himself and his family by farming.[109] But the disagreements over the understanding of the Lord's Supper did not go away with Karlstadt's withdrawal from the arena, for others took up the scriptural understanding and the theological arguments he had advanced. His pamphlets would influence the shape of the early eucharistic controversy and contribute to further divisions within the evangelical movement.

4

Ad Dextram Patris

HUSSITE INFLUENCES ON THE EARLY EUCHARISTIC CONTROVERSY

A CENTURY BEFORE the Protestant Reformation began, the followers of the Czech reformer Jan Hus began a reformation of their own. Although the Hussites attacked the Roman church on several fronts, the Eucharist played an important role in establishing their identity. The demand for communion in both kinds was one of the core ideas uniting what would become a diverse movement. By the early sixteenth century, the Bohemian heresy was especially associated with the rejection of Catholic teaching on the Eucharist and the popular piety associated with it.[1]

In the years between the posting of the Ninety-five Theses and the outbreak of the eucharistic controversy, there were various contacts between reformers and Hussites. Scholars have long been interested in Luther's evolving knowledge of and attitude toward Hus and his later followers, not only because of Johann Eck's adroit linkage of Luther with Hus during their debate in Leipzig but also because Luther addressed his 1523 treatise *On the Adoration of the Sacrament* to the Bohemian Brethren.[2] Erasmus's relations with Bohemia have also received some scholarly attention.[3] In contrast, beyond the pioneering article by Joachim Staedke there are no studies of the influence of Hussite ideas on either the Swiss reformers or the radical groups that emerged in the mid-1520s. Research has instead gone in the other direction, concentrating on the influence of both Zwingli and Calvin in the Czech-speaking lands of Bohemia and Moravia.[4] Several scholars have noted the affinity between Reformed eucharistic theology and that of the Bohemian Brethren, but they have not taken the next step of looking for connections between the two.

In fact, the similarities between certain elements of Hussite teaching on the Eucharist and the arguments advanced by the Swiss and South Germans at the beginning of the eucharistic controversy are more than coincidental. Several of the objections raised by the latter against Christ's corporeal presence in the Lord's Supper originated with the Hussites. Circulated in manuscript form and made more accessible through a variety of works printed in the early decades of the sixteenth century, Taborite arguments against Christ's corporeal presence in the sacrament were adopted and adapted by Cornelis Hoen and Andreas Karlstadt, while Johannes Oecolampadius, Heinrich Bullinger, and eventually Ulrich Zwingli derived what would become a central element of Reformed eucharistic theology from the Bohemian Brethren. This chapter describes the main features of Hussite theology that were relevant to the eucharistic controversy and examines how they were appropriated by others to justify the rejection of Christ's corporeal presence in the sacrament. By so doing, it illuminates yet another aspect of the circulation of ideas in the early Reformation.

HUSSITE VIEWS OF THE EUCHARIST

Although the Hussite movement was loosely united around a single practice, the administration of the chalice to the laity, there was no single Hussite theology of the Eucharist. Instead, in the years following Hus's death at Constance a spectrum of opinions developed, ranging from the conservative Utraquists who accepted transubstantiation to the radical Picards or Adamites who held that the sacrament contained only bread and wine.[5] The militant Taborites held a view lying between these two poles. Their theologians did not fully agree among themselves in their understanding of the Eucharist, but they developed a number of common arguments against Christ's corporeal presence that would be elaborated over the next century and used against both Catholics and Luther at the beginning of the eucharistic controversy.[6]

Influenced as much by John Wyclif and the Waldensians as by Jan Hus, the Taborites denied Christ's corporeal presence in the elements of bread and wine but taught that Christ was spiritually present in them. The confession written in 1431 by the Taborite bishop Nicholas of Pelhřimov (Biscupek) stated that the bread was "the body of Christ, whose true body was in the same truly, sacramentally and spiritually." But it rejected the belief that the substance of bread was converted into the substantial body of Christ, since "that same body of Christ, with all of its properties, both essential and accidental, is seated in heaven at the right hand of God."[7]

The Taborites based their position on ideas they found in Wyclif and elaborated into a more structured system that distinguished between Christ's four modes of existence: in heaven, with the saints in heaven and on earth, throughout the entire universe, and in the sacrament. Concerning the first mode of existence, they argued that Christ's human body had been taken up into heaven, as the angels told the apostles (Acts 1:11), and where Stephen had beheld him at God's right hand (Acts 7:56). Christ had warned his followers not to believe false prophets who claimed that "Christ is here," or "Christ is there" (Mark 13:21; Matt. 24:23).[8] The bread therefore could not be identical to Christ's body, or its substance converted into Christ's natural flesh. Following Wyclif, they held that Christ's words "this is my body" must be understood figuratively, similar to Christ's statement that John the Baptist was Elijah (Matt. 11:14), and Paul's assertion that the rock was Christ (1 Cor. 10:4) and in the same way that the seven ears of grain in Pharaoh's dream were seven years (Gen. 41:26–27).[9] The university-trained Taborite theologians gave qualified support to the adoration of the host, but they emphasized that what was adored was the whole Christ in his divine and human nature, and not his body, which was in heaven, seated at the right hand of God. Because the simple people were prone to misunderstand and so to fall into idolatry, it was better to worship God directly rather than in the signs of bread and wine.[10]

A combination of negotiation and military action led to the elimination of the Taborites by midcentury, but not before their beliefs were spread outside of the Czech-speaking lands, where they mixed with popular forms of late medieval heresy. Contacts between Czech Taborites and German immigrants in Bohemia and Moravia, some of them Waldensian refugees, made it easier for Hussite ideas to cross the ethnic and linguistic barrier. Students and wandering preachers who had contacts with Bohemia also propagated Taborite beliefs.[11] One of the most important of the latter was Friedrich Reiser, a Waldensian who was ordained by the Taborites and who spread heretical ideas from Moravia through southern Germany and into western Switzerland through the second quarter of the fifteenth century.[12] More popular presentation of Hussite ideas also circulated underground in manuscript form.

A treatise by an anonymous "puer Bohemus" illustrates how Taborite eucharistic theology was modified for the common man and woman as it spread to western Europe.[13] Although it taught the same understanding of the sacrament as the Taborites, it omitted their more metaphysical and speculative theological arguments against Christ's corporeal presence and relied chiefly on their scriptural proof texts. It discussed the Eucharist in the larger context of the rejection of images and relics and of the veneration of the saints, which it condemned as forms of idolatry. In the same way, the author argued, it was idolatry to adore and pray to the sacramental bread, for this was to worship a created thing rather than the Creator. Christ called the bread his body not because it was his body in a real sense (*realiter*) but only in a mysterious and participative way (*misterialiter et participative*), in the same way Paul called the cup the communication of Christ's body (1 Cor. 10:17). It was better to believe Paul, who called it bread, than the scholastic theologians, who said it was only the form of bread.[14] Christ's words were not always to be understood literally, and Christ had given the key to understanding his statement "this is my body" when he said "the spirit gives life; the flesh is of no use" (John 6:63). Many who had never substantially eaten Christ's body nor really drunk his blood still possessed the life that is Christ (John 6:54); thus his flesh and blood must be the same spiritual food that the fathers ate (1 Cor. 10:3–4).[15] There was no command in Scripture to adore the consecrated bread, and it was clear from Paul's account in 1 Corinthians 11 that the early church did not do so.[16] As we shall see, many of these arguments would reappear with the outbreak of the eucharistic controversy.

Taborite eucharistic theology was also preserved and further developed in the Czech-speaking lands by the Unitas Fratrum. More generally known as the Bohemian Brethren, this group split from the Utraquists in the 1460s by ordaining their own bishops.[17] Many of the earliest members of the Bohemian Brethren were former Taborites who had renounced the use of violence. Although not a Taborite himself, Peter Chelčický, whose theology helped shape the Bohemian Brethren, shared the Taborite view that Christ's real and essential body was in heaven, at the right hand of God, and would not return to earth until the last judgment. He criticized the Taborites for what he believed was their rejection of Christ's presence in the Eucharist and defended the more moderate position that Christ was indeed present in a spiritual and sacramental way, on the basis of Christ's four modes of existence.[18]

From the 1490s until his death in 1528 the dominant figure within the Bohemian Brethren was Brother Lukas of Prague. In response to growing persecution in the first decade of the sixteenth century, Brother Lukas wrote four confessions or apologies that would make the theology of the Brethren known to a broader audience. The earliest and shortest of these, the *Oratio excusatoria*, was written in 1503 and addressed to King Vladislaus II. Four years later Brother Lukas sent a somewhat lengthier *Confessio fratrum* to King Vladislaus. Attacks by the Moravian humanist Augustin Käsenbrod (Olmucensis) led Brother Lukas to expand on the positions of the 1507 *Confessio* the following year, in his *Excusatio fratrum Valdensium*. Last but certainly not least, the *Apologia verae scripturae* was published in Nuremberg in 1511.[19]

The understanding of the Eucharist presented in all four confessions was similar, although it was developed at greater length in the later, longer works.[20] In them, Brother Lukas combined the more speculative theology derived from Wyclif and the academically trained Taborite theologians with the scriptural proof texts and the critique of eucharistic piety used in works directed to a more popular audience.

He made three assertions: that Christ was spiritually present in the bread and wine; that Christ could not be corporeally present in the sacrament because he had ascended bodily into heaven; and that for this reason, the sacrament was not to be adored. These assertions rested on the distinction between the four modes of Christ's existence discussed in the confessions of 1507 and 1508 and described at greatest length in the *Apologia*. There Brother Lukas differentiated between Christ's personal, true, essential and natural presence (*personalis. vera, substantialis et naturalis*), identified with his physical body now located at the Father's right hand in heaven; his presence in the church, which was in power, spiritual, and ministerial (*virtualis, spiritualis et ministerialis*); his spiritual presence in the soul; and his sacramental and spiritual presence in the elements.[21]

The *Excusatio* acknowledged Käsenbrod's suspicion that the Brethren's talk of Christ's spiritual presence in the bread and wine was simply a trick to hide their rejection of Catholic teaching, but it asserted that Christ's sacramental and spiritual presence in the bread and wine was no less true than his substantial and natural presence in heaven. Like Wyclif and the Taborites, it explained the words of institution by analogy with Christ's statement that John the Baptist was Elijah (Matt. 11:14) and St. Paul's assertion that the rock was Christ (1 Cor. 10:4). In each case, these statements were true if "John" and "rock" were understood spiritually rather than substantially or personally.[22] The soul ate Christ's substance spiritually through faith in his meritorious grace and truth. Christ was not present in the sacrament according to his natural substance but was nevertheless present in power, spiritually, sacramentally, and truly.[23]

Each of these confessions paired the positive statement about Christ's spiritual presence in the elements with the rejection of his corporeal presence. Scripture was full of references to Christ's departure and to his return only at the end of the age. Thus Christ told his disciples that the poor would always be with them, but that he himself would not be (Matt. 26:11), and that it was to their advantage that he left them, for otherwise the Paraclete would not come (John 16:6–7). Christ told his critics that the day would come when the bridegroom would leave them (Matt. 9:15), and in his high priestly prayer before his passion, Christ repeatedly spoke of his going to the Father and the departure of his natural body (John 17). The angels told the disciples that Christ would return from heaven in the same way that he had departed (Acts 1:11). Peter proclaimed that Christ would remain in heaven until the time of restoration of all things (Acts 3:21), while Stephen saw him at the right hand of God (Acts 7:56). The Psalmist had also prophesied that Christ would remain at God's right hand until all his enemies were defeated (Ps. 110:1). Augustine wrote that the body in which Christ rose from the dead must be in one place, in heaven with his Father, but his truth was diffused everywhere.[24] The Apostles'

Creed summarized these truths in its articles concerning Christ's resurrection, ascension, and his coming again. On this basis, Brother Lukas argued that until the close of this age Christ would remain in his personal and natural substance at the Father's right hand in heaven.

This position was the basis for rejecting the adoration of the consecrated host. Because Christ's natural and personal body was in heaven, it could not be adored in the sacrament. The 1507 *Confessio* introduced a number of arguments against such adoration, and these were repeated and expanded in the later works. Several of the arguments were based on the words of Christ. Thus Christ warned his disciples not to believe those who said, "Christ is here," or "Christ is there" (Matt. 24:23). The early church had called the sacrament the Lord's Supper or the breaking of bread rather than Christ's body, and Christians were not commanded to venerate the elements but to remember Christ. Christ told Satan that we were to worship God alone, and then taught his disciples to pray to "Our Father in heaven." The distinction between the Creator and created things meant that adoration of the host was a form of idolatry prohibited by the Decalogue. The 1508 *Excusatio* acknowledged that Christ's promise to be present with his followers (Matt. 18:20 and 28:20) could be used to justify Christ's spiritual but not his corporeal presence, and it pointed out that if Christ were in the sacrament in the same way that he was in the saints, then the latter should also be adored, just as one adored Christ's body in the sacrament and at the Father's right hand.[25]

The three confessions of 1503, 1507, and 1508 were first published not by the Bohemian Brethren but by the Bavarian theologian Jakob Ziegler, who added to them both Käsenbrod's letters and his own refutation of the Brethren's teachings.[26] Ziegler became aware of the 1511 *Apologia* only as he was finishing work on his own book, which was published in Leipzig in 1512. Two years later the Leipzig theologian Hieronymus Dungersheim von Ochsenfurt published a *Confutatio* of the *Apologia*; this was followed in 1514 by his *Reprobatio orationis excusatorae picardorum*, which reprinted the 1503 confession section by section in order to refute its positions.[27] The three confessions, along with several other works concerning both John Wyclif and Jan Hus, were also included with Aeneas Sylvius Piccolomini's history of the Council of Basel published in Basel in the spring of 1523.[28]

In addition to the Latin confessions of the Bohemian Brethren, other Latin and German works concerning Hus and the Hussites were published in the years immediately surrounding the Reformation. Breaking with a long tradition that condemned the Hussites as heretics without specific reference to their teachings, some of these works began to present the Hussites in a somewhat more positive light.[29] They included Poggio Bracciolini's letter to Leonardo Bruni describing the burning of Jerome of Prague at Constance, as well as Hus's treatise *de Ecclesia*, a letter of protest written by the Czech nobility after Hus's execution, and several works attributed to Hus by their editor, Otto Brunfels.[30] These works tended to focus on ecclesiology and the jurisdictional authority of the Roman church, but some of them contained brief statements about the Eucharist. Thus *The Articles and Origin of the Waldensians and the Poor of Lyon, John Wyclif and John Hus* informed its readers that Wyclif rejected transubstantiation, believed that the substance of bread and wine remained after consecration, and taught that Christ was not truly and corporeally in the sacrament. It also described the spread of Wyclif's ideas to Bohemia, and it attributed to Hus's disciple Peter of Dresden the assertion that the laity should receive communion in both kinds.[31] *The Compendious Description of the Origin and of the Condemned Articles of Bohemian or Hussite Heresies* also cited the condemnation at Constance of the views that the substances of bread and wine remained after consecration and that the accidents could not subsist without their substances.[32]

Although it is much harder to track, there is evidence for the circulation of Hussite manuscripts as well. In the preface to his 1524 edition of an explanation of the four Prague articles, the Jena pastor Martin Reinhart stated that he hoped to publish other Hussite texts in his possession.[33] In the prefatory letter for the first volume of Hus's writings, Otto Brunfels told Luther that the texts had belonged to Ulrich von Hutten. The interest shown in Hussite works extended to those of Wyclif as well, and Brunfels was responsible for the publication in 1525 of Wyclif's *Trialogus*, which included a lengthy discussion of the sacraments, that had apparently circulated among humanist circles in south Germany for some time.[34]

In the years immediately preceding the outbreak of the eucharistic controversy, then, it was possible for interested observers to gain some familiarity with Hussite thought in general and with the eucharistic theology of the Bohemian Brethren in particular. Exposure to that theology was often accompanied by a refutation of it, whether in the form of conciliar condemnations or polemical treatises, so that the reader would have no doubts about the errors they contained. Such condemnations did little, however, to prevent the diffusion of Hussite ideas in the early years of the Reformation.[35]

EVANGELICAL USE OF HUSSITE ARGUMENTS

Hussite ideas entered into the evangelical debate over the Eucharist in two forms in the first half of the 1520s. Older Taborite arguments appeared first in a letter by the Dutch jurist Cornelis Hoen rejecting the Catholic belief in transubstantiation, as well as the pamphlets of Andreas Bodenstein von Karlstadt aimed at "the two-fold papists," both Catholics and Luther. The Bohemian Brethren's more detailed confessions were used by the Swiss theologians, contributing to the development of their own Christological argument against Christ's corporeal presence in the Eucharist.

Hoen's brief discussion of the Eucharist was probably written in 1521 and circulated in manuscript before it was finally printed in the summer of 1525 with the title A Most Christian Letter . . . Treating the Lord's Supper Much Differently Than It Has Been Done Until Now.[36] Although its arguments were rejected by Luther, Hoen's significative interpretation of Christ's words of institution was endorsed by Zwingli, and so the letter played a key role in the beginning of the eucharistic controversy.

B. J. Spruyt has pointed to ideas taken from Wyclif and Hus found in Hoen's Most Christian Letter. These include the scriptural proof texts of Matthew 11:14 ("[John] is Elijah"), 1 Corinthians 10:4 ("the rock was Christ"), and Genesis 41:26–27 (Joseph's interpretation of Pharaoh's dream) to illustrate the figurative understanding of "is," and of Matthew 24:23 ("if anyone says to you, 'Lo, here is the Christ'") and John 16:7 ("it is to your advantage that I go away") used against Christ's bodily presence on earth, the opposition to veneration because it entailed worshiping something created rather than the Creator, and the argument that Christ and the apostles used the word "bread," not "body," when referring to the sacrament. Spruyt describes the circulation of Hussite ideas in the Low Countries through the fifteenth century more generally and suggests that Hoen's letter was based on an older heretical work to which Hoen added interpolations reflecting the influence of Luther and Erasmus.[37]

While Spruyt may go too far in reducing Hoen's role to that of redactor, he is certainly correct in identifying the parallels between Hoen's letter and Hussite thought. The Most Christian Letter is not so much a statement of eucharistic theology as it is a collection of arguments against Christ's corporeal presence in the sacrament, and it is possible that Hoen drew those arguments from a variety of sources when he wrote his letter. These sources might also have included one or more of the confessions of the Bohemian Brethren, since they were available in printed works, but there is no evidence for such a link. If Hoen did derive any of his arguments from the Bohemian Brethren, he did so in a piecemeal fashion, selecting only those ideas that could be used against Christ's corporeal presence and the practice of veneration. The first point of the Brethren's confessions, the insistence on Christ's spiritual presence in the Eucharist, is not mentioned in Hoen's letter, although it could be implied on the basis of the analogies Hoen made with a wedding ring and a house key.

The Most Christian Letter may well have been known in Wittenberg as early as 1521, when Andreas Karlstadt published his pamphlet defending the adoration of the sacrament. By the summer of 1524, however, Karlstadt had gone even further than Hoen in not only rejecting Christ's corporeal presence but arguing that the sacrament consisted only of bread and wine. He developed his attack on the traditional understanding of the Eucharist in the pamphlets published in the fall of 1524. While one might read into Hoen's letter a link between Christ's spiritual presence and the elements, Karlstadt's pamphlets left no doubt that the bread and wine conveyed nothing to recipients. Moreover, although in his earlier work he had criticized the "Picards" for regarding the bread of the sacrament like any other bread, he now condemned the "new blind guides" who tried to force the "pious Waldensians" to believe that Christ's body and blood were present in the sacrament.[38]

In his four pamphlets rejecting Christ's corporeal presence in the elements, Karlstadt drew heavily on arguments advanced by Hoen, many of which stemmed from the Hussites.[39] These were expressed most polemically in the *Dialogue . . . on the Horrible and Idolatrous Misuse of the Venerable Sacrament of Jesus Christ,* aimed at a broad popular audience. Like Hoen's *Most Christian Letter*, the *Dialogue* was not so much a reasoned exposition of a theological position as a collection of as many arguments as could be mustered against Christ's corporeal presence. There are a number of parallels between the *Dialogue* and Hussite ideas. Karlstadt stated that according to his divine nature Christ was everywhere, but he denied that Christ's body could be in many places at one time. He cited Matthew 24:23 and John 16:7 as proof texts against Christ's corporeal presence, and he used Acts 1:11 and 3:21 to argue that there were only two comings of Christ, the first at the incarnation and the second at the Last Judgment. Rather than linking this point to the rejection of veneration, however, he used it against the claim that priests had the power to draw Christ down from heaven with their words of consecration.[40]

While there is no direct connection between Karlstadt's eucharistic pamphlets and any specific Hussite works, Karlstadt was at least familiar with some of the objections raised by the Hussites against Christ's corporeal presence. In addition to Hoen's letter, he may have become acquainted with Hussite ideas through Martin Reinhart, one of his closest collaborators while he was in Orlamünde.[41] And his pamphlets, like the translation of Hoen's letter, would help spread Hussite arguments against Christ's corporeal presence among a German-speaking audience that could not read Hussite works published in Latin or circulated in Czech.

There was a more direct connection between Hussite thought and the early eucharistic controversy in Switzerland, where both Johann Oecolampadius and Heinrich Bullinger would borrow ideas from the confessions of the Bohemian Brethren.[42] Oecolampadius was living with Andreas Cratander in the spring of 1523, at the time when the printer was producing the volume that combined Piccolomini's history of the Council of Basel with the Brethren's confessions and other Wyclifite and Hussite material. In a letter to the Waldensians written in 1530, he acknowledged his familiarity with these confessions, stating that many years earlier he had read their response written to King Vladislaus.[43]

In fact, not only was Oecolampadius familiar with the Brethren's confessions, but he used their arguments in his first published defense of the Zwinglian understanding of the Lord's Supper, *On the Genuine Exposition of the Lord's Words, This Is My Body, According to the Oldest Authorities*.[44] As the title suggests, Oecolampadius's primary concern was to demonstrate that the church fathers did not teach Christ's corporeal presence in the elements, but he also incorporated into his book a number of arguments that had already been advanced by Zwingli, Hoen, Karlstadt, and the Bohemian Brethren. For instance, he used 1 Corinthians 10:4 and Matthew 11:14 to defend a figurative understanding of "is," cited Matthew 24:23 against the claim that "Christ is here," and gave the analogy of a house key or a royal scepter as signifying authority over something.[45] Since both Zwingli and Karlstadt had repeated some of Hoen's arguments and Karlstadt had drawn on other Hussite ideas as well, it is impossible to determine where precisely Oecolampadius first encountered these ideas.

There are three passages in his book, however, that point very specifically to Oecolampadius's use of the Brethren's confessions, because in each passage he linked their argument that Christ's body is in heaven with a rejection of adoration of the sacrament. He first addressed the issue of adoration within his broader criticism of the belief that the sacrament involved a miracle, the transformation of bread and wine into Christ's body and blood. Neither the apostles nor the early church saw anything miraculous in the sacrament but rather believed that Christ was in heaven, at the Father's right hand. To support this claim, Oecolampadius referred to the custom in the early church of carrying the Eucharist to the homes of the sick and of communing infants, a practice that implied that they did not believe Christ was corporeally present in it—an argument also made by the Bohemian Brethren. He also cited Christ's statement that he would not always be with his followers (Matt. 26:11) and alluded to the apostles as those who had been robbed of their bridegroom (Matt. 9:15). These statements introduced his more general criticism of the pomp and immoderation associated with the feast of Corpus Christi, in which preaching had been replaced by plays and ceremonies and ignorance of the right use of the sacrament opened the door to idolatry and superstition.[46]

Oecolampadius moved on to defend the figurative understanding of the words of institution but eventually returned to the question of adoration. Picking up on an idea mentioned but not developed by Karlstadt, he argued against the ubiquity of Christ's true, human body. One could not use Christ's promise to be present where two or three were gathered in his name (Matt. 18:20) and with all of his followers to the end of the age (Matt. 28:20) to argue for Christ's corporeal presence, since these passages did not prove Christ's body was everywhere that Christ was. Alluding to John 16:7, he stated that Christ went away so that Christians would have his Spirit. Even if Christ's body were present in the sacrament, this could not justify its adoration, for the Decalogue commanded, "You shall worship the Lord God alone," and one should not worship created things in the place of the Creator. Finally, even if Christ's flesh could be adored, the bread should not be, any more than one worshiped the saints in whose hearts Christ dwelled.[47]

Oecolampadius's third use of arguments from the Bohemian Brethren came near the end of the treatise. Again he rejected the ubiquity of Christ's human body. Scripture taught that Christ came to earth in the flesh only two times, and that his second coming would not be in humility and obscurity as at his birth, but openly before the entire world at the Last Judgment. He listed several chapters from the New Testament, many of them also used by the Brethren, to prove that Christ's body was in heaven, seated at the right hand of the Father.[48] Oecolampadius developed this argument further, claiming that those who taught that Christ's body was present in many places thereby denied the true nature of that body. In his letter to Dardanus, Augustine warned that in attributing divinity to Christ, one must not deny his truly human body. Christ was indeed everywhere as God, but as man he was in heaven. Oecolampadius summarized with approval the argument of "a friend and minister of the word" that it was the property of the Creator alone, and not of any created thing, to be omnipresent. God did not share his glory by granting this power to a created thing.[49]

Oecolampadius's insistence that Christ's truly human body was seated at the right hand of the Father was the first detailed treatment of an argument that would become an essential part of Reformed eucharistic theology. His reputation as a scholar and his connections with reform-minded humanists guaranteed that his book would be widely circulated, and it provoked more detailed refutations from both Lutherans and Catholics than did Zwingli's earliest works on the Lord's Supper.[50]

Heinrich Bullinger was also influenced by the Brethren's arguments against Christ's corporeal presence in the sacrament. According to an entry in his *Diarium*, he first discussed the Lord's Supper with Zwingli in September 1524, shortly before the outbreak of the eucharistic controversy and before the Zurich reformer had made public his own rejection of Christ's corporeal presence in the sacrament. Bullinger told Zwingli that he had formed his opinion after reading "a certain writing of the Waldensians and the books of Augustine." Jarold Zeman's surmise that Bullinger had read the apologies of the Bohemian Brethren from the 1523 Basel edition of Piccolomini's history of the Council of Basel is strengthened by an examination of Bullinger's unpublished treatise "Against the Idolsbread," written in the summer of 1525.[51]

This short work reveals the blending together of several influences on Bullinger's early eucharistic theology. He criticized late medieval preaching on the sacrament, which emphasized that one should believe that Christ's true body was present in the consecrated host in the same way that it had hung on the cross and made the mass into a sacrifice for both the living and the dead. He accused preachers of peddling the benefits of attending mass in the same way that a merchant hawked his wares. In his explanation of 1 Corinthians 11:17–30, Bullinger repeated the chief elements of Zwingli's understanding of the Lord's Supper, including the figurative understanding of the words of institution and the hermeneutical signif-icance of John 6:63, and he praised the new rite for celebrating the Lord's Supper that had recently been introduced in Zurich. In his criticism of popular views of the mass, Bullinger used the same harsh tone and deliberately offensive phrasing that Karlstadt had in his *Dialogue*, accusing priests of putting their "bready God" behind bars, enclosing it, and letting it be eaten by worms and spoiled by the damp. Last but not least, Bullinger drew on arguments made by the Bohemian Brethren to condemn the veneration of the host. Thus he stated that bread was a created thing, and whoever worshiped a created thing instead of the Creator was an idolater. Christ taught his disciples to pray to "Our Father who is in heaven," not to "Our Father who is in a tabernacle or monstrance." More positively, Bullinger argued that Christ, Luke, and the apostles had all called the sacrament bread and had not regarded it as Christ's essential body.[52]

Zwingli too would eventually become familiar with the arguments used by the Bohemian Brethren. In his *Commentary on True and False Religion* published in March 1525, the Zurich reformer stated that he had heard that Wyclif and the Waldensians believed that "is" meant "signifies."[53] The imprecision of this statement reveals that he did not have firsthand knowledge of either Wyclif or the Bohemian Brethren. A year later, however, Zwingli made more explicit use of Hussite arguments in the *Clear Instruction on Christ's Supper*, his first discussion of the sacrament written in German and aimed for a broad audience.[54]

The *Clear Instruction* was organized into four sections: the first argued against a literal understanding of the words of institution; the second explained the broader justification for a figurative understanding of those words based on John 6, 1 Corinthians 10:4, and the Apostles' Creed; the third looked specifically at the accounts of the institution of the Lord's Supper to explain how Christ's words should be understood figuratively; and the final section responded to additional objections against a figurative understanding. Most of Zwingli's arguments were repetitions of what he had said in his earlier works, but his discussion of the Apostles' Creed brought in a new element, the distinction between Christ's divine and human natures as an argument against his corporeal presence in the sacrament.[55]

Zwingli used as the starting point of his discussion the three clauses of the creed, "he ascended into heaven, is seated at the right hand of the Father, and will come again to judge the living and the dead." According to his divine nature, Christ was omnipresent and always with the Father, but in his human nature, he was born, suffered and died, rose, and returned to heaven to take his place at the Father's right hand. Although one could attribute to one nature what belonged only to the other, the characteristics of each nature could not be mixed. For this reason Christ's ascension belonged only to his human nature. Zwingli cited several of Christ's statements to prove the presence of Christ's human nature in heaven, including "you will not always have me" (Matt. 26:11) and "I am going to the Father" (John 16:28). Moreover, Christ promised that he would not come again until the Last Judgment, and this coming would be visible, as the angels had said at his ascension (Acts 1:9–11). Scripture made clear that between his ascension and return, Christ could only be at the Father's right hand (Ps. 110:1). One should therefore not believe false prophets who claimed, "Christ is here" (Matt. 24:23), but should instead await his manifest coming in the future.[56]

Zwingli could have derived his Christological argument against Christ's corporeal presence from a number of sources. It is possible that by early 1526 he had read the confessions of the Bohemian Brethren himself, but it is just as likely that he learned of their arguments and scriptural proof texts more indirectly, from the writings of or in conversations with Oecolampadius, Bullinger, or both. Another possible source of his knowledge may have been Ludwig Hätzer, who translated Oecolampadius's *Genuine Exposition* into German and published it in Zurich in the first few days of 1526. In his preface to Oecolampadius's book, Hätzer argued that it was against "our common faith, learned from childhood from our parents," to believe that Christ's true natural body and blood were in the bread and wine, and he cited the three relevant articles of the Apostles' Creed to support that claim.[57] Both Hoen and Karlstadt may also have served as indirect sources. In his letter to Matthaeus Alber written at the very beginning of the eucharistic controversy, Zwingli stated that he had not read Karlstadt's *Dialogue*, but that Leo Jud and others had told him about its contents. He was also familiar with the general contents of Hoen's argument, for he endorsed the Dutchman's equation of "is" and "signifies."[58]

More important than the exact identification of Zwingli's sources, however, is the fact that together with Oecolampadius he adapted Hussite arguments to support a position that would become one of the cardinal points of difference between Reformed and Lutheran theologians. Zwingli would develop the distinction between Christ's divine and human natures more fully in his *Friendly Exegesis* of 1527, where he argued that the *communicatio idiomatum*, the exchange of divine and human characteristics within the person of Christ, was a grammatical rather than a real transference, and that Christ's finite human body was circumscribed in one place in heaven.[59] At the Marburg Colloquy of 1529 both Zwingli and Oecolampadius would insist that Christ's human body could only be in one place, and that place was in heaven. Twenty years later, Article 25 of the Consensus Tigurinus would state that because "the body of Christ, bearing the nature and mode of a human body, is finite and is contained in heaven as its place, it is necessarily as distant from us in point of space as heaven is from earth."[60] Elaborated especially in the polemical exchange between Johannes Brenz and the Zurich theologians that began in 1561, the differences in Christology would become just as important in the second eucharistic controversy as the disagreement over the interpretation of Christ's words of institution.[61]

Zwingli's use of Hussite arguments illustrates the gradual transformation of those ideas as they were diffused through western Europe. In the most systematic presentation of Hussite eucharistic theology, the confessions of the Bohemian Brethren, Christ's spiritual presence in the elements and his corporeal presence in heaven were linked and then used to reject the adoration of the host. In the early years of the Reformation, though, Hussite ideas were adopted without regard for that connection, and the arguments against Christ's corporeal presence in the elements were used without the parallel emphasis on Christ's spiritual presence. All of the opponents of transubstantiation discussed here cited the scriptural proof texts used by the Hussites to support their contention that Christ's body was seated at God's right hand. Beginning with Karlstadt, however, those texts were used in a different way, not to illustrate the metaphysical distinction between the modes of Christ's existence but rather to argue for the difference between Christ's divine and human natures.

The shift from metaphysics to Christology would effectively prevent any attempt to reintroduce discussion of any closer association between Christ and the sacramental elements during the early years of the eucharistic controversy. Not until 1528, after Luther had introduced the concept of sacramental union in his *Confession Concerning Christ's Supper*, could Martin Bucer argue that it was possible for both sides to agree that Christ was sacramentally united with the elements.[62] In acknowledging Christ's real but spiritual presence in the elements, Bucer would come closer to the view advocated by Wyclif and the Hussite groups influenced by him, but Bucer's understanding of the *unio sacramentalis* as the basis for that presence distanced him from late medieval heresy. The Hussite arguments that would have the greatest impact on the eucharistic controversy were not those advocating Christ's spiritual presence in the bread and wine but instead those concerning the location of Christ's human body at the right hand of the Father.

5

Karlstadt and the Zwinglians

THE EUCHARISTIC CONTROVERSY IN ZURICH, BASEL, AND STRASBOURG

Carlstadt sees the truth but from ignorance of the power of tropes, he fails to arrange the words in the right sequence, and resembles more than anything else a raw recruit who lacks not courage or armor but is without skill in the use of armor and does not know which part of the body one ought to protect with the particular pieces of armor. . . . Thus, I say, Carlstadt comes forth, brave enough and strong enough, but almost wholly destitute of training.[1]

IN VIRTUALLY ALL of his works on the Lord's Supper written in the years immediately following the outbreak of the eucharistic controversy, Ulrich Zwingli took pains to distance himself from Andreas Karlstadt. Karlstadt may have been correct in rejecting Christ's corporeal presence in the bread and wine, but he used the wrong arguments, his exegesis of the words of institution was faulty, and he offended many by his strident tone and his public criticism of Luther.[2] Zwingli's protests had little effect, however; as he wrote to Urbanus Rhegius, "You call everyone a Karlstadtian who disagrees with you; if then we were to show that Christ himself disagreed with you, would he be a Karlstadtian?"[3]

Whether or not Christ was a Karlstadtian, Zwingli had a point in asserting the distinctiveness of his own eucharistic theology. Theologically, Karlstadt had little direct impact on the Zurich reformer, for Zwingli had worked out his own symbolic understanding of the Lord's Supper before Karlstadt published his pamphlets denying Christ's corporeal presence. Karlstadt nevertheless played an important role in the Swiss reformation, for his ideas functioned as a catalyst for Zwingli's first public statement of his eucharistic theology.

Karlstadt had a broader impact on the development of the eucharistic controversy as well, because his ideas were picked up by other reformers and combined with those of Zwingli to create an alternative to the Lutheran understanding of the Lord's Supper. Zwingli's theology is not identical with early Zwinglianism, which was associated as much with the reformers of Basel and Strasbourg as it was with Zurich. Johann Oecolampadius, Wolfgang Capito, and Martin Bucer contributed to the shaping of Zwinglianism in the early years of the eucharistic controversy, drawing on arguments that both Karlstadt and Cornelis Hoen had taken from the late medieval heretical tradition. The result was a deepening of Zwingli's early eucharistic theology to include an array of arguments against Christ's corporeal presence that went along with Zwingli's redefinition of the Lord's Supper as commemoration and public testimony of faith. By following the reactions to Karlstadt in Switzerland and in Strasbourg, we can see more clearly the shaping of early Zwinglian eucharistic theology.[4]

KARLSTADT AND THE SWISS REFORMERS

In August 1524, the Wertheim pastor Franz Kolb wrote to Luther that he, Zwingli, and Leo Jud had reached the conclusion that Christ's words "this is my body" "truly signified what was done, i.e., the giving of Christ's body into death, and not the thing itself, i.e. the true body of Christ."[5] Kolb's letter is the earliest outside evidence of a circle of men who had begun to question the traditional belief in Christ's corporeal presence in the Eucharist. Two years later Oecolampadius would describe the private discussions, whether in person or through letters, of brethren who had questions about the Eucharist. Oecolampadius claimed that he cautioned these friends to examine Scripture diligently and warned them not to teach rashly against received opinion, and he confessed his own initial uncertainty about rejecting what everyone else believed. He had been emboldened, however, by the realization that even the most esteemed teachers were wrong on some points, and it was not necessary to accept the "papist belief." Thus when Karlstadt published his books, Oecolampadius condemned their polemic but found their arguments "not far off the mark."[6]

It is difficult to date precisely when these "more private discussions" took place, but Oecolampadius's biographer Ernst Staehelin observed that after early 1523, Oecolampadius no longer wrote of Christ's real presence. Similarly, Walther Köhler believed that Zwingli moved from an Erasmian view that Christ was present in the sacrament in an ineffable way to the adoption of a symbolic view sometime between mid-1523 and the summer of 1524, and thus at about the same time that

Karlstadt was formulating his own arguments against Christ's bodily presence.[7] The roughly simultaneous development of a symbolic understanding of the Supper in Saxony and in Switzerland helps to explain why Karlstadt's eucharistic theology had little direct influence on the understanding of the Lord's Supper initially formulated by the Swiss theologians.

Oecolampadius may have rejected belief in Christ's corporeal presence at an earlier date than Zwingli, but the Zurich reformer was the first to put his arguments against that presence in writing. His earliest defense of the symbolic interpretation of the Lord's Supper owed almost nothing to Karlstadt. By the time Karlstadt's pamphlets were published, Zwingli had developed his own views and was no longer searching for a theological rationale for his rejection of Christ's corporeal presence. Nor was he likely to derive such a rationale from Karlstadt, for his knowledge of Karlstadt's views was fairly limited at the beginning of the controversy. In his letter to Matthaeus Alber on the sacrament, he claimed that he had read only one of Karlstadt's treatises, *On the Anti-Christian Abuse of the Lord's Bread and Cup*, while his colleagues had told him about the contents of the *Dialogue*.[8] It is therefore only to be expected that the eucharistic theology that Zwingli presented in his publications of 1525 would differ from Karlstadt's.

The key to Zwingli's eucharistic theology was John 6:63, which crowned Christ's discussion of eating his flesh in John 6. Zwingli began both his letter to Alber and the section on the Lord's Supper in the *Commentary on True and False Religion* with a lengthy explanation of this chapter. His interpretation was deeply influenced by St. Augustine's homilies, which stressed the spiritual manducation of faith rather than the corporeal manducation of the sacrament. Interpreting Christ's words to reflect his dualist neoplatonic presuppositions and the spiritualism that resulted, Zwingli argued that nothing physical could provide spiritual benefit. To eat Christ was simply to have faith in him, and corporeal eating contributed nothing to salvation. Moreover, there was no way to combine spiritual and corporeal eating: it was "not only crude but even frivolous and impious" to claim to eat the true body of Christ spiritually, and to refer to Christ's "spiritual body" was an oxymoron that made as little sense as speaking of a "bodily mind" or of "fleshly reason."[9] Although Zwingli did not make this point explicitly in either of his works, one consequence of his sharp separation of spiritual and corporeal eating was the impossibility that an external rite such as the Lord's Supper could convey any kind of spiritual benefit. Zwingli thus could no longer accept Luther's understanding of the sacrament as a means through which communicants were assured of forgiveness or strengthened in faith.

Only after establishing the basic principle of the distinction between flesh and spirit in each of his works did Zwingli take up Christ's words "this is my body." He rejected Karlstadt's claim that "this" referred to "body" and endorsed instead

Hoen's argument that "is" should be understood as "signifies." Scripture provided other examples of this figurative understanding: not only Christ's "I am" statements ("I am the door, the vine, the light"), but also pharaoh's dream (Gen. 41:26) as well as the parables of the sower (Luke 8:11) and of the wheat and the tares (Matt. 13:38).[10] Since eating the physical elements brought no spiritual benefit, Zwingli also had to redefine the purpose of the sacrament. Citing 1 Corinthians 10:16–17 and 1 Corinthians 11:26, he stated that the Supper was instituted in order to remember and to proclaim Christ's death. Participation in the Supper also made clear to others that one was a member of Christ's body, the church, and so gave public testimony to one's faith.[11] Last but not least, Zwingli argued that his understanding of the sacrament was not new but rather was that taught by the church fathers, not only Augustine but also Tertullian, Origen, Hilary, and Jerome.[12]

There were obvious affinities between Karlstadt and Zwingli on the Lord's Supper, not least because of Zwingli's early influence on Karlstadt and their common neo-platonic/Erasmian spiritualist dualism. Zwingli came closest to Karlstadt in his insistence on the complete separation of the physical and the spiritual.[13] Since Luther identified the fundamental difference between himself and Karlstadt as the proper understanding of the relationship between internal and external, the fact that Karlstadt and Zwingli shared the same dualist presuppositions meant that the Wittenberg reformer would see no real difference in their eucharistic theology, despite Zwingli's repeated criticisms of Karlstadt.

Nevertheless, Zwingli and Karlstadt diverged in their understanding of the sacrament in several ways, beginning with the scriptural justification for their spiritualist dualism. Like Zwingli, Karlstadt used John 6:63 to argue against Christ's bodily presence in the Lord's Supper, but it was not as important for his understanding of the sacrament as the schema of Old Testament figure and New Testament fulfillment. Thus Karlstadt cited 1 Corinthians 10:1–4 and Hebrews 9–10 along with John 6 to explain the importance of a spiritual rather than a corporeal reception of Christ. Karlstadt took Erasmus's paraphrase of Hebrews 8–10 as his starting point and under the influence of Zwingli's discussion of Hebrews in the *Exposition of the 67 Articles* developed his understanding of the sacrament in a way that the Zurich reformer did not, for neither of these passages played an important role in Zwingli's eucharistic works of 1525.[14]

Indeed, in the year since publication of the *Exposition*, Zwingli had developed his eucharistic theology in a different direction, one that Karlstadt in turn did not follow, by emphasizing another element of Erasmus's understanding of the Eucharist, its communal and ethical significance. For Karlstadt as for Zwingli, the sacrament was to evoke the heartfelt and meditative remembrance of Christ's suffering and death in the individual recipient. But in early 1525 Zwingli argued just as strongly that reception of the sacrament was a public testimony of faith and of membership in the church, and it obligated Christians to live as Christ prescribed. Karlstadt also recognized both a communal and an ethical aspect of the Supper, but he did not emphasize either to the degree that Zwingli did. On this point, Zwingli remained closer than Karlstadt to their common source, Erasmus.[15]

Zwingli also differed from Karlstadt in drawing an analogy between Passover and Christ's last meal with his disciples in order to explain the meaning of the Lord's Supper. In his *Subsidiary Essay Concerning the Lord's Supper*, published in August, he pointed to the parallel between the Passover lamb, eaten in commemoration of the Israelites' liberation from Egypt, and the bread of the Supper, instituted to commemorate Christ's death on the cross.[16] Although Karlstadt's general approach to the Old Testament was typological, he did not make this specific connection, which would assume an important place in early Zwinglian eucharistic theology.

The most prominent point on which Zwingli and Karlstadt disagreed was their interpretation of the words of institution. In both of his works Zwingli went out of his way to criticize Karlstadt's grammatical and philological exegesis, which had allowed the latter to maintain a literal understanding of the words without accepting Christ's corporeal presence in the Supper. Karlstadt's understanding of the Supper was figural, for he related the sacrament, like the sacrifices of the Old Testament, to Christ's death as figure and fulfillment. Zwingli's understanding was figurative in the sense that he identified a figure of speech, or trope, in the words "this is my body." Despite their different starting points, however, both positions ultimately drew on Augustine's understanding of figures and signs that pointed to an ultimate reality. Furthermore, for both Karlstadt and Zwingli that reality was completely distinct from, rather than contained within, the signs. Their contrasting exegesis of the words of institution therefore hid an underlying agreement that the sacrament should be understood symbolically. Zwingli's embrace of Hoen's figurative interpretation was important because while other reformers would be attracted to Karlstadt's arguments against Christ's bodily presence in the elements, they could not accept Karlstadt's exegesis of "this is my body." Zwingli's equation of "is" with "signifies" gave them an alternative to Karlstadt, which then made it easier for them to accept the latter's other arguments against Christ's corporeal presence.

There was greater agreement between Zwingli and Karlstadt concerning the words describing the cup. Both preferred the wording of Luke (22:20) and Paul (1 Cor. 11:25), "This cup is the new testament in my blood," to that of Matthew (26:27–28) and Mark (14:24), "This is the blood of the new testament." Like Karlstadt, Zwingli argued that something could not be the same as that which contained it, but he applied this philosophical postulate to the linking of cup, testament, and blood rather than to the bread and body as Karlstadt did.[17] More important, however, while Karlstadt interpreted the cup as the new testament through analogy with a testament as a last will, and so within Luther's application of Hebrews 9:15–17 to the sacrament, Zwingli was uncomfortable with this approach. In his *Subsidiary Essay on the Eucharist* he shifted the interpretive framework away from the epistle to the Hebrews, with its discussion of a last will and the sacrificial system of the Old Testament, to Genesis 17:9–14 and the establishment of the covenant with Abraham. This allowed him to introduce the parallel between circumcision and baptism as signs of the covenant and to explain the Lord's Supper as a commemoration of Christ's death on the cross, by which the covenant had been perfected.[18]

A more unexpected difference between Zwingli and Karlstadt is the relative influence of Cornelis Hoen's *Most Christian Letter*. Zwingli did not hesitate to acknowledge his debt to Hoen, but in arguing for a figurative understanding of the words of institution he chose different scriptural proof texts than those Hoen had used. He ignored most of the verses in Hoen's letter that were derived from Wyclif and the Hussites, such as "the rock was Christ" (1 Cor. 10:4) and Christ's reference to John, "he is Elijah" (Matt. 11:14), as well as Christ's statement from the cross, "woman, behold your son" (John 19:26), and he cited instead Christ's parables, which Hoen had not used. In his *Subsidiary Essay* Zwingli added Exodus 12:11 as another example of the figurative use of "is" in Scripture.[19] The difference in choice of Scripture texts suggests that Zwingli did not have a copy of Hoen's letter before him as he wrote these three works and so was initially influenced by its arguments only in a general way.[20] Karlstadt, however, was well acquainted with Hoen's letter, and although he rejected the Dutchman's understanding of the words of institution, he cited several of Hoen's other arguments against Christ's corporeal presence in his pamphlets.

Zwingli also took pains to emphasize that his symbolic understanding of the Supper was taught in the early church and so could not be called heretical. Karlstadt, however, seemed to boast that he taught about the sacrament in a way that no one else had. The frequent citation of patristic sources was a striking element of all defenses of the symbolic interpretation by authors who acknowledged the influence of Zwingli rather than of Karlstadt.

The testimony of the church fathers played an even greater role in Oecolampadius's first entry into the debate over the Lord's Supper. His *Book on the Genuine Exposition of the Lord's Words, "This is my Body," according to the Oldest Authorities* was published in September.[21] Oecolampadius used his formidable knowledge especially of the Greek fathers to argue against Christ's corporeal presence. In addition to the patristic authors quoted by Zwingli, he discussed statements on the sacrament taken from the writings of Hegesippus, Cyprian, Irenaeus, Basil, Gregory of Nazianzus, Ignatius, Cyril, and Chrysostom. As was the case with Zwingli, Oecolampadius's eucharistic theology was fundamentally shaped by Erasmus, and it differed from that of the Zurich reformer only in details, not in essence.[22] Thus, although he preferred Tertullian's interpretation of the words of institution, "this is a figure of my body," to Hoen and Zwingli's "this signifies my body," he asserted that both versions upheld the same figurative rather than literal meaning.[23] Like Zwingli, he insisted that carnal eating accomplished nothing spiritually and emphasized instead the importance of spiritual eating, and he argued for the separation of sign and thing signified.[24] His interpretation of the church fathers was shaped by the conviction that their discussions of the sacrament referred to spiritual rather than sacramental eating, and that when they spoke of Christ's body and blood they actually meant the signs of that body and blood.[25]

Oecolampadius began his treatise by criticizing Peter Lombard, who condemned as heretics those who taught a figurative understanding of 1 Corinthians 10:4 ("the rock was Christ").[26] After arguing that no miracle occurred in the Eucharist, he justified his own figurative understanding of the words of institution and pointed to the many absurdities that resulted from a literal understanding of those words.[27] He incorporated several of the arguments that Zwingli had either already made or would make against Christ's corporeal presence in his *Subsidiary Essay*, such as the parallel between the Passover and the Last Supper, the use of Exodus 12:11 to support a significative understanding of "is," and the fact that in Hebrew the verb "to be" was almost always omitted when the demonstrative pronoun was used.[28] These arguments were circulating already among the Swiss reformers in the spring and summer of 1525, as they further developed and diffused their figurative understanding of the sacrament. Thus Oecolampadius summarized his understanding of the sacrament for the reformer of neighboring Mülhausen (Mulhouse) in April, and Heinrich Bullinger sent Leo Jud a manuscript on the Eucharist to which Jud responded favorably, at the same time explaining Zwingli's use of Exodus 12:11.[29] To this common fund of argumentation Oecolampadius also added ideas taken from the confessions of the Bohemian Brethren, Hoen's *Christian Letter*, and some of Karlstadt's pamphlets.[30]

This comparison of the Swiss reformers with Karlstadt suggests that the latter's importance for the former was not so much his theology as it was his timing and his audience. By publishing his eucharistic pamphlets in German, Karlstadt was the first to argue in print and to a lay audience that Christ was not present bodily in the sacrament. Through the fall of 1524, Zwingli and his colleagues in Zurich had been cautious about publicly rejecting belief in Christ's corporeal presence in the Supper and endorsing an understanding of the sacrament that had long been rejected as heretical. Their discussions with Hinne Rode and Georg Saganus had persuaded the Zurich ministers to endorse Hoen's figurative interpretation of the words of institution, and they shared Hoen's view that adoration of the host was akin to idolatry.[31] They recognized, however, the difficulty they would have in publicly advocating a belief long condemned as heretical and in rejecting the resulting practices that were some of the most common manifestations of popular devotion. For this reason they acted slowly and cautiously in presenting their new understanding of the Supper, restricting their message to their audience in Zurich. In sermons and in their memoranda for the city council, they avoided speaking about Christ's presence in the sacrament and emphasized instead the importance of the sacrament as a remembrance of Christ's death and as a public testimony of one's faith and membership in the Christian community.[32] They also discussed their more radical views with a small group of men outside of Zurich, but they had not yet published anything that would make their views known to a broader audience. Even as late as January 1525, Zwingli continued to refer to the bread and wine in the sacrament as Christ's body and blood.[33]

The publication of Karlstadt's pamphlets destroyed this deliberately cautious strategy by moving the discussion out of a small clerical circle and making it the focus of a public debate that extended even to the illiterate. Zwingli testified to the range of Karlstadt's readership when he wrote that some of the Anabaptists from Zurich "flew to Basel, and carrying [Karlstadt's] books upon their shoulders filled not only the cities, towns and cantons but almost all the farm houses with them."[34] Karlstadt's pamphlets forced Zwingli's hand, causing him to make public his own symbolic understanding of the sacrament earlier than he might otherwise have chosen. As Zwingli acknowledged, he felt compelled to distance himself from Karlstadt's harsh polemics and to spell out his understanding of the sacrament because of its similarity to the contents of Karlstadt's pamphlets. Zwingli did this at first in a gradual way, explaining his views in a letter that circulated in manuscript for four months before it was finally published. By March, however, Zwingli was willing to go public, and he published his letter to Alber in the original Latin as well as in German translation. His Commentary was intended to bring his new understanding of the Lord's Supper to a learned, international audience, but its section on the sacrament was immediately translated into German so that it too would be accessible to those who could not read Latin.[35]

Despite their differences with Karlstadt, the Swiss reformers still found his pamphlets useful because of their arguments against Christ's corporeal presence. In one of his sermons Zwingli urged the Zurich Council to allow the circulation of those pamphlets so that readers could judge his ideas for themselves. In early 1525 Oecolampadius told François Lambert that he did not agree with all that Karlstadt wrote, but he acknowledged the importance of his arguments.[36] The pamphlets were discussed among Basel's humanists and persuaded many of them to reject Christ's corporeal presence in the sacrament. Erasmus disapproved of the turmoil that Karlstadt had caused, but the French nobleman Anémond de Coct wrote to

Guillaume Farel that "all the most pious and learned men" in the city favored Karlstadt's views.[37] And in fact Karlstadt's ideas could not have been entirely new to members of Basel's humanist circles. Oecolampadius had, after all, approved the printing of the *Anti-Christian Abuse*, and in a letter to Zwingli written in mid-November he told the Zurich reformer that he did not think Karlstadt's views on the Eucharist differed from their own.[38] If the Swiss were not Karlstadt's disciples, they were certainly his allies in the campaign against Christ's corporeal presence in the supper.

Perhaps the best indicator of the somewhat reluctant alliance between Karlstadt and the Swiss reformers was the exchange between Johann Bugenhagen and Ulrich Zwingli in the late summer and fall of 1525. In July Luther and Bugenhagen each wrote to the Breslau reformer Johann Hess, warning him about the errors of Karlstadt and Zwingli concerning the sacrament. By the end of August, Bugenhagen's warning had been published as an *Open Letter against the New Error on the Sacrament*.[39]

In his *Open Letter* Bugenhagen took issue with both Zwingli and Karlstadt, mocking their claim to be theologians and asserting that Christ's words "this is my body" must be understood literally.[40] Although he acknowledged the differences between Zwingli and Karlstadt regarding the words of institution, he recognized their agreement on the exegesis of four separate Scripture passages, and to counter that exegesis he repeated the positions Luther had staked out in *Against the Heavenly Prophets*. He rejected their spiritualist understanding of John 6:63 and argued like Luther that "flesh" meant all that came from human understanding rather than from God.[41] He defended Luther's understanding of 1 Corinthians 10:16–17 as the partaking of Christ's body and blood rather than as the fellowship of Christ's mystical body, and he supported this interpretation by citing Paul's account of the Last Supper, 1 Corinthians 11:24–5. Here the apostle had substituted the word "broken" for "given," where "to break" was to be understood as "to distribute by dividing."[42] Bugenhagen also cited Paul's statement that the cup was the new testament and argued that since that new testament consisted of forgiveness of sins, which could not be ascribed to mere wine, Christ's blood must be in the cup. Lastly, he addressed 1 Corinthians 11:27–30, in which Paul spoke of discerning the body, not the bread. Those who claimed to eat simple bread received the sacrament just as unworthily as those who did not receive it as Christ had commanded, in his remembrance.[43]

Zwingli published a *Response to Bugenhagen's Letter* at the end of October, in which he answered Bugenhagen's arguments point by point.[44] As was to be expected, he rejected the assertion that Christ's words of institution must be understood literally, criticized Karlstadt's exegesis, and defended his own figurative understanding of "this is my body." He acknowledged that it was not sufficient merely to recognize that there was a trope in these words, and he credited Hoen's letter for showing him that the key lay in understanding "is" as "signifies."[45]

Despite his differences with Karlstadt regarding the words of institution, however, Zwingli was compelled by Bugenhagen's linkage of their names, as well as by their common understanding of the key scriptural texts, to identify himself with Luther's more notorious opponent. For each of the four texts that Bugenhagen had cited, Zwingli defended positions on which he and Karlstadt agreed against the Wittenbergers, although in each case Zwingli added his own distinctive emphasis. Thus he argued that John 6:63 upheld a sharp distinction between flesh and spirit, but unlike Karlstadt he explicitly cited both patristic sources and Erasmus as support for his significative understanding.[46] With regard to 1 Corinthians 10:16–17, he stated that Paul was speaking of the spiritual communion of the faithful rather than the physical communication of Christ's body, but he emphasized the gathering of Christ's followers, the church, for remembrance and thanksgiving, and he told Bugenhagen to read Oecolampadius's book in order to learn what the church fathers had written in this regard.[47] Turning to 1 Corinthians 11:25, Zwingli agreed with Bugenhagen that the new testament was the forgiveness of sins, but he argued that Christ's blood was not the testament itself but rather that by which the testament was confirmed. The words concerning the cup therefore contained a trope, just as did the words concerning the bread.[48] Last but not least, Zwingli referred Paul's discussion of unworthy eating in 1 Corinthians 11:27–29 to those whose faith and thanksgiving were only feigned or who scorned Christ's church by their sinful lives.[49] Zwingli closed by admonishing Bugenhagen to refrain from insults and contention. He had not criticized the Wittenbergers on other points where he did not think they taught rightly, but if they chose to begin a fight, he would respond in order to defend the evangelical truth.[50]

The exchange between Bugenhagen and Zwingli marked a new stage of the eucharistic controversy. Bugenhagen's *Open Letter* proved particularly effective for disseminating Luther's position: only eight pages long in quarto, it could quickly be reprinted on just one sheet of paper, and it was published in six imprints before the end of the year. The pamphlet was just as popular in German translation, going through five editions.[51] Zwingli's *Response* did not reach the same broad audience. It was published only once in its original Latin, and a German translation by Leo Jud was published at the beginning of 1526.[52]

The two pamphlets made clear the differences in the exegesis of Scripture that underlay the controversy. Neither work introduced new ideas into the debate; instead, they summarized in a brief and clear way the arguments already expressed in the much longer works of Luther and Zwingli and in Karlstadt's various pamphlets. Although the name-calling in the two pamphlets was quite mild in comparison with the earlier polemical exchange between Karlstadt and Luther, as well as with that which would come later in the eucharistic controversy, it produced a sense of righteous indignation on both sides. Those who rejected Christ's corporeal presence understood that, with Bugenhagen's letter, the Wittenbergers had picked up the gauntlet thrown down by Karlstadt's pamphlets. Most important, though, despite the obvious differences in their understanding of "this is my body," both pamphlets linked Zwingli and Karlstadt together for their common rejection of Christ's corporeal presence, while the nuances distinguishing their positions were overlooked or unrecognized. As the eucharistic controversy developed, the link between the two would be strengthened further by the adoption of some of Karlstadt's arguments against Christ's presence not only by Oecolampadius but also by Zwingli's defenders in Strasbourg.

KARLSTADT AND STRASBOURG

Any discussion of the early eucharistic controversy in Strasbourg must take account not only of Karlstadt's impact there but also of the efforts by the city's reformers to mend the breach between Wittenberg and the Swiss that had become apparent with the publication of Bugenhagen's *Open Letter*. Karlstadt's arguments, together with those of Cornelis Hoen, helped persuade Martin Bucer to abandon belief in Christ's corporeal presence. The Erasmianism he shared with his older colleague Wolfgang Capito ultimately led both men to adopt Zwingli's and Oecolampadius's understanding of the Supper, but the Strasbourgers' eucharistic theology retained elements of the arguments introduced by Karlstadt and Hoen. Bucer's Erasmianism combined with veneration for Luther to motivate his efforts to end or at least to mitigate the consequences of the growing controversy.

The Strasbourgers' motives and intentions in the early years of the eucharistic controversy have been interpreted in widely varying ways by scholars. In his magisterial study Walther Köhler focused on the Strasbourgers' desire for evangelical unity and concluded on the basis of the formulations they proposed that "they were not full Zwinglians . . . and if they thought so, this was a self-deception."[53] James Kittelson argued that for Bucer, the precise definition of the elements of the Supper was never important, and it was this indifference that enabled him to mediate between the sides in the fall of 1525 and motivated his later and better-known concord efforts.[54] More convincingly, Ian Hazlett concluded that Bucer was not neutral on the matter of Christ's presence but instead remained true to Zwingli's figurative exegesis. Nevertheless, Hazlett agreed with Köhler that the roots of Bucer's later union formula can be found in the Strasbourger's letters from 1525.[55] Most recently, Reinhold Friedrich has also stressed both Bucer's commitment to Zwingli's understanding of the Supper and his deep desire for concord, based on his concern for a united front against the Catholics and a genuine blending of elements taken from Erasmus, Luther, and Zwingli.[56] Thomas Kaufmann, on the other hand, has emphasized the Strasbourgers' Zwinglian partisanship and described their efforts for concord as only a tactical maneuver.[57] Kaufmann's tendentious conclusion is undermined by his exaggeration of Bucer's and Capito's involvement in the publicistic battles of 1525, but he is correct in emphasizing the Strasbourgers' self-identification as Zwinglians.[58] What these studies have not described is the precise role played by Karlstadt, and by criticisms of transubstantiation coming from late medieval heresy more generally, in the development of the Strasbourgers' eucharistic theology.

Karlstadt's brief visit to Strasbourg in October 1524 and the pamphlets that circulated in that city had a much greater impact on the leaders of the evangelical movement there than they did in either Zurich or Basel. In the Swiss cities, Zwingli and his supporters could control the discussion of the Lord's Supper because they had already reached a position similar to Karlstadt's and could immediately respond with their own justification of a symbolic interpretation of the Lord's Supper. In Strasbourg, however, Karlstadt's arguments came like a bolt out of the blue, forcing the reformers to rethink their own eucharistic theology at the same time that they had to deal with the ferment caused by the spread of Karlstadt's ideas. Moreover, Karlstadt was not the only one to raise questions about the Lord's Supper, for in November Hinne Rode also visited the city, bearing a copy of Hoen's *Most Christian Letter*. Hoen's arguments against Christ's corporeal presence, reinforcing and adding to those first raised by Karlstadt, were the final development that accelerated the division of the evangelical movement in Strasbourg into a small group of individuals who remained loyal to Luther and a more varied assortment of those who rejected Christ's presence, ranging from the moderate position of the city's pastors, who downplayed the importance of this disagreement, through the more vociferous advocates of a symbolic view, to the proto-Anabaptist groups whose disagreements with the others would extend to infant baptism and other issues.[59]

Karlstadt's ideas were welcomed in Strasbourg in part because his concerns rhymed with those already expressed by both clerical and lay advocates of reform in that city. Since March the preachers had been engaged in extended public debates with the Augustinian Konrad Treger and the Franciscan Thomas Murner that included discussion of the Eucharist. In their pamphlets the preachers rejected the sacrifice of the mass, although their public arguments owed more to Luther's understanding of the Supper as a testament than to Zwingli's argument that Christ's sacrifice could not be repeated.[60]

Zwingli's influence is more obvious in other pamphlets published in Strasbourg in 1524, the most polemical of which was Andreas Keller's attack on the sacrifice of the mass.[61] Drawing equally on Erasmus and Zwingli, Keller argued that the essence of the Lord's Supper was fellowship or communion among believers, by which they presented themselves publicly as children of God redeemed through Christ's death.[62] In contrast to this understanding of the sacrament based on Scripture, Keller argued that the papist mass was a blasphemy and abomination. His criticisms catalogue the arguments made by the evangelicals against the mass: the papists had added to it things not specified in Scripture, such as the wearing of vestments and the precise wording and gestures prescribed for the celebrant; the mass was not a sacrifice and certainly should not be bought and sold under the pretense that it forgave sins; the prayers of the canon of the mass contradicted Scripture; private masses, masses said for the Virgin or the saints, and masses for the dead were all illegitimate; when the mass was celebrated it should be in the language of the people, and it should always include a sermon concerning Christ's death and the forgiveness it had obtained.[63] The pamphlet said nothing about Christ's presence in the elements and never referred to the bread and wine as Christ's body and blood, but neither did it explicitly reject such an identification.[64]

There were, however, other elements that contributed to the discussion of the sacrament among the common people, for Strasbourg had been home to a community of heretics through the first half of the fifteenth century. In 1400, twenty-seven suspected Waldensians were expelled from the city on account of their heretical views.[65] The Hussite-Waldensian preacher Friedrich Reiser visited Strasbourg several times over his long career before he was finally arrested by the Inquisition and burned at the stake there in 1458. Some memory of Reiser's activities in Strasbourg survived him, for at the turn of the century the Strasbourg preacher Johann Geiler von Kaysersburg described Reiser's execution for his friend Jakob Wimpheling, mentioned that Reiser had met regularly with his followers in the old wine market to instruct them, and listed the names of Reiser's followers.[66] There is no evidence that heretical cells still existed in Strasbourg in the early sixteenth century, but some of Reiser's teachings may well have survived and contributed to a more general anticlericalism fanned alive by evangelical preaching. Evangelical rejection of purgatory, indulgences, the veneration of the saints, and the adoration of the host may also have had a special resonance in Strasbourg, since these beliefs were rejected by both Waldensians and Hussites. By 1524 Hussite works, both printed and in manuscript, were also circulating in Strasbourg, some of them in German and so accessible to the literate laity.[67]

The pamphlets of the gardener Clemens Ziegler reveal more clearly how one layman synthesized the various treatments of the sacrament that he heard from the pulpit and read in popular pamphlets with his own reading of Scripture. In his *Brief Register . . . in Which One Learns What Idolatry Is*, published in June 1524,

Ziegler rejected the use of images as a form of idolatry, condemned masses for the dead, and criticized private masses because in them the priest did not proclaim the Lord's death to other people.[68] His pamphlet *On the True Eating of Both the Body and Blood of Christ*, published before the end of August, was directed chiefly against the adoration of the consecrated host and the related practices of reservation and its use in processions.[69] Like Luther, he emphasized that the sacrament was a testament, but he also followed Zwingli in rejecting the word "sacrament" as unscriptural and in arguing that the purpose of the Supper was remembrance of Christ's death. On the basis of Christ's words of institution, he believed that the bread was Christ's body, but he rejected the doctrine of transubstantiation.[70] Ziegler's distinctive contribution to the discussion was his rather murky distinction between Christ's body and Christ's flesh. Citing examples of God's appearances in human form in the Old Testament, he argued that God was both spirit and body, but the flesh that Christ talked about in John 6 did not apply to the bread of the Eucharist. Christ himself said that the flesh was of no use, and so his flesh and blood must be understood as spiritual.[71]

Ziegler repeated his condemnation of the reservation and adoration of the host and its use in processions in his *Lovely Book . . . on the Body and Blood of Christ*, published in December.[72] The pamphlet has been seen as an early reflection of Karlstadt's impact on the religious situation in Strasbourg, but it did not endorse Karlstadt's understanding of the sacrament. Although Ziegler insisted that the bread remained after consecration, he still spoke of eating Christ's body under the bread and drinking his blood under the wine, which directly opposed Karlstadt's position.[73] Ziegler's pamphlet might be better understood as a popular (mis-) understanding of the remnants of Waldensian-Hussite heresy.

Ziegler demonstrated his familiarity with Hussite thought with his criticism of "the Bohemians"—more precisely, the Utraquists—who accepted transubstantiation and believed on the basis of John 6:53–54 that communion was necessary for all the baptized, including infants. He rejected infant communion, however, arguing that children were still innocent, and they could not speak and so confess the faith that was necessary for communicants. If Christ's body were received under the bread without faith, then Judas would also have received Christ, but as the evangelist said, he had received the devil (John 13:27).[74]

Ziegler did not refer to either the Taborites or the Bohemian Brethren, but their distinction between the modes of Christ's existence, understood in a very material way, may have influenced his own identification of Christ's divine and human natures with body and flesh, respectively. Expanding on the ideas expressed in his earlier pamphlet, Ziegler differentiated between Christ's first, divine body, which is immortal, imperceptible, and invisible, and the human flesh that he assumed at the incarnation and that suffered hunger and thirst, fear and despair. At the institution of the Supper Christ told his disciples that his human and fleshly body would take up the place promised to it, at the Father's right hand, but his divine and spiritual body would be given as a deposit in the Lord's Supper.[75]

Ziegler's unorthodox understanding of Christ's spiritual body and his human flesh set him apart from the other pamphleteers who would join the debate over the Lord's Supper. His materialistic conception of Christ's divine, preexistent body bears more similarity to the worldview of the miller Menocchio than it does to Karlstadt's spiritualist dualism.[76] There is no echo of Ziegler's ideas in other works published on the sacrament, but his pamphlets may have appealed to the middling and lower levels of society to which Ziegler himself belonged. They help explain why Strasbourg's pastors were so concerned with the abuses of popular piety associated with the consecrated host and why the elements of Karlstadt's thought drawn from late medieval heretical sources were especially potent. There was at least a segment of the broader evangelical movement ready to hear Karlstadt's demands for immediate liturgical reform and more radical action against the presence of images and the elevation of the host. As a consequence, Karlstadt's ideas had the impact of a bombshell in Strasbourg, splitting the evangelical movement along existing fault lines.[77]

In order to preserve a common front against their Catholic opponents, the pastors' first strategy for dealing with Karlstadt's ideas was to downplay the differences within the evangelical party. Already before the end of October, and thus within a few days of Karlstadt's arrival in the city, Capito published a pamphlet in which he emphasized the need for unity based on adherence to Scripture rather than to either Luther or Karlstadt.[78] Most of the pamphlet was directed at those who advocated more immediate and far-reaching reforms, which implies that this was the first issue that Karlstadt had raised in Strasbourg. Capito responded directly and defensively to Karlstadt's *Against the Old and New Papist Masses*, stating that the preachers avoided using the word "mass" and asserting that they hoped to eliminate elevation and the other practices that Karlstadt had condemned.[79]

Only at the end of his discussion did he bring up the disagreement about whether the "this" in the words of institution referred to Christ's body or to the bread. Capito's own spiritualizing tendencies were revealed by his statement that "Christ is internal and invisible and is absolutely not tied to an external thing, whether sign or anything else." This distinction obviously predisposed Capito against Luther's insistence on Christ's bodily presence and toward Karlstadt's and Zwingli's rejection of that presence, once those positions became known in Strasbourg. As of yet, however, Capito was unaware of Zwingli's view and unfamiliar with Karlstadt's argumentation, and he did not consider the matter worth pursuing.

In genuinely Erasmian fashion, he dismissed the discussion over Christ's presence as superfluous and emphasized instead the purpose of the Lord's Supper, the remembrance of Christ through which all believers were united in him.[80]

Capito did not long remain ignorant of the theological arguments against Christ's corporeal presence, however. Over the next few weeks Karlstadt's ideas caused such a stir that by the middle of November the city's pastors had decided to write to their fellow reformers in Nuremberg, Nördlingen, Basel, Zurich, and Wittenberg to ask for their judgment of Karlstadt's arguments against Christ's corporeal presence.[81] Their letters demonstrate their familiarity not only with Karlstadt's pamphlets but also with one of the sources of Karlstadt's ideas, for in the meantime Hinne Rode had arrived in Strasbourg bearing a copy of Hoen's *Most Christian Letter*. In fact, of the ten arguments against Christ's presence that the Strasbourgers listed in their letter to the Swiss and south Germans, only three were unique to Karlstadt. The first concerned his understanding of the words of institution,[82] the second was his insistence that Scripture did not say the body was "in" or "under" the bread,[83] and the third was that the essence of the sacrament was remembrance, not speculation about what the bread was.[84]

Several of the remaining arguments were ones that Hoen had first advanced and that Karlstadt had incorporated into his pamphlets either directly or in modified form. These included Christ's warning not to believe those who claimed that Christ was "here or there" (Matt. 24:23) and his statement that it was necessary for him to go away (John 16:7). Hoen believed that Christ's command "Do this in remembrance of me" (1 Cor. 11:25) implied that Christ was absent; Karlstadt drew the same conclusion from the command to proclaim Christ's death until he comes (1 Cor. 11:26).[85] According to the Strasbourgers, Karlstadt argued that God performed miracles only to confirm doctrine, which was not the case with the conversion of bread into Christ's body; Hoen had first introduced the place of miracles, stating that God did not ask people to believe miracles contrary to sensory experience.[86] Hoen had observed that Paul used the term "bread" rather than "body," a point that may have prompted Karlstadt's argument that the apostles did not speak of the transformation of bread and wine into Christ's body and blood.[87] The Strasbourg pastors pointed to the construction of Christ's words to Peter, "you are Peter, and on this rock I will build my church" (Matt. 16:18), in which the subject of the second clause was not the same as that of the first clause. Hoen had used this verse to argue for a figurative understanding of "is." In his pamphlets Karlstadt did not discuss this verse, but at the end of the *Exegesis* he set it in parallel to "this is my body, which is given for you," with the heading "Similitudes in Scripture."[88] Finally, the Strasbourgers repeated Hoen's assertion that calling the host "bread" would eliminate all superstitions that had become associated with the Lord's table.[89]

As Bucer acknowledged in a letter written a year later, it was difficult for him to abandon Luther's authority, but these arguments—many of them stemming from late medieval heresy—proved compelling. Karlstadt's pamphlets caused him to examine the relevant Scripture passages carefully, while his conversations with Hinne Rode provided further ammunition against Luther.[90] The final shove came when the Strasbourgers received a copy of Zwingli's letter to Alber, which the Zurich reformer sent in response to their letter.[91] By the end of the year Capito could write to Zwingli that Bucer "has submitted to your view with hands and feet."[92]

The Strasbourgers' new understanding of the Lord's Supper was expressed and given quasi-official status in the *Ground and Reasons . . . for the Innovations in the Lord's Supper*, written by Bucer in the name of all the city's ministers and published at the end of 1524. The pamphlet opened with a discussion of the mass that stressed ideas common to Zwingli and Karlstadt, but it defended the more gradual introduction of reforms against Karlstadt's demands for immediate action. Like both Zwingli and Karlstadt, Bucer justified the rejection of the mass on the grounds of Christ's unique sacrifice. He questioned the etymology of "mass" from the Hebrew for "offering," though, and he undermined Karlstadt's criticism of the elevation by finding its origin not in the Old Testament wave and heave offerings but in the various pagan practices adopted by "the Romans." Although the pastors preferred the name "Lord's Supper" to mass and criticized the elevation of the host, they argued that changes should be made only after the weak had been properly instructed and understood the reason for them.[93]

Bucer then took up the issue of elevation more directly. Strasbourg's inhabitants had been sufficiently instructed, and so the time was right to eliminate the practice. Bucer's objections to elevation were based on the abuses of popular piety that grew from the belief in Christ's corporeal presence as well as on an underlying spiritualism justified by John 6:63. Elevation was only an external gesture, but it led people astray by promoting the idea that the priest was offering Christ. Popular preachers had taught the people to believe that they could see the Lord God in the host and that prayers offered at the time of elevation were particularly effective. Christ had instituted the Supper, however, to lead from body to spirit. It was necessary, therefore, to eliminate the physical gestures in order to lead people to spiritual things.[94]

Bucer opposed the vestments and elaborate gestures of the mass for much the same reason. Either people attributed too much to these externals, seeing them as having special merit before God and causing qualms of conscience if they were not performed precisely as prescribed, or they contributed to hypocrisy because those who performed them did so only for the sake of appearances.[95]

The Strasbourgers' endorsement of Zwingli's eucharistic theology came through most clearly in the section describing the celebration of the Lord's Supper. Because the sacrament was "an alliance to Christian fellowship," it was held only on Sundays with the entire congregation. Communion was a public profession of participation in Christ's body, received in remembrance of and thanksgiving for Christ's death.[96] Repeating an idea from Capito's earlier pamphlet, Bucer criticized the disagreement over Christ's corporeal presence as a distraction that drew attention away from the purpose of the Supper, to consider Christ's death in faith. Bucer compared the elements of the Supper to a golden pot left by a father for his sons or the clothing and ornaments given by a lord to his servants to foster remembrance: it was unworthy of the recipients to quarrel over the physical objects rather than remembering and honoring the one who gave them. The only purpose of the bread and the cup was to remember Christ's death so as to be strengthened in faith and love. The flesh was no use, and Christians were to look to the spiritual reality. Bucer did not explicitly endorse Zwingli's equation of "is" and "signifies," but he argued that the bread and the cup were figures or signs of Christ's unique sacrifice and of the new testament established by his death, and he criticized Karlstadt for twisting God's word to support his own interpretation of Christ's words.[97]

By the beginning of 1525, then, Strasbourg's pastors had openly declared their acceptance of Zwingli's understanding of the Lord's Supper. As convinced Erasmians, neither Capito nor Bucer had ever placed much emphasis on Christ's corporeal presence.[98] Their Erasmian concern with spiritual communion and the fellowship of communicants had meshed easily with the early evangelical attacks on the mass and Luther's redefinition of the sacrament as a sign of God's promise of forgiveness. Karlstadt's appearance in the city pushed them to abandon this synthesis of Erasmian and early evangelical ideas, but Karlstadt's own understanding of the meaning and value of the sacrament, as well as his new interpretation of the words of institution, was not a sufficient replacement. It is not surprising, then, that they would endorse Zwingli's view, with its more sophisticated understanding of the purpose and use of the Lord's Supper.[99]

Karlstadt's understanding of the Lord's Supper was not completely without effect in Strasbourg, however, for his arguments against Christ's corporeal presence were a valuable supplement to Zwingli's reinterpretation of the Supper. Karlstadt and Zwingli shared a foundational spiritualistic dualism, and they both used Erasmus's exegetical techniques and insights in formulating their new understanding of the sacrament. While Karlstadt brought arguments against Christ's corporeal presence that had roots in late medieval heresy, Zwingli's positive contribution was a more fully elaborated Erasmian restatement of the purpose of the Supper and evidence that this understanding accorded with the teaching of the church fathers. The Strasbourg reformers could easily synthesize the ideas coming from both men, thereby contributing to the further development of early Zwinglianism.

Although Strasbourg's pastors did not engage in the public debate over the sacrament, they worked behind the scenes to promote their new understanding of the Lord's Supper. Over the fall of 1525, Bucer wrote to several pastors and to the noblemen whose parishes they served, distributing copies of the works by Oecolampadius and Hoen fresh off of Strasbourg's presses. In early October, the Strasbourgers sent the Hebrew instructor Gregor Caselius to Wittenberg in order to defend their position to Luther and his colleagues. They also corresponded with the three brothers, Dieterich, Wolf, and Philipp, the lords of Gemmingen, and with Johannes Brenz in the hope of arranging a meeting to discuss their differences concerning the sacrament, or at the very least to persuade Brenz not to stir up further public controversy.[100]

Their letter writing had two goals. First, it was intended to explain and defend their understanding of the sacrament, in the hope of persuading the recipients to adopt that understanding. The Strasbourgers' debt to Zwingli is clear from their summary of what they taught about the sacrament. John 6:63 served as the key verse through which the Supper was defined. Not bodily eating, but spiritual eating through faith was important.[101] Communicants were told to take and eat the bread in remembrance and proclamation of Christ's death, giving thanks for the redemption it had accomplished.[102] In one seemingly small but very significant difference from the Swiss reformers, however, the Strasbourgers made a clearer connection between bodily and spiritual eating, implying that the two should happen simultaneously. Although they told the lords of Gemmingen that Zwingli and Oecolampadius both taught that believers were truly given the body of Christ through the words "this is my body," neither of the Swiss reformers had ever made a statement that could be interpreted in this way, and indeed, as the Strasbourgers acknowledged, Zwingli and Oecolampadius were careful to distinguish between bread and body so that no one could consider one to be the other.[103] The difference between the Swiss and the Strasbourgers on this point was crucial, however, for it would later make it possible for the Strasbourgers to acknowledge an objective aspect of the sacrament, according to which recipients actually received some spiritual benefit through the Supper that was not available outside of the sacrament, a position that Zwingli strenuously denied.[104]

Despite this difference, both Bucer and Capito clearly identified themselves with the Swiss and against Luther on the issue of Christ's corporeal presence. While Bucer criticized Bugenhagen's *Open Letter* to his friend Jacob Otter, Capito wrote to Bugenhagen himself, listing what he saw to be the weak points in the Wittenberger's exegesis.[105] In all of their letters the Strasbourgers repeated the arguments that had seemed so persuasive to them the year before. Thus they pointed out that the apostles spoke of bread, not of Christ's body, and indeed that Scripture said nothing about the miracle of Christ's carnal presence in the bread, which they repeatedly referred to as "impanation." Moreover, it was not necessary to teach that Christ's body and blood were contained in the bread and wine. Last but not least, 1 Corinthians 10:4 not only supported a figurative understanding of "is" but taught the importance of spiritual eating more generally.[106]

A second reason for the letter-writing campaign was that the Strasbourgers hoped to bring about a truce in the growing war of words over the sacrament. Their efforts were motivated at least in part by the charges of heresy emanating from Wittenberg. Bugenhagen had publicly accused both Karlstadt and Zwingli of error in his *Open Letter*, and according to Capito the Wittenbergers had condemned them as "heretical, schismatic, and seditious" in their private letters.[107] In this regard, the publication of Karlstadt's *Declaration of How Karlstadt Regards His Teaching* in late September 1525 proved a very mixed blessing for the Strasbourgers.[108] On the one hand, Luther left no doubt in his preface that he considered Karlstadt and Zwingli to have dreamed up their understanding of the Lord's Supper, rather than being led by the Spirit of truth, and Karlstadt's rather strained statement that he had published his views only so that they could be compared against Scripture could certainly be interpreted as weakening the arguments of all those opposed to Christ's corporeal presence. On the other hand, Luther's preface could be interpreted as a willingness to bear with one's opponents, if they were genuinely seeking the truth.

It was this latter aspect of Luther's preface that was stressed in the version of Karlstadt's *Declaration* that the Strasbourg pastors published in late October or early November. The pamphlet contained an anonymous additional preface that stressed the importance of spiritual manducation for both sides and downplayed the question of what the elements were.[109] If Christians understood and proclaimed Christ's self-giving love, they would not worry about what was in the elements. Scripture said nothing about a miraculous transformation of the bread and wine into Christ's body and blood, nor did Christ command his disciples to preach that his body and blood were in the bread and wine. Without sure grounds for this belief in Scripture, it was offensive to argue about Christ's bodily presence.[110]

The author put the most positive spin possible on Luther's preface. He claimed, for instance, that Luther's acceptance of Karlstadt's explanation of his teaching, like his acceptance of the Waldensians in his *On the Adoration of the Sacrament*, proved that the Wittenberger did not want to destroy fraternal unity with those who did not agree with him, a position he could not hold if he considered Karlstadt a heretic.[111] Luther's statement that it was dangerous to doubt the articles of the faith was qualified by the claim that Luther did not consider the presence of Christ's body to be an article of faith necessary for salvation. Similarly, the author regarded Luther's assertion that the Holy Spirit gave certainty as applying only to the chief articles of the faith, and he pointed out that in lesser things the Holy Spirit often proceeded by gradual illumination. Thus Luther himself had spoken tentatively about the papal mass in his earlier works but had eventually moved to a bolder proclamation of the truth in later ones. Luther's warning against Karlstadt, Zwingli, and those who agreed with them was qualified by the clause "as far as their view is without God's word," and his assertion that the sacramentarians did not have God's Spirit was flatly contradicted. Any hesitation that the Swiss reformers had in expressing their own views was due not to their uncertainty but rather to their desire to treat holy matters with reverence.[112]

In his correspondence, Bucer repeated the essence of this preface. As he told Johann Landschad, the church fathers had disagreed about whether Satan's appearance as a snake in Genesis 3 should be understood figuratively or literally, Luther and Bugenhagen differed in their interpretation of some of the Psalms, and even Luther himself had changed his understanding of Psalm 120 over the course of time. One simply could not expect that all Christians would understand every part of the Bible in the same way. It was therefore best for each to be sure of his own understanding and to maintain unity in the essentials.[113] Each side should recognize the sincerity of the other party, acknowledge that Christians could legitimately disagree in their understanding of Scripture, continue to accept each other as brethren, and refrain from criticizing those who taught differently.[114]

The Strasbourgers' rosy picture of Luther's willingness to tolerate disagreement over Christ's corporeal presence was smashed at the end of November, when Caselius returned home from Wittenberg, bearing letters from Luther and Bugenhagen. Luther stated in no uncertain terms that belief in Christ's corporeal presence was indeed a necessary article of faith. Either the Wittenbergers or the Swiss were wrong in their understanding of the words of institution, and there was no middle ground on the issue. The Swiss had started the controversy by publishing their books on the sacrament, and they were the first to resort to insults, calling the Wittenbergers flesh-eaters, idolaters, and eaters of an impanated God. Their call for a truce was therefore disingenuous, and in fact their writings had so fanned the controversy that Luther saw no hope of restoring the peace.[115]

The Wittenbergers' response to Strasbourg made clear how central they regarded the question of Christ's corporeal presence to be. Their rejection of the Strasbourgers' attempts to portray the issue of Christ's presence as an *adiaphoron* was thus categorical, and Luther's statement "I will consider all those who argue that the body is not present to be alien from the faith" was a virtual sentence of excommunication for all who disagreed with his understanding of the Supper.[116] The tentative plans to meet with Brenz to discuss differences concerning the Supper also came to nothing, and the publication in January of the *Syngramma . . . on the Words of the Lord's Supper*, written by Brenz as a response to Oecolampadius and signed by fourteen Swabian pastors, only sharpened the controversy. Over the next few years, the polemical battle would focus almost exclusively on the corporeal presence of Christ in the elements, and the issue of Christ's spiritual presence in the sacrament, touched on ever so briefly by the Strasbourgers, was ignored.

WHAT'S IN A NAME?

By the beginning of 1526, virtually all of the arguments for and against Christ's corporeal presence had been made public, and the reformers of Zurich, Basel, and Strasbourg had emerged as the chief opponents to Luther's view. Their common opposition to Luther brings us back to the problem raised at the beginning of this chapter, but now posed in a broader way: What was the relationship between Zwinglianism and "Karlstadtianism"?

The answer to the question depends on how both terms are defined. To begin with "Zwinglianism," the eucharistic theology espoused in all three cities was an elaboration of the views first publicly expressed by Zwingli, enriched by arguments taken from late medieval heresy and supported by a particular interpretation of the church fathers. Zwingli may have given his name to this theology, but Oecolampadius and the Strasbourgers, and through them Karlstadt, Hoen, Wyclif, and various Hussite groups, also contributed to its formation. Zwingli endorsed this development in both his public commendation of Oecolampadius's book and his private correspondence with Oecolampadius and Capito. He acknowledged that there were differences among them—thus in 1527 he would tell Luther that he did not agree with Bucer's assertion that one could disagree on the Lord's Supper without detriment to the faith.[117] Such differences were minor, however, in comparison to the agreement on the chief issue of whether Christ was corporeally present in the elements and on the redefinition of the sacrament required by a rejection of that presence. It is thus an unnecessary narrowing of the term "Zwinglian" to restrict it only to the views of the Zurich reformer.

A similar problem arises with the definition of "Karlstadtian." At one end of the spectrum, using Rhegius's definition but stated less polemically as someone who rejected Christ's corporeal presence in the Supper, then Zwingli was certainly a Karlstadtian. Such a label is far too broad to be useful, however, for it suggests Zwingli's dependence on Karlstadt and obscures the differences between the two men. At the other extreme, if the term is defined as someone whose ideas were derived from or close to those of Karlstadt, Zwingli was clearly not a Karlstadtian— but by this definition, there were very few genuine Karlstadtians. To begin with, it was difficult even for those who favored Karlstadt's views to gain a full picture of his eucharistic theology. Karlstadt presented his understanding of the Supper piecemeal in a series of pamphlets published at different times and in different places. If Zwingli and Oecolampadius could obtain copies of only one or two of those works, it must have been even more difficult for those not living in a major printing center to read all of Karlstadt's pamphlets. Furthermore, unlike the reformers of Zurich, Basel, and Strasbourg, Karlstadt did not hold a public position protected by the magistrate from which to disseminate his views. Instead, he spent much of the year between his exile from Saxony and his reconciliation with Luther as a refugee in hiding. As a consequence, the general understanding of Karlstadt's eucharistic theology was bound to remain vague and imprecise. His name was associated with the rejection of Christ's corporeal presence, and his critics were aware of his unusual exegesis of the words of institution, but there was no separate group that derived its understanding of the sacrament from Karlstadt.

There are, however, important connections between Karlstadt and the Zwinglians. Karlstadt contributed to the development of early Zwinglianism in two ways. First, he made public an understanding of key scriptural texts that differed significantly from that of the Lutherans. Although Karlstadt and the Zwinglians disagreed in their interpretation of the words of institution, they agreed in their exegesis of other central passages: John 6:63, 1 Corinthians 10:3–4, 1 Corinthians 10:16–17, Luke 22:20/1 Corinthians 11:25, and 1 Corinthians 11:27–29. Bucer explicitly stated that Karlstadt's pamphlets had caused him to examine the relevant Scripture texts and to abandon the interpretation defended by Luther in his treatise *On the Adoration of the Sacrament*, which discussed not only the words of institution but also 1 Corinthians 10:4 and 1 Corinthians 10:16–17.[118] His older colleagues may have already held their variant understanding of the relevant passages before this became an issue separating them from Wittenberg, for they could all be found in Erasmus, particularly in the Dutch humanist's paraphrases. Erasmus's paraphrase of 1 Corinthians 10:4, for instance, stated that Christ "was the dry and sterile rock," a phrasing that required a figurative understanding of "is." Similarly, his paraphrase of 1 Corinthians 10:16 described the cup which "declared a fellowship of those redeemed by Christ's blood" and the bread which "declared an alliance and highest society" among Christians.[119] These readings precluded the Lutheran understanding of each text, and those who relied on Erasmus in their study of the New Testament would therefore be inclined to disagree with the Wittenbergers. It was Karlstadt, however, who brought these differences out into the open and gave them a central role in the eucharistic controversy. For a German-reading audience, the new understanding of these Scripture texts thus became associated with Karlstadt and Zwingli, not with Erasmus.

Second, Karlstadt introduced into the public discussion a host of arguments against Christ's bodily presence that Oecolampadius and the Strasbourgers would incorporate into early Zwinglianism either directly or in modified form. Karlstadt derived some of these arguments from late medieval heresy, especially as it was mediated by Hoen's letter; others he had developed himself, sometimes on the basis of Erasmus's exegesis. Whatever their origin, though, they provided additional support for Zwingli's rejection of Christ's corporeal presence, originally justified chiefly by a figurative understanding of the words of institution.

Zwingli may have wanted to distance himself from Karlstadt, and his protests against being labeled a Karlstadtian were certainly made in good faith. Nevertheless, Zwinglian eucharistic theology owed a great deal to Karlstadt as pathbreaker, catalyst, and source of some of its arguments. To use Zwingli's own analogy, Karlstadt may not have been "skilled in the use of armor," but he produced much of the weaponry that would be used by the Zwinglians in their battle against Wittenberg.

6

"One Body and Many Heads"

THE DIFFUSION OF SACRAMENTARIAN IDEAS

BY THE END of 1524 Karlstadt's pamphlets had made clear his differences with
Luther on the Lord's Supper. Zwingli's understanding of the sacrament became
public knowledge in the spring of 1525, with the printing of his letter to Matthaeus
Alber and the publication of his *Commentary on True and False Religion.*
Oecolampadius joined the debate in September with his book *On the Genuine
Exposition of the Lord's Words, "This is my Body."* Over the course of the summer and
fall, more pamphlets rejecting Christ's corporeal presence were published, and the
Strasbourgers tried to win, if not Luther's approval, at least his toleration of their
position. Last but not least, in December the Wittenbergers became aware that the
reforming circle centered around Kaspar Schwenckfeld and Valentin Crautwald in
Silesia had developed an understanding of the Supper at variance with their own.
The eucharistic controversy had begun in earnest.

Luther regarded the ideas of Karlstadt, Zwingli, Oecolampadius, and all others
who denied Christ's corporeal presence as simply variations on the same theme,
but he also recognized that differences existed between them. In his preface to the
first Wittenberg translation of the *Syngramma . . . on the Lord's Supper,* he compared
his opponents to the beast of the Apocalypse, which had "one body with many
heads, just as these sects in sum hold one view and have one body, but in their
causes and reasons each sect has its own head and its own way, although all have
arisen to blaspheme the one single Christian truth." Their disagreements over the
exegesis of the words "this is my body" only proved that they were all in error.[1]

Luther's judgment highlights the problem of labeling all of his evangelical opponents as Zwinglians. Just as Zwingli and his allies adopted ideas taken from Hoen, Karlstadt, and the Bohemian Brethren, so pamphlet authors outside of Zurich, Basel, and Strasbourg used ideas from a variety of sources to explain or defend their understanding of the Lord's Supper. Unlike Oecolampadius and the Strasbourgers, these pamphleteers did not contribute to the elaboration of early Zwinglianism. They were important, however, for the popular diffusion of an understanding of the Supper at variance with Luther's. Luther used "sacramentarian" as a term of opprobrium, but if its negative connotation can be set aside the term allows us to acknowledge the input of others besides Zwingli to the eucharistic controversy.[2]

We can learn a good deal about the gradual diffusion and development of the sacramentarian movement by analyzing the pamphlets published in the year after the outbreak of the eucharistic controversy. After describing these publications more generally, this chapter will look specifically at those pamphlets written by authors outside of the two centers of Wittenberg and Zurich to see how they responded to the controversy and formulated their own understanding of the Lord's Supper. It will also discuss the earliest statements of Kaspar Schwenckfeld and Valentin Crautwald concerning the Lord's Supper. Although not published until several years later, their writings give yet another view of the debate concerning the Lord's Supper over the course of 1525. This analysis will allow us to evaluate the spread and evolution of the eucharistic controversy in the year after its outbreak.

THE PAMPHLET WAR

Karlstadt's pamphlets touched off a propagandistic battle over the evangelical understanding of the Lord's Supper. The 52 percent increase in the number of pamphlets on the Lord's Supper published between 1524 and 1525 can be attributed entirely to the outbreak of the eucharistic controversy (table 6.1). Seventy-two of the 172 pamphlets printed in 1525 dealt directly with the question of Christ's corporeal presence or advocated a sacramentarian understanding of the Lord's Supper, while several other works addressed the issue at least tangentially.[3] As in the years before 1525, Luther was the single most important author, but the number of pamphlets written by other evangelical authors continued to increase.

Most accounts of the eucharistic controversy give the impression that the two parties were roughly balanced in terms of their audience and argumentation, but a survey of the publications of 1525 suggests that this picture must be revised.

TABLE 6.1

Pamphlets on the Lord's Supper, 1524–1525

		OTHER						NUMBER OF
	LUTHER	EVANGELICALS		CATHOLICS		TOTAL		AUTHORS
	Titles[1] Imprints	Titles Imprints		Titles Imprints		Titles Imprints		
1524	13	29	30	72	6	13	49	114	26 + 2 anon.
1525	10	52	51	110	9	10	70	172	30 +1

1. German and Latin versions of the same work are counted as separate titles because they were intended for different audiences.

Whether one looks at the number of publications, the uniformity of the message they conveyed, the ability to distribute their own views and to suppress those of their opponents, or the perceived authority of their authors, the Lutherans had a tremendous advantage over the sacramentarians. By almost any standard, the defenders of Christ's corporeal presence were more successful than their opponents at publicizing their position.

To begin with absolute numbers, there were more imprints opposing the sacramentarians (40) than there were defending their understanding of the Lord's Supper (32). Only when one adds in the nine editions of Karlstadt's eucharistic pamphlets published in 1524, as well as the four imprints of pamphlets from 1524 that responded to Karlstadt, do the numbers of pamphlets produced by each side become more even.[4]

The defenders of the traditional view had an even more important advantage over their opponents in that they disseminated their view through multiple reprints of a small number of titles. There were only six titles published in 1525 that defended Christ's presence or attacked the sacramentarian position. In addition to the four imprints of Rhegius's *Warning against the New Error of Dr. Andreas Karlstadt Concerning the Sacrament* and the five of Luther's letter to the Strasbourgers, both of which first appeared in 1524, there were a dozen imprints of the first part of Luther's *Against the Heavenly Prophets* and another ten of the second part. Johann Bugenhagen's *Open Letter against the New Error Concerning the Sacrament* went through six editions of its Latin original and another five editions in German, while Nicolaus von Amsdorf's *Admonition to the Magdeburgers* saw two editions.[5] In comparison, their opponents produced nineteen titles by ten different authors advocating a sacramentarian understanding of the Supper; most of these were printed only once.[6] The diversity of views they presented was perceived as disunity and therefore as weakness. While the sacramentarians fielded a host of arguments made by several different authors, the defenders of the Wittenberg position presented a single uniform message. This uniform message was all the more convincing because it had the weight of tradition behind it, while the sacramentarians constantly had to defend themselves against charges of heresy.[7]

A third factor was that none of the sacramentarian authors could equal Luther's reputation and positive image. John Wyclif was a well-known heretic, Andreas Karlstadt had become notorious through his disagreement with Luther, and Balthasar Hubmaier was discredited by his involvement in the Peasants' War and his rejection of infant baptism. Other authors shied away from being publicly associated with a sacramentarian view. Two of the authors, Conrad Ryss and Matthaeus Frey, used pseudonyms, while Hoen's *Most Christian Letter* was attributed only to "a certain Batavian";[8] a fourth author, Caspar Turnauer, was so obscure that he remains largely unknown today. As one of Augsburg's preachers, Michael Keller held a more visible post, but he did not have the theological stature of his colleague and theological opponent Urbanus Rhegius. Only Zwingli and Oecolampadius had established reputations as reformers before the outbreak of the controversy, and neither of them could command the same respect and authority as Luther and, by association, his colleagues in Wittenberg.[9]

A final factor contributing to the shape of the controversy was the effectiveness of censorship measures, whether formal or informal, in the cities where the pamphlets were printed. This can be seen by examining the eucharistic pamphlets published in each of the most important printing centers (figure 6.1). In the years up through 1524 Augsburg publishers produced almost a quarter of all those pamphlets that discussed the Eucharist. Strasbourg printers produced another 17 percent of the total, with Wittenberg (16 percent) a close third. Erfurt, Nuremberg, Basel,

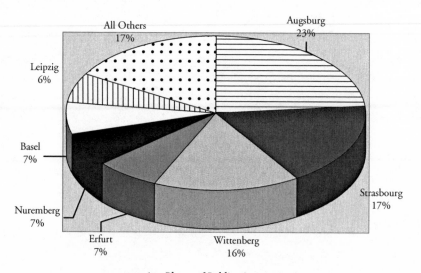

FIGURE 6.1 Places of Publication, 1518–1524

and Leipzig each published about 7 percent of the pamphlets; no other city published more than a few pamphlets.[10] These relative proportions remained the same in 1525, with the exception that Zurich replaced Basel as a major center for publication of pamphlets on the Lord's Supper.[11]

With the outbreak of the eucharistic controversy, however, a clear divergence developed in the publications produced in each of these cities. The printers in Saxony limited their publications on the Lord's Supper to Lutheran works. Leipzig's printers published works by Bugenhagen, Osiander, four imprints of Rhegius's 1523 *Corpus Christi* sermon and two of his *Warning against the New Error*, and nothing by Catholic authors. Erfurt's printers seemed to pay little attention to the controversy over the Lord's Supper. The largest proportion of their publications were reprints of pamphlets that addressed the proper preparation for communion and advocating or justifying moderate liturgical reform, along with Luther's *Against the Abomination of the Secret Mass*.[12] The only pamphlet published in Erfurt that might be seen as a challenge to Luther's understanding was Capito's *What One Should Think about the Disagreement between Martin Luther and Andreas Karlstadt*. This was more than balanced by two imprints of each part of Luther's *Against the Heavenly Prophets* and Karlstadt's *Declaration of How Karlstadt Regards His Teaching*, with its preface by Luther.

Karlstadt's *Declaration* was also published in Nuremberg, where it was one of several works intended to uphold Luther's understanding of the sacrament. The association of Zwingli and his supporters with both the Anabaptists and the unrest of the Peasants' War had turned the city's authorities against the Swiss. As a consequence, not only did the Nuremberg Council enforce its earlier ban on Karlstadt's eucharistic pamphlets, but it also suppressed Zwingli's works as heretical.[13] Nuremberg's printers thus published only the works of Luther and Bugenhagen aimed against the "fanatics." In addition to two imprints of Part One and one of Part Two of *Against the Heavenly Prophets*, they printed two editions of Luther's *Open Letter to the Strasbourgers*, while Bugenhagen's *Open Letter against the New Error about the Sacrament* was published in both Latin and German. At the same time, the Nurembergers continued to publish attacks on the Catholic mass by Luther and Osiander.[14]

On the other side of the controversy, Basel's disappearance from the market for eucharistic pamphlets was also due to the tighter censorship measures imposed in that city after the arrest and interrogation of the printers who had produced Karlstadt's eucharistic pamphlets. The only works on the sacrament published there in 1525 were the two parts of Luther's *Against the Heavenly Prophets*. Zurich's printers were more than happy to fill the gap. All of the imprints concerning the sacrament published in that city were either works by

Zwingli or editions of the city's new liturgy for celebrating the Lord's Supper, introduced in time for Easter of 1525.

Because Strasbourg's pastors supported Zwingli, its printers were free to publish a range of sacramentarian works. The Strasbourg Council's effort to prohibit the sale of Karlstadt's pamphlets proved ineffective, and three of Karlstadt's five eucharistic pamphlets were reprinted there before the end of 1525.[15] Not all of Strasbourg's evangelical inhabitants shared the pastors' convictions that the question of Christ's presence was of secondary importance, and they took advantage of Strasbourg's many printers to publish works rejecting that presence. Otto Brunfels, who was so taken by Karlstadt that he accompanied him from Strasbourg to Heidelberg in November 1524, was responsible for the publication of John Wyclif's *Trialogus* in March 1525.[16] Unable to publish his *Genuine Exposition* in Basel, Oecolampadius sent the manuscript to Guillaume Farel in Strasbourg, asking him and Capito to see it through the press, and the book duly appeared in September.[17] Hoen's *Most Christian Letter* was also published in Strasbourg in late August or early September, both in the original Latin and in German translation.[18] There was also a disinclination to publish works defending Christ's corporeal presence in the sacrament. Luther's works were too profitable to suppress, and the city's printers reprinted both parts of *Against the Heavenly Prophets*, but they did not publish Bugenhagen's attack on Zwingli.[19]

Augsburg's printers were by far the most varied in their publications. In addition to printing Karlstadt's last two eucharistic pamphlets, they published works by authors ranging from Amsdorf to Zwingli. The city's printers produced forty-one pamphlets on the Lord's Supper in 1525, nineteen more than they had published in 1524. Nineteen of these works related directly to the eucharistic controversy: eight imprints defending Christ's corporeal presence, and eleven upholding a sacramentarian view.[20] In fact, the only contributions to the eucharistic controversy written in 1525 that were not printed or reprinted in Augsburg were Balthasar Hubmaier's *Some Theses . . . of Instruction on the Mass*,[21] which was published in nearby Ulm, Oecolampadius's *Genuine Exposition*, and Hoen's *Christian Letter*—and a German translation of the letter would be published in Augsburg in 1526. In comparison, the older controversy with the Catholics virtually disappeared, although there were six pamphlets from 1525 concerning the mass.[22]

If one looks only at the place of publication, it is clear that the works of Luther and his supporters were more broadly distributed than those of their opponents. Interested readers could obtain copies of their pamphlets from the same places and through the same channels as existed before the controversy began. Because of the limited number of cities where sacramentarian works were published, it was more difficult to obtain the pamphlets of Luther's opponents. This does not mean that sacramentarian works were unknown outside of South Germany. The existing mechanisms for the distribution of books, especially the Frankfurt book fair, assured that copies of Zwingli's and Karlstadt's pamphlets could be found in places as distant as Magdeburg and Silesia, as the examples of Wolf Cyclops and Kaspar Schwenckfeld demonstrate. But the variety of authors and titles, combined with the limited number of print runs of sacramentarian pamphlets, contributed to a more heterogeneous presentation of that position and opened up the possibility that its reception would be correspondingly diverse.

To assess the diversity of the sacramentarian pamphlets, however, we must examine their contents more closely. As a first step, let us look at the exchanges over the Lord's Supper presented in the pamphlets of three Augsburg pastors: the Carmelite preacher Johann Landsperger, the cathedral preacher Urbanus Rhegius, and Michael Keller, the preacher at the Franciscan church. This will alert us to characteristics of the debate as it was carried on in other pamphlets concerning the sacrament published in 1525.

CONTRASTING VIEWS OF THE LORD'S SUPPER

Landsperger's *Useful Report on the Reception of the Venerable Sacrament or Testament of Christ in both Signs of Bread and Wine, and What Has Until Now been Hidden from Both Parties (Contending Against Each Other)* was published at the very end of 1524.[23] In contrast to Luther, Landsperger used John 6:53 ("unless you eat the flesh of the Son of man and drink his blood, you have no life in you") to argue for communion in both kinds and to emphasize the necessity of spiritual communion.[24] Although Karlstadt's pamphlets were already circulating in Augsburg by the time the *Useful Report* was published, Landsperger's only allusion to divisions within the evangelical party occurred in his pamphlet's lengthy title.[25] The pamphlet reflects Landsperger's evangelical eclecticism: he combined Luther's understanding of the sacrament as Christ's testament in which divine grace was offered to recipients with a Zwinglian emphasis on remembrance as the purpose of the Supper and a rejection of the mass as a repeated sacrifice. His exegesis of John 6, and especially his use of John 6:63 to highlight the importance of spiritual communion, reflected a strong late medieval and Erasmian bent and moved him close to Zwingli's early writings on the sacrament.[26] There is also a possible reflection of Karlstadt's 1521 pamphlets in Landsperger's statement that each element of the Supper had its particular meaning, and so it was not sufficient to receive only one sign.[27] The pamphlet concluded with a strong endorsement of both the objective (the presence of Christ's body and blood) and the subjective (the recipient's faith) aspects of the Supper: it was an article of faith that Christ was truly and essentially within the bread to strengthen and feed the soul, but he was there as food for the soul, not the body. Reinforcing many of the ideas expressed in Rhegius's earlier publications on the sacrament, Landsperger's pamphlet provides a good indication of how Augsburg's preachers balanced ideas drawn from a variety of sources when discussing the sacrament on the eve of the eucharistic controversy.

The publication of the pamphlets first of Karlstadt and then of Zwingli destroyed this balance. Rhegius was the first to attack Karlstadt in print; his *Warning against the New Error* was published by the end of December 1524.[28] The first part of the pamphlet was a response to Karlstadt's *Anti-Christian Abuse* and the *Dialogue*. Rhegius chastised Karlstadt for the offensiveness of his language and his arrogance in rejecting the views of others. Although his own pamphlet was certainly not free from polemic, for the most part he avoided the name-calling and bitter invective that characterized Karlstadt's two pamphlets and that Luther would use in *Against the Heavenly Prophets*.

Rhegius criticized Karlstadt on three issues, but on each point he was willing to recognize that they shared common ground. In response to Karlstadt's assertion that the sacrament did not forgive sins, Rhegius declared that Karlstadt had willfully misrepresented evangelical teaching. In fact, no one taught that the sacrament forgave sins, strictly speaking. Forgiveness came only through faith, but one received the sacrament as assurance of the grace given in Christ.[29] To Karlstadt's claim that the sacrament did not give assurance, Rhegius pointed out that the self-examination that preceded communion must result not only in recognition of one's faith but also in awareness of one's sinfulness, and the sacrament was given especially to reassure those oppressed by their sins. He did not dispute Karlstadt's assertion that the Holy Spirit assured one internally, and he acknowledged that without this assurance no external thing could grant peace of conscience. But he also argued that as physical beings, humans also needed external signs or pledges, and thus God had instituted the sacraments.[30]

Rhegius took a harsher line in his refutation of Karlstadt's claim that the sacrament consisted only of natural bread and wine. He had no patience whatsoever for Karlstadt's new exegesis of the words of institution. One could not separate "take and eat" from the following, "this is my body," as Karlstadt tried to do. Rhegius defended the traditional understanding that Christ authorized the church's ministers to bring his body into the bread using the words of consecration, and he criticized Karlstadt's arguments that Christ remained in heaven and could not be brought down to earth in the sacrament.[31]

In the last part of his pamphlet Rhegius summarized his teaching on the sacrament, beginning with Adam's fall and humanity's need for redemption, and continuing through Christ's unique sacrifice on the cross and the necessity of faith in the Christ promised by the prophets. Rhegius echoed Karlstadt in stating that one must have the right knowledge and ardent remembrance of the salvation Christ brought, but he went beyond Karlstadt to argue that the sacrament was instituted to strengthen faith in God's promise of salvation. If Christ's words were spoken rightly in faith over the bread and wine, there was no doubt that Christ's body and blood were present. Citing John 6:63, Rhegius acknowledged that the flesh alone was of no use, and body and blood only became food and drink when they were received with faith, but he also argued that Christ's body and blood were given under visible signs to help our weak faith.[32]

With his emphasis on both Christ's bodily presence and the importance of spiritual communion, Rhegius tried to restore the balance between objective and subjective aspects of the sacrament. Michael Keller moved more clearly to the subjective side in *Some Sermons on Christ's Supper*. Keller published the pamphlet in response to the discord surrounding his series of sermons on the account of the Last Supper in Luke 22:14–23, and particularly concerning his explanation of the use and purpose of the external signs of the sacrament.[33]

Keller's discussion of those signs was circumspect, but it clearly followed Zwingli's understanding of the sacrament's purpose. The elements were symbols and signs of Christ's love, seals of the new testament established through Christ's death. They caused his followers to remember, give thanks for, and proclaim his passion and death and bound them in mutual love and good works. Like Zwingli, Karlstadt, and Erasmus, Keller understood 1 Corinthians 10:16–17 as referring to the fellowship that existed among Christians rather than to the sharing of Christ's body and blood. The self-examination that Paul spoke of was done to make sure that one recognized that Christ had given his body and blood for the forgiveness of sins and set one's confidence in Christ. Only then could one eat and drink to proclaim one's firm faith, knowledge of, and trust in the new testament that had been established.[34]

Despite his obvious agreement with Zwingli on the purpose of the sacrament, Keller stopped short of stating in print that the elements consisted only of bread and wine. Rather than criticizing other evangelicals, Keller directed all of his polemic against the Catholics, rejecting the sacrifice of the mass, masses for the dead, and the withholding of the chalice. He also condemned what he called "the three great abuses of the papists"—the reservation of the consecrated host, its adoration, and its use in processions—but he did not directly attack the belief in Christ's corporeal presence that underlay these practices.[35] In this regard, Keller's pamphlet was Zwinglian implicitly rather than explicitly, by what it failed to say about Christ's corporeal presence and the sacrament's ability to confirm faith, rather than by an open rejection of these two aspects of Luther's eucharistic theology.

If we step back from the specific situation in Augsburg and look at other early sacramentarian pamphlets, we see the same endorsement of Zwingli's under-standing of the purpose of the Lord's Supper combined with an unwillingness to put in print a clear rejection of Christ's corporeal presence. Like Keller, the pastor Mathaeus Frey acknowledged the dissension that had arisen over the Lord's Supper, and he lamented the tendency to follow "doctors and masters" rather than Scrip-ture in his *Lovely Instruction and Teaching in Consideration of the Supper of Our Dear Lord Jesus Christ*.[36] Christ's highest commandment was to love God and neighbor, and if one sought the salvation of others above all else, then such arguments would disappear. Frey attributed no inherent benefit to the reception of the sacrament per se. Instead, the Supper was a remembrance of Christ's death, and the bread and wine were external signs whereby recipients obligated themselves to serve others in Christian love. Frey was particularly concerned with the ethical aspect of communion. All who partook of the Supper had fellowship with Christ and with one another, and receiving communion did no good if one did not love one's neighbor. Even the self-examination before communion had an ethical and com-munal purpose, to determine whether one was properly disposed toward his or her neighbor.[37]

Despite this strong emphasis on the subjective and ethical aspects of the Lord's Supper, Frey drew back from an open rejection of any objective element. Instead he drew on the older concept of spiritual communion to link the reception of Christ's body with the word, rather than with the elements of bread and wine:

> When Christ says, "take, eat, this is my body which is given for you," he sig-nifies and presents his mortal body, which then suffered for us naturally and with all its senses. This same he also presented to us invisibly in his holy word, to comprehend and to grasp by grace through faith in the Spirit.[38]

Frey's concern with receiving Christ's body spiritually was closer to the view of the Strasbourgers than it was to Zwingli, who in his publications from 1525 carefully avoided any explicit linkage between spiritual communion and reception of the elements.

Balthasar Hubmaier's *Theses Instructing All Christians on the Mass* also endorsed Zwingli's understanding of the Lord's Supper as remembrance of Christ's passion and proclamation of his death, in which Christians publicly pledged themselves to each other. Although he did not attack the belief in Christ's presence, he echoed Zwingli's terminology when he called the elements external signs that signified

Christ's body and blood. Hubmaier was familiar with the arguments being circulated against the traditional understanding of Christ's words of institution, and his own interpretation of "take, eat, this is my body, which is given for you" mixed arguments from both Zwingli and Karlstadt: with these words Christ "signified his mortal body, for he himself, and not the table bread that he gave them to eat, suffered for us."[39]

Most prominent in Hubmaier's discussion of the sacrament, however, was the use of 1 Corinthians 10:16–17 to argue for the centrality of the fellowship established among Christians through partaking of Christ's Supper. Christians were to examine themselves before the Supper to see if they were united and willing to share all with their neighbors; if such an attitude was lacking, their reception of the sacrament made them hypocrites who ate and drank eternal death.[40] Hubmaier's emphasis on the communal aspect of the Supper went beyond what Zwingli had expressed in either his letter to Alber or the *Commentary*, although it paralleled ideas that the Zurich reformer would express in his liturgy for the Lord's Supper, and it is very similar to the view of the Supper expressed by Conrad Grebel and his friends in their letter to Thomas Müntzer the previous September.[41]

Those pamphlets that were willing to address directly the issue of Christ's presence in the sacrament showed a greater debt to Karlstadt than to Zwingli. Caspar Turnauer, who may have been the pastor of Mindelheim, a small town near Augsburg, was particularly concerned with what it meant to discern Christ's body and so receive the bread and wine worthily.[42] In *The Words of Paul on the Lord's Supper*, he stated his belief that no one had understood Paul rightly, and so he presented his own exegesis of 1 Corinthians 11:17–34. Like Karlstadt, Turnauer made the point that Christ gave, and his disciples ate, bread. Christ told them to remember his body, which would be given in the future, and he explained what Christ meant by "giving his body" using Christ's prediction of his passion and death, his surrender to Judas and his captors, and Pilate's handing him over to the executioners. Turnauer's interpretation of unworthy eating, or not discerning the body, took on a strong social cast: he defined it as not recognizing that fellow believers were part of the body of the Lord, and particularly as despising and overlooking that body's poorer members.[43]

The author most obviously influenced by Karlstadt was Conrad Ryss (or Reyss) zu Ofen, who wrote his pamphlet as an *Answer to the Highly Learned Doctor Johann Bugenhagen . . . Concerning the Sacrament*.[44] This pamphlet was the only one written by any of these secondary figures to argue openly and at length against Christ's bodily presence in the Lord's Supper. Ryss began with a consideration of the words of institution. According to its natural sense, the word "this" must refer to the following phrase, "which will be given for you." Christ's words should thus be understood as, "Take and eat. This which will be given for you is my body; do this in my remembrance." Ryss was here taking the logical next step suggested by Karlstadt's exegesis and rearranging the clauses to make the point more clearly that "this" referred to Christ's body, not the bread.[45] Ryss supported this interpretation with an application to the bread of a point that Karlstadt had made about the wine: Christ no longer held the bread in his hands when he spoke the words of institution. He thus told his disciples to eat the bread before he could have converted it into his body.[46]

Ryss also echoed Karlstadt in asserting that neither Christ nor any prophet before him had said anything about his body being given in natural baker's bread. Picking up on a point first made by Hoen and elaborated on by Karlstadt, Zwingli, and Oecolampadius, he asserted that the disciples had eaten the bread without assuming it was anything else, nor had they ever taught that it was bread. Their very silence demonstrated this, since elsewhere in Scripture they had asked Christ to clarify something they did not understand. Like Hoen and Karlstadt, Ryss also argued that Christ's command to "do this" referred to eating the bread in remembrance, and not to making the bread into his body.[47] Ryss followed Karlstadt's argumentation with regard to the meaning of Christ's words concerning the cup. Mark stated that Christ did not speak the words "this is my blood" until after the disciples had drunk from the cup. It was nonsense to argue that "the cup is in the blood," even if by "cup" one understood what the cup contained, and so here "is" must be understood as "signifies."[48]

Bugenhagen had mocked both Zwingli and Karlstadt for their interpretation of John 6:63. Ryss responded with a pointed defense of their spiritualist understanding of the passage. As Zwingli had done in his response to Bugenhagen, Ryss emphasized that throughout John 6, Christ had spoken of his flesh, and he did not suddenly change his meaning to refer to fleshly understanding.[49] Ryss also defended the metaphorical interpretation of 1 Corinthians 10:16 to refer to the fellowship of Christians rather than the sharing of Christ's body in the bread. He introduced Paul's subsequent discussion about food offered to idols (1 Cor. 10:18– 21) as evidence that the preceding verses could not be understood as the eating of Christ's physical body and blood, a point Karlstadt had made in two of his pamphlets.[50]

With regard to worthy eating and discerning the Lord's body (1 Cor. 11:27–29), Ryss accused Bugenhagen of translating one phrase to suit his own position, and then using it to misinterpret the entire passage. Paul did not teach the Corinthians to believe that Christ's body was in the bread, but rather rebuked them for not holding the Lord's Supper rightly. Like Karlstadt, he defined worthy eating as the remembrance of Christ's passion.[51]

In the final section of his pamphlet, Ryss condemned the adoration of the sacrament as a form of idolatry, citing the same scriptural proof texts used by the Bohemian Brethren, Hoen, Karlstadt, and Oecolampadius. Beginning with a discussion of Christ's warning not to believe those who claimed, "here is Christ" (Matt. 24:23), he criticized those who built pilgrimage chapels or showed "the bready Lord God" to individuals on their sickbeds. Scripture taught that Christ was in heaven, but there was no Scripture text that taught the daily coming of Christ's body into the bread. In light of the many passages that opposed belief in Christ's corporeal presence, one could not rely on an ambiguous verse, "this is my body," to determine the understanding of the Supper. Those who did so made an idol out of bread, just as the Jews had made a golden calf and called it their god.[52] As his parting shot, Ryss returned to a point Karlstadt had also made. Christ had commanded his disciples to heal the sick, cleanse lepers, and raise the dead; if the clergy wanted to insist on the basis of the words of institution that they brought Christ's body into the bread, why couldn't they perform these other miracles?[53]

Ryss's pamphlet, published at the end of 1525, proved to be more effective at spreading Karlstadt's ideas than Karlstadt's own pamphlets had been.[54] It provided a brief and readable summary of the chief exegetical arguments against Christ's corporeal presence without having the disadvantage of Karlstadt's name. The pamphlet was quickly reprinted in Augsburg, as well as in both Zurich and Strasbourg.[55] Only Hoen's *Most Christian Letter*, which was ultimately published in three Latin and three German editions, and two works by Zwingli—his *Commentary* and his *Clear Instruction on Christ's Supper*, first published in February 1526—would go through as many editions.[56] Ryss's outspoken criticism of the Lutheran position could also be perceived as a drawback, however. Zwingli, for instance, acknowledged that the pamphlet's author was learned but wished that he had been a bit more cautious.[57]

Zwingli's concern demonstrates the vulnerable position of the sacramentarians a year after the outbreak of the eucharistic controversy, as they tried to avoid accusations of heresy with all of its repercussions. All of these authors were eager to endorse the understanding of the Lord's Supper as remembrance of and thanksgiving for Christ's death, a public testimony of faith, a visible demonstration of Christian unity, and a spur to greater love of neighbor. There was nothing heretical about this view of the Supper, focusing as it did on the subjective aspects of the sacrament and its horizontal, communal purpose. Indeed, Luther's 1519 *Sermon on the Venerable Sacrament* also taught that the sacrament included these subjective and horizontal aspects, although Luther did not develop this position in such detail.

Much more difficult was the public rejection of belief in Christ's corporeal presence, a view condemned not only by the Catholic church but also by Luther and his followers. Keller's and Frey's references to public debate over the sacrament suggest that sacramentarian preachers may have been more forthright about their rejection of Christ's corporeal presence from the pulpit, but they were extremely cautious about rejecting that presence in print. Perhaps the most striking example of this caution is the pamphlet of the Magdeburg physician Wolf Cyclops. Nicolaus von Amsdorf had accused Cyclops of preaching without authorization and of teaching that "this is my body" should be understood as "this signifies my body." Cyclops's response, *On the Most Venerable Supper of Jesus Christ*, says nothing about the sacrament but is instead a defense of his character against von Amsdorf's attacks.[58]

This caution with regard to the denial of Christ's corporeal presence had significant implications for the spread of the sacramentarian movement. These pamphlets transmitted only a partial version of the sacramentarian understanding of the Lord's Supper and omitted its central concern. While readers in Augsburg familiar with Keller's preaching may have read into his pamphlet an implicit rejection of Christ's presence, those farther from the center of the debate might not. As a result, the more cautious pamphlets could never be as effective as sacramentarian propaganda as the handful of works—those by Karlstadt, Zwingli, Oecolampadius, Hoen, and Ryss—that tackled the issue of Christ's presence head-on.

The rejection of Christ's presence in the elements precluded any possibility that partaking of the elements could establish a vertical link between God and the communicant, and so the sacramentarians denied the consolatory and strengthening power of the sacrament. Again, most of the pamphleteers did not draw attention to this fact by explicitly rejecting the sacrament's consolatory function; they simply failed to discuss it. Because Luther understood this consolation and assurance as the chief purpose of the sacrament, however, he and his followers would necessarily see the sacramentarians' silence on this point as a serious failing. Lutherans responded by ignoring those aspects of the Lord's Supper common to both sides and focusing on those aspects that the sacramentarians rejected, whether openly or tacitly: Christ's bodily presence in the elements, and the consolatory and strengthening power of sacramental communion.

The sacramentarian pamphlets differed among themselves not only in the extent to which they challenged traditional beliefs but also in their style and intended audience. The acknowledged leaders of the movement, Zwingli and Oecolampadius, chose to disseminate their eucharistic theology in Latin treatises addressed to the scholarly community.[59] They employed an irenic and persuasive tone, and they avoided extended polemics. All of the lesser-known figures aimed their vernacular pamphlets directly at a popular audience. Those whose views most closely followed Zwingli presented their positions in the most positive fashion possible, and they decried the discord among evangelicals generated by disagreements over the Supper. Most of them adopted a pastoral tone intended to strengthen their credibility as spiritual authorities. In striking contrast to this strategy, Conrad Ryss, who was Karlstadt's most loyal supporter, did not shy away from offensive language and name-calling. Under the circumstances, it might have been justifiable to employ a polemical style to attack a traditional belief so entrenched in popular piety, and Ryss's forthright argumentation may have appealed to the common people. Nevertheless, it was also divisive and likely to alienate further those who saw the evangelical movement as a threat to public order. As Zwingli recognized, this pamphlet was a two-edged sword for the sacramentarian movement. [60]

Ryss's pamphlet suggests that by the end of 1525 the distinctions between the views of Karlstadt and Zwingli had begun to dissolve. Like clear streams flowing into a larger and muddier river, the arguments against Christ's corporeal presence and the elements that contributed to a fully subjective and communal understanding of the Supper merged into the larger public debate. We have already seen how early Zwinglianism absorbed some of Karlstadt's arguments against Christ's presence and how Bugenhagen's *Open Letter* associated the two men. Ryss's "Karlstadtian" arguments were presented as a defense of Zwingli against Bugenhagen, blurring the differences even further. One might argue that with the important exception of how the words of institution were understood, "sacramentarianism" and "early Zwinglianism" had become virtually synonymous. This does not mean, however, that the sacramentarian position had ceased to evolve. The view of the Lord's Supper advocated by Kaspar Schwenckfeld and Valentin Crautwald and their circle in Silesia illustrates the potential that still existed for the further elaboration of sacramentarian theology.

THE SILESIAN CONTRIBUTION

The Silesian understanding of the Lord's Supper represented yet another combination of evangelical beliefs with Erasmian humanism and Hussite heresy, this time tempered by an awareness of the differences between Luther, Karlstadt, and Zwingli. Works by both Luther and Zwingli—although none dealing with the sacrament—had been published in Breslau as early as 1520, and by 1524 evangelical reforms had been introduced in the city. Kaspar Schwenckfeld, a nobleman in the service of Count Frederick II of Liegnitz, played a key role in promoting evangelical teachings in Frederick's lands, and his earliest writings demonstrate his deep concern for moral reform and the need for Christians to demonstrate their inner faith by their outward actions.[61]

Reports of the disagreements concerning the Lord's Supper spread quickly to Silesia. In June 1525 Schwenckfeld wrote to Paul Speratus that divisions had developed among the evangelical party, and there were plans to seek the advice of the Wittenbergers concerning Zwingli's views, "which the Picards (otherwise a pious people), held previously."[62] A month later, Bugenhagen sent his letter criticizing Karlstadt and Zwingli to the Breslau reformer Johann Hess; a German translation was reprinted in Breslau before the end of the year. In September Schwenckfeld reported to Speratus that some were claiming that many scriptural passages concerning communion and the breaking of bread were not rightly understood, and that a true Christian church could not be restored if one retained the older understanding of the Lord's Supper.[63] A few weeks later he first mentioned to Speratus what would become one of his chief objections to Christ's corporeal presence: the claim that even the godless received Christ's body.[64] As he later wrote, concern about this issue led him to a closer study of John 6 until, enlightened by the Holy Spirit, he realized that Christ was speaking here not of baker's bread, "nor did he want to be in bread or under wheaten bread or with bread," but that he was himself the true and heavenly bread.[65]

Schwenckfeld's first written presentation of his new understanding came in the form of "Twelve Questions or Arguments on Impanation," which he circulated among his friends in the fall of 1525.[66] The key to his position was John 6:54 ("he who eats my flesh and drinks my blood has eternal life"). Christ's body and blood were a heavenly, spiritual food and drink that bestowed eternal life. They were distributed through God's word, and they were received only by a true, living faith and not by mouth. The godless who partook of the sacrament outwardly were incapable of eating and drinking this flesh and blood, and to claim otherwise would be to say that they received eternal life despite their unbelief.[67]

Schwenckfeld found confirmation of this view in the distinction frequently made in Scripture between the godless and the faithful. Throughout the "Twelve Questions" he highlighted the difference between the old and new man, the members of Christ's body and the members of Satan, those who hungered for Christ's righteousness and those who did not seek the things above, God's children and the children of wrath. Only the former could be united with Christ's body and drink the blood of Christ's new testament; the uncircumcised, the impure, and strangers were separated from Christ. It followed, therefore, that "unbelieving false Christians" had no share or participation in Christ's body and blood.[68]

In the "Twelve Questions" Schwenckfeld discussed only obliquely the importance of the Lord's Supper for believers. Spiritual communion was the chief point of the Supper, but no one was able truly to eat Christ's body and blood unless he was a disciple and had a genuine, living faith. The godless received "only the bread of the

Lord, and not the bread that is the Lord himself." At no point, however, did Schwenckfeld link spiritual eating with the bread and the wine. Christ's spiritual body and blood were distributed and received through God's word, not through the external elements. Schwenckfeld warned against leading Christians astray from the one, spiritual eating of Christ's body to a different, physical eating of his body.[69]

Schwenckfeld wrote the "Twelve Questions" just as he was beginning to think through the consequences of his rejection of Christ's corporeal presence.[70] Although he was aware of Zwingli's disagreements with Luther, he did not use any of Zwingli's most characteristic arguments, particularly John 6:63, the lens through which Zwingli interpreted the sacrament.[71] His concern with spiritual communion reflects the same ideas taken from late medieval preaching and devotional practice that were also common in early Reformation pamphlets on the mass.[72] More strikingly, his discussion of whether Judas ate Christ's body and his insistence that the godless could have nothing to do with Christ are similar to one of Karlstadt's arguments expressed in both the *Exegesis* and the *Explanation*.[73] Schwenckfeld did not discuss any of the other positions advocated in either treatise, which suggests that he may have learned of these arguments indirectly. It is possible that Karlstadt's ideas circulated in Silesia through word of mouth more widely than in written form.

Although he rejected the traditional belief in Christ's corporeal presence, Schwenckfeld could offer no alternative understanding of Christ's words of institution. That was the contribution of his friend Valentine Crautwald. Crautwald, who held the post of lecturer in theology at the Liegnitz cathedral, was both more highly educated and more directly influenced by humanism than Schwenckfeld.[74] He was drawn into the debate in September, when Schwenckfeld gave him a copy of the "Twelve Questions" and asked him to consider how his new understanding of Christ's body as spiritual bread could be reconciled with Christ's words "this is my body."[75]

Crautwald knew of and rejected Zwingli's equation of "is" with "signifies," and his initial reaction was to oppose Schwenckfeld as well. Nevertheless, to oblige Schwenckfeld he again took up both Zwingli's and Luther's writings on the Lord's Supper. His reading only raised the possibility that both men might be wrong in their understanding of Christ's words. In that frame of mind he went to sleep, and the next morning, as he returned to his studying, he felt a "mighty power, like light shining suddenly in the darkness," that revealed a new understanding of the text. Christ's words spoken during his Last Supper were to be interpreted in tandem with John 6:55 ("for my flesh is food indeed, and my blood is drink indeed"). "This is my body given for you" meant the same as "my flesh is food indeed," and so it could be understood as "my body, which is given for you, is this [sc. bread]." Encouraged by this revelation, Crautwald sought confirmation of his new understanding through prayer and further study not only of the scriptural accounts of the Last Supper but also of canon law and the church fathers. Prompted by the works of Oecolampadius and Zwingli, he found that his inverted reading of the words could be supported by "the earliest church fathers."[76]

Like Karlstadt, Crautwald came to a new understanding of "this is my body" by rearranging the order of Christ's words, which allowed him to retain a literal understanding of "is" and still reject the belief that the bread became Christ's body.[77] The use of John 6:53–57 rather than John 6:63 as the hermeneutical key to understanding the words of institution imparted a distinctive twist to Silesian eucharistic theology, for it shifted the focus away from the elements and onto the recipient. It thus accorded with Schwenckfeld's primary concern, which was not *whether* one could receive Christ's body and blood through external means but *who* was able to receive that body and blood.

Schwenckfeld had sent a copy of his "Twelve Questions" to Luther in the fall of 1525, but he received no answer. In early December Duke Frederick sent him to Wittenberg on an errand, and he took with him another copy of the "Twelve Questions" as well as Crautwald's letter and other documents concerning the Lord's Supper generated by the Silesian circle. While in Wittenberg he spent three days discussing the sacrament with Justus Jonas, Bugenhagen, and Luther.[78]

The timing of Schwenckfeld's visit to Wittenberg set the tone for the discussions themselves. The Silesian arrived less than a month after Gregor Caselius brought letters from Strasbourg's pastors asking for a suspension of the controversy over the Lord's Supper.[79] The Wittenbergers mentioned these letters several times in their discussions, and Schwenckfeld's appearance so soon after the Strasbourg mission must have heightened their alarm at the spread of sacramentarian views. For his part, Schwenckfeld wanted to know more about the Strasbourgers' position on the Lord's Supper and seemed encouraged by the fact that their criticisms of the abuses associated with traditional beliefs echoed his own.[80]

The discussions themselves were carried out in an open and friendly manner. Both sides initially expressed their willingness to learn from the other. Bugenhagen twice stated that he would retract his earlier writings if he believed Schwenckfeld was right. Schwenckfeld presented himself to Bugenhagen as someone desiring instruction on such a weighty issue.[81] Ultimately, though, each was sure of his own position and entered into the debate primarily in order to persuade the other that he was mistaken.

At the center of the discussion was the new exegesis Crautwald had suggested for the words of institution. As Luther acknowledged, if Schwenckfeld could prove the identity of the two propositions, "my flesh is food indeed" and "this is my body," he would establish his case.[82] Neither Luther nor Bugenhagen believed such an equation could be proved. Crautwald's approach did not work for Christ's words concerning the cup, it ignored the context of Christ's taking and blessing the bread, and it could not be reconciled with Paul's words about unworthy eating and discerning Christ's body.[83] As far as the Wittenbergers were concerned, this took care of the issue and ended the discussion. Schwenckfeld, however, was unmoved by the Wittenbergers' arguments. After three days of meetings, he told Luther that he had only become more convinced that his own view was the correct one.[84]

Schwenckfeld also introduced a number of other arguments against Christ's corporeal presence. The most important of these revealed the same spiritualistic dualism that shaped the views of Karlstadt and Zwingli. Schwenckfeld expressed this not so much as the contrast between flesh and spirit on the basis of John 6:63, as Zwingli did, but rather as the contrast between sign and spirit, and between the dead letter and the living word of God. To Bugenhagen's claim that God's word was joined to the sacrament as a seal, Schwenckfeld responded that one could not bind God's word to such signs. It was the role of the Holy Spirit to strengthen and confirm faith; Christ did not institute any external signs to do this. The earthly bread was an image or representation of the heavenly bread that was Christ and that could only be eaten by faith. Christ did not want us to place our faith in external, physical things, nor did faith require a strictly literal understanding of Christ's words. For this reason, the purpose of the Supper was to remember and proclaim Christ's death, not to assure consciences.[85]

Schwenckfeld also brought up the popular abuses associated with belief in Christ's bodily presence, especially the idolatry implied by the elevation and the adoration of the host.[86] On this issue he was decisively influenced by the Bohemian Brethren. Schwenckfeld not only discussed "the Picards" with Bugenhagen but gave him a copy of "the Picards' pamphlet in which they present their apology [*entschuldigung*] to the king and the lords of Bohemia." He also introduced several of the Brethren's arguments concerning Christ's bodily departure from earth and his session at the Father's right hand to support his assertion that Christ's invisible body could not be contained within or eaten as part of a visible thing. These included the angel's statement in Acts 1:11; Christ's words about his departure, John 16:7; the portions of the Apostles' Creed concerning Christ's ascension, session, and return; and the warning against regarding a created thing as the Creator.[87]

A final issue that came up repeatedly over the course of the discussions was the role of revelation. The Wittenbergers were unmoved by Crautwald's letter describing how he had come to his new understanding of the words of institution. As they pointed out, Zwingli also claimed that his understanding of the words was confirmed by a revelation. Since he and Crautwald disagreed on the interpretation of "this is my body," one or both of them had to be wrong.[88] Moreover, the

Wittenbergers regarded the differences between Karlstadt, the Swiss, and the Silesians as obvious proof that all of them were in error. They dismissed Schwenckfeld's assertion that at base all three parties agreed, just as they had dismissed Oecolampadius's claim that he and Zwingli understood the words of institution to mean the same thing, although they explained that meaning with different words.[89]

The Wittenberg discussions allowed Schwenckfeld to elaborate on a broader range of issues than he had discussed in the "Twelve Questions." For the first time he described the relationship between word and signs, the proper understanding of the elements of bread and wine, and the purpose of the Supper.[90] Schwenckfeld's frequent citation of John 6 obscured the fact that like both Luther and Zwingli, he separated the spiritual eating of Christ's flesh and blood from reception of the Lord's Supper. God worked through his word, not through any external thing. While that word was certainly present at the celebration of the Supper, it had no more prominence there than at any other time. The public breaking of bread gave Christians the opportunity to remember and to proclaim the Lord's death, but it had no further spiritual significance, whether for the individual or for the congregation. It would therefore not be difficult for Schwenckfeld to suggest only a few months later that celebration of the Lord's Supper be suspended.[91]

Schwenckfeld apparently departed from Wittenberg in the belief that he had made a positive impression on Luther and his colleagues. It is an open question whether the Silesian nobleman was misled by the Wittenbergers' deference toward him, but in fact Luther had no sympathy for Schwenckfeld's view. In April he wrote to Schwenckfeld, asserting that he could find no connection between John 6 and the words of institution, admonishing him to abandon his error, and warning him not to lead others astray.[92] Luther's admonition came too late, for both Schwenckfeld and Crautwald had continued to elaborate their own understanding of the Supper and to circulate their writings in Silesia. In April they also entered into direct contact with the Swiss and the Strasbourgers, and they would increasingly be drawn into the theological orbit of the Zwinglians.[93]

DIVERSITY AND DYNAMISM

The developments in Silesia demonstrate the diversity and the dynamic nature of the sacramentarian understanding of the Lord's Supper. The sacramentarian movement was indeed "one body with many heads," not in Luther's negative sense of a group divided among itself but in the more positive sense of a common core of beliefs that were elaborated in various ways by many individuals. The sacramentarians were obviously united in their rejection of Christ's corporeal presence, but this view was only the logical consequence of a more significant common understanding of the nature of reality. Karlstadt, Zwingli, the Silesians, and their supporters all shared a neoplatonic dualism that separated physical from spiritual, external from internal, and old from new, and that subordinated the former to the latter. Their metaphysical presuppositions caused them to reject Christ's corporeal presence in the elements, which in turn required them to answer a host of related questions concerning the Lord's Supper. Table 6.2 summarizes the way the major players in the eucharistic controversy addressed these issues over the course of 1525.

The first and most fundamental of these issues was the interpretation of Christ's statement "this is my body." To avoid the traditional literal understanding of these words, they all insisted that Christ's words had to be interpreted in the light of other scriptural texts or principles that upheld their dualist metaphysic. For Karlstadt, the hermeneutical key was the distinction between the figures and prophecies of the Old Testament and their fulfillment in the New Testament; the former were material, and the latter were spiritual. Like Erasmus, he found this dualism at the heart of the epistle to the Hebrews, especially Hebrews 9–10; it was also supported by John 6:63, which contrasted the value of flesh and spirit. Zwingli placed even more emphasis on John 6:63, making it the foundation of his view of the Supper. The Silesians chose John 6:53–57, highlighting the spiritual communion enjoyed by believers and denied to the godless. While the Zwinglians accepted Hoen's argument that "is" meant "signifies," both Karlstadt and the Silesians changed the order of Christ's words in order to come up with a literal use of "is" that allowed them to interpret the words of institution in a nonliteral way.

Luther and his colleagues rejected both the dualist metaphysic of the sacramentarians and their argument that the words of institution needed an interpretive lens in order to be understood properly. They argued that it was incorrect to use John 6:63 to teach a sharp division between flesh and spirit and that John 6:53–57 had nothing to do with the Supper. The words of institution were clear and had to be interpreted literally and directly. Because they regarded Christ's words of institution as the basis for understanding the sacrament, rather than as a text to be interpreted by means of other Scripture, they were bound to consider the disagreements among the sacramentarians concerning the interpretation of those words as more significant than the sacramentarians themselves did.

In addition to their interpretation of Christ's words, the major contributors to the controversy all used a metaphor or series of metaphors to explain the significance of the Supper. Luther's early understanding of the sacrament as Christ's testament, based on Hebrews 9:15–17, was enormously influential in the early years of the Reformation, although Luther had ceased to use the concept by the time the

TABLE 6.2

Interpretations of the Lord's Supper, 1524–1525

Issue	Hoen	Karlstadt	Luther	Zwingli/ Oecolampadius	Schwenckfeld/ Crautwald
Interpretation of words of institution	Figurative: this [bread] signifies my body	Literal: this [body] is my body given for you	Literal: this [bread] is my body	Figurative: this [bread] signifies my body (Z); this [bread] is [a figure of] my body (O)	Literal: my body is this [spiritual bread]
Hermeneutical key		OT figure/NT fulfillment; John 6:63	Words of institution: This is my body	John 6:63: [my] flesh is of no avail	John 6: 54–57: my flesh is food indeed
Interpretation of John 6:63		*Visible flesh does not make holy*	Flesh is carnal understanding	Flesh is Christ's physical body	
Dominant metaphor	Wedding ring; key or staff transferring authority	Meal of remembrance	*Testament; mass not a good work*	Meal of remembrance; *mass not a sacrifice*	
Purpose of Lord's Supper	Pledge of assurance; Christ giving self through bread	Ardent remembrance	*Assurance of consciences; appropriation of forgiveness*	Remembrance, public testimony, fraternal union	Remembrance and proclamation in public assembly
Chief actor		Individual	*God acting through word and signs/elements*	Individual and congregation	Individual
Luke 22:20/ 1 Cor. 11:25 (cup is new testament)		Blood not bodily in cup; cup is vessel to recall shed blood	Cup is new testament because of blood it contains	Cup is sign of new testament	

1 Cor. 10:16 (koinonia of blood/body)	Bread signifies participation in Christ's body	Fellowship with Christ and other Christians	Distribution/sharing of physical body	Spiritual communion of the faithful
1 Cor. 11:27–29 (worthy eating/discerning the body)	Recognition of eating more than what is taken by the mouth	Sincere remembrance of passion	*Awareness of sinfulness, desire for assurance;* belief in Christ's corporeal presence	Unfeigned faith, renouncing sinful life
Other scriptural proof texts	1 Cor. 10:3–4; Matt. 16:18; John 6:49–51; Matt. 24:23; John 16:17	1 Cor. 10:3–4; Heb. 9–10		Gen. 41:26–7; Exod. 12:11; 1 Cor. 10:3–4
Other arguments against corporeal presence	—Miracles always visible —Corporeal presence not in Creed	—"Bless" does not mean "consecrate" —Externals cannot sanctify —Judas/godless do not partake of body/blood —Christ not brought down from heaven	—Testimony of church fathers —Christ's body at Father's right hand (from Bohemian Brethren) —Lord's Supper as replacement for or parallel to Passover	—Christ's body received spiritually through word —Judas/godless do not partake of body/blood —Spirit not tied to externals —Testimony of earliest church fathers

Table based on Hoen, Most Christian Letter, Spruyt, Hoen, pp. 226–235; Karlstadt's pamphlets of 1524–1525; Luther, Sermon on the New Testament, WA 6: 353–378, On the Adoration of the Sacrament, WA 11: 417–456, and Part II of Against the Heavenly Prophets, WA 18: 134–214; Zwingli, Epistle to Alber, Z 3: 335–354, Commentary on True and False Religion, Z 3: 773–820, Action oder Bruch des Nachtmals, Z 4: 13–24; and Subsidium, Z 4: 458–504; Oecolampadius, Genuine Exposition; Crautwald, Letter to Schwenckfeld, CS 2:194–209; Schwenckfeld: IIII. Sendbrief, CS 2: 240–282, "Twelve Questions"/Christlich Bedencken, CS 3: 498–507. Views expressed before 1524 are in italics.

eucharistic controversy began.[94] Hoen used the traditional analogy of the wedding ring and of a key or staff transferring authority. He may have been influenced by Luther's view of the elements as a pledge of forgiveness, for he implied that something of spiritual significance was actually given along with the elements of the Supper, but unlike Luther he abandoned belief in Christ's corporeal presence. His metaphors of the ring and the staff were transformed by the Zwinglians to emphasize the representational power of physical objects or the remembrance they prompted, rather than the transfer of anything by means of them.[95] Both Karlstadt and Zwingli used Christ's last meal with his disciples as the basis for understanding the sacrament. The Lord's Supper was both a reenactment and a remembrance of that meal, and no further metaphor was necessary to explain its significance.

The sacramentarians also had to redefine the purpose of the Lord's Supper, because their separation of external and internal precluded the possibility that the elements could convey any spiritual benefit. Echoing St. Paul, they described the Supper as the remembrance and proclamation of Christ's death, but they weighted those terms differently. Although Karlstadt acknowledged the fellowship that existed among those who celebrated the Supper together, his focus remained on the individual recipient. Zwingli also recognized the purpose of the sacrament as recalling Christ's passion, but he gave more emphasis to the corporate aspect of the Supper. Influenced by the etymological links between *sacramentum* and oath, he associated proclamation with the public testimony of faith made when one received the Supper in the presence of other Christians.[96] In comparison to Karlstadt and Zwingli, Schwenckfeld's discussion of the Supper's purpose was still superficial at the end of 1525, and he did not attempt to define or elaborate on what either remembrance or proclamation entailed. His focus on spiritual communion, however, inclined him to the same concern for the individual that characterized Karlstadt's thought rather than the corporate emphasis apparent in Zwingli's writings.

Just as the purpose of the meal was redefined, so too was its worthy reception. In all of his early works Luther emphasized that worthy preparation consisted of the recognition of one's own sinfulness and need for grace. Only after the outbreak of the controversy did it become clear that he shared the medieval assumption that worthy eating also required a belief in Christ's corporeal presence in the elements. Although Hoen rejected Christ's corporeal presence in the elements, he still recognized a spiritual manducation associated with reception of the elements, so that those who thought they received only what they took by mouth ate judgment upon themselves.[97] Karlstadt's emphasis on ardent remembrance was so strong that he virtually equated it with faith, and if this ardor was lacking, one could not receive the sacrament worthily.[98] Zwingli held that worthy reception required genuine faith and the desire to live a sinless life befitting a child of God. The public character of the Supper meant that those who did not have such a mind-set were hypocrites who received the Supper unworthily.[99]

The question of worthy reception illustrates the importance of differences in interpreting key Scripture texts. Just as Luther and the sacramentarians disagreed fundamentally on their exegesis of 1 Corinthians 11:27–29, so they disagreed in their understanding of the communion or communication of Christ's body and blood (1 Cor. 10:16–17) and of Christ's reference to the cup as the new testament in his blood (1 Cor. 11:25/Luke 22:20). The sacramentarians introduced other Scripture passages to support their views as well. Some of these, such as St. Paul's statement that "the rock was Christ" (1 Cor. 10:3–4) were associated with medieval heresy; once introduced into the discussion, they were used by almost everyone. Other passages, most notably Zwingli's understanding of "[the lamb] is the Passover" (Exod. 12:11), were introduced at a specific point in the debate and so can be used as markers to detect the influence of the work in which they were introduced.

Last but not least, there were a number of arguments derived only secondarily from Scripture or based on reason that became part of the common arsenal against Christ's corporeal presence. Some of these came from the late medieval heretical tradition and were introduced into the broader public discussion of the sacrament by Hoen and Karlstadt, such as the claim that the creeds of the early church did not require belief in Christ's corporeal presence or that Christ's body was located in heaven at the right hand of the Father. The interpretation of the church fathers advanced by Zwingli and especially Oecolampadius would prove attractive to the humanistically trained reformers in Strasbourg and Silesia. The Strasbourgers and the Silesians also took up Karlstadt's argument that neither Judas nor any godless person could partake of Christ's body but received only bread in the Supper. Finally, the analogy drawn by Zwingli and Oecolampadius between Passover and the Lord's Supper as celebrations instituted to commemorate and give thanks for God's saving actions in the past would be frequently repeated in the polemical battle with Luther and his followers.

This summary reveals the diversity of the early sacramentarian movement and, by extension, the complexity of the debate over the Lord's Supper from its very beginning. Too often the eucharistic controversy is depicted as a static contest between two sides, the one following Luther and the other Zwingli. One cannot so easily identify the sacramentarian position with Zwingli, however. The Zurich reformer certainly played a key role, but others also contributed to the formulation of sacramentarian theology, as they drew out the logical consequences of their rejection of Christ's corporeal presence. The variety of authors who formulated these elements led inevitably to greater diversity and mutual influence than was true among Luther's supporters.

On the surface, it seems less problematic to characterize the Lutheran position as both uniform and static. As the single most influential figure within the evangelical movement, Luther dominated the discussion of the sacrament, and the works by his colleagues Bugenhagen and von Amsdorf only strengthened the appearance of cohesion among the Wittenbergers. Moreover, Luther and his supporters could draw on a long theological tradition to support their defense of Christ's corporeal presence, which made it easier to formulate a uniform response to the sacramentarians.

Careful consideration of the developments, however, shows that assumptions about the static nature and uniformity of the Lutheran party are misleading. Urbanus Rhegius defended Christ's corporeal presence, but he was surprisingly open to some of Karlstadt's arguments.[100] These differences would become more apparent in early 1526 with the publication of several works by authors outside of Wittenberg arguing in support of Christ's corporeal presence. From Nuremberg, Willibald Pirckheimer would endorse Luther's arguments against Karlstadt, but in some ways his defense of the miraculous transformation that occurred in the Lord's Supper sounded closer to Catholic teaching than to Luther, and he was far more concerned with refuting the Zwinglians' use of the church fathers than the Wittenbergers were. Theobald Billican echoed the Wittenbergers' insistence that the meaning of the Lord's Supper was based on a literal understanding of Christ's words of institution, but his examination of those words betrayed the greater influence of humanist philology. The *Syngramma on the Words of the Lord's Supper*, written by Johannes Brenz in the name of his Swabian colleagues, presented a defense of Christ's corporeal presence that also agreed with Luther but that stood out by its emphasis on the consecratory power of Christ's words and that could be interpreted as denying the *manducatio impiorum*.[101] Most important for the long run would be the small but significant differences between Luther and Melanchthon over the way to describe the relationship of Christ's body to the bread—"in" and "under," as opposed to "with"—that emerged over the course of 1527.[102] Oecolampadius would soon be able to claim that those supporting Christ's corporeal presence were as divided among themselves as Luther believed his opponents to be.[103]

Just as important, the issues being debated would change over time. There are indications already in 1525 of an alternative to the two options of either Luther's "corporeal presence" or Zwingli's "real absence" of Christ's body: that of Christ's real but spiritual presence in or with the elements. Karlstadt had acknowledged in his *Dialogue* that no one questioned whether Christ was present in the sacrament according to his divinity, since as God he could be everywhere. He decisively shaped the ensuing debate, however, by asking whether Christ was corporeally present in the bread and wine, a question that could only be answered either yes or no.[104] In the wake of the Marburg Colloquy of 1529, as individuals on both sides sought common ground, the debate shifted back to the question of Christ's presence more generally, particularly *the way in which* Christ was present in the sacrament (whether to the eyes of faith, in the actions of the sacrament, through the word, or in the elements of bread and wine) and *how* that presence could be described (as real, substantial, true, virtual, sacramental, or some other term).

These developments lie beyond the chronological limits of this study and so will not be pursued further. But just as individuals are shaped by the events of their youth, so the course of the eucharistic controversy would be shaped by the positions, polemics, and personalities so important at its very beginning. The eucharistic controversy took root in the rich soil of late medieval piety and heresy, it was watered by various understandings of the sacrament circulating in the early years of Reformation, and its later growth would be characterized by the diversity and dynamism apparent already in 1525.

Appendix

THE PUBLICATION OF KARLSTADT'S EUCHARISTIC PAMPHLETS, 1524–1525

The printing history of Karlstadt's eucharistic pamphlets is closely linked to two of Karlstadt's closest associates, his brother-in-law Gerhard Westerburg and the Jena pastor Martin Reinhart, as well as to his own travels after his banishment from Saxony. Most accounts of Karlstadt's movements rely on the itinerary suggested by Hermann Barge in his biography of Karlstadt, but Barge's account needs to be revised in light of more recent findings.

Shortly after his meeting with Luther on 22 August 1524, Karlstadt dispatched Westerburg to Zurich with manuscripts of eight pamphlets, five of them dealing with the Lord's Supper. The Zurich humanist and soon-to-be Anabaptist Conrad Grebel had established contact with Karlstadt sometime during that summer, and Karlstadt apparently hoped that Grebel and his friends in Zurich would help with the publication of these pamphlets.[1] Westerburg arrived in the Swiss city perhaps as early as mid-September and certainly no later than the first week of October. He stayed in Zurich for six days before leaving for Basel to have the pamphlets printed. He was accompanied by Felix Manz and possibly by Andreas Castelberger, who would eventually take copies of the printed pamphlets back to Zurich.[2]

More information about Westerburg's activities comes from the two Basel printers, Thomas Wolff and Johann Bebel, who were questioned by the city authorities in early December. Bebel's statement confirms this general time frame, for he said that he had been contacted by Westerburg "a week or two after the Frankfurt fair," which ended on 21 September.[3] Westerburg's first contact with the printer thus occurred in late September or early October. According to Wolff, Westerburg had come to Basel looking for the printer Adam Petri. Petri not only had published many of Luther's works but also had reprinted three of Karlstadt's pamphlets, and so it is logical that he would be the first printer that Westerburg would seek out. Petri was out of town at the time, however, and so after waiting a week, Westerburg approached Wolff, who was a logical alternative to Petri. Over the previous few years he had printed four editions of Luther's New Testament as well as a few of Luther's Latin pamphlets; he had also published several of Melanchthon's New Testament commentaries and Erasmus's paraphrase of Luke. He had thus demonstrated that he was sympathetic to the evangelical cause and willing to print the works of those associated with Wittenberg. Most of Wolff's publications were in Latin, however, and the printer told Westerburg that he did not want to print anything in German that might offend the authorities. Westerburg assured him that the pamphlets contained nothing that criticized secular rulers, only "the evil priests who have many benefices and [attack] the gospel." Westerburg also volunteered to serve as corrector, since Wolff's regular corrector was out of town, and he promised to purchase 300 copies of each pamphlet himself.[4]

Wolff eventually printed four pamphlets, including the three that said nothing about Christ's presence in the Lord's Supper: *Whether We Should Go Slowly and Avoid Offending the Weak, How Belief and Unbelief Relate to Light and Darkness*, and *Against the Old and New Papistic Masses*.[5] Wolff claimed that he did not remember their titles, and since Westerburg served as corrector, it is likely that the printer did not read any of them and was therefore unaware of the radical nature of the fourth pamphlet, *Whether One . . . Can Prove*.

The most polemical pamphlets were given to Johann Bebel. Bebel had set up his press in Basel the previous year and printed mostly Latin works, in part as a subcontractor for Andreas Cratander.[6] Westerburg may have sought Bebel out for these very reasons: as a relative new-comer with a low profile, he may have been more willing to print controversial works, but his ties with Cratander were also evidence of evangelical sympathies. Nevertheless, Westerburg took the precaution of giving Bebel only one of the remaining four pamphlets at a time, and he accompanied Bebel when the printer took the first pamphlet, the *Anti-Christian Abuse*, to Johann Oecolampadius to get his approval. After a hasty reading, Oecolampadius allowed the pamphlet to be printed at Westerburg's expense; for this reason Bebel produced only 300 copies. Westerburg then persuaded Bebel to print a thousand copies of the *Dialogue*, promising to pay for 300 of them and swearing that "it was Christian and good and not against anyone but only contained the pure truth."[7]

In the meantime, Karlstadt himself had arrived in Basel. He was banished from Saxony on 18 September. Although Barge assumed that Karlstadt did not leave until 26 September, the day after the duke rejected a request to rescind that banishment, he was apparently in Rothenburg ob der Tauber by 22 September, and he remained in that area through 8 October.[8] Over the next month he traveled to Strasbourg, Basel, and Zurich, but the next documented evidence of his whereabouts is a brief visit to Heidelberg on 7 November.

Barge believed that Karlstadt traveled from Rothenburg to Strasbourg and then on to Zurich, where he met with Grebel and his circle, and that he did not arrive in Basel, where Westerburg was overseeing the publication of Karlstadt's pamphlets, until the end of October.[9] This reconstruction of Karlstadt's movements is problematic from a number of per-spectives, however. To begin with, the time involved in traveling from Saxony to the upper Rhine and Zurich and then back to Heidelberg simply does not allow for so many detours and side trips. It took Strasbourg's messenger three weeks to travel from Strasbourg to Wittenberg just a few weeks later.[10] If Karlstadt traveled at the same pace, he could not have arrived in Strasbourg before the third week of October. This leaves only two weeks for his visits to the other cities, taking into account not only his stays in each but also the time needed for travel between them. Barge cited Strasbourg's reputation as a printing center as the justification for Karlstadt's visit, but Karlstadt had no reason to seek out Strasbourg's printers when he had already sent the pamphlets with Westerburg to Zurich.[11] Karlstadt may have hoped that his

Zurich contacts could arrange to have the pamphlets printed in that city. Even if he anticipated that Westerburg would continue on to Basel to publish the pamphlets, however, the easiest way to find his colleague was to go to Zurich first, so that his contacts there could tell him how to find Westerburg. Furthermore, the major trade routes from Saxony ran directly south through Nuremberg, Augsburg, and Zurich. A trip to Strasbourg would have made sense only if Karlstadt knew that Westerburg was going to Basel and was confident of his ability to find him in that city.[12]

It seems more likely that Karlstadt followed in Westerburg's footsteps, going first to Zurich and then on to Basel. Nine months later, Zwingli would write that Karlstadt came to Zurich "for no other reason than to confer with me upon a thing unfamiliar to the ears of the people" and was deterred from that meeting by "the melancholic spirit of certain people." Since the Zurich reformer did not meet with Karlstadt, he may not have realized that Karlstadt's visit to Zurich was motivated by his contact with Grebel and his need to find Westerburg rather than by a desire to meet Zwingli.[13]

Karlstadt must have arrived in Zurich in mid-October, probably within a few days after Grebel wrote to Vadian about Westerburg's visit.[14] From Zurich he went on to Basel, where he finally met up with Westerburg. There he added his postscript to the *Exegesis* before it was printed by Bebel. By this time, though, the printer was worried that printing these pamphlets would get him into trouble with the authorities. In fact, the fourth pamphlet he was given, a dialogue on infant baptism, proved to be the last straw. After the typesetter warned him that the pamphlet attacked Luther, Bebel took the pamphlet to Oecolampadius for approval. This time Oecolampadius told him not to print it. Manz then took the manuscript to Wolff, who also refused to print the pamphlet, and so it remained unpublished.[15] Karlstadt and Westerburg did not know about the problem with the printers, though, for they had already left Basel for Strasbourg, bearing with them copies of the seven pamphlets already printed. According to this reconstruction, then, all of the eucharistic pamphlets were in print by the last week of October, when Karlstadt arrived in Strasbourg.[16]

Karlstadt stayed in Strasbourg for four days, during which time he may have made preliminary arrangements to publish another pamphlet, *The Reasons Why Andreas Karlstadt Was Expelled from Saxony*. Although he avoided Capito and the other pastors, Karlstadt did meet with some of the more radical circles of laity in the city. Accompanied by "a certain physician," probably Otto Brunfels, he then left Strasbourg, stopping only briefly in Heidelberg on his way to Schweinfurt, where he wrote Duke John Frederick to ask if he could return to Saxony to be with his pregnant wife.[17]

On 9 November, two days after Karlstadt's visit to Heidelberg, Martin Frecht wrote to the Ulm physician Wolfgang Rychart summarizing Karlstadt's new understanding of the Eucharist. The letter is important not only for what it tells us about Karlstadt's travels but also about how his ideas were both transmitted and received.[18] According to Frecht, Karlstadt left copies of four eucharistic pamphlets with the Greek professor Simon Grynaeus. Frecht did not mention either the *Anti-Christian Abuse*, whose entire print run had probably been taken by Westerburg and the Zurichers who had paid for them, or the two pamphlets on other topics, and he specified that the pamphlets on the Lord's Supper were being distributed clandestinely. Frecht mentioned Karlstadt's supporters in both Strasbourg and Rothenburg, but he was apparently unaware of the role played by the Zurich proto-Anabaptists in distributing Karlstadt's pamphlets in Switzerland.[19] The letter is therefore strong evidence that all of the eucharistic pamphlets were in clandestine circulation by early November. Although the Strasbourg Council prohibited both the printing and the sale of Karlstadt's works, *Against the Old and New Papistic*

Masses was reprinted there before the end of the year, while the other three that Frecht listed were published in that city in 1525.[20]

Basel and Strasbourg were not the only cities where Karlstadt's eucharistic pamphlets were printed, however, and this brings us to the activities of another of Karlstadt's disciples, the Jena pastor Martin Reinhart.[21] Reinhart was responsible for publishing the account of Karlstadt's meeting with Luther and of the latter's visit to Orlamünde two days later. *What Dr. Andreas Bodenstein von Karlstadt Discussed with Doctor Martin Luther in Jena* was printed in Wertheim within a month of that meeting; Luther had a copy of the pamphlet by the beginning of October.[22] Reinhart was also expelled from Saxony, possibly at the same time as Karlstadt in September but most certainly by the end of October. When he left he must have had manuscript copies of Karlstadt's two last eucharistic pamphlets.[23] Traveling via Bamberg, Reinhart was in Nuremberg by early November, where Hieronymus Höltzel printed the *Anti-Christian Abuse* and began work on the *Dialogue*.[24] When this came to the attention of the authorities in mid-December, they expelled Reinhart and forbade the sale of any books not on a list that they had approved.[25] Reinhart took the pages of the *Dialogue* that Höltzel had printed to the Bamberg printer Georg Erlinger, who finished the pamphlet.[26] From Nuremberg and Bamberg copies of these pamphlets spread to other cities in southeastern Germany, and the *Anti-Christian Abuse* was reprinted in Augsburg before the end of 1524.

The diffusion of Karlstadt's pamphlets in Franconia had an impact similar to developments in Strasbourg. Karlstadt's ideas had reached the region by the fall of 1524, when the Nuremberg Council received reports that various individuals were propagating erroneous beliefs about the sacrament. The painter Hans Greiffenberger was arrested at the end of October for his views on the Lord's Supper. His confession shows some similarities to Karlstadt's ideas, including an emphasis on remembrance as the purpose of the Supper and the definition of unworthy eating as not eating the bread and wine "in unity and blessedness." Two months later Erasmus Wisberger was arrested after reading aloud from Karlstadt's pamphlets in the marketplace. The "godless painters" and Hans Denck were also questioned about their views concerning the sacrament in January 1525 and expelled soon afterward.[27] In contrast to the situation in Strasbourg, then, the Nuremberg city council took prompt and firm action against those who questioned Christ's presence in the sacrament, and the city remained relatively untroubled by controversy over the Lord's Supper.[28]

Karlstadt had in the meantime returned to Rothenburg. At the end of January, the Rothenburg Council forbade its citizens to shelter Karlstadt, who then left the city for the area around Nördlingen. By mid-February, however, he had returned to Rothenburg, where he lived in secret with the former Burgermeister Ehrenfried Kumpf.[29] While there, he received a copy of the second part of *Against the Heavenly Prophets* and wrote his response, the *Explanation of 1 Cor. 10*. The pamphlet was printed by the Augsburg publisher Philipp Ulhart and was circulating in the area by the middle of April. Karlstadt wrote his final eucharistic pamphlet, *On the New and Old Testament*, in mid-March but was not able to have it printed before mid-April, when he entrusted it to the book peddler Lienhart Götz. Götz in turn took the manuscript to Ulhart in Augsburg, who printed it soon thereafter. By this time Karlstadt had developed a circle of disciples in Rothenburg, and he even preached on the sacrament himself at Easter time.[30] His influence on the development of the South German Anabaptist movement was thus distinct from his influence on the early Anabaptist movement in Switzerland and Strasbourg not only chronologically but also with regard to publication of his pamphlets.

Karlstadt was forced to leave Rothenburg at the end of May by the events of the Peasants' War. With Luther's intervention, and at the price of writing two pamphlets in which he disassociated himself from the peasant unrest and urged readers to compare his writings on the Lord's Supper to Scripture, he was allowed to resettle in Saxony. He did not abandon his views, however, and in early 1529 he fled Saxony in order to avoid imprisonment.[31] After a year of wandering in Holstein and East Frisia, he went south to Strasbourg, and then to Switzerland, where he was welcomed with open arms. He was given a temporary position in the Zurich church upon his arrival in that city in 1530. Four years later he was appointed professor of Old Testament at the university of Basel, and in 1535 he was given a pastorate in the city as well.[32]

Karlstadt published nothing further about the Lord's Supper, but along with the rest of Basel's ministers he signed the Wittenberg Concord in 1536. His later career in Basel was not without controversy, but the issue at stake shifted from the sacrament to the magistrate's right to intervene in ecclesiastical affairs and his own position within Basel's church. Even his death of the plague at the end of 1541 contributed to his notoriety, for it was reported that he had seen a demon several times in the months before his final illness.[33]

⌒———

PREFACE

1. E. Gordon Rupp, *Patterns of Reformation* (Philadelphia: Fortress, 1969), pp. 141–142.

INTRODUCTION

1. The incident is described in WA 15: 338–339; English translation in Sider, *Battle*, pp. 47–48.

2. The two classic accounts are both in German: Walther Köhler, *Zwingli und Luther: Ihre Streit über das Abendmahl nach seinen politischen und religiösen Beziehungen*, 2 vols., Quellen und Forschungen zur Reformationsgeschichte 6–7 (Gütersloh: Bertelsmann, 1924–1953); and Ernst Bizer, *Studien zur Geschichte des Abendmahlsstreits im 16. Jahrhundert*, 2nd ed. (Darmstadt: Wissenschaftliche Buchgesellschaft, 1962). Both need to be updated to reflect the research of the last few generations. The most detailed study in English, Hermann Sasse, *This Is My Body: Luther's Contention for the Real Presence in the Sacrament of the Altar* (Minneapolis: Augsburg, 1959), is written from a confessional Lutheran perspective, while the older work of Alexander Barclay, *The Protestant Doctrine of the Lord's Supper: A Study in the Eucharistic Teaching of Luther, Zwingli and Calvin* (Glasgow: Jackson, Wylie & Co., 1927), is more sympathetic to Zwingli.

3. I use the comparison to archaeology as a metaphor rather than in conscious opposition to the history of ideas, as Michel Foucault does in *The Archaeology of Knowledge and the Discourse on Language*, trans. A. M. Sheridan Smith (New York: Pantheon, 1972), pp. 135–140. My approach comes closer to his understanding of "genealogy," hence the plural "origins" in the book's subtitle; Michel Foucault, "Nietzsche, Genealogy, History," in *Language, Counter-Memory, Practice: Selected Essays and Interviews*, ed. D. F. Bouchard (Ithaca: Cornell University Press, 1977),

pp. 139–164. Ultimately, however, I am here more interested in the social history of ideas than in analysis of the discourse concerning the Lord's Supper.

4. In addition to Sasse, *This Is My Body*, pp. 143–186, and Barclay, *Protestant Doctrine*, pp. 38–106, see Robert H. Fischer, "Luther's Stake in the Lord's Supper Controversy," *Dialogue* 2 (1963): 50–59, W. Peter Stephens, *The Theology of Huldrych Zwingli* (Oxford: Clarendon, 1986), pp. 235–250, and Alasdair I. C. Heron, *Table and Tradition* (Philadelphia: Westminster, 1983), pp. 108–122.

5. My thinking in this respect has been influenced by the approach of the Cambridge school to the study of early modern political thought, especially the essays collected in Quentin Skinner, *Visions of Politics*, vol. 1, *Regarding Method* (Cambridge: Cambridge University Press, 2002), and the example of J. G. A. Pocock, *The Machiavellian Moment: Florentine Political Thought and the Atlantic Republican Tradition* (Princeton: Princeton University Press, 1975).

6. Roger Chartier, "Texts, Printings, Readings," in *The New Cultural History*, ed. Lynn Hunt (Berkeley: University of California Press, 1989), pp. 154–175. For a useful summary of how researchers understand the construction of learning, see the first two chapters of the report of the National Research Council, John Bransford et al., *How People Learn: Brain, Mind, Experience, and School: Expanded Edition* (Washington, D.C.: National Academy Press, 2000).

7. Barge, *Karlstadt*; see also his "Luther und Karlstadt in Wittenberg: Eine kritische Untersuchung," *Historische Zeitschrift* 99 (1907): 256–324. August Wilhelm Dieckhoff's chapter on Karlstadt and Luther in his history of the eucharistic controversy is a good example of the earlier approach, comparing Karlstadt's "false reformatory movement" with the "true evangelical Reformation represented by Luther," *Die evangelische Abendmahlslehre im Reformationszeitalter* (Göttingen: Vandenhoeck & Ruprecht, 1854), pp. 299–351, citation at p. 299.

8. Karl Müller, *Luther und Karlstadt: Stücke aus ihrem gegenseitigen Verhältnis* (Tübingen: Mohr, 1907); Hermann Barge, *Frühprotestantisches Gemeindechristentum in Wittenberg und Orlamünde: Zugleich eine Abwehr gegen Karl Müllers "Luther und Karlstadt"* (Leipzig: Heinsius, 1909). A useful summary and evaluation of the points debated by Barge and Müller is the untitled review article by Walther Köhler, *Göttingische gelehrte Anzeigen* 174 (1912): 515–550; a discussion of the larger significance of the debate, Jens-Martin Kruse, "Karlstadt als Wittenberger Theologe. Überlegungen zu einer pluralen Darstellungsweise der frühen Reformation," *Mennonitische Geschichtsblätter* 57 (2000): 7–30.

9. Müller, WB. The documents were also assembled and published together as a separate book (Leipzig: Heinsius, 1911). I have used the first edition, but to make it easier to consult the second edition I have cited both pages and document numbers.

10. Sigrid Looß summarizes much of this research in "Andreas Bodenstein von Karlstadt (1486–1541) in der modernen Forschung," in Sigrid Looß and Markus Matthias, eds., *Andreas Bodenstein von Karlstadt (1486–1541): Ein Theologe der frühen Reformation. Beiträge eines Arbeitsgesprächs vom 24–25. November 1995 in Wittenberg* (Wittenberg: Drei Kastanien Verlag, 1998), pp. 9–23. The most important works in English include Hans J. Hillerbrand, "Andreas Bodenstein of Carlstadt, Prodigal Reformer," *Church History* 35 (1966): 379–398; James S. Preus, *Carlstadt's "Ordinaciones" and Luther's Liberty: A Study of the Wittenberg Movement 1521–22*, Harvard Theological Studies 27 (Cambridge, Mass.: Harvard University Press, 1974); Sider, *Karlstadt*; and Calvin Pater, *Karlstadt as Father of the Baptist Movements: The Emergence of Lay Protestantism* (Toronto: University of Toronto Press, 1984). E. Gordon Rupp's discussion of Karlstadt's eucharistic ideas, like the rest of his biography of Karlstadt, is more superficial; *Patterns of Reformation* (Philadelphia: Fortress, 1969), pp. 49–153, esp. pp. 141–148.

11. The tendency is evident in both Ralf Ponader, "'Caro nichil prodest. Joan. vi. Das fleisch ist nicht nutz/sonder der geist.' Karlstadts Abendmahlsverständnis in der Auseinandersetzung mit Martin Luther," in Looß and Matthias, *Andreas Bodenstein von Karlstadt*, pp. 223–245; and Crerar Douglas, "The Coherence of Andreas Bodenstein von Karlstadt's Early Evangelical Doctrine of the Lord's Supper, 1521–1525" (Ph.D. diss., Hartford Seminary Foundation, 1973).

12. Spruyt, *Hoen.*

13. The *Oxford English Dictionary* points out that the term is understood by Roman Catholics and Lutherans to mean the presence of Christ's actual body and blood, while the Church of England understands it as the presence of body and blood in a "heavenly and spiritual manner"; s.v. "real," A. adj., 2a.

14. This is at least implied in Stephens's account of Zwingli's eucharistic theology, *Theology*, pp. 218–259, and it can be seen in the correspondence of the Strasbourg reformers from the fall of 1525; see chapter 5.

CHAPTER 1

1. In addition to the works cited in the introduction, see Martin Brecht, *Martin Luther*, vol. 2, *Shaping and Defining the Reformation, 1521–1532*, trans. James L. Schaaf (Minneapolis: Fortress, 1990), pp. 25–45, and Heinz Scheible, *Melanchthon. Eine Biographie* (Munich: Beck, 1997), pp. 59–74.

2. The best brief overview of Luther's early eucharistic theology is Hans Grass, *Die Abendmahlslehre bei Luther und Calvin. Eine kritische Untersuchung*, 2nd ed., Beiträge zur Förderung christlicher Theologie, 2. Reihe, 47. Band (Gütersloh: Bertelsmann, 1954), pp. 17–37; see also Wolfgang Schwab, *Entwicklung und Gestalt der Sakramentstheologie bei Martin Luther*, Europäische Hochschulschriften: Reihe 23, Theologie 79 Frankfurt am Main: Lang, 1977), pp. 169–226, and Thomas J. Davis, "'The Truth of the Divine Words': Luther's Sermons on the Eucharist, 1521–1528 and the Structure of Eucharistic Meaning," in Davis, *This Is My Body: The Presence of Christ in Reformation Thought* (Grand Rapids, Mich.: Baker Academic, 2008), pp. 41–63. Frido Mann, *Das Abendmahl beim jungen Luther*, Beiträge zur ökumenischen Theologie 5 (Munich: Hueber, 1971), examines Luther's views up through 1520. The most exhaustive discussion of Luther's understanding of the sacrifice of the mass in his earliest works is Wolfgang Simon, *Die Messopfertheologie Martin Luthers. Voraussetzungen, Genese, Gestalt und Rezeption*, Spätmittelalter und Reformation, Neue Reihe 22 (Tübingen: Mohr Siebeck, 2003), pp. 170–389.

3. Sider, *Karlstadt*, p. 147.

4. *Sermo de digna praeparatione ad sacramentum eucharistiae*, WA 1: 325–334; *Ein Sermon von dem hochwürdigen Sakrament des Leichnams Christi und von den Bruderschaften*, WA 2: 738–758, LW 35: 49–73; *Ein Sermon von dem neuen Testament, das ist von der heiligen Messe*, WA 6: 353–378, LW 35: 79–111; *Sermon von der würdigen Empfahung des heiligen wahren Leichnams Christi, gethan am Gründonnerstag*, WA 7: 692–697; as notes taken from the sermon as preached rather than its published form, WA 9: 640–649.

5. Peter Browe, S.J., "Die Kommunionvorbereitung im Mittelalter," *Zeitschrift für katholische Theologie* 56 (1932): 375–415; Amy Nelson Burnett, "The Social History of Communion and the Reformation of the Eucharist," *Past and Present*, forthcoming.

6. WA 1: 330–333; WA 2: 750, 752–753; LW 35: 61, 65–66.

7. WA 6: 358–359; LW 35: 86; Hartmut Hilgenfeld, *Mittelalterlich-traditionelle Elemente in Luthers Abendmahlsschriften*, Studien zur Dogmengeschichte und systematischen Theologie 29

(Zurich: Theologischer Verlag, 1971), pp. 86–97; Reinhard Schwarz, "The Last Supper: The Testament of Jesus," *Lutheran Quarterly* 9 (1995): 391–403.

8. WA 6: 512–526; LW 36: 35–57.

9. WA 6: 503–512, citation at p. 508; LW 36: 20–35, citation at p. 31. Melanchthon was the first to argue that the church could not make the rejection of transubstantiation into a heresy, in a disputation held in September 1519; Wilhelm H. Neuser, *Die Abendmahlslehre Melanchthons in ihrer geschichtlichen Entwicklung (1519–1530)*, Beiträge zur Geschichte und Lehre der Reformierten Kirche 26 (Neukirchen-Vluyn: Neukirchener Verlag, 1968), pp. 20–22.

10. WA 7: 692–694, 696.

11. *Recipients*, Köhler MF 357, no. 996; Burnett, *Pamphlets*, pp. 21–38.

12. Barge, *Karlstadt*, 1: 42–44. Karlstadt left for Denmark toward the end of May, but he was back in Wittenberg by the middle of June; Barge, *Karlstadt*, 1: 256–262. The dedication of the pamphlet is dated 24 June 1521.

13. Karlstadt, *Recipients*, fol. a4r–b1r; Burnett, *Pamphlets*, pp. 25–26. The comparison of revealing one's sins to a priest with revealing one's symptoms to a doctor derived from early monastic practice; it was used, for instance, in both the Pseudo-Ambrosius *Liber de Penitentia* and in Alain of Lille's *Liber poenitentialis*; Oscar D. Watkins, *A History of Penance, Being a Study of the Authorities* (New York: Franklin, 1961), 2: 565–566, 747. The medical analogy was not unknown in late medieval sermons on the Eucharist, but the emphasis tended to be on reception of the sacrament as medicine, and the comparison to a physician was made not only of Christ but also of the priest distributing the host; Otto Gecser, "The Social Significance of Communion: Eucharistic Preaching in the Fifteenth-Century Hungarian Sermon Collection *Sermones Dominicales*," *Annual of Medieval Studies at the CEU* 7 (2001): 113–134.

14. *Recipients*, fol. b4r–v; Burnett, *Pamphlets*, p. 30.

15. E. Gordon Rupp draws attention in a general way to Augustine's influence on Karlstadt; *Patterns of Reformation* (Philadelphia: Fortress, 1969), pp. 55–63. Sider is more specific about that influence; *Karlstadt*, pp. 21–44. The most detailed study is Ernst Kähler, *Karlstadt und Augustin: Der Kommentar des Andreas Bodenstein von Karlstadt zu Augustins Schrift De Spiritu et Litera*, Hallische Monographien 19 (Halle: Niemeyer, 1952), pp. 1*–45*; see also Carter Lindberg, "The Conception of the Eucharist According to Erasmus and Karlstadt," in *Les Dissidents du XVIe siècle entre l'Humanisme et la Catholicisme*, ed. Marc Lienhard (Baden-Baden: Koerner, 1983), pp. 79–94.

16. Jens-Martin Kruse also argues that the Wittenberg theologians were essentially in agreement and that the differences between Luther and Karlstadt at this time should not be overemphasized; *Universitätstheologie und Kirchenreform: Die Anfänge der Reformation in Wittenberg, 1516–1522* (Munich: Philipp von Zabern, 2002), pp. 301–305, 315–317. On Karlstadt's earliest publishing activity, Alejandro Zorzin, *Karlstadt als Flugschriftenautor*, Göttinger theologische Arbeiten 48 (Göttingen: Vandenhoeck & Ruprecht, 1990), pp. 24, 35–37.

17. For a description of the leading figures of the Wittenberg movement during Luther's absence, Kruse, *Universitätstheologie*, pp. 282–287.

18. WA 6: 524–525; LW 36: 53–54.

19. Barge, *Karlstadt*, 1: 290–291; Neuser, *Abendmahlslehre Melanchthons*, pp. 124–126.

20. Luther to Melanchthon, 1 August 1521, WA Br 2: 370–372, no. 424; LW 48: 279–281.

21. Barge gives a detailed account of the events described here; *Karlstadt*, 1: 313–328; more recent accounts in Ulrich Bubenheimer, "Scandalum et ius divinum: Theologische und rechtstheologische Probleme der ersten reformatorischen Innovationen in Wittenberg 1521/1522," *Zeitschrift der Savigny-Stiftung für Rechtsgeschichte* 90, kanonistische Abteilung 59 (1973):

263–342, esp. 277–286; with a focus on Melanchthon, Neuser, *Abendmahlslehre Melanchthons*, pp. 114–228; Sider, *Karlstadt*, pp. 153–173; Mark U. Edwards, *Luther and the False Brethren* (Stanford: Stanford University Press, 1975), pp. 6–33. James S. Preus, *Carlstadt's "Ordinaciones" and Luther's Liberty: A Study of the Wittenberg Movement 1521–22*, Harvard Theological Studies 27 (Cambridge, Mass.: Harvard University Press, 1974), pp. 8–11, provides a useful chronology of the most important developments between August 1521 and May 1522.

22. The immediate context of Zwilling's sermon was a series of student disturbances in response to permission given to the chapter of All Saints to display its relic collection in order to promote the sale of indulgences; Neuser, *Abendmahlslehre Melanchthons*, pp. 119–120.

23. Müller, WB 6: 174–183, nos. 3–5. These contemporary reports of the sermon reflect the consternation caused by Zwilling's ideas.

24. Gregor Brück's report to the elector on 8 October and Melanchthon to Link on 9 October; Müller, WB 6: 179–183, no. 5–6; Melanchthon's letter also in MBW, T1: 358–360, no. 173.

25. Bubenheimer, "Scandalum," pp. 282–283. The letter was published anonymously in 1525 with the title *Epistola christiana admodum ex Bathavis missa*. Simon raises three objections against Bubenheimer's hypothesis; *Messopfertheologie*, 446–449. I agree with his first objection, that Karlstadt's reference to "strange expositions" in *Forms*, fol. d2v, Burnett, *Pamphlets*, p. 64, does not necessarily allude to Hoen's letter as Bubenheimer suggests it does, but Karlstadt's condemnation of those rejecting adoration of the host in *Adoration*, fol. A4r–v; Burnett, *Pamphlets*, pp. 42–43, does suggest that the one who opposed such adoration was not from Wittenberg, and so Karlstadt was not referring to Zwilling. Simon's second objection was also advanced by Neuser, *Abendmahlslehre Melanchthons*, p. 122, who believed that Zwilling did not reject Christ's presence in the sacrament because he reportedly used the phrase "ut panem et vinum, carnem et sanguinem sumere." This amplification may have been added, however, by the author of the report, the student Sebastian Hellmann; Müller, WB 6: 177, no. 4, and so it is not compelling. Simon's third objection, that Hoen's letter may not have been known in Wittenberg, is the crux of the argument. Bubenheimer's position is supported by Dölsch's report that there were some who claimed that Christ was "not essentially or truly" in the form of bread and wine and therefore argued that those forms should not be adored; Müller, WB 6: 203, no. 17.

26. Bubenheimer, "Scandalum," pp. 280–283. Rupp asserts that Karlstadt was unaware of and so not influenced by Hoen, but he was looking for ideas Karlstadt may have adopted from Hoen rather than arguments introduced to counter him; *Patterns*, p. 142. In an essay first published in 1898, Otto Clemen placed Rode's visit to Wittenberg sometime in 1521, "Hinne Rode in Wittenberg, Basel, Zürich und die frühesten Ausgaben Wesselscher Schriften," in Clemen, *Kleine Schriften zur Reformationsgeschichte (1897–1944)* (Leipzig: Zentralantiquariat der DDR, 1982), 1: 24–52, a dating followed by later scholars. The most recent study of Hoen's letter discusses the difficulties of dating Rode's visit and concludes that it probably occurred in the spring of 1521, Spruyt, *Hoen*, pp. 197–202. Luther certainly knew of the letter by early 1523, for he refuted its main argument in his treatise *On the Adoration of the Sacrament*, published in the spring of that year. One might expect that Luther would have voiced his opposition to Hoen's understanding of the sacrament when he first read the letter, but if Rode's visit occurred while Luther was at the Wartburg, the reformer would have received only secondhand reports of the controversy it generated in Wittenberg. Luther's silence on the matter in 1521 is thus an additional bit of evidence supporting Bubenheimer's hypothesis concerning the date of Rode's visit.

27. Later in the letter Hoen applied the same argument, that "is" means "signifies," to Christ's words of institution ("this is my body"), but it is worth noting that the first use of this argument concerned the words of Paul, not those of Christ.

28. Spruyt, *Hoen*, pp. 226–228; Oberman, *Forerunners*, pp. 268–271.

29. Spruyt, *Hoen*, pp. 228–230; Oberman, *Forerunners*, pp. 271–272.

30. Spruyt, *Hoen*, pp. 230–233; Oberman, *Forerunners*, pp. 272–276.

31. Spruyt, *Hoen*, pp. 233–235. This passage is not included in Oberman's translation because it was attributed to Zwingli as the editor of the letter; Spruyt rejects this attribution and argues that the entire text was written by Hoen, pp. 169–176.

32. MBW T1: 360–370, no. 174; they replaced Brück's first point, concerning adoration of the sacrament, with rejection of the sacrifice of the mass. Both Bubenheimer, "Scandalum," 279–280, and Neuser, *Abendmahlslehre Melanchthons*, p. 122, point out that Zwilling was pressured by the university commission to retract his statements about adoration. The number of contemporary accounts mentioning the condemnation of adoration in the sermon raises questions about the veracity of the commission's claim that Zwilling had not rejected the practice, and Johann Dölsch's statement that Zwilling had preached only once against the practice of adoration is more credible; Müller, WB 6: 204, no. 17.

33. Barge, *Karlstadt*, 1: 485–487.

34. Barge, *Karlstadt*, 1: 485–486. The "little books on logic" (*parvis logicalibus*) to which Karlstadt referred were a series of treatises used for instruction in dialectic.

35. Barge, *Karlstadt*, 486–487; Luther's view of elevation in the *Babylonian Captivity*, WA 6: 524, LW 36: 53–54, and his *Sermon on the New Testament*, WA 6: 366, LW 35: 95; on the linkage of the Old Testament wave and heave offerings with elevation, Johannes Reuchlin, *Principivm Libri II Ioannis Revchlin Phorcensis LL. Doc ad Dionysivm fratrem svvm Germanvm de Rvdimentis Hebraicis* . . . (Pforzheim: Anshelm, 1506), p. 314. This link would become increasingly important for Karlstadt, see p. 59.

36. On Melanchthon's agreement with Karlstadt, Müller, WB 6: 206–208, no. 18; the theses in CR 1: 477–481.

37. Ralf Ponader, "'Caro nichil prodest. Joan. vi. Das fleisch ist nicht nutz/sonder der geist.' Karlstadts Abendmahlsverständnis in der Auseinandersetzung mit Martin Luther," in *Andreas Bodenstein von Karlstadt (1486–1541): Ein Theologe der frühen Reformation. Beiträge eines Arbeitsgesprächs vom 24.–25. November 1995 in Wittenberg*, ed. Sigrid Looß and Markus Matthias (Wittenberg: Drei Kastanien Verlag, 1998), pp. 223–245, esp. pp. 224–225, rightly acknowledges the anti-Catholic thrust of Karlstadt's eucharistic works from 1521/22, but he does not see the antisymbolic emphasis of the works published in November.

38. *Adoration*, Köhler MF 791, no. 1995; English translations in Furcha, *Carlstadt*, pp. 40–50, and Burnett, *Pamphlets*, pp. 39–48. The preface is dated 1 November 1521. The preface of the second and longer work was dated 11 November, but Karlstadt refers to it in *Adoration*, so the two pamphlets must have been written at about the same time. As with his earlier pamphlet on the proper preparation for communion, the length, format, and simple expression of ideas in *Adoration* suggest that it may have originated as a sermon.

39. Spruyt, *Hoen*, p. 227; Oberman, *Forerunners*, 269; *Adoration*, fol. A3r–A4r; Burnett, *Pamphlets*, pp. 41–42. Crerar Douglas understands Karlstadt's statement as a rejection of adoration, "The Coherence of Andreas Bodenstein von Karlstadt's early Evangelical Doctrine of the Lord's Supper, 1521–1525" (Ph.D. diss., Hartford Seminary Foundation, 1973), p. 103. He overlooks the important point that Karlstadt is talking not about whether the sacrament should be adored but rather about the purpose of the sacrament. In fact, Karlstadt's subsequent

discussion of the obligation to honor Christ, and of the identity of bread and body, is an affirmation of adoration; see his later assertion, "And so I may worship the bread that is Christ and ask help from it, although it was instituted for eating and given as a sign, because I worship Christ with whom the bread has become one thing, as God and man are one person." *Adoration*, fol. B1r; Burnett, *Pamphlets*, p. 43.

40. *Adoration*, fol. A4r–v; Burnett, *Pamphlets*, pp. 42–43.

41. *Adoration*, fol. A4v; Burnett, *Pamphlets*, p. 43. Sider interprets this as implying that Karlstadt had doubts about Christ's physical presence in the sacrament as early as 1521, *Karlstadt*, p. 294. Since rejection of Chalcedonian Christology was virtually unthinkable to any of the reformers, I see it more as an affirmation and argument by analogy in favor of the scholastic understanding of remanence; on this doctrine, see n. 46.

42. *Adoration*, fol. B1r–B2r; Burnett, *Pamphlets*, pp. 44–45.

43. This was a reference to the distinction in Peter Lombard's *Sentences* between the *sacramentum tantum*, the bread and wine, and the *sacramentum et res*, the body and blood which were both signified and contained in the consecrated elements, *Sent*. IV, Dist. VIII, 4; MPL 192, col. 857.

44. *Adoration*, fol. B2r–B3r; Burnett, *Pamphlets*, pp. 45–46. "Picard" was a term applied to the Bohemian Brethren; see p. 176 n. 5. Karlstadt's insistence throughout this pamphlet that his position was found in Scripture could also be seen as a counter to Hoen's claim that the "Romanist" understanding of the sacrament had no scriptural basis, Spruyt, *Hoen*, p. 232; Oberman, *Forerunners*, p. 275.

45. I used the edition published in Strasbourg by Prüss in 1522, Köhler MF 92, no. 249; translation in Burnett, *Pamphlets*, pp. 49–77.

46. The pamphlet is thus another example of what Hans Hillerbrand has seen as Karlstadt's significance for the Reformation movement: his ability to draw out the implications of Luther's theology—and in this case, going beyond Luther himself; Hans J. Hillerbrand, "Andreas Bodenstein of Carlstadt, Prodigal Reformer," *Church History* 35 (1966): 379–398. Remanence (or consubstantiation), annihilation/succession (the belief that the substances of bread and wine were destroyed and replaced by those of body and blood), and conversion (transubstantiation proper, or the transformation of the substance of bread and wine into body and blood) were the three alternative ways of explaining the doctrine, endorsed at the Fourth Lateran Council in 1215, that Christ's body and blood were truly contained under the forms of the bread and wine; Ian Christopher Levy, *John Wyclif: Scriptural Logic, Real Presence, and the Parameters of Orthodoxy* Marquette Studies in Theology 36 (Milwaukee, Wis.: Marquette University Press, 2003), pp. 172– 175. In addition to Pierre d'Ailly, whom Luther cited, both John Duns Scotus and William of Ockham believed that remanence was philosophically preferable to conversion, although they all accepted the authority of the church to endorse the latter as the correct interpretation, James F. McCue, "The Doctrine of Transubstantiation from Berengar through Trent: The Point at Issue," *Harvard Theological Review* 61 (1968): 385–430.

47. WA 6: 510–511; LW 36: 33–34.

48. *Forms*, fol. a4v; Burnett, *Pamphlets*, p. 53: "Sich Christus spricht nit/gestalt des brots ist mein leip sonder also/das brot das ich in meine hende genommmen vnd gebenedeyet/gebrochen/ vnd euch geben hab/das ist mein leyp;" fol. b1r, Burnett, *Pamphlets*, p. 54: "Der text sagt nit also. Gestalt des brots ist meyn leyp/sonder klar/brot ist meyn leip."

49. *Forms*, fol. a4r–b4r; citation at fol. b3v–b4r; Burnett, *Pamphlets*, pp. 53–57, citation at p. 57: "Alßo ists gott nicht minder müglich/dz er mit einen wörtlin/tzuwo substanz/ein ding magt/vnd last dem seine eygen weßen bleiben. Nemlich das brot macht got/durchs wort/den

leip Christi/und den wein das bluot Christi. Alßo dz uß dem brot und fleisch Christi ein ding wirt . . . Demnach sag ich auch/brot vnd fleisch sind zuwo naturen. Jdoch ist gesegnet brot/der leyp Christ. Das natürlich brot/ist himelisch brot/das vnlebendig brot ist leendig brot/vnd des beckers brot/ist gottis brot."

50. *Forms*, fol. b4r–d1v; Burnett, *Pamphlets*, pp. 57–63.

51. Karlstadt had also argued this position in the disputation of mid-October, Barge, *Karlstadt*, 1: 487–488. In a disputation held in the summer of 1521 Melanchthon had argued that the body and the blood signified different things; Kruse, *Universitätstheologie*, p. 303. He made the same distinction between the body or sacrifice, which made satisfaction for God, and the blood, which cleansed from sin, in the lectures on 1 Corinthians that he was giving in the fall of 1521, *Melanchthons Werke in Auswahl*, ed. Robert Stupperich et al. (Gütersloh: Bertelsmann, 1951–1975), 4: 59–60; Neuser, *Abendmahlslehre Melanchthons*, p. 116.

52. *Forms*, fol. d4r–e4v; Burnett, *Pamphlets*, pp. 66–71.

53. *Forms*, fol. e1v–e2v; f1r–f2v; Burnett, *Pamphlets*, pp. 67–69, 71–74.

54. Without making this specific connection, Bubenheimer also argues that Karlstadt's defense of Christ's presence and so of the adoration of the sacrament was based on a strict biblicism rather than spiritualism, "Scandalum," 285–286.

55. CR 21: 208–210, 221. Yet another indication of the common fund of ideas among Wittenberg's reformers comes from the letter that several of the Catholic canons sent to the elector in early November, in which they reported that Zwilling had compared the sacrament to a rainbow—an analogy used by both Luther and Karlstadt—and to "a carved or painted crucifix," as Melanchthon did in the October disputation; Müller, WB 6: 219, no. 25; CR 1: 478.

56. Müller, WB 6: 195–200, no. 16. In addition to Karlstadt and Melanchthon, the commission consisted of the three theologians Justus Jonas (who was also provost of the chapter of All Saints), Johann Dölsch, and Nicolas von Amsdorf, the jurist Hieronymus Schurf, and the university's vice-rector Tileman Plettner.

57. MBW T1: 399–403, no. 186, which corrects Müller, WB 6: 203, no. 17; on the dating, Bubenheimer, "Scandalum," pp. 311–313, n. 191. Dölsch had signed the commission's memo written in October but did not sign the second memo written in December.

58. Müller, WB 6: 287–288, no. 44 (=MBW T1: 405–407, no. 187), 6: 304–308, no. 51.

59. The elector raised this point in his response to the commission's October report, Müller, WB 6: 210–212, no. 20 (=MBW T1: 375–380, no. 177).

60. Karlstadt's legal training, as well as his dependence on the traditional financial structures of the chapter, may have contributed to his differences with Melanchthon; Müller, WB 6:193–194, no. 15; 6: 207–208, no. 18; Neuser, *Abendmahlslehre Melanchthons*, pp. 132–136.

61. Müller, WB 6: 279–285, no. 43 (=MBW T1: 390–398, no. 185); a detailed analysis of both the October and the December reports, as well as the dissenting opinions from December, in Richard Wetzel, "Melanchthon und Karlstadt im Spiegel von Melanchthons Briefwechsel," in Looß and Matthias, *Andreas Bodenstein von Karlstadt*, pp. 159–222, esp. 170–175.

62. Barge, *Karlstadt*, 1: 352–353; Müller, WB 6: 218–219, no. 25; 6: 272–273, no. 36; 6: 290, no. 44 (=MBW T1: 408–409, no. 187); 6: 407–408, no. 68. Luther also intervened in the debate, sending the pamphlet *De abroganda missa privata sententia*, in which he restated his understanding of the sacrament as a testament rather than as a sacrifice and argued that it was contrary to Christ's institution to celebrate the mass without allowing all present to communicate. The pamphlet was translated into German, and both versions were published in January 1522; WA 8: 482–563; LW 36: 133–230. To Luther's great displeasure and despite his complaints

to Spalatin, the canons continued to celebrate mass over the next few years, which led him first to preach against private masses and then to publish the sermon as *Vom Greuel der Stillmesse* at the turn of 1524/25; WA 18: 8–36; LW 36: 311–328.

63. MBW T1: 359–360, no. 173; 369, no. 174. Karlstadt's title was a repetition of a thesis he had already defended the previous summer.

64. *Forms*, fol. f2r; Burnett, *Pamphlets*, pp. 72–73; Karlstadt himself was using an argument advanced by Luther in *On the Babylonian Captivity*, WA 6: 502–503; LW 36: 20.

65. MBW T1: 396, no. 185.

66. Müller, WB 6: 283, no. 43 (=MBW T1: 396, no. 185); 6: 222, no. 25; 6: 267, no. 31.

67. Müller, WB 6: 204, no. 17 (=MBW T1: 401–402, no. 186); 6: 298, no. 49; 6: 222, no. 25; 6: 308–309, no. 51; 6: 418, no. 68.

68. Müller, WB 6: 215, no. 23; 6: 283 no. 43 (=MBW T1: 396, no. 185); 6: 301, no. 49.

69. The December reports of the university committee and of the canons illustrate this exchange of name-calling, Müller, WB 6: 280, no. 43 (=MBW T1: 393–394, no. 185); 6: 286, no. 44 (=MBW T1: 404–405, no. 187); and 6: 303–304, no. 51. Karlstadt's *Sendbryff . . . Erlutterung Pauli, Ich bitt euch brüder das yhr alle sampt ein meinung reden welt* (Wittenberg, 1521), published in December, followed the same tactic of accusing his opponents of causing division by their refusal to follow the gospel; Barge, *Karlstadt*, 1: 355–356. The changing position of Karlstadt and Melanchthon on this issue is the theme of Bubenheimer, "Scandalum," especially pp. 286–326.

70. Bubenheimer, "Scandalum," pp. 297–298, 306–309. Karlstadt appealed to both levels of local authority. During the October disputation he suggested that Wittenberg's citizens be assembled to vote on eliminating the abuses associated with the mass, but he also stated that this should be done with the magistrate's consent, Müller, WB 6: 194, no. 15; 6: 207–208, no. 18.

71. Müller, WB 6: 266–272, nos. 32–34. These disturbances occurred at about the same time that Luther secretly returned to Wittenberg for a brief visit. His visit prompted him to write a pamphlet warning against insurrection, but his general support for developments in the city is reflected in the pamphlet condemning private masses that he had written a month earlier. Both pamphlets were published in early January 1522; Brecht, *Martin Luther*, 2: 27–32.

72. Other provisions called for the abolition of confraternities and the closure of taverns and brothels; Müller, WB 6: 416–418, no. 68.

73. Müller, WB 6: 318–320, no. 56.

74. Müller, WB 6: 320–321, no. 57; 6: 407–408, no. 68. The statutes specified which festival masses each of the chapter's leading members were to celebrate; that for the circumcision of Christ was the responsibility of the archdeacon. In addition to the festival masses prescribed for the highest ranking members of the chapter, each canon was expected to say mass at least twice a week; Barge, *Karlstadt*, 2: 527. The timing of Karlstadt's announcement is crucial, because it has been used to determine whether or not his announcement was made in deliberate disobedience of the elector's injunction. He announced his intention in a sermon given on either 15 or 22 December; Barge, *Frühprotestantisches Gemeindechristentum in Wittenberg und Orlamünde: Zugleich eine Abwehr gegen Karl Müllers "Luther und Karlstadt"* (Leipzig: Heinsius, 1909), pp. 64–65, n. 4. If it was on the earlier date, he clearly announced his decision before the elector's decree. The injunction was sent from the elector's court in Lochau to his counselor Christian Beyer in Eilenburg, about fifty kilometers to the east; Beyer then had to travel another fifty kilometers north to Wittenberg and meet with university representatives

to tell them of the decree. It is therefore possible that even if Karlstadt made his announcement on the later date, the decree had not yet been publicized in Wittenberg.

75. *Sermon*, Köhler MF 334, no. 943; partially translated in Sider, *Battle*, pp. 7–15, and fully
translated in Burnett, *Pamphlets*, pp. 78–88. Karlstadt's preface to the sermon is dated Christmas
1521; he was well aware of the significance of his actions and published his sermon as quickly as
he could. Karlstadt's rhetorical style is analyzed in Neil R. Leroux, "Karlstadt's 'Christag Predig':
Prophetic Rhetoric in an 'Evangelical' Mass," *Church History* 72 (2003): 102–137.

76. Most modern narratives assume that Karlstadt's sermon was part of the Christmas Day
high mass. The mass for Christmas Day was the responsibility of the chapter's provost, Justus
Jonas, and Barge assumed that Karlstadt substituted for him; *Frühprotestantische
Gemeindechristentum*, p. 65. Contemporary accounts suggest, however, that the mass was an
unanticipated addition to a vespers or preaching service, and not the high mass for Christmas
Day. Karlstadt was not wearing the appropriate vestments in which to celebrate mass, he began
the mass with the Confiteor *after* the sermon rather than giving the sermon after the reading
of the Gospel, where it would normally be held within the mass, and a large proportion of the
audience had already broken their fasts, which they would not have done if they had planned to
attend mass. On the separation of the medieval mass and preaching services, Michael Menzel,
"Predigt und Predigtorganisation im Mittelalter," *Historisches Jahrbuch* 111 (1991): 337–384.

77. Descriptions of Karlstadt's celebration of this mass sometimes read too much into the
sources and assert that he was wearing "street clothes." It is much more likely that he wore his
university robe while preaching and he did not remove it to celebrate the mass.

78. Müller, WB 6: 387, no. 61; 6: 409, 418, no. 68.

79. On the broader reforms that are the context for the following discussion of the mass,
Stefan Oehmig, "Die Wittenberger Bewegung 1521/22 und ihre Folgen im Lichte alter und
neuer Fragestellungen. Ein Beitrag zum Thema (Territorial-) Stadt und Reformation," in *700
Jahre Wittenberg. Stadt, Universität, Reformation*, ed. Stefan Oehmig (Weimar: Herman Böhlaus
Nachfolger, 1995), pp. 97–130.

80. Müller, WB 6: 406–419, no. 68; see also 6: 390–391, nos. 62–63; 6: 419–422, no. 69; citation at pp. 410–411.

81. Barge, *Karlstadt*, 1: 362–364; Müller, WB 6: 425, no. 73; 6: 415–416, no. 68; anonymous
report to Wolfgang Capito, January 1522, Erika Rummel and Milton Kooistra, eds., *The
Correspondence of Wolfgang Capito* (Toronto: University of Toronto Press, 2005–), 1: 183–186,
no. 125. Any influence of the Zwickau prophets on events was due less to their teachings than
to their timing. Sider has shown that Karlstadt's writings from January 1522 argued for the
authority of Scripture in opposition to the prophets' claims of direct revelation; *Karlstadt*,
pp. 161–166. Melanchthon, too, became more confident of his ability to criticize their teachings after he and Amsdorf met with the elector's counselors; Neuser, *Abendmahlslehre
Melanchthons*, pp. 158–164; protocol of the meeting, Müller, WB 6:392–400, no. 64 (MBW T1:
426–433, nos. 201–204).

82. There had been a plan to make Melanchthon the preacher of the parish church in October,
but the canons, who held patronage rights, opposed this because Melanchthon was not
ordained; Müller, WB 6: 223–224, no. 25. Karlstadt was later accused of having preached without
authorization; on the accuracy of this charge, Sider, *Karlstadt*, pp. 168–171. Neither Jonas nor
von Amsdorf had the same stature as Karlstadt and Melanchthon, while Dölsch had already
demonstrated his reluctance to endorse the innovations. Zwilling had forfeited his legal right to
a pulpit in the city when he left the Augustinian order, a point that would be used against him
when the sermons he preached over the next month were seen as too inflammatory.

83. Under Zwilling's influence, the Augustinians had removed and destroyed the images from their church on 8 January; Bubenheimer, "Scandalum," pp. 265–277. Barge takes pains to show that Zwilling was more strident and more radical than Karlstadt, both in Eilenburg and in Wittenberg; *Frühprotestantisches Gemeindechristentum*, pp. 67–70. The radical nature of events in Eilenburg is described by Volkmar Joestel, "Auswirkungen der Wittenberger Bewegung 1521/22: Das Beispiel Eilenburg," in Oehmig, ed., *700 Jahre Wittenberg*, pp. 131–142.

84. Müller, WB 6: 429, no. 75; Hans Lietzmann, *Die Wittenberger und Leisniger Kastenordnung* (Berlin: de Gruyter, 1935), pp. 5–6.

85. Müller, WB 6: 432–436, nos. 81–83 (=MBW T1: 442–443, no. 208). Melanchthon, who had been asked to intervene with Zwilling, also supported the preachers, noting that "in such matters concerning the salvation of souls, we must act with earnestness"; Müller, WB 6: 436–437, no. 84 (=MBW T1: 443–444, no. 209).

86. Müller, WB 6: 445–461, nos. 92–97 (=MBW T1: 445–454, nos. 211–215). Brecht says this compromise "virtually annulled" the earlier ordinance; *Martin Luther*, 2: 40–41, but in fact the compromise was in most things an endorsement of the evangelical mass prescribed by the ordinance; Preus, *Carlstadt's "Ordinaciones,"* p. 44. The meeting also concerned Karlstadt's preaching responsibilities and the removal of images.

87. These concerns emerge clearly from the elector's instruction to Luther from the end of February, WA Br 2: 449–452.

88. Müller, WB 6: 438, no. 85 (=MBW T1: 440–441, no. 206); on Melanchthon's evolving understanding of scandal, Bubenheimer, "Scandalum," pp. 292–294, 311–320.

89. In his report to von Einsiedeln, he said he had argued in favor of retaining the crucifix; Müller, WB 6: 429, no. 47.

90. Luther specifically mentioned the developments in Eilenburg; WA Br 2: 443–444; Brecht, *Martin Luther*, 2: 41–45. For an analysis of the older debate concerning Luther's motives for returning to Wittenberg, Köhler, review article, pp. 525–534; Preus, *Carlstadt's "Ordinaciones,"* pp. 53–63; Edwards, *Luther*, pp. 17–20.

91. These issues were the focus of sermons five through seven of the *Acht Sermon D. M. Luthers von jm geprediget zu Wittemberg in der Fasten*, better known as the Invocavit sermons, WA 10/3: 40–58, LW 51: 88–96. On the publication of *Von beider Gestalt*, WA 10/2: 1. The Maundy Thursday sermon was preached on 17 April; it was published as *Das Hauptstück des neuen Testaments von dem Sakrament beider Gestalt*, WA 10/2: 68–71.

92. WA 10/3: 9–10, 15–18, 21; LW 51: 73, 76–77, 79.

93. WA 10/3: 40–47; LW 51: 88–91.

94. WA 10/2: 11–41; LW 36: 237–267.

95. WA 10/3: 48–58; LW 51: 92–96; WA 10/3: 68–71.

96. Barge, *Karlstadt*, 1: 452–459. The pamphlet itself is lost; these statements were the portions excerpted by the censors as particularly controversial; Barge, *Karlstadt*, 2: 562–565.

97. Barge, *Frühprotestantisches Gemeindechristentum*, pp. 217–220.

98. Wolfgang Simon also underlines the importance of this disagreement, looking chiefly at the issues of monastic vows and clerical celibacy but also touching on the mass; "Karlstadt neben Luther. Ihre theologische Differenz im Kontext der 'Wittenberger Unruhen' 1521/22," in *Frömmigkeit, Theologie, Frömmigkeitstheologie: Contributions to European Church History: Festschrift für Berndt Hamm zum 60. Geburtstag*, ed. Gudrun Litz et al. (Leiden: Brill, 2005), pp. 317–334.

99. Both Bubenheimer, "Scandalum," 326–331, and Carlos M.N. Eire, *War against the Idols: The Reformation of Worship from Erasmus to Calvin* (Cambridge: Cambridge University Press,

1986), pp. 65–73, recognize the fundamental nature of this disagreement concerning the priority of law and liberty; Martin Brecht looks at the later disagreement between the two men and draws out the implications of their disagreement concerning the relationship between external and internal, "Luther und Karlstadt. Der Beginn des Abendmahlsstreites 1524/25 und seine Bedeutung für Luthers Theologie," *Zeitschrift der Savigny-Stiftung für Rechtsgeschichte* 101, kanonistische Abteilung 70 (1984): 196–216.

100. Müller, WB 6: 324, no. 59; Preus, *Carlstadt's "Ordinaciones,"* 60–62.

101. WA Br 3: 345–346, no. 776.

102. Hans Peter Rüger, "Karlstadt als Hebraist an der Universität Wittenberg," *Archiv für Reformationsgeschichte* 75 (1984): 297–308.

103. Simon, "Karlstadt neben Luther"; Lindberg, "Conception."

CHAPTER 2

1. To cite two examples, Wolfgang Simon, *Die Messopfertheologie Martin Luthers. Voraussetzungen, Genese, Gestalt und Rezeption*, Spätmittelalter und Reformation, Neue Reihe 22 (Tübingen: Mohr Siebeck, 2003), and Thomas Hohenberger, *Lutherische Rechtfertigungslehre in den reformatorischen Flugschriften der Jahre 1521–22*, Spätmittelalter und Reformation Neue Reihe 6 (Tübingen: Mohr Siebeck, 1996), focus only on Luther's influence in their consideration of early Reformation pamphlets.

2. Information based on the online version of the *Verzeichnis der im deutschen Sprachbereich erschienenen Drucke des 16. Jahrhunderts* (VD16, http://www.vd16.de), as well as Josef Benzing, ed., *Lutherbibliographie. Verzeichnis der gedruckten Schriften Martin Luthers bis zu dessen Tod* (Baden-Baden: Heitz, 1966) and the bibliographies of Michael A. Pegg, ed., *A Catalogue of German Reformation Pamphlets . . .*, Bibliotheca Bibliographica Aureliana (Baden-Baden: Koerner, 1973– 2004). The numbers in Table 2.1 are intended to be indicative rather than authoritative. I have counted variant printings as separate imprints as a way to compensate for imprints that are no longer extant or that are not included in these bibliographies. Pamphlets were identified on the basis of their titles. Influential works that contain discussions of the sacrament but do not mention it in their titles are also included. The mass was sometimes discussed within shorter pamphlets whose titles did not refer to it, especially in summaries of preaching or in defenses of evangelical teachings more generally; some of these are discussed in Simon, *Messopfertheologie*, pp. 553–587, 608–645. The focus of this study, however, is on those pamphlets that readers would easily identify as contributing to the discussion of the sacrament, whether because this was clear from the title or because this became known in the process of public debate.

3. The only author besides Luther to publish a pamphlet on the sacrament in 1518 was Anton Engelbrecht, at that time a chaplain in the Basel cathedral. His *Ein andechtige leer von dem hochwyrdigen sacrament vnsers herren/gar nutzlich vnd fruchtbar zuo lesen* (Basel: Petri, 1518) is dated 19 March 1518 and so was published before Luther's earliest work on the sacrament. On Engelbrecht, who became a pastor in Strasbourg but eventually returned to the Catholic church, Cornelis H. W. Berg, "Anton Engelbrecht, un 'épicurien' strasbourgeois," in *Croyants et sceptiques au XVIe siècle: Le dossier des "Epicuriens": actes du colloque organisé par le GRENEP, Strasbourg, 9– 10 juin 1978*, ed. Marc Lienhard (Strasbourg: Librairie ISTRA, 1981), pp. 111–120.

4. Statistics on Luther's publications taken from Mark U. Edwards, *Printing, Propaganda, and Martin Luther* (Berkeley: University of California Press, 1994), pp. 18–20. The largest percentage of the 1524 imprints were versions of Luther's *Formula Missae et Communionis*, whether in its original Latin or in German translation.

5. *Sermo de digna praeparatione ad sacramentum eucharistiae* (WA 1: 325–334). The sermon was first published in Latin. Most of these imprints were independent pamphlets, but the Latin sermon was also included with *Ad Leonem X. Pontificem Maximum Resolutiones disputationum de virtute indulgentiarum*, first published in Basel in 1518 and reprinted twice in Strasbourg the following year.

6. There were six Latin imprints, either alone or with the *Resolutiones*, and nine Latin imprints in 1519; two more German imprints appeared in 1520.

7. *Ein Sermon von dem hochwürdigen Sakrament des heyligen waren Leychnams Christi* (WA 2: 738–758; LW 35: 49–73).

8. *Eyn Sermon von dem newen testament, das ist Von der heyligen Messe* (WA 6:353–378; LW 35: 79–111).

9. *De Captivitate Babylonica Ecclesiae Praeludium Martini Lutheri* (WA 6: 484–573). There were also seven imprints of Luther's defense of his 1519 sermon, *Verclerung Doctoris Martini Luther etlicher Artickell yn seynem Sermon von dem heyligen sacrament* (WA 6: 76–83).

10. Augustin Alveldt, *Tractactus de communione Sub vtraque Specie . . .* (Leipzig: Stöckel, 1520); Thomas Murner, *Ein christliche vnd briederliche ermanung zuo . . . Martino Luther . . . Dz er etlichen reden von den newen testament der heiligen messen gethon abstanden* (Strasbourg: Grüninger, 1520). This work was reprinted once in 1520 and again in 1521; a modern edition in *Thomas Murners Deutsche Schriften*, vol. 6, *Kleine Schriften*, pt. 1 (Berlin: de Gruyter, 1927), 31–87.

11. There were five imprints of *Eyn sermon von der wirdigen emphahung des heyligenn waren leychnamß Christi gethann am gruendornstag* (WA 7: 689–697); it was also included in *Ettliche Sermones D. Martini Lutheri* (Basel: Petri, 1521).

12. *De Abroganda Missa Privata Martini Lvtheri Sententia* (WA 8: 477–568; LW 36: 133–230). There were four imprints of the original Latin and eight of the German translation.

13. *Recipients* appeared in four editions in 1521; *Adoration* was reprinted in both Augsburg and Strasbourg before the end of that year, and it was included in one of the imprints of *Recipients*. *Forms* was reprinted four times in 1522, as was the *Sermon*; there was a fifth edition of the latter work in 1524.

14. Karlstadt's *Articuli super celebratione Missarum, Sacramenti Panis et Vini . . .* (Wittenberg: Schirlentz, 1521) was also included in a collection of Wittenberg disputations published in 1522; the memorandum was printed a total of five times under two different titles; MBW, T1:360–370, no. 174.

15. *De Sacramento Eucharistiae* (Augsburg: Grimm & Wirsung, 1521), Köhler MF 695, no. 1797; *Ain Predig . . . von wirdiger ereenbietung dem Sacrament des fronleichnam christi* (Augsburg; Grimm & Wirsung, 1521).

16. *Ain Sermon von dem hochwirdigen sacrament des Altars* (Augsburg: Otmar, 1521), Köhler MF 694, no. 1797.

17. Georg Fener, *Sturm wider ain laymen thurn ains Römischen predigers/der auß der hayligenn Meß gern ain opffer mächte* (Augsburg: Grimm & Wirsung, 1521); Joannes Mansberger, *Joannes Manberger Pfarrher ze Thun Costenzer bystumbs vff den Leimen thurn Gerg fenere von weil: das die meß ein opffer sy: Antwort* (Basel: Gengenbach, 1521).

18. Johann Eckart, *Ain Dialogus . . . das Höchst goldtrain opfer der heyligen Meß betreffent* (Ingolstadt: Lutz, 1521).

19. *Das Hauptstuck des ewigen vnd newen Testaments von dem hochwirdigen Sacrament* (WA 10/3: 68–71); *Von beyder gestalt des Sacraments tzu nemen* (WA 10/2: 1–41; LW 36: 237–267).

20. *Von anbeten des Sacraments des heyligen leychnams Christi* (WA 11: 417–456; LW 36: 275–305) went through thirteen editions in 1523 and two more in 1524; the *Formula Missae et*

Communionis (WA 12: 205–220; LW 53: 22–30) went through one Latin and twelve German editions in 1524 in addition to the two Latin imprints published at the end of 1523.

21. *Contra Henricum Regem Angliae* (WA 10/2: 184–222); *Acht sermon D. M. Luther von ihm gepredigt . . . in den Fasten* (WA 10/3: 1–64). The 1523 *Sermon . . . am gruenen Donnerstag gepredigt* was also published as *Ein Sermon von der Empfahung vnd Zubereitung des hochwür-digen Fronleichnam* and *Ein Sermon von der frucht und nutzbarkeit des heiligen Sacraments* (WA 12: 472– 483). The *Sermon auf das Euangeli Johannis vi*, preached for Corpus Christi 1522 (WA 12: 580–74), was published three times in 1523–1524, and the 1524 Holy Week *Sermon von der Beicht und dem Sakrament* (WA 15: 481–505) was published three times in German and once in Latin during that year.

22. For a discussion of their works, Erwin Iserloh, *Der Kampf um die Messe in den ersten Jahren der Auseinandersetzung mit Luther*, Katholisches Leben und Kämpfen im Zeitalter der Glaubensspaltung 10 (Münster: Aschendorff, 1952).

23. Mathias Kretz, *Von der Mesz/vnnd wer der recht priester sey* (Augsburg: Simprecht, 1524); the work was reprinted in 1525. There were two imprints of the *Christenlich vnderrichtung des Hochwirdigen Fürsten . . . Hugo Bischoffen zuo Constanz* (Freiburg/Br: Wörlin, 1524).

24. Ziegler's pamphlets are discussed in chapter 5, pp. 103–105.

25. In addition to the authors discussed individually below, they include Otto Brunfels, *Vereum* [sic] *Dei multo magis expedit audire, quam missam* (Strasbourg: Schott, 1523); Martin Bryßgauer, *Wie man Christlicher weysz beychten: Sacrament emtpfahen: Messz halten/vnd das Sacrament anbetten sol* (Strasbourg: Schwan, 1524); Nikolaus Krumpach, *Eyn auszerwöllt Byechlin . . . mit schönen gebeten So eyn mensch dz Sacrament empfahen will . . .* (Augsburg: Ramminger, 1524); Wolfgang Oechsner, *Ein kurtzer vnterricht . . . von dem geplerre vnd mißbrauch der Seelmessen* (Nuremberg: Hergot, 1524); and two anonymous pamphlets, *Dialogus von Zweyen pfaffen Köchin/Belangendt den abbruoch des opffers . . .* (Erfurt: Buchfürer, 1523), and *Was schedlicher früchte der Bepstler Messz bracht hat* (Strasbourg: Schwan, 1524).

26. Moeller first posited a "lutherische Engführung" in "Was Wurde in der Frühzeit der Reformation in den deutschen Städten Gepredigt?" *Archiv für Reformationsgeschichte* 75 (1984): 176–193; he clarified his use of the phrase in "Die Rezeption Luthers in der frühen Reformation," in *Reformationstheorien: Ein kirchenhistorischer Disput über Einheit und Vielfalt der Reformation*, ed. Bernd Moeller et al. (Göttingen: Vandenhoeck & Ruprecht, 1995), pp. 9–29. For a summary of the discussion of the early reception of Luther's ideas, Hohenberger, *Rechtfertigungslehre*, pp. 1–12.

27. WA 1: 325–334; WA 2: 738–758, LW 35: 49–73. Thomas J. Davis has argued that Luther's evangelical understanding of the sacrament was present already in his lectures on Hebrews from 1518–1519, " 'His Completely Trustworthy Testament': The Development of Luther's Early Eucharistic Teaching, 1517–1521," in Davis, *This Is My Body: The Presence of Christ in Reformation Thought* (Grand Rapids, Mich.: Baker Academic, 2008), pp. 19–39, but this understanding is not evident in the sermons.

28. WA 6: 353–378, LW 35: 79–111; WA 6: 502–526, LW 36: 19–57. Detailed analysis of the *Sermon von dem Neuen Testament* in Eberhard Grötzinger, *Luther und Zwingli. Die Kritik an der mittelalterlichen Lehre von der Messe, als Wurzel des Abendmahlsstreites*, Ökumenische Theologie 5 (Zurich: Benziger, 1980), pp. 17–45, and of both works in Simon, *Messopfertheologie*, 262–327.

29. *Das Hauptstück des ewigen und neuen Testaments von dem hochwürdigen Sakrament beider Gestalt*, preached on Maundy Thursday, 1522, WA 10/3: 68–71.

30. *Sermon am Grünen Donnerstag*, 1523, WA 12: 472–493.

31. *Sermon auf unsers Herrn Fronleichnamstag,* 1522, WA 12: 580–584; see note in WA 11: 125 concerning the year. John 6:56–59 was the Gospel text appointed for the feast of Corpus Christi. Luther had first rejected the relevance of John 6 for an understanding the sacrament in *On the Babylonian Captivity,* WA 6: 502, LW 36: 19.

32. On the background to the publication of the *Formula Missae et Communionis,* Martin Brecht, *Martin Luther,* vol. 2, *Shaping and Defining the Reformation, 1521–1532,* trans. James L. Schaaf (Minneapolis, Minn.: Fortress, 1990), pp. 122–126.

33. Engelbrecht recommends all of these activities, as well as a series of meditations and prayers, as appropriate preparation for worthy reception; *Andechtige leer,* fol. a3r–d4r.

34. On the development of the understanding of spiritual communion, Gary Macy, *The Theologies of the Eucharist in the Early Scholastic Period: A Study of the Salvific Function of the Sacrament According to the Theologians, ca. 1080– ca. 1220* (Oxford: Clarendon, 1984), pp. 73–105; Willi Massa, *Die Eucharistiepredigt am Vorabend der Reformation. Eine material-kerygmatische Untersuchung zum Glaubensverständnis von Altarssakrament und Messe am Beginn des 16. Jahrhunderts als Beitrag zur Geschichte der Predigt,* Veröffentlichungen des Missionspriester-seminars St. Augustine, Siegburg 15 (St. Augustin: Steyler Verlag, 1966), pp. 195–204; Amy Nelson Burnett, "The Social History of Communion and the Reformation of the Eucharist," *Past and Present,* forthcoming.

35. Francis Rapp, "Notes sur l'eucharistie à la veille de la Réformation: Ce que nous apprennent quelques documents sur la communion," *Revue d'histoire et de philosophie religieuses* 85 (2005): 5–16; Charles M. A. Caspers, "The Western Church during the late Middle Ages: Augenkommunion or Popular Mysticism?" in *Bread of Heaven: Customs and Practices Surrounding Holy Communion. Essays in the History of Liturgy and Culture,* ed. Charles M. A. Caspers and G. Lukken (Kampen: Kok Pharos, 1995), pp. 83–97; Robert W. Scribner, "Popular Piety and Modes of Visual Perception in Late Medieval and Reformation Germany," in Scribner, *Religion and Culture in Germany (1400–1800),* ed. Lyndal Roper, Studies in Medieval and Reformation Thought 81 (Leiden: Brill, 2001), pp. 104–128. An example of a prayer for spiritual communion, said immediately before the priest's communion, in Franz Rudolf Reichert, ed., *Die älteste Deutsche Gesamtauslegung der Messe,* Corpus Catholicorum 29 (Münster: Aschendorff, 1967), p. 186; see also Anne T. Thayer, "Learning to Worship in the Later Middle Ages: Enacting Symbolism, Fighting the Devil, and Receiving Grace," *Archiv für Reformationsgeschichte* 99 (2008): 36–65, esp. pp. 59–61.

36. Massa, *Eucharistiepredigt,* pp. 150–168; Thayer, "Learning to Worship," pp. 58–59.

37. The most detailed treatment of Erasmus's view of the Eucharist is Gottfried G. Krodel, "Die Abendmahlslehre des Erasmus von Rotterdam und seine Stellung am Anfang des Abendmahlsstreites der Reformatoren" (Ph.D. dissertation, Universität Erlangen, 1955). The shorter presentation in John B. Payne, *Erasmus: His Theology of the Sacraments* (Richmond, Va.: John Knox Press, 1970), pp. 126–154, is also useful.

38. ASD VII/6, pp. 76–77; CWE 44, p. 240.

39. Krodel, "Abendmahlslehre," pp. 86–88, 115–125, 144–147; Payne, *Erasmus,* pp. 127–130.

40. Canon Five, on moving from the visible to the invisible; LB V, col. 27–39, esp. col. 30F– 31C; CWE 66: 65–84, esp. pp. 70–71. Erasmus's paraphrase of John 6:44–64 has the same emphasis on moving from material things to spiritual truth; LB VII, col. 548E–551D; CWE 46, p. 82; Payne, *Erasmus,* p. 133.

41. On Erasmus's Christology and its implications for his eucharistic theology, Krodel, "Abendmahlslehre," pp. 32–42.

42. Krodel, "Abendmahlslehre," pp. 91–102. Erasmus highlighted the importance of the sacrament for establishing fellowship and promoting remembrance of Christ's death among Christians in his paraphrase of Matt. 26:26–29; LB VII, col. 133E–134E; CWE 45: 348–351.

43. Krodel, "Abendmahlslehre," pp. 102–105, 108–115.

44. Köhler, *Zwingli und Luther*, 1: 51–52; Krodel, "Abendmahlslehre," pp. 125–130.

45. The *Annotations* were first published in 1516, as a supplement to Erasmus's edition of the Greek New Testament, and they were expanded in each subsequent edition published during his lifetime, in 1519, 1522, 1527, and 1535. On his treatment of the Eucharist in the *Annotations*, Erika Rummel, *Erasmus' Annotations on the New Testament: From Philologist to Theologian* (Toronto: University of Toronto Press, 1986), pp. 156–160. The paraphrase of 1–2 Cor. was published in February 1519, that on Hebrews in January 1521, and those on the four Gospels between March 1522 and February 1524; CWE 44: 380; CWE 42: xx–xxix. They also proved extremely popular. His collected paraphrases of all the New Testament epistles, for instance, were printed a dozen times between 1521 and 1523; ASD VII/6, pp. 4–9.

46. *Ein nützlicher Sermon zu allen Christenmenschen von der rechten evangelischen Meß* (Augsburg: Steiner, 1522), Köhler MF 393, no. 1071. On Diepold, see Christian Peters, "Luthers Einfluß auf die frühreformatorische städtische Predigt: das Beispiel des Ulmer Kaplans Johann Diepold (gest. vor 1539)," in *Luthers Wirkung: Festschrift für Martin Brecht zum 60. Geburtstag*, ed. W.-D. Hauschild et al. (Stuttgart: Calwer, 1992), pp. 111–133; Simon, *Messopfertheologie*, pp. 599–608. Hohenberger reproduces an excerpt of Luther's 1520 *Sermon on the New Testament* in order to compare it with excerpts not only from Diepold's pamphlet but from the pamphlets of Rhegius and Strauss discussed below; *Rechtfertigungslehre*, pp. 398–402.

47. *Ein nützlicher Sermon*, fol. A1v–A2v, citation at A2r: Darumb wenn der priester die wort Christi das seind das testament/ gesprochen hat/ hebt er das Sacrament auff/ als wolt er gegen dem volck sagen. O yr lieben Christen sehent an das zeichen/ die bestettigung/ die sicherheyt/ das pfandt/ die brieff vnnd sygel ewers testaments/ das ist der genad vnd barmhertzigkeyt gottes vnd des ewigen heyls.

48. *Ein nützlicher Sermon*, fol. A2v: Es mag auch der mensch also alle tag das Sacrament geystlich entpfahen durch den glawben/ wan die geystlich empfahung mit dem glawben der zusagung Christi ist nütz/ vnd die leiblich entpfahung des Sacraments an den glawben ist nith nutz/ ist nur ein erdicht ding/ vnd gespöt.

49. *Ein nützlicher Sermon*, fol. A4r–v.

50. Johann Herolt, *Sermones discipuli de tempore* (London, 1510), sermon for Corpus Christi, fol. 108; Reinhard Schwarz, "Abendmahlsgemeinschaft durch das Evangelium, obwohl der Tisch des Herrn 'durch menschliche Irrung versperrt ist,'" *Lutherjahrbuch* 59 (1992): 38–78.

51. *Ein verstendige tröstlich Leer/ über das wort Sanct Paulus/ Der mensch sol sich selbs probieren . . .* (Strasbourg: Knoblauch, 1522), Köhler MF 982, no. 2481, fol. A2r–B1v. The pamphlet originated as a sermon that Strauss preached to his congregation in Hall, Tyrol, for Pentecost 1522.

52. *Ein verstendige tröstlich Leer*, fol. B2v–B4r.

53. *Ein verstendige tröstlich Leer*, fol. B4v–B5r.

54. *Ain schöne liepliche Unndericht/zuo bedencken vnnd enpfahenn/der kostbarlichen hayligesten leib Christi/vnd sein roßenfarbes pluot zuo nyessenn* (Augsburg: Steiner, 1524).

55. Martin Reinhart, *Vnderrichte wie sich ein frumer Christ bey den Papistischen Messen/so yetz noch vil gehalten werden . . . halten sol* (Jena: Buchfürer, 1524).

56. For a description of this broadsheet and a more general discussion of the influence of Strauss's pamphlet, Schwarz, "Abendmahlsgemeinschaft."

57. *Von der Euangelischen Meß/ was die Meß sey . . . Auch wie man Meß soll hören/vnd das hoch-wirdig Sacrament empfahen/vnd warumb mann es empfachet* (Augsburg: Steiner, 1524), Köhler MF 328, no. 925. This work was reprinted four times; it also included a vernacular evangelical mass liturgy that combined a translation of Luther's *Formula Missae* with the German liturgy of the Nördlingen reformer Kaspar Kantz; Julius Smend, ed., *Die evangelischen deutschen Messen bis zu Luthers deutscher Messe*, reprint ed. (Nieuwkoop: de Graaf, 1967), pp. 72–89.

58. *Von der Euangelischen Meß*, fol. A2r: Wilt du recht meß hören/ so gedenck/ das hie ain speyß vnd tranck ist/ darumb muost du essen vnd tricke oder din meß hören ist nichts. Nym die wortt der meß für dich vnd betracht sy recht im glauben/ dz du nit zweifelest/ wie Christus dir verhaist/ also geschehe dir/ vnd im glauben der selbigen wort/ empfahe dz hochwirdig Sacrament/ als ain gewyß hailigs zaichen vnder welchem söllichs zuosagen/ dir geschicht/ dadurch dein hertz gewisen wirt/ auff die wort zuo glauben/ das hayst gaistlich vnd leyplich zuo gots tisch gangen.

59. *Von der Euangelischen Meß*, fol. A4r–B2v. This prayer was attributed to Kantz.

60. *Underricht wie sich ain Christen mensch halten sol das er frucht der Meß erlang und Christlich zu gotz tisch ganng* (Augsburg: Grimm & Wirsung, 1522), Köhler MF 1353, no. 3562, and *Vom hochwürdigen Sakrament des Altars vnderricht was man auß hayliger geschryfft wissen mag* (Augsburg: Ruff, 1523), Köhler MF 694, no. 1798; the 1523 sermon was reprinted once. For analyses of Rhegius's early writings on the sacrament, Hellmut Zschoch, *Reformatorische Existenz und konfessionelle Identät. Urbanus Rhegius als evangelischer Theologe in den Jahren 1520 bis 1530*, Beiträge zur historischen Theologie 88 (Tübingen: Mohr, 1995), pp. 15–24, 59–69; Simon, *Messopfertheologie*, pp. 587–598.

61. *Ain Sermon*, fol. A3v–A4v; *Underricht*, fol. A2r–A4v; *Vom hochwürdigen Sacrament*, fol. D4v–E2v. The 1523 sermon also reflects the influence of Luther's *Von Anbeten des Sacraments* in its distinction between external and internal adoration, cf. *Vom hochwürdigen Sacrament*, fol. D2r–D4v, and possibly of Strauss's *Ein verstendige tröstlich Leer* in its criticism of a complete auricular confession as preparation for receiving the sacrament; *Vom hochwürdigen Sacrament*, fol. B3v–C3v.

62. *Vom hochwürdigen Sacrament*, fol. D4v–E1v; citation at E1r–v: Ich bin tailhafftig aller deren/dye dich fürchten/vnd deine gepot halten. Wz gepetet würt in vngern/österrich/ Engelland/Schotland/Franckreich/Hispania/Italia/Teütschland überal/kompt dir auch zum trost vnd zuo hilff.

63. *Vom hochwürdigen Sacrament*, fol. B1v–B3r.

64. *Underricht*, fol. B1r–v, citation at B1v: "laß in mir geschehen was das hochwürdig Sacrament bedeut das ich in rechter warer liebe veraint werd dir vnd allen deinen hayligen hie vnd dort ewigklich."

65. *Vom hochwürdigen Sacrament*, fol. B1v; cf. E2r: "Und das du ain gewiß zaichen habest söllicher brüderschafft/empfach in allen anligen das hochwürdig Sacrament des altars gei-stlich/oder leiplich/glaub den worten und dem zaychen/in aller not/hiw würdt dir gewißlich bedeut/verhaissen/geben/gemeinschafft/hülff/liebe/trost   vnd   beystand   aller   gottes hayligen."

66. *Ain Predig vnd ermanung . . . von wirdiger ereenbietung dem Sacrament des fronleichnam christi* (Augsburg: Grimm & Wirsung, 1521). Staehelin gives a detailed summary of the sermon, *Theologische Lebenswerk*, pp. 142–146.

67. *Ein Predig vnd ermanung*, fol. A4v–B1v.

68. *Ein Predig vnd ermanung*, fol. C1r–v.

69. *Ein Predig vnd ermanung*, fol. D3v–E1v.

70. WA 6: 512–526; LW 36: 35–57.

71. WA 8: 506–537, citation at p. 512; LW 36: 162–198, citation at p. 169.

72. Carl Fr. Wislöff summarizes, "Die Messefrömmigkeit ist ein Ausfluß der Selbstrechtfertigung des natürlichen Menschen. Damit ist die Kritik Luthers an der Messe auf den kürzesten Ausdruck gebracht;" *Abendmahl und Messe: Die Kritik Luthers am Meßopfer*, Arbeiten zur Geschichte und Theologie des Luthertums 22 (Berlin: Lutherisches Verlaghaus, 1969), p. 90.

73. The earliest appearance of this argument is a passing reference in Melanchthon's *Annotationes . . . in Evangelium Matthaei* where Melanchthon discusses the error of calling the mass an offering and sacrifice; CR 14: 1008. He condemns the former term as contradicting the principle of justification by faith alone and the latter as contradicting the unique sacrifice described in Hebrews. Melanchthon gave his lectures on Matthew in Wittenberg from late 1519 through early 1520, but the *Annotationes* was not published until 1523. Notker M. Halmer, O.P., mentions Melanchthon's use of Heb. 10 in his disputation on the mass from the fall of 1521, "Der literarische Kampf Luthers und Melanchthons gegen das Opfer der Messe," *Divus Thomas* 21 (1943): 63–78. The first use of Hebrews 10 in a vernacular pamphlet occurs in Georg Fener's *Sturm wider ain laymen thurn*, published in 1521; for a summary of the exchange between Fener and Johannes Manberger on the mass, Hohenberger, *Rechtfertigungslehre*, pp. 356– 359; Simon, *Messopfertheologie*, pp. 646–659.

74. *Auslegen und Gründe der Schlußreden*, Z 2: 112–120, 127–130, citation at p. 114; HZW 1: 92–98, 103–105, citation at p. 94. There were two imprints of this work in 1523; a detailed analysis in Grötzinger, *Luther und Zwingli*, pp. 47–70.

75. Z 2: 131–132, 144; HZW 1: 106–107, 116.

76. Z 2: 141–143; HZW 1: 113–115; see also his letter to Thomas Wyttenbach, Z 8: 84–89.

77. Z 2: 120–122, 150–151; HZW 1: 98–100, 120. Zwingli repeated his criticisms of the mass in *De Canone Missae . . . Epichiresis* (one imprint in 1523, Z 2: 556–608), *De Canone Missae libelli Apologia* (one imprint in 1523, Z 2: 617–625), and *Adversus Hieronymum Emservm . . . Antibolon* (one imprint in 1524, Z 3: 241–287, esp. pp. 280–282).

78. WA 8: 486, 493.

79. WA 8: 506; *Von dem Greuel der Stillmesse* (WA 18: 8–36); Simon, *Messopfertheologie*, pp. 390–406. Wislöff discusses Luther's use of the single sacrifice from Heb. 10, but he does so entirely from a systematic perspective, without considering when and under what circumstances Luther made his statements. Nevertheless, it is clear from his citations from the WA that they date from after 1524; Wislöff, *Abendmahl und Messe*, 90–110.

80. Grötzinger, *Luther und Zwingli*, pp. 61–65. This ambiguity in German was matched in scholastic theology by a growing tendency to stress the offering rather than the act of sacrifice; Caroline Walker Bynum, *Wonderful Blood: Theology and Practice in Late Medieval Northern Germany and Beyond* (Philadelphia: University of Pennsylvania Press, 2007), pp. 218–219.

81. Ludwig Hätzer, *Acta oder geschicht wie es vff dem gesprech . . . in der Christenlichen Statt Zürich*, Z 2: 669–803, esp. pp. 731ff. (one imprint); *Cristenlich antwurt burgermeysters und radtes zuo Zürich, dem hochwirdigen etc. herren Hugen, byschoffe zu Costanz*, Z 3: 155–229, esp. 185ff. (three imprints); Leo Jud, *Ein Christenlich widerfechdung Leonis Jud/ wider Mathyß Kretzen zuo Ougspurg/ falsche/ Endchristliche Mäß* (Zurich: Hager, 1524), Köhler MF 8222, no. 48 (two imprints).

82. Simon downplays the theological significance of this difference between Luther and Zwingli, although he acknowledges that there were Christological implications; he does not

take into account the polemical importance of Zwingli's argument; *Messopfertheologie*, pp. 285–287.

83. *Priesthood*, Köhler MF 67, no. 175; translation in Burnett, *Pamphlets*, pp. 89–109. The pamphlet went through three imprints; see pp. 57–58.

84. "Das D. Luthers und seiner nachfolger leer . . . christlich und gerecht ist," BDS 1:329–332; *Grund und Ursach*, BDS 1: 212–213 (one edition in 1524 and a second in 1525). In contrast to these two works, Bucer did not use Zwingli's argument against the sacrifice of the mass in *De Caena Dominica* (Strasbourg: Herwagen, 1524), BOL 1: 17–58. Thomas Kaufmann rightly recognizes Luther's influence on Bucer, but he says nothing about Zwingli's influence before the end of 1524; *Die Abendmahlstheologie der Strassburger Reformatoren bis 1528*, Beiträge zur historischen Theologie 81 (Tübingen: Mohr, 1992), pp. 174–176.

85. Theobald Billican (Gerlacher), *Von der Mess Gemayn Schlußred* (Augsburg: Ulhart 1524), Köhler MF 393, no. 1068 (two imprints), fol. A2v–A3r; Johann Landsperger, *Ain nutzlicher berücht von nyessung des hochwirdigen Sacraments* (Augsburg: Ramminger, 1524), Köhler MF 681, no. 1776 (one imprint), fol. C3r–v, D4v–E1v.

86. *Grund und Ursach*, Osiander, GA 1: 209–216 (two editions in 1524 and nine more in 1525–1526). Brenz's pamphlet, *Libellus insignis de Missah*, was not published until 1526, and so it is not included in the statistical overview above, but its editors suggest that the pamphlet was written before the outbreak of the eucharistic controversy; Johannes Brenz, *Werke. Eine Studienausgabe*, vol. 1/1: *Frühschriften* (Tübingen: Mohr, 1970), pp. 207–219.

87. Iserloh has observed that these works are better characterized as polemical defenses of traditional teaching than theological justifications of that teaching; *Kampf*, 56–57.

88. Karlstadt, *Priesthood*, fol. E2v–F1r, Burnett, *Pamphlets*, pp. 106–107.

89. Billican, *Von der Mess Gemayn Schlußred*, fol. A3r–v.

90. Andreas Keller, *Ein anzeygung was für Gottzlesterung in der Papisten Messz ist/ vnd das sich alle fromen Christen daruor als vor der aller grösten gotzlesterung hyeten sollent* . . . (Strasbourg: Schürer, 1524). Köhler MF 67, no. 174, fol. B3v–C2v. There was only one edition of this pamphlet; see pp. 102–103.

91. *Das Testament Jesu Christ, Das man bißher genent hat die meß*; reprinted and discussed in Smend, *Die evangelischen deutschen Messen*, pp. 49–71. An eighth edition appeared in 1525. Luther's prescription for an evangelical weekday service without communion, *Von ordnung gottes dienst in der gemein*, was also published nine times in 1523.

92. *Von der Euangelischen Messz mitt schönen Christlichen gebetten*; Smend, *Die evangelischen deutschen Messen*, pp. 72–94.

93. *Von der Euangelischen Messz was die Messz sey/ wie vnd durch wenn/ vnd warumb sy auffgesetzt sey . . . durch herr Johan Pommer zu Wittenberg*; this pamphlet was published eight times in 1524 and once in 1525. Bugenhagen disavowed any association with this order of the mass in a postscript to his *Contra novum errorem de Sacramento Corporis et sanguinis Domini* (Wittenberg: Lotter, 1525), fol. A3v–A4r.

94. Smend, *Die evangelischen deutschen Messen*, pp. 123–159; Friedrich Hubert, *Die Straßburger liturgischen Ordnungen im Zeitalter der Reformation, nebst einer Bibliographie der Straßburger Gesangbücher* (Göttingen: Vandenhoeck & Ruprecht, 1900), pp. 57–115.

95. Thirty-seven out of 100 pamphlets.

96. Jakob Strauss, *Wider den vnmilten Jrrthum Maister Vlrichs zwinglins so er verneünet die warhafftig gegenwirtigkait dess allerhailigsten leybs vnd bluets Christi im Sacrament* (Augsburg: Ramminger, 1526), Köhler MF 293, no. 652.

97. This was certainly the case for Martin Bucer, who read a Zwinglian (and Erasmian) understanding of John 6:63 into Luther's sermon on John 6, BCorr 2: 51; BDS 3: 414.

98. Z 8: 276. The editors identify the book Zwingli refers to as one of Karlstadt's pamphlets, but it is a clear reference to Luther's work, in which the Wittenberger rejected the understanding of "is" as "signifies."

99. Luther was also capable of polemical outbursts against the mass, as illustrated by Rudolf Padberg, "Luther und der Canon Missae," *Catholica* 37 (1983): 288–305, but such attacks were balanced by the more pastoral emphasis of his sermons and of Bugenhagen's pamphlets, especially in comparison to the pamphlets from South Germany.

CHAPTER 3

1. Hermann Barge, "Zur Chronologie und Drucklegung der Abendmahlsschriften Karlstadts," *Zentralblatt für Bibliothekswesen* 21 (1904): 323–331; see also Barge's introduction to Luther's *Wider die himmlischen Propheten*, WA 18: 37–46.

2. Calvin Pater suggested that there was sufficient internal evidence to assume that at least some of the pamphlets were written before Karlstadt's confrontation with Luther, but he did not give any more precise indication of when the pamphlets were written; *Karlstadt as Father of the Baptist Movements: The Emergence of Lay Protestantism* (Toronto: University of Toronto Press, 1984), pp. 160–161. More recent studies of Karlstadt's eucharistic pamphlets have acknowledged Pater's comments but continued to follow Barge's chronology; see, for instance, Thomas Kaufmann, *Die Abendmahlstheologie der Strassburger Reformatoren bis 1528*, Beiträge zur historischen Theologie 81 (Tübingen: Mohr, 1992), pp. 181–184; Ralf Ponader, "'Caro nichil prodest. Joan. vi. Das fleisch ist nicht nutz/sonder der geist.' Karlstadts Abendmahlsverständnis in der Auseinandersetzung mit Martin Luther," in *Andreas Bodenstein von Karlstadt (1486–1541): Ein Theologe der frühen Reformation, Beiträge eines Arbeitsgesprächs vom 24.–25. November 1995 in Wittenberg*, ed. Sigrid Looß and Markus Matthias (Wittenberg: Drei Kastanien Verlag, 1998), pp. 223–245, at p. 228. In his dissertation Ponader suggests a rough chronology for the composition of the eight Basel pamphlets, all between 24 August and early October, which I do not find persuasive; Ralf Ponader, "Die Abendmahlslehre des Andreas Bodenstein von Karlstadt in den Jahren 1521–1524: Die Kritik an der Realpräsenz durch Karlstadt untersucht vor dem Hintergrund der Chorismos-Problematik" (Ph.D. diss., Universität Greifswald, 1993), pp. 114–121. Alejandro Zorzin discusses publication but not the date of composition of the pamphlets; *Karlstadt als Flugschriftenautor*, Göttinger theologische Arbeiten 48 (Göttingen: Vandenhoeck & Ruprecht, 1990), pp. 101–102, 123–125.

3. These pamphlets were all published in Augsburg; Zorzin, *Karlstadt*, 96–100; on the influence of German mysticism, Sider, *Karlstadt*, pp. 180–181.

4. 14 January 1524, WA Br 3: 232–233.

5. The latter two pamphlets were published in Nuremberg and Strasbourg; Zorzin, *Karlstadt*, pp. 98–99. On Buchführer, Siegfried Hoyer, "Martin Reinhart und der erste Druck hussitischer Artikel in Deutschland," *Zeitschrift für Geschichtswissenschaft* 18 (1970): 1597–1615; Volkmar Joestel, *Ostthüringen und Karlstadt: Soziale Bewegung und Reformation im mittleren Saaletal am Vorabend des Bauernkrieges (1522–1524)* (Berlin: Schelzky & Jeep, 1996), pp. 106–107.

6. Amedeo Molnár, "Luthers Beziehungen zu den Böhmischen Brüdern," in *Leben und Werk Martin Luthers von 1526 bis 1546. Festgabe zu seinem 500. Geburtstag*, ed. Helmar Junghans (Göttingen: Vandenhoeck & Ruprecht, 1983), 1: 627–639.

7. WA 11: 434–437; LW 36: 279–282. In rejecting a figurative understanding of 1 Cor. 10:4, Luther was repeating the position stated by Peter Lombard, *Sent.* IV, Dist. 10, c. 1; MPL 192, col. 859. On the significance of this verse for Wyclif and the Hussites, see pp. 79–81.

8. WA 11: 437–442, citation at p. 441; LW 36: 282–289, citation at pp. 287–288.

9. *Priesthood*; Köhler MF 67, no. 175; translation in Burnett, *Pamphlets*, pp. 89–109. The pamphlet was first published at the end of 1523; it was reprinted once in 1524. There is also a variant version of the first printing.

10. Volkmar Joestel, "Neue Erkenntnisse zu Jenaer Karlstadtschriften 1524," in *Andreas Bodenstein von Karlstadt (1486–1541): Ein Theologe der frühen Reformation. Beiträge eines Arbeitsgesprächs vom 24.–25. November 1995 in Wittenberg*, ed. Sigrid Looß and Markus Matthias (Wittenberg: Drei Kastanien Verlag, 1998), pp. 121–142, at pp. 123–124. There are strong parallels between the first section of *Priesthood* and Karlstadt's discussion of God's internal call in his *Ursachen, daß Andreas Karlstadt eine Zeit stillschweig*, which Buchführer had just finished printing; English translation of the latter pamphlet in Furcha, *Carlstadt*, pp. 169–184.

11. ASD VII/6, pp. 72–78; CWE 44: 236–240.

12. Z 2: 111–120; HZW 1: 92–98; see pp. 48–49. On the difference between Luther and Zwingli on this point, Eberhard Grötzinger, *Luther und Zwingli. Die Kritik an der mittelalterlichen Lehre von der Messe, als Wurzel des Abendmahlsstreites*, Ökumenische Theologie 5 (Zurich: Benziger, 1980), pp. 61–65.

13. Z 2: 137–138, 141–144, 150–153; HZW 1: 110–111, 113–116, 120–122. The (mistaken) etymology of "mass" came from Reuchlin's Hebrew grammar, *Principivm Libri II Ioannis Revchlin Phorcensis LL. Doc ad Dionysivm fratrem svvm Germanvm de Rvdimentis Hebraicis . . .* (Pforzheim: Anshelm, 1506), pp. 336–337.

14. Zwingli based his argument entirely on the Hebrews passage, which is itself a figural interpretation of the Old Testament sacrifices. Karlstadt, however, focused primarily on the Old Testament, in which Moses and the prophets taught about Christ's future sacrifice. For a useful discussion of figural interpretation, which links concrete events in the past and present, as opposed to a more abstract allegorical interpretation, Erich Auerbach, "Figura," in *Scenes from the Drama of European Literature: Six Essays* (Gloucester, Mass.: Peter Smith, 1973), pp. 11–76.

15. *Priesthood*, fol. A4v–B4r; C3r–D3v; Burnett, *Pamphlets*, pp. 92–96, 98–103.

16. *Priesthood*, fol. D4v–E1r; F1v; Burnett, *Pamphlets*, pp. 104–105, 107. Because Karlstadt had criticized the use of the word "mass" already in his censored pamphlet of 1522 and had used Reuchlin's lexicon to link the wave and heave offerings with the elevation of the consecrated host even earlier, in the fall of 1521, it is likely that he took this etymology directly from Reuchlin, and that Zwingli's rejection of the word only confirmed his earlier position.

17. *Priesthood*, fol. D4r; Burnett, *Pamphlets*, pp. 103–104.

18. Jacob and Wilhelm Grimm, *Deutsches Wörterbuch* (Leipzig: Hirzel, 1962) (http://urts55.uni-trier.de:8080/Projekte/DWB/), 4: 1927ff., emphasizes the connotations of meditation and devotion associated with *Gedächtnis* in the sixteenth century. *Wiedergedächtnis* is literally a "re-remembrance," Zwingli's translation of the Greek *anamnesis*, which also has a sense of re-calling or re-presenting; Gregory Dix, *The Shape of the Liturgy* (London: Dacre Press, 1945), pp. 161–162. On the neoplatonic/Augustinian background of Zwingli's use of remembrance, Gottfried W. Locher, "Zwingli's Theology Compared with Luther and Calvin," in Locher, *Zwingli's Thought: New Perspectives*, Studies in Medieval and Reformation Thought 25 (Leiden: Brill, 1981), pp. 142–234, esp. pp. 222–223. Dorothea Wendebourg discusses the understanding of remembrance in both Karlstadt and Zwingli, but she does not consider the possibility of the

latter's influence on the former, *Essen zum Gedächtnis: Der Gedächtnisbefehl in den Abendmahlstheologien der Reformation*, Beiträge zur historischen Theologie 148 (Tübingen: Mohr Siebeck, 2009), pp. 61–85.

19. Barge, *Karlstadt*, 2: 151, argues that Karlstadt had abandoned Christ's corporeal presence in this work, a view that Karl Müller rejects; *Luther und Karlstadt: Stücke aus ihrem gegenseitigen Verhältnis* (Tübingen: Mohr, 1907), pp. 227–229. Douglas is kinder, referring to Barge's view as "a slight exaggeration"; "The Coherence of Andreas Bodenstein von Karlstadt's Early Evangelical Doctrine of the Lord's Supper, 1521–1525" (Ph.D. diss., Hartford Seminary Foundation, 1973), p. 179. Ponader claims that Karlstadt's criticism of the sacrifice of the mass was also a criticism of Christ's real presence, "Karlstadts Abendmahlsverständnis," pp. 225–226, but the rejection of the former does not necessarily entail a rejection of the latter. Zwingli used the same arguments against the sacrifice of the mass in his *Auslegung der Schlußreden* but at that time still held to the presence of Christ's body and blood in the sacrament; Köhler, *Zwingli und Luther* 1: 19–20, 29–37.

20. The closest he came was "the bread and blood of the Lord"; *Priesthood*, fol. D4r; Burnett, *Pamphlets*, p. 103.

21. *Priesthood*, fol. D1r–v; Burnett, *Pamphlets*, pp. 100–101.

22. Luther referred to his plans to revise the liturgy in his letters to Hausmann over the course of the fall; WA Br 3: 182–184, 194–195.

23. WA 12: 208–214; LW 53: 22–30. On the broader context of these liturgical reforms, Martin Brecht, *Martin Luther*, vol. 2, *Shaping and Defining the Reformation, 1521–1532*, trans. James L. Schaaf (Minneapolis: Fortress, 1990), pp. 122–126.

24. *Masses*; Köhler MF 95, no. 256; translation in Burnett, *Pamphlets*, pp. 110–115. The pamphlet was written after the publication of *Priesthood*, which is mentioned in the text. As Calvin Pater has noted, the pamphlet concluded by telling the recipient to write back with his objections so that Karlstadt could respond to them, which presupposes that Karlstadt was at that time in a stable situation; *Karlstadt*, p. 161. On the censored pamphlet, see p. 31.

25. *Masses*, fol. A1v–A2r, A4v, citation at fol. A2r; Burnett, *Pamphlets*, pp. 111–115, citation at p. 111.

26. Luther to Spalatin, 14 March 1524, WA Br 3: 254–255; Karlstadt's successor in Orlamünde reported to Luther that Karlstadt had translated some of the Psalms from Hebrew into German for the congregation to sing; WA Br 3: 424–425; Martin Brecht, "Luther und Karlstadt. Der Beginn des Abendmahlsstreites 1524/25 und seine Bedeutung für Luthers Theologie," *Zeitschrift der Savigny-Stiftung für Rechtsgeschichte* 101, kanonistische Abteilung 70 (1984): 196–216.

27. WA Br 3: 265–266, no. 727; 3: 305–306; Melanchthon to Spalatin, MBW T2: 122–123, no. 316; T2: 125–126, no. 318. On the efforts to force Karlstadt back to Wittenberg, Sider, *Karlstadt*, pp. 190–194; he did not actually resign his position until July. These innovations caused concern elsewhere as well, for Karlstadt wrote his pamphlet *Whether We Should Go Slowly* in response to the cautions of a friend in Joachimstal about proceeding with too much haste. Although much of the treatise was devoted to the removal of images, Karlstadt drew a clear parallel between removal of images and liturgical reform when he advocated "the removal of God-blaspheming and Christ-blaspheming images or masses in places where we are in control"; *Ob man gemach faren, vnd des ergernüssen der schwachen verschonen soll* ([Basel: Wolf,] 1524); English translation in Furcha, *Carlstadt*, pp. 247–268, citation at pp. 257–258.

28. WA Br 3: 314–316, no. 756.

29. *Prove*, Köhler MF 48, no. 133, fol. A3r–B4r; Burnett, *Pamphlets*, pp. 117–123. Hoen also refuted the claim that priests had the authority, on the basis of Christ's words, "do this," to transform the elements, but he used a different line of reasoning; Spruyt, *Hoen*, pp. 96–97, 108–112, 230–231; Oberman, *Forerunners*, pp. 272–274.

30. *Prove*, fol. B4r–C2r; Burnett, *Pamphlets*, pp. 123–126. Karlstadt consistently used *Geimeinschaft* as his translation of the Greek word *koinonia*, rendered in various English translations as communion, participation, or sharing. His understanding of 1 Cor. 10:16 may have been influenced by Erasmus, whose paraphrase referred to the *consortium* and *foedus* among believers testified to by the bread and cup; LB VII, col. 893 A–B.

31. *Prove*, fol. C2r–E1r; Burnett, *Pamphlets*, pp. 126–133; cf. Erasmus's annotation on Mark 14:24, ASD VI/5, 424, and on 1 Cor. 11:24, ASD VI/8, p. 230; John B. Payne, *Erasmus: His Theology of the Sacraments* (Richmond, Va.: John Knox Press, 1970), p. 127. Hoen also noted that Christ had spoken the words after the apostles drank from the cup, explicitly citing Erasmus, and stated that the apostles did not speak of the sacrament as "the Roman faith" did; Spruyt, *Hoen*, pp. 227, 230; Oberman, *Forerunners*, pp. 269, 272–273.

32. *Prove*, fol. E1r–E3r; Burnett, *Pamphlets*, pp. 133–135.

33. *Prove*, fol. F2r–F4r; Burnett, *Pamphlets*, pp. 139–141; cf. Spruyt, *Hoen*, p. 229; Oberman, *Forerunners*, p. 272. On John 6 in Karlstadt's eucharistic theology more generally, Ponader, "Karlstadts Abendmahlsverständnis," pp. 229–235.

34. *Prove*, fol. B3r–v; Burnett, *Pamphlets*, p. 122; Spruyt, *Hoen*, pp. 232–233; Oberman, *Forerunners*, pp. 275–276.

35. *Prove*, fol. F4r–v; Burnett, *Pamphlets*, pp. 141–142. Karlstadt compared this intermediate form of existence to purgatory, which supposedly lay between heaven and hell—and whose existence he likewise rejected.

36. *Prove*, fol. F4v–F6r; Burnett, *Pamphlets*, pp. 142–143.

37. *Prove*, fol. A3r–A4r, E4r–F1r; Burnett, *Pamphlets*, pp. 117–118, 136–137.

38. *Prove*, fol. F1r–v; Burnett, *Pamphlets*, pp. 137–138. Gottfried Krodel has suggested that Karlstadt's reevaluation of the relationship of the parts of the words of institution to each other was first suggested by Erasmus in his annotation on Mark 14:24. There the Dutch humanist stated that Mark's placing the words of institution after the disciples drank from the cup might be explained as a *figura prothysteron*, or the transposition of phrases within a sentence in order to change the meaning; Gottfried G. Krodel, "Figura Prothysteron and the Exegetical Basis of the Lord's Supper," *Lutheran Quarterly* 12 (1960): 152–158. Karlstadt was only beginning to make use of this exegetical technique in *Prove*, but the reordering of phrases within the words of institution was a prominent polemical device in his final eucharistic pamphlet.

39. *Exegesis*, Köhler MF 1446, no. 3833, fol. a1v–a2v; Burnett, *Pamphlets*, pp. 144–145.

40. *Exegesis*, fol. a3r–a4r; Burnett, *Pamphlets*, pp. 146–147.

41. *Exegesis*, fol. a4r–b2r; Burnett, *Pamphlets*, pp. 147–149.

42. *Exegesis*, fol. b2r–c2r; Burnett, *Pamphlets*, pp. 149–153.

43. Z 2: 141–144; HZW 1: 113–116. In his *Auslegung*, Zwingli described God's word as food for the soul, and eating was faith in Christ's saving death.

44. *Exegesis*, fol. c2v–c3r; c4r–d1r; Burnett, *Pamphlets*, pp. 154–156; Spruyt, *Hoen*, pp. 94–95, 228–229; Oberman, *Forerunners*, pp. 271–272.

45. See chapter 2, pp. 41–42.

46. *Exegesis*, fol. d1v–d3v; Burnett, *Pamphlets*, pp. 157–159.

47. For a comparison of Luther and Zwingli on this point, Helmut Gollwitzer, "Zur Auslegung von Joh. 6 bei Luther und Zwingli," in *In Memoriam Ernst Lohmeyer*, ed. Werner Schmauch (Stuttgart: Evangelisches Verlagswerk, 1951), pp. 143–168; David C. Steinmetz, "Scripture and the Lord's Supper in Luther's Theology," in *Luther in Context* (Grand Rapids, Mich.: Baker Academic, 2002), pp. 72–84.

48. The exception is the final several pages of *Exegesis*, which were added later; see the discussion below.

49. WA 15: 334.

50. WA 15: 335. Sider translates "nach den Aposteln" as "in conformity with the apostles"; Sider, *Battle*, 40, but the context here, as well as Karlstadt's earlier polemic against those who would cite the authority of the church fathers against him (*Priesthood*, fol. D4v–E1v; Burnett, *Pamphlets*, pp. 104–105), and his awareness that his position was opposed by "so many thousand scribes" (*schrifftgelerten*), leads me to translate the "nach" in a temporal sense. Mark U. Edwards describes the deteriorating relationship between Luther and Karlstadt both before and after their Jena meeting, *Luther and the False Brethren* (Stanford: Stanford University Press, 1975), pp. 34–48.

51. WA 18: 135–139; see below.

52. Ernst Koch, "Das Sakramentsverständnis Thomas Müntzers," in *Der Theologe Thomas Müntzer. Untersuchungen zu seiner Entwicklung und Lehre*, ed. Siegfried Bräuer and Helmar Junghans (Göttingen: Vandenhoeck & Ruprecht, 1989), pp. 129–155; William W. McNiel, "Andreas von Karlstadt and Thomas Muentzer: Relatives in Theology and Reformation" (Ph.D. diss., Queen's University, 1999), pp. 135–173; Brecht, *Martin Luther*, pp. 146–157.

53. *Dialogue*, fol. a1v–a2r; Burnett, *Pamphlets*, pp. 165–166. the German text is reprinted in Hertzsch, *Schriften* 2: 5–49 (citation at pp. 7–9). Hertzsch transposed fol. A4v of the Basel imprint so that it wrongly appears on pp. 40.33–41.25; it should follow the sentence that ends p. 11.34. There are two English translations based on the Hertzsch edition, Furcha, *Carlstadt*, pp. 269–315, and with a lengthier introduction in Carter Lindberg, "Karlstadt's Dialogue on the Lord's Supper," *Mennonite Quarterly Review* 53 (1979): 35–77. The translation in Burnett, *Pamphlets*, pp. 163–204, follows the Basel imprint and so corrects the transposition of the text.

54. Pater's comment that the *Dialogue* was "the most humorous work Karlstadt ever published" and so not likely to have been written at a time when he was facing exile (*Karlstadt*, p. 160), misses the polemical thrust of the dialogue. A modern reader might find the pamphlet amusing, but as the comments of Zwingli and others demonstrate, contemporaries were incensed and offended by its language and tone.

55. Gemser initially sounds like a Catholic, mentioning seven sacraments and encouraging the invocation of the saints, and he uses scholastic arguments to support Christ's corporeal presence in the sacrament. Later in the *Dialogue*, though, he cites the authority of Luther and Wittenberg more generally, and he introduces Luther's argument that the sacrament was intended to assure one of forgiveness. He can thus best be described as one of "the old and new papists," reflecting the fact that on the issue of Christ's corporeal presence in the sacrament, Karlstadt saw no difference between Catholics and Lutherans.

56. Victus's "reappearance" in modern versions of the *Dialogue* is the result of Hertzsch's transposition of pages and does not occur in the sixteenth-century imprints; Hertzsch, *Schriften*, 2: 40–41; Furcha, *Carlstadt*, pp. 306–307; see n. 53 above.

57. *Sent*. IV, Dist. 1, c. 2, MPL 192, col. 839; Zwingli also cited the meaning of "sacrament" as a military oath in *Auslegung*; Z 2: 120–122, 124–125, HZW 1: 98–102; Hertzsch, *Schriften*, 2: 9–11; Burnett, *Pamphlets*, pp. 167–168.

58. Hertzsch, *Schriften*, 2: 11–17; Burnett, *Pamphlets*, pp. 168–175.

59. Barge, *Karlstadt*, 2: 170–171, demonstrates that the Cathars and Waldensians had earlier argued that Christ pointed to himself when he said, "this is my body."

60. Hertzsch, *Schriften*, 2: 17–18, 24, 29–30, 33–35, 39–40, 42–43; Burnett, *Pamphlets*, pp. 175–176, 182, 187–188, 190–191, 195–197,

61. Hertzsch, *Schriften*, 2: 24, 42–43; Burnett, *Pamphlets*, pp. 181–182, 197. Hoen used John 16:7 to argue against Christ's corporeal presence; Spruyt points to the possible influence of Erasmus on Hoen at this point, although Erasmus did not use the passage to argue for Christ's absence from the elements; *Hoen*, pp. 105–106, 232; Oberman, *Forerunners*, pp. 269, 274. On Matt. 24:23, Spruyt, *Hoen*, pp. 92, 227; Oberman, *Forerunners*, p. 269. On the Hussite source of these ideas, see pp. 79, 81–82, 84.

62. Hertzsch, *Schriften*, 2: 49; Burnett, *Pamphlets*, p. 204. Karlstadt gives the title of *Masses* between the second and the third title/section heading of *Abuse*, which supports the argument that he had not yet written *Abuse* and intended instead to write three separate works. There is a good deal of overlap between *Exegesis* and *Abuse*, which suggests that the latter was written some time after the former: such repetition would be unlikely if the two pamphlets had been written within a few weeks of each other.

63. *Abuse*; Köhler MF 1949, no. 4973. The pamphlet is reprinted in Walch 20: 93–109; English translations in Sider, *Battle*, pp. 72–91, and Burnett, *Pamphlets*, pp. 205–218.

64. *Abuse*, fol. a1v; Burnett, *Pamphlets*, pp. 205–206.

65. *Abuse*, fol. a4r; Burnett, *Pamphlets*, pp. 208–209.

66. *Abuse*, fol. a2r–v; a3v–b2v; c1v–c2r; Burnett, *Pamphlets*, pp. 206–212, 215–216. Sider sums this up as "both an intellectual understanding of the cross and inner regeneration"; he gives several examples of Karlstadt's use of adjectives to strengthen "remembrance"; *Karlstadt*, pp. 296–297.

67. The main section of the *Exegesis* ends with "Amen" near the bottom of fol. d3v; the postscript continues through the last two pages of the gathering, plus three pages from a final sheet of paper (d4r–d6r), Burnett, *Pamphlets*, pp. 159–162. Luther told Spalatin that the letters to Orlamünde were signed, "Andres Bodensteyn unverhort vnd vnvberwunden durch Martinum Luther vertrieben"; 30 October 1524, WA Br 3: 365. There are also close parallels in phrasing between the conclusion to the *Exegesis* and the *Vrsachen der halben Andres Carolstatt auß den landen zuo Sachsen vertryben* (Strasbourg: Prüß, 1524), which was printed in early November; see the appendix.

68. On Karlstadt's travels, see the appendix, pp. 144–147.

69. See pp. 102–107.

70. The editor of Luther's published response to the Strasbourgers assumes that Luther received all five of the Basel eucharistic pamphlets from Strasbourg, but he gives no basis for this assumption; WA 15: 382. The editors of *Wider die Himmlischen Propheten* are much more careful in demonstrating Luther's knowledge of Karlstadt's pamphlets; WA 18: 45–46; see Kaufmann, *Abendmahlstheologie*, pp. 217–237, for a broader discussion of the context and content of the Strasbourg letter.

71. Luther first used the word *Schwärmerei* against Karlstadt in his letter to the Strasbourgers from November 1524; WA 15: 393; LW 40: 67. On his broad use of the term, Günter Mühlpfordt,

"Luther und die 'Linken.' Eine Untersuchung seiner Schwärmerterminologie," in *Martin Luther. Leben—Werk—Wirkung*, ed. Günter Vogler (Berlin: Akademie Verlag, 1986), pp. 325–345.

72. Brecht, "Luther und Karlstadt"; Luther's response was published as *Ein Brief an die Christen zu Straßburg wider den Schwärmergeist*, WA 15: 391–397; LW 40: 65–71.

73. WA 18: 62; LW 40: 79.

74. WA 18: 102–110; LW 40: 119–127.

75. WA 18: 113–122; LW 40: 130–140.

76. WA 18: 123–125; LW 40: 141–143.

77. WA 18: 134–139; LW 40: 144–149.

78. WA 18: 139–142; LW 40: 149–152.

79. WA 18: 143–144; LW 40: 153–154.

80. WA 18: 145–151; LW 40: 155–161.

81. WA 18: 152–157; LW 40: 161–168.

82. WA 18: 166–172, citation at p. 166; LW 40: 177–182, citation at p. 177. Luther was here repeating the position he had already stated in *On the Adoration of the Sacrament*, but in a much more polemical way. Karlstadt had in fact discussed 1 Cor. 10:16 in *Prove*, which Luther had not read.

83. WA 18: 172–180; LW 40: 182–190.

84. WA 18: 192–193; LW 40: 202–203.

85. WA 18: 194–198; LW 40: 204–208.

86. WA 18: 200–205; LW 40: 210–215.

87. WA 18: 209; LW 40: 218. While writing the second part of his book, Luther also read Urbanus Rhegius's response to Karlstadt, *Wider den newen irrsal Doctor Andres von Carlstadt/ des Sacraments halb/warnung* (Augsburg: Ruff, 1524), Köhler MF 252, no. 705; see his letters to Spalatin asking to have the pamphlet sent to him, 29 December 1524, and returning the pamphlet, 13 January 1525, WA Br 3: 409, 421–422. Rhegius's pamphlet was directed against both the *Dialogue* and *Abuse*, and so Luther had a secondhand knowledge of Karlstadt's arguments in the latter work, derived from Rhegius.

88. *Explanation*, Köhler MF 106, no. 275; modern edition in Adolf Laube et al., eds., *Flugschriften vom Bauernkrieg zum Täuferreich (1526–1535)* (Berlin: Akademie Verlag, 1992), 1: 51–70; English translation in Burnett, *Pamphlets*, pp. 205–237; *Testament*, Köhler MF 107, no. 277; reprinted in Walch 20: 286–311; English translation in Burnett, *Pamphlets*, pp. 238– 257. Karlstadt listed the fifteen propositions drawn from Luther's work that he intended to refute in *Explanation*, fol. A2r-v; Laube, *Flugschriften*, pp. 51–52; Burnett, *Pamphlets*, pp. 219–221.

89. This characterization is especially true of the *Explanation*, written under the immediate impression of *Against the Heavenly Prophets*. The two pamphlets were written between 27 February, the date Karlstadt says he began the *Explanation*, and mid-March; the preface of *Testament* is dated 16 March. The marked stylistic contrast between these two pamphlets and the *Exegesis* and *Prove* is further evidence that the latter were not written under similar time pressure in the few weeks after the Jena confrontation.

90. *Explanation*, fol. A2v–B2v, citation at fol. A4r; Laube, *Flugschriften*, pp. 52–57; Burnett, *Pamphlets*, pp. 221–225, citation at p. 223.

91. *Explanation*, fol. B2v–B3v; Laube, *Flugschriften*, pp. 57–58; Burnett, *Pamphlets*, pp. 225–227.

92. *Explanation*, fol. C1r–C2r; Laube, *Flugschriften*, pp. 60–62; Burnett, *Pamphlets*, p. 229. Hoen first proposed that "est" meant "significat" with regard to 1 Cor. 10:16, and he made the

comparison with other metaphors in Scripture; Spruyt, *Hoen*, pp. 227–228; Oberman, *Forerunners*, pp. 269–271.

93. *Explanation*, fol. C2v–C4r, D2r–D3r; Laube, *Flugschriften*, pp. 62–64, 67–69; Burnett, *Pamphlets*, pp. 230–232, 234–236.

94. *Explanation*, fol. D3r–D4r; Laube, *Flugschriften*, pp. 69–70; Burnett, *Pamphlets*, pp. 236–237.

95. *Testament*, fol. A3r–A4r, C2v–C3v; Burnett, *Pamphlets*, pp. 239–241, 248–250. Krodel, "Figura Prothysteron," does not discuss this pamphlet, but Karlstadt's various transpositions of this phrase reflect Erasmus's suggestion of applying this exegetical technique to understand the passage.

96. *Testament*, fol. B1r–B1v; Burnett, *Pamphlets*, pp. 242–243; ASD VII/6, pp. 66–80, perhaps best summed up in Erasmus's paraphrase of Heb. 10:22: "For our bodies have not been sprinkled beforehand with the blood of an animal, but our minds and spirits have been sprinkled with the blood of Jesus Christ," p. 78; CWE 44: 233–243, citation at p. 241.

97. *Testament*, fol. B2v–B3r, D1r–v; Burnett, *Pamphlets*, pp. 244–245, 251–252.

98. *Testament*, fol. B4r–C2r; Burnett, *Pamphlets*, pp. 246–248.

99. *Testament*, fol. C4r, E1r–E2v; Burnett, *Pamphlets*, pp. 250–251, 254–256.

100. Ponader also emphasizes the importance of a metaphysical dualism for Karlstadt's eucharistic theology; "Abendmahlslehre," pp. 198–203.

101. In *Forms*, fol. b4r, Burnett, *Pamphlets*, p. 58, for instance, Karlstadt referred to the difference between natural signs, such as smoke signifying a fire, and conventional signs; this distinction comes from Augustine's *de Doctrina Christiana*, II, 1,2. On Augustine's figural interpretation of the Old Testament, Auerbach, "Figura."

102. The difference between Luther and Karlstadt might be loosely characterized as a particular instance of the difference between an Aristotelian metaphysic that saw reality as located within the material world and a (neo-)Platonic dualism that separated what was real and eternal from the material world. On the neoplatonic roots of Reformation spiritualism, R. Emmet McLaughlin, "Reformation Spiritualism: Typology, Sources and Significance," in *Radikalität und Dissent im 16. Jahrhundert/Radicalism and Dissent in the Sixteenth Century*, ed. James M. Stayer and Hans-Jürgen Goertz (Berlin: Duncker & Humblot, 2002), pp. 123–140. Richard A. Beinert discusses the implications of this difference between Luther and Karlstadt for practical theology, "Another Look at Luther's Battle with Karlstadt," *Concordia Theological Quarterly* 73 (2009): 155–170.

103. There were twelve imprints of Part One and ten imprints of Part Two of *Against the Heavenly Prophets*.

104. WA Br 3: 409, 451–452, 456–457.

105. *Erklerung wie Carlstat sein lere von dem hochwirdigen Sacrament vnd andere achtet vnd geacht haben wil* (Wittenberg: Rhau-Grunenberg, 1525), WA 18: 453–466; translation in Burnett, *Pamphlets*, pp. 258–269. The work appeared in print in late September; Barge, *Karlstadt*, 2: 366–369. It was printed separately in five editions as well as together with his *Entschuldigung D. Andres Carlstats des falschen names der auffruor* and so circulated more widely than any of Karlstadt's other eucharistic pamphlets.

106. WA 18: 455–462; Burnett, *Pamphlets*, pp. 260–266.

107. WA 18: 453–454; citation at p. 454; Burnett, *Pamphlets*, pp. 259–260, citation at pp. 259–260.

108. WA 18: 455–456; Burnett, *Pamphlets*, pp. 260–261.

109. Barge, *Karlstadt*, 2: 376–379.

CHAPTER 4

1. David R. Holeton surveys the development of various aspects of Hussite eucharistic theology, drawing attention to the importance not only of the lay chalice but also frequent communion and the communion of all baptized, including infants; "The Bohemian Eucharistic
Movement in Its European Context," in *The Bohemian Reformation and Religious Practice: Papers
from the XVIIth World Congress of the Czechoslovak Society of Arts and Sciences, Prague 1994*, ed.
David R. Holeton (Prague: Academy of Sciences of the Czech Republic, 1996), pp. 23–47.

2. The foundational study is Walther Köhler, *Luther und die Kirchengeschichte nach seinen
Schriften, zunächst bis 1521*, Beiträge zu den Anfängen protestantischer Kirchengeschichtsschreibung (Erlangen: Junge, 1900), pp. 162–236, supplemented by Erhard Peschke, *Die Theologie
der böhmischen Brüder in ihrer Frühzeit*, vol. 1, *Das Abendmahl*, Forschungen zur Kirchen- und
Geistesgeschichte 5 (Stuttgart: Kohlhammer, 1935), pp. 334–374. More recent scholarship is
reflected in Bernhard Lohse, "Luther und Huß," *Luther. Zeitschrift der Luthergesellschaft* 36
(1965): 108–122; Amedeo Molnár, "Luthers Beziehungen zu den Böhmischen Brüdern," in *Leben
und Werk Martin Luthers von 1526 bis 1546. Festgabe zu seinem 500. Geburtstag*, ed. Helmar
Junghans (Göttingen: Vandenhoeck & Ruprecht, 1983), 1: 627–639; and Thomas Kaufmann,
"Jan Hus und die frühe Reformation," in *Biblische Theologie und historisches Denken.
Wissenschaftsgeschichtliche Studien, aus anlass der 50. Wiederkehr der Basler Promotion von Rudolf
Smend*, ed. Martin Kessler and Martin Wallraff (Basel: Schwabe, 2008), pp. 62–109.

3. Frantisek M. Bartos, "Erasmus und die böhmische Reformation," *Communio Viatorum* 1
(1958): 116–123, 246–257; Konrad Bittner, "Erasmus, Luther und die böhmischen Brüder," in
Rastloses Schaffen: Festschrift für Dr. Friedrich Lammert, ed. Heinz Seehase (Stuttgart:
Kohlhammer, 1954), pp. 107–129.

4. Joachim Staedtke, "Voraussetzungen der Schweizer Abendmahlslehre," *Theologische
Zeitschrift* 16 (1960): 19–32. Jarold K. Zeman looks at the contacts between the Bohemian
Brethren and the Swiss reformers in the early years of the Reformation, but he is more
concerned with Balthasar Hubmaier and the Swiss Anabaptists in the period after the outbreak of the eucharistic controversy; *The Anabaptists and the Czech Brethren in Moravia 1526–
1628: A Study of Origins and Contacts*, Studies in European History 20 (The Hague: Mouton,
1969). Joseph Th. Müller, "Die böhmische Brüderunität und Zwingli," *Zwingliana* 3 (1920):
514–524, is also concerned primarily with the period after 1525.

5. The range of Hussite thinking is described by Peschke, *Theologie*, I/1: 1–16; see also the
two articles by Amedeo Molnár, "L'évolution de la théologie hussite," *Revue d'histoire et de philosophie religieuses* 43 (1963): 133–171, and "Bekenntnisse der böhmischen Reformation,"
Jahrbuch für die Geschichte des Protestantismus in Österreich 96 (1980): 310–332. Hus's own
views on the sacrament were conventional. He accepted the substantial presence of Christ's
body and blood in the consecrated elements as well as the doctrine of concomitance, and only
after his arrival in Constance in 1414 did he begin to defend the lay chalice; Alexander Kolesnyk,
"Hussens Eucharistiebegriff," in *Jan Hus. Zwischen Zeiten, Völkern, Konfessionen. Vorträge des
internationalen Symposions in Bayreuth vom 22. bis 26. September 1993*, ed. Ferdinand Seibt
(Munich: Oldenbourg, 1997), pp. 193–202. The Picards were a heretical group from the
Low Countries that came to Bohemia in 1418. Their views were rejected even by the radical
Taborites, and they were virtually eliminated in the early 1420s. There was no direct connec-
tion between these Picards and the later Bohemian Brethren, who were commonly called
"Picards" or "Pighards" by the beginning of the sixteenth century; Frantisek M. Bartos,
"Picards et Pikarti," *Bulletin de la Société de l'histoire du Protestantisme Français* 80 (1931):

465–486; 81 (1932): 8–28; Peschke, *Theologie*, I/1: 80–81; Howard Kaminsky, *A History of the Hussite Revolution* (Berkeley: University of California Press, 1967), pp. 418–433.

6. On the disagreements concerning the Eucharist, Kaminsky, *Hussite Revolution*, pp. 460–466. In addition to Nicholas of Pelhřimov, the most important Taborite theologians were the exiled Englishman Peter Payne and the German Hussite priest Jan Němec (Johann Teutonicus) of Saaz.

7. Amedeo Molnár and Romolo Cegna, eds., *Confessio Taboritarum*, Fonti per la storia d'Italia 105 (Rome: Istituto storico italiano per il medio evo, 1983), pp. 78–79; the disputation for which the confession was written is described in F. M. Bartos, *The Hussite Revolution, 1424–1437* (Boulder, Colo.: East European Monographs, 1986), p. 63.

8. Johannis de Zacz, "Tractatulus [de eucharistia]," in *Táborské traktáty eucharistické*, ed. Jan Sedlak (Brno: Nákl. Papezské Knihtisk. Benedktinu Rajhradskych, 1918), pp. 4–15; Peter Payne, "Tractatus II de corpore Christ," ibid., p. 32; "Tractatus de 4 modis essendi," ibid., pp. 38–50; Peschke, *Theologie*, I/1: 85–96. On Wyclif's influence, William R. Cook, "John Wyclif and Hussite Theology, 1415–1436," *Church History* 42 (1973): 335–349; Erhard Peschke, "Die Bedeutung Wiclefs für die Theologie der Böhmen," *Zeitschrift für Kirchengeschichte* 54 (1935): 462–483. On Wyclif's understanding of Christ's presence in the sacrament, Ian Christopher Levy, *John Wyclif: Scriptural Logic, Real Presence, and the Parameters of Orthodoxy*, Marquette Studies in Theology 36 (Milwaukee, Wis.: Marquette University Press, 2003), pp. 288–304; Stephen Penn, "Wyclif and the Sacraments," in *A Companion to John Wyclif, Late Medieval Theologian*, ed. Ian Christopher Levy (Leiden: Brill, 2006), pp. 241–291, esp. pp. 267–272.

9. Sedlak, *Táborské traktáty*, pp. 6–7; Karl Adolf Constantin Höfler, ed., *Geschichtsschreiber der husitischen Bewegung in Böhmen*, vol. 2, Fontes Rerum Austriacarum. 1. Abt.: Scriptores, Bd. 6,2 (New York: Johnson Reprint, 1969), pp. 777–779, a portion of the Taborite chronicle recounting a debate between Jan Rokycana, the leader of the Utraquists, and the Taborite theologians at a synod held in 1443; see also the confession of the Taborite clergy, pp. 798–804. In the *Trialogus*, which Peter Payne cited against the Utraquists associated with the university of Prague, *Geschichtsschreiber*, pp. 705–707, Wyclif introduced these three Scripture texts to demonstrate the figurative language of Scripture, Book IV, chap. 7, John Wyclif, *Trialogus cum supplemento Trialogi*, ed. Gotthard Lechler (Oxford: Clarendon, 1869), pp. 266–267. The figurative understanding of the words of institution, including the parallel to "[John] is Elijah," was one of the articles drawn from Wyclif's works condemned by the Council of Constance.

10. Höfler, *Geschichtsschreiber*, pp. 780–791; "de adorare et colere," Sedlak, *Táborské traktáty*, pp. 51–55.

11. Frederick G Heymann, "The Hussite Revolution and Reformation and Its Impact in Germany," in *Festschrift für Hermann Heimpel zum 70. Geburtstag am 19. September 1971* (Göttingen: Vandenhoeck & Ruprecht, 1971), 2: 610–626; Ferdinand Seibt, *Hussitica. Zur Struktur einer Revolution* (Cologne: Böhlau, 1965), pp. 92–97; Peter Segl, "Die Auswirkungen der hussitischen Bewegung auf Europa," in *Reformer als Ketzer: Heterodoxe Bewegungen von Vorreformatoren*, ed. Günter Frank and Friedrich Niewöhner (Stuttgart/Bad Cannstatt: Frommann-Holzboog, 2004), pp. 197–213; Bart Jan Spruyt, "Das Echo des Jan Hus und der hussitischen Bewegung in den burgundischen Niederlanden, ca. 1420-ca. 1530," in *Jan Hus. Zwischen Zeiten, Völkern, Konfessionen. Vorträge des internationalen Symposions in Bayreuth vom 22. bis 26. September 1993*, ed. Ferdinand Seibt (Munich: Oldenbourg, 1997), pp. 283–301; Frantisek Smahel, *Die Hussitische Revolution*, trans. Thomas Krzenck, MGA Schriften 43 (Hannover: Hahnsche Buchhandlung, 2002), 3: 1913–1936.

12. On Reiser, see the essays in Albert de Lange and Kathrin Utz Tremp, eds., *Friedrich Reiser und die "waldensisch-hussitische Internationale" im 15. Jahrhundert. Akten der Tagung Ötisheim-Schönenberg, 2. bis 4. Oktober 2003* (Heidelberg: Verlag Regionalkultur, 2006). Contacts between the Waldensians and the Hussites came to an end after the execution of the most important Waldensian preachers, including Reiser, and the formation of the Bohemian Brethren during the later 1450s and 1460s; Amedeo Molnár, *Die Waldenser. Geschichte und europäisches Ausmaß einer Ketzerbewegung* (Göttingen: Vandenhoeck & Ruprecht, 1980), pp. 283–293. A general sense of the relationship between the Waldensians and the Bohemian heretics was the origin of the usual name in Germany for the Unitas Fratrum, the "Waldensian Brethren"; Zeman, *Anabaptists*, 149.

13. Franticek M. Bartos, ed., "Puer Bohemus. Dva projevy husitské propagandy," *Věstník Královské České Společnosti Nauk. Třída filosophicko-historicko-jazykozpytná. Ročník 1523, II* (Memoires de la Société Royale des Sciences de Bohême. Classe des lettres. Année 1923, II) (1924): 1–58. Bartos believed that the anonymous treatise originated in the Low Countries, but the manuscripts he edited were found in Karlsruhe and Stuttgart, which suggests the spread of Hussite ideas up the Rhine into South Germany. The treatise is also discussed by Spruyt, *Hoen*, pp. 157–159.

14. Bartos, "Puer Bohemus," pp. 23–25; cf. Payne, "Tractatus I," Sedlak, *Táborské traktáty*, p. 25.

15. Bartos, "Puer Bohemus," p. 27.

16. Bartos, "Puer Bohemus," p. 30.

17. For an overview of political and religious developments in the Czech lands in the later fifteenth century, Frederick G. Heymann, "John Rokycana—Church Reformer between Hus and Luther," *Church History* 28 (1959): 240–280; Heymann, "The Hussite-Utraquist Church in the Fifteenth and Sixteenth Centuries," *Archiv für Reformationsgeschichte* 52 (1961): 1–16; Winfried Eberhard, "Zur reformatorischen Qualität und Konfessionalisierung des nachrevolutionären Hussitismus," in *Häresie und vorzeitige Reformation im Spätmittelalter*, ed. Frantisek Smahel (Munich: Oldenbourg, 1998), pp. 213–238.

18. Peter Chelčický, "Vom Leibe Christi," in Erhard Peschke, *Die Theologie der böhmischen Brüder in ihrer Frühzeit*, vol. 1, *Das Abendmahl*, pt. 2, *Texte aus alttschechischen Handschriften übersetzt*, Forschungen zur Kirchen- und Geistesgeschichte 20 (Stuttgart: Kohlhammer, 1940), pp. 132–137; see also Peschke, *Theologie*, I/1: 107–123; Pavel Kolář, "Petr Chelčický's Defense of Sacramental Communion: Response to Mikuláš Biskupec of Tábor," in *The Bohemian Reformation and Religious Practice*, vol. 6, *Papers from the Sixth International Symposium on the Bohemian Reformation and Religious Practice*, ed. Zdenek V. David and David R. Holeton (Prague: Academy of Sciences of the Czech Republic, 2007), pp. 133–142. On Chelčický more generally, Howard Kaminsky, "Peter Chelčický: Treatises on Christianity and the Social Order," *Studies in Medieval and Renaissance History* 1 (1964): 104–179, esp. pp. 107–136; Matthew Spinka, "Peter Chelčický: The Spiritual Father of the Unitas Fratrum," *Church History* 12 (1943): 271–291.

19. Zeman, *Anabaptists*, pp. 132–136; Erhard Peschke, *Die Böhmischen Brüder im Urteil ihrer Zeit; Zieglers, Dungersheims und Luthers Kritik an der Brüderunität*, Arbeiten zur Theologie, 1. Reihe 17 (Stuttgart: Calwer Verlag, 1964), pp. 12–14. The *Apologia* is photomechanically reproduced in Alfred Eckert, ed., *Bekenntnisse der Böhmischen Brüder*, Nikolaus Ludwig von Zinzendorf Materialen und Dokumente Reihe 1, Quellen und Darstellung zur Geschichte der böhmischen Brüder-Unität 3 (Hildesheim: Olms, 1979), unpaginated.

20. An overview of Brother Lukas's understanding of the Eucharist in Peschke, *Theologie*, I/1: 272–304.

21. I used the confessions of 1503, 1507, and 1508 printed in Aeneas Sylvius Piccolomini (later Pope Pius II), *Commentariorum Aeneae Sylvii Piccolominei Senensis De Concilio Basileae celebrato libri duo, olim quidem scripti, nunc vero primum impressi* (Basel: Cratander, 1523): 1503 *Oratio*, pp. 125–133, 1507 *Confessio*, pp. 135–136, 1508 *Excusatio*, pp. 152–153; Eckert, *Bekenntnisse*, "Apologia," fol. H4v–I4v. See also Peschke, *Die Böhmischen Brüder*, pp. 22–24; Milos Strupl, "The Confessional Theology of the Unitas Fratrum," *Church History* 33 (1964): 279–293.

22. Piccolomini, *Commentariorum*, 1508 *Excusatio*, pp. 152–154.

23. Eckert, *Bekenntnisse*, "Apologia," fol. I2v: "Anima quidem christi subsistentia potitur spiritualiter per fidem in meritoria gratia et veritate: vt prous patuit: in sacramentis autem sacramentali modo. . . . Naturalis tamen subsistentia in vsum nunquam venit: sed tantummodo spiritualiter: virtualiter: sacramentaliter et vere."

24. This quotation was cited in the *Decretum*, pars III (*De consecratione*), Dist. 2, c. 44; Emil Friedberg, ed., *Corpus Iuris Canonici* (Leipzig: Tauchnitz, 1879–81), 1: 1330. The proper understanding of this passage, particularly in light of the differences between the original text and the excerpt in the *Decretum*, would be hotly contested between the two sides of the debate over the Lord's Supper in the later 1520s. Philipp Melanchthon would consider it to be one of the strongest patristic citations used by his opponents, and so he devoted a lengthy section of his *Sentenciae Veterum aliquot scriptorum de Coena Domini* of 1530 to it; CR 23: 744–752.

25. Piccolomini, *Commentariorum*, 1507 *Confessio*, pp. 135–136; 1508 *Excusatio*, pp. 151–155; Eckert, *Bekenntnisse*, "Apologia," fol. I1r–v. The Wycliffite origin of these ideas is suggested by the fact that trials of English Lollards raised the same arguments about seeing God more clearly in other people than in the consecrated host and arguing that priests, as created beings, could not make God, the Creator; Ann Hudson, "The Mouse in the Pyx: Popular Heresy and the Eucharist," *Trivium* 26 (1991): 40–53.

26. Jakob Ziegler, *In hoc volumine haec continentur . . . Contra haeresim valdensium libri quinque* (Leipzig, 1512).

27. Peschke, *Die Böhmischen Brüder*, pp. 28–30, 65–66.

28. Piccolomini, *Commentariorum*. VD16 (P 3111) identifies the editor as the Cologne humanist Jakob Sobius; on Sobius, see Peter Bietenholz, ed., *Contemporaries of Erasmus: A Biographical Register of the Renaissance and Reformation* (Toronto: University of Toronto Press, 1985–1987), 3: 262–263. The *Commentariorum* also contained a list of articles drawn from Wyclif's works and refuted by the English theologian William Woodford; the Wyclifite articles condemned at the Council of Constance along with a justification of their condemnation; an excerpt from Piccolomini's history of Bohemia concerning Wyclif, Hus, and Jerome of Prague; Leonardo Bruni's *adversum hypocritas libellus*; a description of the discussions with the Bohemians at the Council of Basel; the petition of the Bohemians at the Council along with the response to it; and the interrogation of John of Wesel by the Inquisition in 1479.

29. Siegfried Hoyer, "Jan Hus und der Hussitismus in den Flugschriften des ersten Jahrzehnts der Reformation," in *Flugschriften als Massenmedium der Reformationszeit*, ed. Hans-Joachim Köhler (Stuttgart: Klett-Cotta, 1981), pp. 291–307; Hans-Gert Roloff, "Die Funktion von Hus-Texten in der Reformations-Polemik (Erster Teil)," in *De captu lectoris. Wirkungen des Buches im 15. und 16. Jahrhundert, dargestellt an ausgewählten Handschriften und Drucken*, ed. Wolfgang Milde and Werner Schuder (Berlin: de Gruyter, 1988), pp. 219–256. On the negative depiction of the Hussites, Frantisek Matous, "Johannes Hus in den Schweizer Chroniken des 15. und 16. Jahrhunderts," in *Jan Hus. Zwischen Zeiten, Völkern, Konfessionen. Vorträge des internationalen Symposions in Bayreuth vom 22. bis 26. September 1993*, ed. Ferdinand Seibt (Munich: Oldenbourg, 1997), pp. 367–374.

30. *Wie Hieronymus von Prag ain anhänger Johannis Huß durch das concilium zuo Costentz für ain Ketzer verurtailt vnd verpränt worden ist* (Augsburg, 1521), two imprints in 1521 and one in 1525; [Paul Phrygio, ed.], *De Causa Boemica* (Hagenau: Anshelm, 1520); also printed with the title *Liber Egregius de unitate Ecclesiae, Cuius autor periit in concilio Constantiensi* (Basel: Petri, 1520); *Epistola quinquagintaquattuor nobilium Moraviae, pro defensione Johannis Hussi, ad concilium Constantiense, commendata literis adulescentis cuiusdam, argumenti vice appositis . . .* [Basel: Cratander, 1524]; Otto Brunfels, ed., *Ioannes Hvss De Anatomia Antichristi, Liber Unus ...; Ioannis Huss Locorum aliquot ex Osee, & Ezechiele prophetis . . . Tomus Secundus*; and *Sermonum Ioannis Huss ad Populum, Tomus Tertius* (Strasbourg: Schott, 1524). These texts were actually written by Matthias of Janov, a precursor of Hus. Roloff, "Function," describes several of these works and their reception by the reformers.

31. *Artickel und Ursprung der Waldenser und der armen von Lugdun, auch Joannis Wicleffen, und Joannis Hussen* (Nuremberg: Gutknecht, 1524), fol. B2r–B4r.

32. Theophilus Tectonus, *Compendiosa Boemice seu Hussitane Hereseos ortus & eiusdem damnatorum Articulorum descriptio* (Strasbourg: Grüninger, 1524), fol. A4r.

33. Hoyer, "Jan Hus und der Hussitismus"; Siegfried Hoyer, "Martin Reinhart und der erste Druck hussitischer Artikel in Deutschland," *Zeitschrift für Geschichtswissenschaft* 18 (1970): 1597–1615. Reinhart's book was titled *Antzeygung wie die gefallene Christenheit widerbracht mügen werden . . .* (Jena: Buchfürer, 1524). The Prague articles were the four demands made by the Hussite delegation at the Council of Basel: free preaching of the gospel, punishment of public mortal sins, prohibition of wealth and secular lordship for the clergy, and communion in both kinds for the laity.

34. Brunfel's preface to Luther, WA Br 3: 335. The work was published in March 1525 as *Io. Wiclefi Viri vndiqvaque pijs. dialogorum libri quattuor . . .* (Hagenau: Schöffer, 1525); the first ten chapters of Book 4 concerned the Eucharist, fol. 99v–117v. In a letter dated by its editors toward the end of 1524, Melanchthon advised against the printing of Wyclif's *Trialogus*, which he had seen "long ago," presumably while still a student; MBW T2: 220, no. 363. In the polemics of the period, Hus and Wyclif were generally mentioned together.

35. György Székely, "Das Erbe von Jan Hus in der Reformation Martin Luthers," *Annales Universitatis Scientiarum Budapestinensis, sectio historica* 24 (1985): 3–21, gives examples of several scholars, including the young Luther, who had access to these heretical ideas before the Reformation.

36. *Epistola Christiana admodum . . . longe aliter tractans Cenam Dominicam quam hactenus tractata est*; on the publication history of the pamphlet, Spruyt, *Hoen*, pp. 167–186. The contents of the pamphlet are summarized in chapter 1, pp. 17–18.

37. Spruyt, "Das Echo," Spruyt, *Hoen*, pp. 127–165, esp. pp. 163–165.

38. *Adoration*, fol. B3r; Burnett, *Pamphlets*, p. 46; *Exegesis*, fol. a2v; Burnett, *Pamphlets*, pp. 145–146. This passage alluded to Luther's *On the Adoration of the Sacrament*, which was addressed to "the Waldensians" or Bohemian Brethren.

39. The similarites are described more fully in chapter 3, pp. 60–64, 66–68; see also chapter 5, p. 106.

40. Spruyt, *Hoen*, p. 157; Hertzsch, *Schriften*, 2: 24.6–7, 42.18–43.2; Burnett, *Pamphlets*, pp. 181–182, 197–198. Karlstadt's distinction between Christ's divine and human natures is obscured in Hertzsch's edition by the transposition of fol. A4v in the Basel edition from its proper place (p. 11.7) to pp. 40.33–41.25 (the reappearance of Victus). Because Furcha used Hertzsch's text for his translation, he made the same transposition; *Carlstadt*, pp. 275 and 306–307.

41. Hoyer, "Martin Reinhart"; Smahel, *Hussitische Revolution*, 3: 1971.

42. These connections were first pointed out by Staedtke, "Voraussetzungen"; a more precise description of the Swiss reformers' knowledge of Hussite ideas in Zeman, *Anabaptists*, pp. 137–155.

43. B&A 2: 511, 13 October 1530. Oecolampadius's statement suggests that he was not aware of either the historical or the theological differences between the Waldensians and the Bohemian Brethren.

44. *De genvina verborum domini, Hoc est corpus meum, iuxta uetutissimos authores expositione liber* (Strasbourg: Knoblauch, 1525). Oecolampadius finished the manuscript in late June, and the printed version was available by mid-September; Ernst Staehelin, *Das theologische Lebenswerk Johannes Oekolampads*, Quellen und Forschungen zur Reformationsgeschichte (Leipzig: Heinsius, 1939), pp. 276–284.

45. *De genvina . . . expositione*, fol. B8v–C1r, R7r. Oecolampadius also cited Christ's command to Mary to "behold your son," John 19:26, another proof text used by Hoen, but not by either Zwingli or Karlstadt. Hoen's letter was not published until after Oecolampadius had finished his own book, but it is possible that the Basler had a manuscript copy of it.

46. *De genvina . . . expositione*, fol. B4r–v. On the Brethren's use of early church practices, Piccolomini, *Commentariorum: 1507 Confessio*, p. 135; *1508 Excusatio*, pp. 141, 151.

47. *De genvina . . . expositione*, fol. D6v–D7v.

48. Oecolampadius listed Mark 16 [:9], Matt. 26 [:11], Luke 24 [:51], John 13 [:1], 16 [:7] and 17, Acts 1 [:11] and 7 [:56], Rom. 8 [:34], Eph. 1 [:20], 2 Cor. 6 (possibly a reference to 2 Cor. 5:16, used by the Bohemian Brethren), Heb. 8–10 and 12 [:2], 1 Thes. 4 [:16] and 1 Pet. 2; *De gevuina . . . expositione*, fol. K7r.

49. *De genvina . . . expositione*, fol. K6v–K8r. Oecolampadius had earlier cited the statement of Augustine, taken from the Decretum and also used by the Brethren, that Christ's body was above but his truth was diffused everywhere; fol. C6v.

50. A group of Swabian clergy, led by Johannes Brenz, responded to Oecolampadius's treatise in their *Syngramma . . . super uerbis Coenae Dominicae*, written in October 1525 and published twice in 1526; there were also three different German translations of the *Syngramma* published in 1526. Oecolampadius's treatise was attacked by Josse Clicthove in his 1526 *De Sacramento Evcharistiae*, reprinted in Cologne in 1527, as well as by John Fisher in his *De veritate Corporis et Sanguinis Christi in Eucharistia libri quinque* of 1527, and by Willibald Pirkheimer, whose *De vera Christi carne et uero eius sanguine, ad Ioan. Oecolampadium responsio* (Nuremberg: Petreius, 1526) provoked a further published exchange with Oecolampadius. Pirckheimer recognized the Hussite origin of the argument concerning Christ's body, and he accused Oecolampadius of sharing the "Pighard" belief that Christ's glorified body could not be in many places simultaneously; fol. F5r–v, cf. fol. B6v.

51. Zeman, *Anabaptists*, pp. 148–150; the treatise in HBTS 2: 49–65. Joachim Staedtke gives a more detailed analysis of Bullinger's early eucharistic theology; *Die Theologie des jungen Bullinger*, Studien zur Dogmengeschichte und systematischen Theologie 16 (Zurich: Zwingli-Verlag, 1962), pp. 234–254.

52. Bullinger also claimed that a god who let himself be eaten daily by such impure, drunken, and evil priests must himself be evil; HBTS 2: 51–53; 60.

53. Z 3: 795; *Commentary*, p. 224.

54. *Eine klare Unterrichtung vom Nachtmahl Christi*, Z 4: 789–862; Geoffrey W. Bromiley, ed., *Zwingli and Bullinger*, Library of Christian Classics 24 (Philadelphia: Westminster, 1953), pp. 176–238; the preface is dated 17 February 1526. For a summary, Köhler, *Zwingli und Luther*, 1: 301–310. Zwingli's earlier Latin discussions of the sacrament were all available in German translation, but this was his first work written specifically for a non-Latin reading public.

55. Zwingli's earliest allusion to the location of Christ's body in heaven occurred in the letter to the Strasbourgers with which he enclosed his letter to Alber, where he referred to Ps. 110:1 as cited in Heb. 1:13; BCorr 1: 313. He also mentioned that Christ's body was seated at the right hand of the Father in his *Subsidium*, Z 4: 467, HZW 2: 197, but he did not elaborate further on this idea in either work.

56. Z 4: 827–830; Bromily, *Zwingli*, p. 212–215.

57. The translation was titled *Vom Sacrament der Dancksagung. Von dem waren nateurlichen verstand der worten Christi...* (Zurich: Froschauer, 1526); Hätzer's preface in B&A 1: 437–447, citation at pp. 438–439. In a letter to Zwingli from 14 September 1525, Hätzer had criticized Bugenhagen for wanting to show Christ "at some place other than at the Father's right"; Z 8: 361.

58. Z 3: 336, 344–345; HZW 2: 131, 138–139. In the *Commentarius* he said that he had read only one of Karlstadt's pamphlets, the *Anti-Christian Abuse*; Z 3: 793; *Commentary*, p. 221. Zwingli's writings from 1527 betray greater familiarity with Karlstadt's works, but there is no direct evidence to show he had read any of Karlstadt's other pamphlets before early 1526. Zwingli did read Hoen's letter before it was published, however, and he could easily have obtained a printed copy of either the Latin or the German version, which were both published in the late summer of 1525.

59. *Amica Exegesis*, Z 5: 679–701; HZW 2: 319–336; Richard Cross, "'Alloiosis' in the Christology of Zwingli," *Journal of Theological Studies* N.S. 47 (1996): 105–122.

60. Köhler, *Zwingli und Luther*, 2: 100–110; Consensus Tigurinus cited from the translation of Henry Beveridge in John Calvin, *Treatises on the Sacraments: Catechism of the Church of Geneva, Forms of Prayer, and Confessions of Faith*, Christian Heritage Society (Grand Rapids, Mich.: Reformation Heritage, 2002), p. 220. This clause of the Consensus Tigurinus was the inspiration for Theodore Beza's more pointed and (in)famous statement at the 1561 Colloquy of Poissy that Christ's body was as distant from the bread and wine as heaven is distant from earth; Alain Dufour, *Théodore de Bèze. Poète et théologien*, Cahiers d'Humanisme et Renaissance 78 (Geneva: Droz, 2006), pp. 78–79.

61. On the Christological debate between Brenz and the Zurich theologians, Hans Christian Brandy, *Die späte Christologie des Johannes Brenz*, Beiträge zur historischen Theologie 80 (Tübingen: Paul Siebeck, 1991), pp. 45–69.

62. Walther Köhler argued that Zwingli first suggested that Christ was spiritually present in the sacrament in the *Amica Exegesis, Zwingli und Luther*, 1: 483–484, but the mention is so slight as to be negligible. Bucer first advanced the idea of agreement on the basis of a sacramental union in his *Vergleichung D. Luthers und seins Gegentheyls* of 1528, BDS 2: 305–383, esp. pp. 312–320. On the development of Bucer's eucharistic theology, Reinhold Friedrich, "'Eine Streit um Worte?' Bucers Position in der Abendmahlsfrage im Jahr 1530," in *Martin Bucer zwischen Luther und Zwingli*, ed. Matthieu Arnold and Berndt Hamm (Tübingen: Mohr Siebeck, 2003), pp. 49–65; Wilhelm H. Neuser, "Bucers konfessionelle Position," in *Martin Bucer and Sixteenth Century Europe. Actes du colloque de Strasbourg, 28–31 août 1991*, ed. Christian Krieger and Marc Lienhard (Leiden: Brill, 1993), 2: 693–704; Wilhelm H. Neuser, "Martin Bucer als Mittler im Abendmahlsstreit (1530/31)," in *Kaum zu Glauben. Von der Häresie und dem Umgang mit ihr*, ed. Athina Lexutt and Vicco von Bülow (Rheinbach: CMZ-Verlag, 1998), pp. 140–161.

CHAPTER 5

1. *Amica Exegesis*, Z 5: 632; HZW 2: 287.

2. *Ad Matthaeum Alberum . . . epistola*, Z 3: 335–336; HZW 2: 131

3. *Ad Theobaldi Billicani et Urbani Rhegii epistolas responsio*, Z 4: 933.

4. I distinguish early Zwinglianism, in which there was no discussion whatsoever of Christ's spiritual presence in the Supper, from late Zwinglianism, which included such discussion. On Zwingli's public statements concerning the Supper from 1529 on, W. Peter Stephens, *The Theology of Huldrych Zwingli* (Oxford: Clarendon, 1986), pp. 250–255. This "late Zwinglianism" continued to evolve after Zwingli's death; Paul Sanders, "Heinrich Bullinger et le 'zwinglianisme tardif' aux lendemains du 'Consensus Tigurinus,'" in *Reformiertes Erbe. Festschrift für Gottfried W. Locher zu seinem 80. Geburtstag*, ed. Heiko A. Oberman et al. (Zurich: Theologische Verlag, 1992), pp. 307–323.

5. WA Br 3: 329–332.

6. *Ioannis Oecolampadii ad Billibaldum Pyrkhaimerum de re Eucharistiae responsio* (Zurich: Froschauer, 1526), Köhler MF 355–356, no. 992, fol. A6r–v; *Apologetica Ioann. Oecolampadii . . . ad Theobaldvm Billicanvm quinam in uerbis Caenae alienum sensum inserant* (Zurich: Froschauer, 1526), Köhler MF 717–720, no. 1829, fol. C2v–C3v; German translation by Ludwig Hätzer, *Vom Nachtmal Beweisung ausz Euangelischen schrifften* (Augsburg: Ulhart, 1526), reprinted in Walch 17: 635–709, citation at col. 641–642. In his translation, Hätzer added parenthetically that the "papist belief" to which Oecolampadius referred was that Christ is substantially in the bread.

7. Ernst Staehelin, *Das theologische Lebenswerk Johannes Oekolampads*, Quellen und Forschungen zur Reformationsgeschichte (Leipzig: Heinsius, 1939), pp. 269–270; Köhler, *Zwingli und Luther*, 1: 49, 61–63; see also Köhler's debate with Karl Bauer concerning Zwingli's early eucharistic theology: Karl Bauer, "Die Abendmahlslehre Zwinglis bis zum Beginn der Auseinandersetzung mit Luther," *Theologische Blätter* 5 (1926): 217–226; Walther Köhler, "Zu Zwinglis ältester Abendmahlsfassung," *Zeitschrift für Kirchengeschichte* 45 (1926): 399–408; Karl Bauer, "Symbolik und Realpräsenz in der Abendmahlsanschauung Zwinglis bis 1525," *Zeitschrift für Kirchengeschichte* 46 (1927): 97–105; and Walther Köhler, "Zur Abendmahlskontroverse in der Reformationszeit, insbesondere zur Entwicklung der Abendmahlslehre Zwinglis," *Zeitschrift für Kirchengeschichte* 47 (1928): 47–56.

8. Z 3: 335–336; HZW 2: 131. While Zwingli was obviously trying to distance himself from Karlstadt, this does not make his claim unreliable. The letter was written in November 1524 and circulated in manuscript for several months before its publication.

9. *Epistola*, Z 3: 336–340; HZW 2: 132–135; *Commentarius*, Z 3: 775–784, 818, citation at p. 787; *Commentary*, pp. 200–211, 250, citation at p. 214. Zwingli had expressed a similar understanding of John 6 already in his *Auslegung der Schlussreden*, Z 2: 141–143; HZW 1: 113–115. Helmut Gollwitzer clearly brings out the importance of Zwingli's neoplatonic spirit/flesh dualism for understanding this passage as well as for his eucharistic theology more generally, and he points out that for Zwingli, just as for Luther, Christ's discourse in John 6 did not pertain directly to the sacrament; "Zur Auslegung von Joh. 6 bei Luther und Zwingli," in *In Memoriam Ernst Lohmeyer*, ed. Werner Schmauch (Stuttgart: Evangelisches Verlagswerk, 1951), pp. 143–168.

10. *Epistola*, Z 3: 343–345; HZW 2: 137–139; *Commentarius*, Z 3: 793–798; *Commentary*, pp. 222–227.

11. *Epistola*, Z 3: 345, 347–349; HZW 2: 139, 141–142; *Commentarius*, Z 3: 801–803, 807–809; *Commentary*, pp. 231–233, 238–239.

12. *Epistola*, Z 3: 346–347; HZW 2: 139–140; *Commentarius*, Z 3: 809–816; *Commentary*, pp. 239–248.

13. Erasmus had applied John 6:63 to the physical eating of the sacrament already in his *Enchiridion*, LB V, col. 30F–31C; CWE 66: 70–71. For Erasmus's influence on Zwingli, J. V. Pollet,

Huldrych Zwingli et le Zwinglianisme. Essai de synthèse historique et théologique mis à jour d'après les recherches récentes (Paris: Vrin, 1988), pp. 8–14. Zwingli, like Karlstadt, went beyond Erasmus in applying this dualism to the sacrament; Gottfried G. Krodel, "Die Abendmahlslehre des Erasmus von Rotterdam und seine Stellung am Anfang des Abendmahlsstreites der Reformatoren" (Ph.D. diss., Universität Erlangen, 1955), pp. 213–220. For Zwingli's influence on Karlstadt, see chapter 3, pp. 57–58.

14. The importance of the epistle to the Hebrews is especially apparent in both *Priesthood* and *Testament*; see chapter 3, p. 73.

15. For a comparison of Erasmus's influence on Karlstadt and Zwingli that highlights the communal and ethical role of the Supper, Krodel, "Abendmahlslehre," pp. 200–205, 207–220.

16. Z 4: 484–487; HZW 2: 210–213. The analogy between the Passover lamb and the bread of the Last Supper was not new; it was taught, for instance, in Nicolas de Lyra's comment on Matt. 26:28; *Textus Biblie cum Glossa ordinaria, Nicolai de lyra Postilla, Moralitatibus eiusdem Pauli Burgensis . . . Sexta Pars* (Basel: Petri and Froben, 1508), fol. 79v.

17. Z 3: 800, *Commentary*, p. 230; cf. *Exegesis*, fol. a2r; Burnett, *Pamphlets*, p. 145.

18. Z 4: 499–502; HZW 2: 223–226.

19. Like Hoen, Zwingli did cite Christ's "I am" statements—the most obvious figurative use of "is" in the New Testament—and Joseph's dream interpretations (Gen. 41). His opponents in Zurich used his reliance on parables against him, arguing that their necessarily metaphorical interpretation differed from Christ's clear statement, "this is my body." The applicability of Exod. 12:11 came to Zwingli in a dream following two days of discussion with the Council about the abolition of the mass in April 1525; he described the discussion and his revelation in *Subsidium sive coronis de eucharistia*, Z 4: 480–487; HZW 2: 207–213.

20. Z 4: 513–514; Spruyt, *Hoen*, p. 228; Oberman, *Forerunners*, 270. These differences provide additional support for Spruyt's argument that Zwingli was not responsible for the initial publication of Hoen's letter; *Hoen*, pp. 169–170.

21. *De genuina verborum domini, Hoc est corpus meum, iuxta uetutissimos authores expositione liber* (Strasbourg: Knoblauch, 1525).

22. On Erasmus's influence on Oecolampadius, Krodel, "Abendmahlslehre," pp. 221–239. Köhler summarizes earlier discussions of possible differences between Zwingli and Oecolampadius and suggests that the latter acknowledged that Christ could work through the sacrament, which distinguished his position from Zwingli's; *Zwingli und Luther* 1: 122–125. Thomas Kaufmann, *Die Abendmahlstheologie der Strassburger Reformatoren bis 1528*, Beiträge zur historischen Theologie 81 (Tübingen: Mohr, 1992), pp. 301–302, argues that Köhler's view was based on a faulty translation of a sentence in *De genuina . . . expositione*, and maintains, rightly in my view, that on the issues that mattered—Christ's corporeal presence in the elements, and the purpose and significance of the Lord's Supper—Zwingli and Oecolampadius held the same position. It should at least be asked whether and to what extent Oecolampadius influenced Zwingli, rather than the other way around; only a careful study of the Basler's eucharistic theology before 1525 can answer this question.

23. *De genuina . . . expositione*, fol. B8r. In the *Commentarius*, Zwingli cited Tertullian as support for his interpretation of 1 Cor. 11:25 and Luke 22:20 as "this cup is the symbol of my blood"; Z 3: 801; *Commentary*, p. 230.

24. *De genuina . . . expositione*, fol. E4r–E6r, K1r–v. Oecolampadius would be even more outspoken about the distinction between sign and signified in his later works.

25. It is beyond the purpose of this chapter to discuss Oecolampadius's interpretation of the church fathers, but see Gottfried Hoffmann, "Sententiae Patrum. Das patristische

Argument in der Abendmahlskontroverse zwischen Oekolampad, Zwingli, Luther und Melanchthon" (Ph.D. diss., Heidelberg, 1971), pp. 25–29, 78–106.

26. *De genvina . . . expositione*, fol. A2v–A4r; in rejecting the Lombard's understanding of the passage, Oecolampadius was also rejecting Luther's view expressed in *von Anbeten des Sacraments*.

27. *De genvina . . . expositione*, fol. A4r–B5r, C8v–E7v.

28. *De genvina . . . expositione*, fol. C2r, I1r–I34; cf. Z 4: 484–488, HZW 2: 210–213. Oecolampadius also argued, as Zwingli had in his *Commentarius*, that Luke 22:20 should be interpreted as "this cup is a figure of the new testament"; *De genvina . . . expositione*, fol. I4r–v, and he cited with approval Zwingli's interpretation of John 6 in his letter to Alber, fol. K6v.

29. Oecolampadius to Nikolaus Prugner, 19 April 1525, B&A 1: 362–363; Jud to Bullinger, 20 April 1525, HBBW 1: 75–76. Zwingli's *Subsidium* was published in early August, more than a month after Oecolampadius had finished his manuscript and sent it to Strasbourg for printing. It is therefore quite possible that Zwingli derived some of his arguments from Oecolampadius and not vice versa.

30. On the Basler's use of arguments from these sources, see chapter 4. At the end of 1524, Oecolampadius told François Lambert that he had not been able to find copies of all of Karlstadt's pamphlets; B&A 1: 336–338, no. 235. Nevertheless, he was certainly more familiar with Karlstadt's arguments than Zwingli was. He had read Karlstadt's *Abuse* in his role as censor, and his assertion that miracles must be unique, public, and intended to strengthen faith, *De genvina . . . expositione*, fol. A8v, bears more than a passing resemblance to Karlstadt's discussion of miracles, *Prove*, fol. B3r–v; Burnett, *Pamphlets*, pp. 122–123.

31. Köhler, *Zwingli und Luther*, 1: 61–62. Zwingli identified Hoen and Saganus in his *Amica Exegesis*, Z 5:738; HZW 2: 357.

32. See, for instance, the *Vorschlag wegen der Bilder und der Messe* from May 1524, Z 3: 123–131; Köhler, *Zwingli und Luther*, 1: 67–69.

33. Grebel to Vadian, 14 January 1525, QGTS 1: 33–34, no. 23; see also Zwingli's response to the Strasbourg pastors, 16 December 1524, Z 8: 275: "We shared with only a few people what we have thought for some years about this bread and cup, and only with those friends whose faith was well-known to us."

34. Z 4: 464; HZW 2: 195.

35. The *Commentarius* was dedicated to the king of France; its section on the Lord's Supper was hastily translated by three students so that, like the *Commentarius*, it would be available at the spring book fair in Frankfurt. It was published as *Von dem Nachtmal Christi widergedechtnus* (Zurich: Froschauer, 1525).

36. Barge, *Karlstadt*, 2: 260–263; the letter of Oecolampadius to which Barge refers was written to François Lambert, B&A 1: 340–341.

37. Erasmus to Melanchthon, 10 December 1524, MBW T2: 212–213, no. 360; de Coct to Farel, 17 December 1524, Herminjard, 1: 308–310; cf. Luther to Spalatin, 13 January 1525, WA Br 3: 421–422. De Coct was perhaps a bit premature in his portrayal of the unity among the city's elite, for in April Zwingli wrote to Basel's pastors urging them to unite behind a symbolic understanding of the Lord's Supper, 5 April 1525, Z 8: 315–320.

38. Z 8: 251–253, no. 352.

39. Luther to Hess, 19 July 1525, WA Br 3: 544–545; the publication date of Bugenhagen's letter is discussed in both Ernst Koch, "Johannes Bugenhagens Anteil am Abendmahlsstreit zwischen 1525 und 1532," *Theologische Literaturzeitung* 111 (1986): 705–730, and Volker Gummelt, "Die Auseinandersetzung über das Abendmahl zwischen Johannes Bugenhagen und Huldrych Zwingli im Jahre 1525," in *Die Zürcher Reformation: Ausstrahlungen und Rückwirkungen*.

Wissenschaftlicher Tagung zum hundertjährigen Bestehen des Zwinglivereins (29. Oktober bis 2. November 1997 in Zürich), ed. Alfred Schindler and Hans Stickelberger (Bern: Peter Lang, 2001), pp. 189–201. There is a German translation of Bugenhagen's *Sendbrief* in Walch 20: 500–506.

40. Johann Bugenhagen, *Contra novum errorem de Sacramento Corporis et sanguinis domini nostri Iesu Christi Epistola* (Wittenberg: Lotter, 1525), Köhler MF 1744, no. 4533, fol. A2r: "Atque hic ridemus magnum illum Theologum [sc. Zwingli] cum suo Carlstadio." This line would be repeated as particularly offensive by all who wrote to defend either Zwingli or Karlstadt. Bugenhagen himself was incensed that Zwingli had referred to those who taught Christ's corporeal presence as "voratores et carnivoras," fol. A2v; cf. Zwingli's *Commentarius*, Z 3: 794; *Commentary*, p. 223.

41. *Contra novum errorem*, fol. A1v–A2v; cf. WA 18: 192–193; LW 40: 202–203.

42. *Contra novum errorem*, fol. A2v–A3r; cf. WA 18: 166–168; LW 40: 177–178, where Luther defined "breaking" as "breaking into pieces and distributing," based on Isa. 58:7 and Lam. 4:4.

43. *Contra novum errorem*, fol. A3r–v; WA 18: 72–77; LW 40: 182–187.

44. *Ad Ioannis Bugenhagii Pomerani Epistolam Responsio*, Z 4: 546–576; German translation in Walch 20: 506–520.

45. Z 4: 558–561; Zwingli did not mention Hoen by name but referred only to "the letter of a learned and pious Batavian." Hoen's letter had by this time been published as an anonymous *Epistola . . . ex Batavis Missa*. In addition to the parables of the sower (Luke 8:11) and "this is the Passover" (Exod. 12:11), which he had earlier used to support his figurative understanding, Zwingli for the first time cited Matt. 11:14 (John is Elijah), the verse that played an important role for Wyclif and his followers.

46. Z 4: 561–566.

47. Z 4: 567–572.

48. Z 4: 572–573.

49. Z 4: 573–575.

50. Z 4: 575–576.

51. There were at least two different translations of Bugenhagen's letter, the first published in Wittenberg, *Eyn Sendbrieff widder den newen yrrtumb bey dem Sacrament*; and the second published in Augsburg as *Wider den newen irsal vom Sacrament* (Augsburg: Ruff, 1525). Both Gummelt, "Auseinandersetzung," and Kaufmann, *Abendmahlstheologie*, pp. 282–284, emphasize the importance especially of Bugenhagen's pamphlet.

52. *Ein Antwurt Huldrychs Zuinglins vff die Epistel Joannis Pugenhag vss Pomeren das Nachtmal Christi betreffende* (Zurich: Froschauer, 1526).

53. Köhler, *Zwingli und Luther*, 1: 213–223; citation at p. 222.

54. James M. Kittelson, "Martin Bucer and the Sacramentarian Controversy: The Origins of His Policy of Concord," *Archiv für Reformationsgeschichte* 64 (1973): 166–183. Kittelson attributes Bucer's emphasis on communion as establishing fellowship among believers to the Strasbourger's reading of Luther's earliest sermons on the sacrament, but the understanding of the Eucharist as communion is much more prominent in Erasmus and Zwingli than it is in Luther.

55. Ian Hazlett, "The Development of Martin Bucer's Thinking on the Sacrament of the Lord's Supper in Its Historical and Theological Context, 1523–1534" (Ph.D. diss., Universität Münster, 1977), pp. 97–133.

56. Reinhold Friedrich, *Martin Bucer—"Fanatiker der Einheit"? Seine Stellungnahme zu theologischen Fragen seiner Zeit (Abendmahls- und Kirchenverständnis) insbesondere nach seinem*

Briefwechsel der Jahre 1524–1541, Biblia et symbiotica 20 (Bonn: Verlag für Kultur und Wissenschaft, 2002), pp. 24–29.

57. Kaufmann, *Abendmahlstheologie*, pp. 303–310, 318–333. The differences between Friedrich and Kaufmann are summarized in their two contributions to Christian Krieger and Marc Lienhard, eds., *Martin Bucer and Sixteenth Century Europe: Actes du colloque de Strasbourg, 28–31 août 1991*, Studies in Medieval and Reformation Thought 52–53 (Leiden: Brill, 1993): Thomas Kaufmann, "Streittheologie und Friedensdiplomatie: Die Rolle Martin Bucers im frühen Abendmahlsstreit," 1: 239–256, and Reinhold Friedrich, "Martin Bucer—Ökumene im 16. Jahrhundert," 1: 257–268.

58. For a discussion of the eucharistic pamphlets published in Strasbourg, see chapter 6, p. 120.

59. Karlstadt's impact in Strasbourg and the early development of the eucharistic controversy in that city have been examined most recently and thoroughly by Kaufmann, *Abendmahlstheologie*, pp. 181–268, with details to be corrected by what follows. Of the accounts in English, James M. Kittelson, *Wolfgang Capito, From Humanist to Reformer*, Studies in Medieval and Reformation Thought 17 (Leiden: Brill, 1975), pp. 143–150, is unreliable because it ignores the influence of Erasmus on Capito's thought; a more accurate discussion of the developments in Strasbourg is found in Martin Greschat, *Martin Bucer: A Reformer and His Times* (Louisville, Ky.: Westminster John Knox Press, 2004), pp. 70–79. See also Barge, *Karlstadt*, 2: 206–233; Hans-Werner Müsing, "Karlstadt und die Strasbourger Täufergemeinde," in *Origins and Characteristics of Anabaptism*, ed. Marc Lienhard (The Hague: Martinus Nijhoff, 1977), pp. 169–195; and Sigrid Looß, "Zu einigen Aspekten des Verhältnisses zwischen Luther und Karlstadt, vorwiegend dargestellt an Karlstadts Straßburgaufenthalt im Oktober 1524," in *Martin Luther—Leistung und Erbe*, ed. H. Bartel (Berlin: Akademie-Verlag, 1986), pp. 142–147.

60. Kaufmann, *Abendmahlstheologie*, pp. 152–179; on the differences between Luther and Zwingli concerning the sacrifice of the mass, see chapter 2, pp. 48–49.

61. Andreas Keller, *Ein anzeygung was für gottzlesterung in der Papisten Messz ist/ vnd das sich alle fromen Christen daruor als vor der aller grösten gotzlesterung hyeten sollent* (Strasbourg: Schürer, 1524); Köhler MF 65, no. 174. In his preface to Rosina von Eschenau, Keller identified himself as the pastor of Wasselheim, a suburb of Strasbourg, fol. A2r. The pamphlet is analyzed by Wolfgang Simon, *Die Messopfertheologie Martin Luthers. Voraussetzungen, Genese, Gestalt und Rezeption*, Spätmittelalter und Reformation, Neue Reihe 22 (Tübingen: Mohr Siebeck, 2003), pp. 682–697.

62. Keller, *Anzeygung*, fol. A3v–B1v. Keller cited Erasmus's paraphrase of Acts 2:42, fol. B1r.

63. Keller, *Anzeygung*, fol. B1v–D2v.

64. The pamphlet may have been written after Karlstadt's visit to Strasbourg, but its silence concerning whether or not Christ's body was present implies that it was written before the question of Christ's presence became an issue in Strasbourg.

65. Georg Modestin, "'Dass sie unserer Stadt und diesem Land grosse Schmach und Unehre zugefügt haben.' Der Strassburger Waldenserprozess von 1400 und seine Vorgeschichte," in *Friedrich Reiser und die "waldensisch-hussitische Internationale" im 15. Jahrhundert. Akten der Tagung Ötisheim-Schönenberg, 2. bis 4. Oktober 2003*, ed. Albert de Lange and Kathrin Utz Tremp (Heidelberg: Verlag Regionalkultur, 2006), pp. 189–204.

66. Albert de Lange, "Friedrich Reiser und die 'waldensisch-hussitische Internationale.' Quellen und Literatur zu Person und Werk," in de Lange and Tremp, *Friedrich Reiser*, pp. 29–74, esp. pp. 39–41; see also, in the same volume, Martin Schneider, "Friedrich Reiser—Herkunft, Berufung und Weg," pp. 75–86.

67. See chapter 4, pp. 82–83. At least two works concerning the Hussites were published in Strasbourg, Hieronymus Gebweiler's edition of a work attributed to Theophilus Tectonus, *Compendiosa Boemice seu Hussitane Hereseos . . . Articulorum descriptio*, and Otto Brunfels's edition of *De Anatomia Antichristi*, attributed to Jan Hus. Others were printed in nearby Basel.

68. Clemens Ziegler, *Ein kurtz Register vnd auszzug der Bibel in welchem man findet was abgötterey sey* (Strasbourg: Schwan, 1524), excerpts in Manfred Krebs and Hans Georg Rott, eds., *Elsass I*, Quellen zur Geschichte der Täufer 7 (Gütersloh: Mohn, 1959), pp. 8–10. On Ziegler, Rodolph Peter, "Le Jardinier Clément Ziegler, l'homme et son oeuvre," *Revue d'histoire et de philosophie religieuses* 34 (1954): 255–282.

69. See his criticisms of these practices, *Von der waren nyessung beyd leibs vnd bluots Christi . . . Vnd von dem Tauff . . .* (Strasbourg: Schott, 1524), fol. A3r–v, B4r–v. Kaufmann believes that Ziegler's pamphlet was written in October 1524 and so reflects Karlstadt's influence in the city; *Abendmahlstheologie*, pp. 192–196; see also Kaufmann, "Nouvelles sources de la controverse eucharistique à Strasbourg en automne 1524," *Revue d'histoire et de philosophie religieuses* 73 (1993): 137–153. The ideas that Kaufmann attributes to Karlstadt, however, were already being discussed in the Upper Rhine before Karlstadt's appearance. Erasmus had linked John 6:63 to the sacrament in his *Enchiridion* and his *Paraphrases on John*, and Zwingli had criticized the word "sacrament" in his *Exposition of the 67 Articles*; Conrad Grebel's letter to Thomas Müntzer shows that his circle had rejected infant baptism before Karlstadt's arrival, 5 September 1524, QGTS 1: 17–18. More decisive for an earlier date for the pamphlet is a passage in the letter of Urbanus Rhegius to Capito, 16 September 1524: "ante aliquot septimanas publicis declamationibus errorem Hortulani de eucharistia et baptismo scripturarum testimoniis confutavi, et ecclesiam a lectione tam stultorum libellorum magna contentione absterrui"; English translation in Erika Rummel and Milton Kooistra, eds., *The Correspondence of Wolfgang Capito* (Toronto: University of Toronto Press, 2005–), 2: 45, no. 215. This can only be a reference to Ziegler's pamphlet. Kaufmann saw only a summary of this letter, which led him to misinterpret its contents and so assume it was not a reference to Ziegler's work; "Nouvelles sources," p. 138, n. 7.

70. *Nyessung*, fol. B1v, B4v–C1v; cf. B3v: "wann ein mensch den leib Christi will nyessen so soll er das brot/ in dem er den leib Christi neusszt vnderscheydlich halten/ gegen dem anderen brot das noch vff demn tisch ligt/ ja er sols halten als den leib Christi/nit in einer einfalt/ oder in einem schlechten won/ sonder in einem starcken und steiffen vnd vesten glauben. Dann Christus hat gesprochen/ das ist mein leib."

71. *Nyessung*, fol. A4v–B2r.

72. *Ein fast schon büchlin . . . von dem leib vnd bluot Christi* (Strasbourg: Schwan, 1525), fol. A4r, B3v. Capito knew of the pamphlet by 17 December 1524; see his letter to Ambrosius Blarer, Traugott Schiess, ed., *Briefwechsel der Brüder Ambrosius und Thomas Blaurer 1509–1548* (Freiburg i.Br.: Fehsenfeld, 1908–1912), 1: 115; Rummel, *Correspondence*, 2: 88–90, no. 232.

73. *Büchlin*, fol. C4v; Kaufmann argues for Karlstadt's influence, *Abendmahlstheologie*, pp. 197–203.

74. *Büchlin*, fol. C3v–C4v; David R. Holeton, "The Communion of Infants and Hussitism," *Communio Viatorum* 27 (1984): 207–225. Peter notes Ziegler's discussion of the Moravian (i.e., Bohemian) Brethren, but he does not seem aware of the differences between the Utraquists and the Brethren, nor does he comment on Ziegler's critical comments about the former; "Maraîcher," pp. 260, 269. In his *Sermon auf das Euangeli Johannis vi*, preached for the feast of Corpus Christi and published in 1523, Luther also criticized those who used John 6:53 to argue for infant communion, but he did not identify them with the Hussites; WA 12: 584.

75. *Büchlin*, fol. D2v–D4r. Much of the rest of the pamphlet is devoted to expanding on the distinction between Christ's divine and human natures, described as spiritual body and human flesh. On the various modes of Christ's existence, see chapter 4, pp. 78–79, 81.

76. Carlo Ginzburg, *The Cheese and the Worms: The Cosmos of a Sixteenth-Century Miller*, trans. John and Anne Tedeschi (Baltimore: Johns Hopkins University Press, 1982).

77. On the iconoclasm and violence against Catholic clergy that broke out in the months preceding Karlstadt's arrival, Müsing, "Karlstadt."

78. Wolfgang Capito, *Was man halten/ vnnd antwurten soll/ von der spaltung zwischen Martin Luther vnd Andres Carolstadt* (Strasbourg: Köpfel, 1524); reprinted in Walch 20: 340– 351; translation of preface in Rummel, *Correspondence* 2: 68–74; Kaufmann, *Abendmahlstheologie*, pp. 207–217. The title page gives the publication date as October, while in the pamphlet Capito referred to the decision of the Senate on 24 October that images were to be removed from the cathedral and the church of St. Aurelia. Hence the pamphlet could only have been written in the last week of October. On the date of Karlstadt's visit to Strasbourg, see the appendix, pp. 144–145.

79. Capito, *Was man halten . . . soll*, fol. B2v–B3v. Kaufmann, *Abendmahlstheologie*, pp. 208– 209, is justifiably cautious about assuming that Capito had read any of Karlstadt's pamphlets, although he agrees that the specific nature of Capito's comments implies a direct literary dependence. This dependence is even more probable since *Masses* was only a few pages long and so could be read quickly.

80. Capito, *Was man halten . . . soll*, fol. B3v–B4r.

81. BCorr 1: 281–297. Kaufmann, *Abendmahlstheologie*, pp. 217–237, analyzes these letters and draws attention to the parallels with Karlstadt's pamphlets, pp. 227–228; he does not discuss the similarities with Hoen's letter.

82. BCorr 2: 282–283.

83. BCorr 2: 283.69–70. This argument is only briefly mentioned in the *Dialogue*, fol. F1v, Hertzsch, *Schriften*, 2: 38.11–14; Burnett, *Pamphlets*, pp. 193–194, but it had a prominent place at the beginning of *Exegesis*, fol. A1v–A2r; Burnett, *Pamphlets*, pp. 145–146.

84. BCorr 2: 283.73–75; Karlstadt's discussion of remembrance in the *Dialogue*, fol. d1v–d2r; Hertzsch, *Schriften*, 2: 25; Burnett, *Pamphlets*, pp. 183–184, and at greater length in both *Exegesis*, fol. d3r; Burnett, *Pamphlets*, p. 159; and *Abuse*, fol. a3v–b2v; Burnett, *Pamphlets*, pp. 208–212. The dismissal of speculation about the manner of Christ's presence is, however, more typical of Capito than of Karlstadt, who mocked the belief that Christ's body could be in the consecrated host in the same way that it hung on the cross; *Dialogue*, fol. a4v–b1r; Hertzsch, *Schriften*, 2: 11.34–12.34, 40.35–41.4 (the second citation is part of the section transposed in Hertzsch's edition; in the original pamphlet it directly precedes the first section on p. 11); Burnett, *Pamphlets*, p. 169.

85. BCorr 1: 283.52–55, 65; Spruyt, *Hoen*, pp. 227–228, 231–232, Oberman, *Forerunners*, pp. 269–270, 274–275; *Dialogue*, fol. c4r, e2r, f4r; Hertzsch, *Schriften*, 2: 24.5–7, 32.22–37, 42.28–34; Burnett, *Pamphlets*, pp. 180–181, 189, 197.

86. BCorr 1: 283.71–72; Spruyt, *Hoen*, pp. 232–233, Oberman, *Forerunners*, pp. 275–276; *Prove*, fol. B3r–B3v, Burnett, *Pamphlets*, p. 122.

87. BCorr 1: 283.52–53, 60–61; Spruyt, *Hoen*, pp. 227–228; Oberman, *Forerunners*, pp. 269, 274, 276; 270; *Prove*, fol. C1v–C2r, C4r; Burnett, *Pamphlets*, pp. 125, 128. Kaufmann, *Abendmahlstheologie*, p. 228 n. 630, associates this statement with a passage in the *Dialogue*, Hertzsch, *Schriften*, p. 47.4ff., *Dialogue*, fol. g2v–g3r, Burnett, *Pamphlets*, pp. 201–202, but that passage says nothing about the apostles' terminological preference,

88. Spruyt, *Hoen*, p. 228; Oberman, *Forerunners*, p. 270; *Exegesis*, fol. D6r; Burnett, *Pamphlets*, p. 162. It is, however, quite likely that Karlstadt explained this parallel in discussions with others while in Strasbourg.

89. BCorr 1: 283.76–77; Spruyt, *Hoen*, pp. 233.5–15; Oberman, *Forerunners*, p. 275.

90. The letter was written either to Martin Germanus (as the editors of BCorr surmise) or to Martin Schalling (Kaufmann, *Abendmahstheologie*, p. 305, n. 214), sometime between late October and early December 1525; BCorr 2: 50–54. In this letter Bucer acknowledged the heretical origins of some of the arguments. He also cited Wyclif along with Wessel Gansfort, Zwingli, and Oecolampadius as those who shared the same understanding of Scripture, to the knight Johann Landschad von Steinach, 22 October 1525, BDS 3: 440, and he added Hus and the "Waldensians" (presumably the "Waldensian Brethren" or Bohemian Brethren) to a similar list in a letter he and Capito sent to the lords of Gemmingen, 1 December 1525; BCorr 2: 81.

91. BCorr 1:298–314, esp. pp. 312–313.

92. Capito to Zwingli, 31 December 1524, Z 8: 279; summarized in Rummel, *Correspondence*, 2: 94–95, no. 234.

93. BDS 1: 205–220. The discussion was clearly directed against Karlstadt's *Masses*.

94. BDS 1: 225–230.

95. BDS 1: 236–241.

96. BDS 1: 242–243.

97. BDS 1: 248–254.

98. This, at least, is what they claimed in their letters written in the fall of 1525. Capito told Bugenhagen that he had never preached that one must believe in Christ's corporeal presence in the Supper; 8 October 1525, Otto Vogt, Eike Wolgast, and H. Volz, eds., *Dr. Johann Bugenhagens Briefwechsel* (Hildesheim: Olms, 1966), pp. 32–50, esp. pp. 37–38; summarized in Rummel, *Correspondence* 2: 156–157, no. 248. At about the same time Bucer told Martin [Germanus or Schalling] that he had never believed in Christ's carnal presence in the bread; BCorr 2: 51.

99. Kaufmann points out that some of the Strasbourg pastors may not have been as solidly committed to Zwingli's eucharistic theology, but Capito and Bucer, working together, were able to influence decisively the direction of the city's church; *Abendmahlstheologie*, pp. 273–277.

100. On this correspondence, Kaufmann, *Abendmahlstheologie*, pp. 304–310, 318–333; Friedrich, *Martin Bucer*, pp. 23–29.

101. Bucer to Jacob Otter, BDS 3: 413–414; to Johann Landschad, BDS 3: 433.

102. Bucer to Landschad, BDS 3: 434.

103. Bucer to Landschad, BDS 3: 433; Capito and Bucer to the lords of Gemmingen, BCorr 2: 80, 82; Rummel, *Correspondence* 2: 172.

104. This difference is what both Köhler and Hazlett see as the beginnings of Bucer's later concord efforts. Underlying Bucer's view is the fact that he understood the discourse of John 6 as applying to the Lord's Supper and not just to spiritual manducation more generally; on Bucer's difference from both Luther and Zwingli on this point, Ian Hazlett, "Zur Auslegung von Johannes 6 bei Bucer während der Abendmahlskontroverse," in *Bucer und seine Zeit: Forschungebeiträge und Bibliographie*, ed. Marijn de Kroon and Friedhelm Krüger (Wiesbaden: Steiner, 1976), pp. 74–87.

105. Bucer to Otter, BDS 3: 412–418; Capito to Bugenhagen, Vogt et al., *Bugenhagens Briefwechsel*, pp. 32–50, summarized in Rummel, *Correspondence*, 2: 156–157, no. 248.

106. Bucer's advice to Caselius, BDS 3: 423, 424; Bucer to Landschad, BDS 3: 433; Capito to Bugenhagen, Vogt, *Bugenhagens Briefwechsel*, pp. 32–50; Rummel, Correspondence, 2: 156–157.

Oecolampadius had introduced the term "impanation" in his *De genvina . . . expositione*, stating that a new concept required a new term; fol. C6v.

107. Capito to Zwingli, 20 November 1525, Z 8: 428–429; summarized in Rummel, *Correspondence* 2: 168, no. 258. See also Luther's response to the Strasbourgers delivered orally by Caselius, BCorr 2: 76; Lazarus Spengler to the Strasbourg *Stadtschreiber* Peter Butz, 24 October 1525, in Berndt Hamm and Wolfgang Huber, eds., *Lazarus Spengler Schriften*, Quellen und Forschungen zur Reformationsgeschichte, 61, 70 (Gütersloh: Gütersloher Verlagshaus, 1995–1999), 2: 8–12; and Capito to Osiander, 18 November 1525, Osiander, GA, 2: 201–204; summarized in Rummel, *Correspondence* 2: 167–168, no. 257. The insult perceived by Bugenhagen's reference to Karlstadt and Zwingli as "masters of error" (Bugenhagen, *Contra novum errorem*, fol. A1v) comes out repeatedly in Bucer's instructions to Caselius for his mission to Wittenberg, BDS 3: 421–430.

108. WA 18: 448–449.

109. On 28 October, Capito reported to Zwingli that the Strasbourgers were editing Karlstadt's pamphlet, "adding suitable scholia with a preface"; Z 8: 405, summarized in Rummel, *Correspondence* 2: 163–164, no. 250. Thomas Kaufmann noted that this preface is identical with the anonymous pamphlet, *Frolockung eins Christliche bruders von wegen der vereynigung Zwischen D.M. Luther und D. Andres Carlostat* (Speyer: Eckhart, 1526), and he identified Capito as the author, "Zwei unerkannte Schriften Bucers und Capitos zur Abendmahlsfrage aus dem Herbst 1525," *Archiv für Reformationsgeschichte* 81 (1990): 158–188. On the basis of strong textual parallels between the preface/*Frolockung* and Bucer's letter to Landschad, I believe that the author may have been Bucer rather than Capito. For the purposes of determining the collective position of the Strasbourg pastors, however, the question of authorship is secondary. The *Frolockung* is reprinted in Adolf Laube et al., eds., *Flugschriften vom Bauernkrieg zum Täuferreich (1526–1535)* (Berlin: Akademie Verlag, 1992), 1: 102–115.

110. *Frolockung*, fol. A3r–A4r; Laube, *Flugschriften*, pp. 103–105.

111. *Frolockung*, fol. B1v–B2r; Laube, *Flugschriften*, pp. 107–108.

112. *Frolockung*, fol. B3r–B4r; Laube, *Flugschriften*, pp. 110–111.

113. BDS 2: 434–435.

114. This was the bottom line of Bucer's instruction to Caselius, as well as of Bucer's initial letter to Brenz, as is clear from the opening lines of Brenz's response, 3 October 1525, BCorr 2: 39–40; one need not interpret it as "a tactical smokescreen," as Kaufmann does, *Abendmahlstheologie*, p. 323.

115. Luther's letter and his instructions for Caselius, both dated 5 November 1525, BCorr 2: 55–58; Caselius's oral report, 29 November 1525, BCorr 2: 71–78 (WA Br 3: 599–612).

116. BCorr 2: 76.

117. *Amica Exegesis*, Z 5: 624–625; HZW 2: 280–281.

118. BCorr 2: 51; BDS 3: 415–416

119. LB VII, col. 891E; col. 892A–B. Zwingli explicitly cited Erasmus's paraphrase for a defense of his understanding of 1 Cor. 10:16–17 in his *Subsidium*, Z 4: 498; HZW 2: 223. In his annotation on 1 Cor. 10:4, Erasmus cited Augustine to support his understanding that the rock signified Christ, ASD VI/8, pp. 210–212.

CHAPTER 6

1. WA 19: 458–459, where Luther identified "five or six" groups and speculated about the emergence of a seventh; see also his open letter to Reutlingen, WA 19: 121, and his *Sermon von*

dem Sakrament . . . wider die Schwarmgeister, WA 19: 484; LW 36: 337. Both Luther and Johann Bugenhagen pointed out the divisions among their opponents to Kaspar Schwenckfeld during the latter's visit to Wittenberg in December, 1525; CS 2: 253, 277.

2. George Huntston Williams, *The Radical Reformation*, 3rd ed., Sixteenth Century Essays and Studies 15 (Kirksville, Mo.: Sixteenth Century Journal Publishers, 1992), pp. 95–108, suggests that both sacramentarianism and "sacramentism," his term for spiritual communion, bordered on heresy and that these movements were particularly strong in the Netherlands on the eve of the Reformation. As we have seen, the emphasis on spiritual communion was both orthodox and widespread outside of the Low Countries; it should not be discussed in this context. More recent Dutch scholarship also questions the existence of a distinctly Dutch form of pre-Reformation "sacramentarianism"; Spruyt, *Hoen*, pp. 36–41. Trapman has found no occurrences of the term "sacramentarian" before Luther; when the word did begin to be used in the Netherlands, it was used broadly for all types of heretics, including Lutherans; J. Trapman, "Le rôle des 'sacramentaires' des origines de la Réforme jusqu'en 1530 aux Pays-Bas," *Nederlands archief voor kerkgeschedenis* 63 (1983): 1–24.

3. Thus, for instance, Martin Bucer's *Grund und Ursach*, published in two editions at the turn of the year, and Theodor Billican's *Renovatio Ecclesiae Nordlingiacensis*, published twice in 1525, were defenses of the liturgical innovations introduced in Strasbourg and Nördlingen, respectively, but both works also criticized Karlstadt's understanding of the Lord's Supper and explained what was taught in their churches; BDS 1: 194–278, esp. pp. 248–254, and Ernst Sehling, ed., *Die evangelischen Kirchenordnungen des XVI. Jahrhunderts* (Göttingen/Leipzig/Tübingen, 1902–), 12/2: 289–306, esp. pp. 298–306.

4. The four works responding to Karlstadt were two imprints of Luther's *Ein brieff an die Christen Zu Straspurg widder den schwermer geyst*, WA 15: 380–397, LW 40: 61–71, and two of Urbanus Rhegius, *Wider den newen irrsal Doctor Andres von Carlstadt des Sacraments halb warnung* (Augsburg: Ruff, 1524), reprinted in Walch 20: 110–131.

5. Nicolaus von Amsdorf, *Vermanung Nicolai von Amsdorf an die von Magdeburg widder den rotten secten geyst Doctor Cyclops* (Wittenberg: Weiß, 1525).

6. The pamphlets were written by Matthaeus Frey, Cornelis Hoen, Balthasar Hubmaier, Andreas Karlstadt, Michael Keller, Johann Oecolampadius, Conrad Ryss zu Ofen, Caspar Turnauer, John Wyclif, and Ulrich Zwingli.

7. Z 3: 790, 795, 819, *Commentary*, pp. 218, 224, 252; Oecolampadius, *De genvina verborum domini, Hoc est corpus meum, iuxta uetutissimos authores expositione liber* (Strasbourg: Knoblauch, 1525), fol. A3r–v, B8r, D4r; cf. the complaint of Conrad Ryss that those who recognized the true meaning of Christ's words were condemned as heretics; *Antwort dem Hochgeleerten Doctor Johann Bugenhage . . . das Sacrament betreffend* (Augsburg: Ulhart, 1525), Köhler MF 737, no. 1880, fol. B3r–v. Although they had downplayed disagreements on the Lord's Supper from the very beginning of the controversy, the Strasbourgers' argument that belief in Christ's corporeal presence was a secondary issue on which Christians could differ was also used to counter the accusations of heresy emanating from Wittenberg and Nuremberg in the fall of 1525.

8. When a German translation of Hoen's letter was published in Augsburg in 1526, the editor included a preface justifying his decision not to identify either himself or the author; Spruyt, *Hoen*, pp. 237–241. Hoen was already dead by the time the letter was first published.

9. For a comparison and discussion of leading evangelical pamphleteers, Alejandro Zorzin, *Karlstadt als Flugschriftenautor*, Göttinger theologische Arbeiten 48 (Göttingen: Vandenhoeck & Ruprecht, 1990), pp. 19–52.

10. Between 1518 and 1524, 88 pamphlets were published in Augsburg, 65 in Strasbourg, 59 in Wittenberg, 27 in Erfurt, 26 in Nuremberg, 25 in Basel, and 23 in Leipzig; 62 pamphlets were published in other cities. Leipzig's prominence may seem surprising, since Duke George had taken a firm stand against Luther at the beginning of the Reformation. Nevertheless, the city was a major center for the publication of Luther's early eucharistic pamphlets. Its printers produced seventeen of Luther's pamphlets between 1518 and 1520, and only one work against Luther, Augustin Alveldt's *Tractatus de communione sub vtraque specie*, in 1520. Duke George's opposition to Luther did have an effect over the next few years, and only six eucharistic pamphlets—Johann Diepold's *Nutzlicher Sermon*, a German translation of Henry VIII's attack on Luther, and four works by Hieronymus Emser—were published between 1522 and 1524. Heinrich R. Schmidt points out that in both Nuremberg and Strasbourg, censorship measures against Luther's works in the wake of the Edict of Worms were not very effective because the censors in each city favored Luther; *Reichstädte, Reich und Reformation: Korporative Religionspolitik 1521–1529/30*, Veröffentlichungen des Instituts für europäische Geschichte Mainz 122 (Stuttgart: Steiner, 1986), pp. 45–51.

11. In 1525, Augsburg produced 22 percent (40 pamphlets), Strasbourg 15 percent (25 pamphlets), Wittenberg 13 percent (22 pamphlets), Erfurt 10 percent (18 pamphlets), Nuremberg and Zurich each 8 percent (13 pamphlets each), and Leipzig 6 percent (10 pamphlets) of the total; the remaining 18 percent (31 pamphlets) were produced in cities that published only a few pamphlets.

12. These included Bugenhagen's *Antwurt . . . vber eyn frage vom hochwirdigen Sacrament* (two imprints) and his *Vas die Euangelisch Meß . . . sey*, Osiander's *Grund vnd vrsach*, GA 1: 174–254, Justus Menius's *Jn was glauben die Tauff . . . zu fordern seyen. Jtem wie des heyligen leichnambs . . . fruchtbarlich zu niessen kurtzer vnd eynfaltiger vnterricht*, Luther's *Ordenung vnd Bericht*, WA 12: 472–493, and his *Von dem grewel der Stillmesse*, WA 18: 22–36, LW 36: 311–328.

13. Heinrich R. Schmidt, "Die Häretisierung des Zwinglianismus im Reich seit 1525," in *Zugänge zur bäuerlichen Reformation*, ed. Peter Blickle (Zurich: Chronos, 1987), pp. 219–236. On the 1524 Nuremberg imprints of Karlstadt's pamphlets, see the appendix, p. 146.

14. There were two editions of Osiander's *Wider Caspar Schatzgeyer . . . daß die Messz eyn opffer sey* (Osiander, GA 1: 480–500), and one of Luther's *Von dem grewel der Stillmesse*.

15. The prohibition was issued on 12 November 1524; Manfred Krebs and Hans Georg Rott, eds., *Elsass I*, Quellen zur Geschichte der Täufer 7 (Gütersloh: Mohn, 1959), pp. 21–22, no. 12. Karlstadt's *Exegesis, Dialogue*, and *Prove* were all published by Johann Prüss in 1525. There were also two different imprints of his *Declaration*, one by Prüss, which included Capito's *Frolockung eins christlichen bruders*, and the other by Knobloch.

16. Published as *Io. Wiclefi viri undiquaque piis.dialogorum libri quattuor* (Hagenau: Schöffer, 1525). The preface is dated 7 March 1525; Brunfels admitted to editing Wyclif's work in the letter of dedication to Luther in the third volume of *Ioannes Hvss De Anatomia Antichristi*, WA Br 3: 477. On Brunfels's travels, see the appendix, p. 145. Thomas Kaufmann is thus wrong to suggest that Capito was responsible for the publication of Wycif's work, *Die Abendmahlstheologie der Strassburger Reformatoren bis 1528*, Beiträge zur historischen Theologie 81 (Tübingen: Mohr, 1992), p. 267, n. 909, but he is correct in pointing to Capito's early familiarity with Wyclif's works. Capito may even have been the original owner of the manuscript that Brunfels published, which would explain Capito's reference to a work by Wyclif, "which I do not now have at home"; Capito to Zwingli, 31 December 1524, Z 8: 280; The summary in Erika Rummel and

Milton Kooistra, eds., *The Correspondence of Wolfgang Capito* (Toronto: University of Toronto Pres, 2005–), 2: 94–95, does not mention Wyclif.

17. 1 July 1525, B&A 1: 376, and 25 July 1525, B&A 1: 378.

18. Kaufmann sees this publishing activity as an indication of the Strasbourgers' avid partisanship, *Abendmahlstheologie*, pp. 284–302, but he attributes more direct responsibility for these publications to the pastors than is warranted by the sources. The marginal glosses added to Oecolampadius's *De genvina . . . expositione* were probably added not by Capito but by Farel, who was far more insistent than the city's pastors on the need to abandon belief in Christ's corporeal presence; cf. his letter to Bugenhagen, 8 October 1525, Herminjard 1: 393–398; this is indirectly confirmed by Zwingli, who told Rhegius that the term "deus impanatus" was coined by "the French in Germany," chief among whom was Farel, Z 4: 933. Spruyt, *Hoen*, pp. 176–181, rejects Kaufmann's arguments for Bucer's involvement in the publication of the Hoen letter and proposes instead Otto Brunfels as the editor. In both cases, although Strasbourg's pastors may have agreed with the views expressed in these works, they were not the individuals responsible for the active anti-Lutheran propaganda that Kaufmann attributes to them. Kaufmann sees the publication of Hoen's letter as a response to Bugenhagen's *Contra novum errorem*, but it is more likely that both letters were published so that they could be sold at the Frankfurt book fair, which began in early September. On the pamphlet of Conrad Ryss, which Kaufmann also attributes to Bucer, *Abendmahlstheologie*, p. 333, see below.

19. They also published Luther's *Sermon von der Beycht vnd dem Sacrament* (WA 15: 481–505), preached during Holy Week of 1524 and so before the outbreak of the eucharistic controversy, and his *Sermon von der höchsten gotzslesterung* (WA 15: 758–774), an attack on the mass. On the publication of sacramentarian, as opposed to Lutheran, works in Strasbourg, Kaufmann, *Abendmahlstheologie*, 280–281.

20. The works defending Christ's presence were those of Amsdorf, Bugenhagen, and Luther; the sacramentarian pamphlets included Karlstadt's two last eucharistic pamphlets, *Explanation* and *Testament* (two imprints), Zwingli's *Vonn dem nachtmal Christi widergedechtnus*, which was the German translation of the section on the Lord's Supper in his *Commentarius*, as well as the works by Frey, Michael Keller, Ryss, and Turnauer discussed below. Augsburg's importance as a printing center is discussed in Lee Palmer Wandel, *The Eucharist in the Reformation: Incarnation and Liturgy* (Cambridge: Cambridge University Press, 2006), pp. 67–70, but she does not analyze the contents of any of these works, and her characterization of the views of Zwingli, Oecolampadius, and Schwenckfeld in the opening years of the eucharistic controversy is misleading. More useful is the discussion in Köhler, *Zwingli und Luther*, 1: 255–270.

21. *Ettlich beschluszreden . . . allen christen von vndricht der meß*, Balthasar Hubmaier, *Schriften*, edited by Gunnar Westin and Torsten Bergsten, Quellen zur Geschichte der Täufer 9 (Gütersloh: Gütersloher Verlagshaus, 1962), pp. 102–104.

22. There were two Catholic works, one by Leopold Dick, *De mysterio venerabilis Sacramenti Eucharistiae*, and the other by Kaspar Schatzgeyer, *Von dem hayligisten Opffer der Meß*, reprinted in Erwin Iserloh and Peter Fabisch, eds., *Kaspar Schatzgeyer OFM Schriften zur Verteidigung der Messe*, Corpus Catholicorum 37 (Münster: Aschendorff, 1984), pp. 148–198; those attacking the mass were Leo Jud, *Ain Christenlich widerfechdung Leonis Jud/ wider Mathis Kretzen zuo Augspurg falsche Endchristische Meß* (Augsburg: Ulhart, 1525), Andreas Osiander, *Wider Caspar Schatzgeyer* (Augsburg: Ulhart, 1525), Osiander, GA 1: 480–500; Philipp Melhofer, *Offenbarung der alerheimlisten haimlichait . . . genannt Canon oder die Styllmess* (Augsburg: Ulhart, 1525), and Zwingli's *Antwort wider Hieronimii Emser*, a translation of his *Antibolon*, Z 3: 230–287.

23. Johann Landsperger, *Ain nützlicher berücht von nyessung Des hochwirdigen Sacraments oder Testaments Christi in bayerlay zaichen da brots vnd weins/Vnnd was baide parthey (wider ainander streytend) filen bißher verborgen* (Augsburg: Ramminger, 1524), Köhler MF 681, no. 1776. The pamphlet is dated 23 December 1524 at the end; Max Wilhelm Martin, *Johann Landtsperger: Die unter diesem Namen gehenden Schriften und ihre Verfasser* (Augsburg: Lampart, 1902), pp. 39–44.

24. Luther had used this verse to argue that John 6 did not concern the sacrament of the altar, since this would mean that everyone, including infants, must receive sacramental communion; moreover, there were clearly many who ate the sacrament physically to their own death and judgment. WA 6: 502–503, LW 36: 19–20; WA 12: 580–582.

25. Rhegius's *Wider den newen irrsal*, published in December, responded to Karlstadt's arguments in *Abuse* and *Dialogue*, both of which had been published in nearby Nuremberg.

26. I agree with Köhler, *Zwingli und Luther*, 1: 261, and against Martin, *Landtsperger*, pp. 39–40, that Landsperger probably had not read Zwingli's letter to Alber. Köhler describes Landsperger's pamphlet as unclear and confused. This is an unfair assessment that can be made only if one ignores the purpose of the pamphlet, which is to help readers prepare for worthy reception—a goal that is clearly expressed in both the title and the opening lines—and instead tries to find in it a clear endorsement of either Luther's or Zwingli's (or Karlstadt's) position on Christ's presence.

27. *Berücht*, C4r–v; cf. Karlstadt, *Forms*, fol. d4r–v; Burnett, *Pamphlets*, pp. 66–67.

28. Luther to Spalatin, 29 December 1524, WA Br 3: 409. For a theological analysis of the pamphlet, Hellmut Zschoch, *Reformatorische Existenz und konfessionelle Identität. Urbanus Rhegius als evangelischer Theologe in den Jahren 1520 bis 1530*, Beiträge zur historische Theologie 88 (Tübingen: Mohr, 1995), pp. 171–181.

29. *Irrsal*, fol. A3r–A4v.

30. *Irrsal*, fol. A3r–A4v, C1r–C4v.

31. *Irrsal*, fol. A4v–C1r.

32. *Irrsal*, fol. D1v–E4v.

33. Michael Keller, *Ettlich Sermones von dem nachtmal Christi* (Augsburg: Ulhart, 1525), fol. A2r–v. I used a microfilm of the copy held by the Bodleian Library, Oxford, made available through the Thrivent Reformation Research Library in Minneapolis; the pamphlet is also available as Köhler MF 993, no. 2522. Keller's pamphlet is dated 25 May; the sermons on which it was based were probably preached during the week before Easter, which fell on 16 April in 1525.

34. *Sermones*, fol. B3v–C1r, F1v. As if to emphasize the pamphlet's agreement with Zwingli, its title page reproduces a woodcut of Christ and his disciples celebrating the Last Supper that was also the title page of the new liturgy for the Lord's Supper introduced in Zurich for Easter 1525, *Action oder Bruch des Nachtmals* (Zurich: Froschauer, 1525). The woodcut was also used for the title pages of both the Zurich and Augsburg imprints of *Von dem nachtmal Christi/widergedechtnus oder Dancksagung* (the German translation of the section on the Lord's Supper in Zwingli's *Commentarius*) as well as of Zwingli's *Subsidium*. It is reproduced and discussed by Lee Palmer Wandel, "Envisioning God: Image and Liturgy in Reformation Zurich," *Sixteenth Century Journal* 24 (1993): 21–40, who notes only its appearance as the title page of the Zurich liturgy.

35. *Sermones*, fol. C4v–D1r, D2v–D3v, E3v–F3v; citation at F3v. Keller would be more outspoken in his rejection of Christ's corporeal presence in the expanded edition of *Ettlich Sermones* published in 1526; Köhler, *Zwingli und Luther* 1: 264–266.

36. Matthaeus Frey, *Ain Schöne vnderweysung vnd leer/zubetrachten das nachtmal vnsers lieben herren Jhesu Christ* (Augsburg: Ramminger, 1525), Köhler MF 1204, no. 3046. Frey identi-

fied himself only as "a sinful shepherd of his sheep." It has generally been assumed that Frey was a pseudonym for Michael Keller, and VD16 lists the work under his name, but Köhler rightly questioned this identification; *Zwingli und Luther* 1: 264.

37. *Vnderweysung*, fol. A4v–B1v.

38. *Vnderweysung*, fol. A4r: So dann Christus redt/ Nemend/ essend/ das ist mein leib/ der für euch hingeben würt/ bedeut vnd dargibt er seinen sterplichen leib/ der dann also natur-tlich/entpfintlich für vns gelitten hat/ den selbigen hat er unns also vnsichtparlich im hailigen wort/ durch die gnad im gayst/ dasselbig haylig wort im glauben zuobegreyffen vnd fassen dargeraicht.

39. Hubmaier, *Schriften*, p. 102; he cited Matt 16:18 and 1 Cor. 10:4, passages also used by both Hoen and Karlstadt, as parallel constructions for understanding the words of institution.

40. Hubmaier, *Schriften*, p. 103.

41. According to the editors, Hubmaier's pamphlet was published before Easter 1525; Hubmaier, *Schriften*, p. 101. Grebel's letter in QGTS 1: 15; a translation in Michael G. Baylor, ed., *The Radical Reformation*, Cambridge Texts in the History of Political Thought (Cambridge: Cambridge University Press, 1991), p. 38.

42. Turnauer studied in Ingolstadt, Leipzig, and Wittenberg. In early 1525 he published a translation of Bugenhagen's commentary on the Pauline epistles, and he would later translate a portion of Oecolampadius's commentary on Ezekiel that was published with Caspar Schwenckfeld's *De Cursu Verba Dei*, CS 6: 271. On his possible connection with Mindelheim, see the reference to "Turnauer" in the letter of Wilhelm von Zell of Mindelheim to Zwingli, Z 9: 328; Köhler, *Zwingli und Luther*, 1: 270–271. My thanks to Reiner Henrich for helping me track down this information.

43. *Die Wort Pauli vom Nachtmal des Herren Cor. xi. Außgelegt* (Augsburg: Otmar, 1525), Köhler MF 738, no. 1885; cf. Karlstadt, *Exegesis*, fol. a3r–v, b3r–v; Burnett, *Pamphlets*, pp. 146–147, 150–151.

44. *Antwort . . . das Sacrament betreffend*, Köhler MF 737, no. 1880. Even at the time that the pamphlet was published, the author's name was assumed to be a pseudonym. Martin rejected the attribution to Johann Landsperger and suggested that Michael Keller was the author, *Landtsperger*, pp. 108–110, a suggestion followed by VD16. Köhler believed the pamphlet was influenced by Schwenckfeld and so doubted Keller's authorship; he proposed Jörg Regel, a wealthy Augsburg patrician and later follower of Schwenckfeld; *Zwingli und Luther* 1: 274–275. Thomas Kaufmann believed that Martin Bucer was the author, "Zwei unerkannte Schriften Bucers und Capitos zur Abendmahlsfrage aus dem Herbst 1525," *Archiv für Reformationsgeschichte* 81 (1990): 158–188, but I am not persuaded by his arguments. Not only are Ryss's style and lan-guage quite different from Bucer's—admittedly, a subjective judgment—but the pamphlet's clear dependence on Karlstadt makes Bucer's authorship improbable. If one were going to make an attribution on the basis of parallels with works known to be written by an individual, Karlstadt himself would be a more logical choice than Bucer. Spruyt, *Hoen*, p. 177, suggests that the name was not a pseudonym, since a priest by the name of Conrad Ryss bought citizenship in Strasbourg in 1528, but as Kaufmann points out, this would not explain the appellation "zu Ofen" ([Buda-] Pest). It was this appellation that caused Gottfried Locher to suggest either Simon Grynaeus, who had served as school rector in Budapest for several years, or an unnamed individual who succeeded Grynaeus in that position; *Die Zwinglische Reformation im Rahmen der europäischen Kirchengeschichte* (Göttingen: Vandenhoeck & Ruprecht, 1979), pp. 307, 657. The Wittenbergers recognized the pamphlet as "gut Carlstadtisch," and Melanchthon suspected that the author was Karlstadt's ally, the exiled Jena pastor Martin Reinhart; Justus Jonas to Johann von Dolzig, 4

January 1526, Gustav Kawerau, ed., *Der Briefwechsel des Justus Jonas* (Hildesheim: Olms, 1964), 1: 97–98. I am most inclined to agree with Melanchthon.

45. It was this rearrangement of the words of institution that caused Köhler to see Schwenckfeldian influence. The argument developed by Crautwald and endorsed by Schwenckfeld was somewhat different from that of Ryss, however; see below. A better way to explain this rearrangement of words is Erasmus's application of the *figura prothysteron* to the words of institution; Gottfried G. Krodel, "Figura Prothysteron and the Exegetical Basis of the Lord's Supper," *Lutheran Quarterly* 12 (1960): 152–158. It is just as likely, however, that Ryss applied his common sense to the understanding of the words of institution that Karlstadt had proposed in both *Prove*, fol. F1r–v; Burnett, *Pamphlets*, pp. 137–138, and *Exegesis*, fol. a3r–a4r; Burnett, *Pamphlets*, pp. 146–147. Karlstadt had also used this technique in his discussion of the words concerning the cup, *Testament*, fol. C2v–C4r; Burnett, *Pamphlets*, pp. 249–251, and Ryss may have been inspired to apply it to the words concerning the body.

46. *Antwort*, fol. A2r–v; Karlstadt, *Prove*, fol. C3r–v; Burnett, *Pamphlets*, pp. 249–250. Karlstadt, in turn, owed this observation to Erasmus.

47. *Antwort*, fol. A2v–A4r. For similar passages, Spruyt, *Hoen*, pp. 227, 230–231 Oberman, *Forerunners*, pp. 269, 272–273; *Subsidium*, Z 4: 468–469, HZW 2: 198–199; Oecolampadius, *De genvina . . . expositione*, fol. B3v. Karlstadt insisted that the apostles never wrote that Christ's body and blood were in the sacrament, *Prove*, fol. C1v–C2r, C4r; Burnett, *Pamphlets*, pp. 125, 127–28.

48. *Antwort*, fol. A4r; cf. Karlstadt, *Prove*, fol. C3r–v; Burnett, *Pamphlets*, p. 127.

49. *Antwort*, fol. A4v–B2r; Z 4: 563–565.

50. *Antwort*, fol. B3v–B4r; cf. Karlstadt, *Prove*, fol. C2r; Burnett, *Pamphlets*, p. 125; *Explanation*, fol. C2v; Burnett, *Pamphlets*, p. 230.

51. *Antwort*, fol. B4v–C2r; cf. Karlstadt, *Exegesis*, d1v–d3v; Burnett, *Pamphlets*, pp. 157–159; *Abuse*, fol. a2v–a4v; Burnett, *Pamphlets*, pp. 207–209.

52. *Antwort*, fol. C2r–C3v; for the comparison with the Israelites' worship of the golden calf, cf. Spruyt, *Hoen*, p. 233; Oberman, *Forerunners*, p. 276. Ryss cited Acts 1:11, Acts 3:21, Rom. 8:34, Ps. 110:1, and Matt. 26:11, opposed John 16:7 to Matt. 18:20, argued that God's promise that his holy one would not see corruption (Ps. 16:10) proved that consecrated hosts, which decayed and were consumed by mice, could not be Christ's body, and cited both the Lord's Prayer, addressed to "Our Father in heaven" and the articles of the Apostles' Creed concerning Christ's ascension, session at the Father's right hand, and return in judgment. On the Hussite source of these arguments and their use in sacramentarian works, see chapter 4, pp. 79–87.

53. *Antwort*, fol. C4r; Karlstadt, *Prove*, fol. B2r–B4r; Burnett, *Pamphlets*, pp. 121–123.

54. The earliest references to Ryss's pamphlet in the reformers' correspondence come from the end of 1525. Zwingli received a copy from Ludwig Hätzer, who brought the pamphlet from Augsburg; Zwingli to Vadian, 23 December 1525, Z 8: 470–472. The Wittenbergers received a copy at the turn of the year; Justus Jonas to von Dolzig, 4 January 1526, Kawerau, *Briefwechsel* 1: 97–98. Luther did not mention Ryss's exegesis of the words of institution when describing the disagreement among his opponents in his open letter to Reutlingen, dated 4 January 1526, WA 19: 120–121; contra Kaufmann, "Schriften," 183, he was here referring to Schwenckfeld's exegesis. Luther did refer to Ryss, however, in a letter to Spalatin, 27 March 1526, WA Br 4: 42. Theodore Billican had also read Ryss's work by mid-January; Billican to Oecolampadius, 16 January 1526; B&A 1: 452.

55. Kaufmann, "Schriften," pp. 166–168, argued that the pamphlet was first printed in Strasbourg. He claimed that the Strasbourg and Zurich imprints predated the Augsburg

imprints, but it is hardly likely that Zwingli would have been unaware of the pamphlet, as Kaufmann suggests, if it had already been printed in Zurich. The differences between the Augsburg and the Zurich/Strasbourg imprints can be used just as easily to argue that the pamphlet was first printed in Augsburg, and the Zurich and Strasbourg editions were reprints.

56. The *Commentarius* was published in two Latin imprints, two imprints of a complete German translation, and two imprints of the excerpt on the Lord's Supper in German. One of these excerpts was printed in Augsburg; the others were all published in Zurich. There were four German imprints of the *klare Vnderrichtung*, two printed in Zurich and two in Strasbourg; Z 4: 782–783.

57. To Vadian, 17 January 1526, Z 8: 505–507.

58. *Vermanung Nicolai von Amsdorf an die von Magdeburg*, Köhler, MF 53, no. 152, fol. A2r–A3r; Cyclops, *Von dem aller hochwirdigsten Nachtmahl Jesu Christi* (Magdeburg: Oettinger, 1525), Köhler MF 423, no. 1160. On the conflict, Ernst Koch, "Zwinglianer zwischen Ostsee und Harz in den Anfangsjahren der Reformation (1525–1532)," *Zwingliana* 16 (1983–85): 517– 545. Koch suggests that Cyclops may have been influenced by Hoen's letter rather than by Zwingli, but this is unlikely in view of the publication dates of the relevant pamphlets. Hoen's letter was published sometime in August, while Amsdorf's letter, first published in Wittenberg, was reprinted in Augsburg in the first part of September, Hätzer to Zwingli, 14 September 1525, Z 8: 363–364. While Amsdorf may have responded immediately to Cyclops's unauthorized preaching, it is more likely that the latter had read one or both of Zwingli's pamphlets published in March.

59. This is not to say that either of them opposed the translation of their works. Zwingli's colleague Leo Jud, the Zurich schoolmaster Georg Binder, and Ludwig Hätzer translated all of their Latin discussions of the sacrament into German, all within a few months of their initial publication.

60. In striking contrast to Ryss (and to Karlstadt), Zwingli pleaded with his readers not to reject his words out of hand but to pray for illumination at the end of the section on the Lord's Supper in his *Commentarius*, Z 3: 819–820, *Commentary*, pp. 252–253.

61. R. Emmet McLaughlin, *Caspar Schwenckfeld, Reluctant Radical: His Life to 1540*, Yale Historical Publications Miscellany 134 (New Haven, Conn.: Yale University Press, 1986), pp. 22–56.

62. 23 June 1525, CS 2: 120–125.

63. 14 September 1525, CS 2: 169–171.

64. 1 October 1525, CS 2: 367–374.

65. Schwenckfeld described how he came to this new insight in a letter to Marx Zimmermann written in June 1556; CS 14: 801–805; citation at pp. 802–803.

66. The "Twelve Questions" was not published until 1529, as *Ein Christlich bedencken*, CS 3: 498–507. For a discussion, see R. Emmet McLaughlin, "The Genesis of Schwenckfeld's Eucharistic Doctrine," *Archiv für Reformationsgeschichte* 74 (1983): 94–121, esp. pp. 99–104.

67. CS 3: 499–500.

68. CS 3: 502–505.

69. CS 3: 504–505, 501. McLaughlin, "Genesis," pp. 101–102, does not catch this distinction and so believed that Schwenckfeld attributed more to reception of the elements than is warranted by the text.

70. McLaughlin cited what he saw as inconsistencies with earlier statements and an allusion to Crautwald's exegesis of the words of institution to argue that the last two pages, as well as the introduction, were added when the pamphlet was published in 1529 and were not part of the original "Twelve Questions"; "Genesis," pp. 99, 102. I am not fully persuaded by his

arguments, but because there are doubts that these pages represent Schwenckfeld's earliest position on the Lord's Supper, I will not consider them here.

71. Horst Weigelt, *Spiritualistische Tradition im Protestantismus: Die Geschichte des Schwenckfeldertums in Schlesien* (Berlin: de Gruyter, 1973), pp. 51–52, sees a Zwinglian influence, which McLaughlin disputes, "Genesis," pp. 102–103. Douglas H. Schantz, *Crautwald and Erasmus: A Study in Humanism and Radical Reform in Sixteenth Century Silesia*, Bibliotheca Dissidentium Scripta et Studia 4 (Baden-Baden: Koerner, 1992), pp. 79–83, accused McLaughlin of downplaying Zwingli's influence and endorses Weigelt's interpretation, but in fact McLaughlin's understanding of Zwingli's theology as presented in the works published in 1525 is more accurate than Weigelt's.

72. McLaughlin pointed to parallels in Wessel Gansfort's discussion of spiritual communion but found no direct connection between Gansfort and Schwenckfeld; "Genesis," pp. 104–106. Such a connection is not necessary, though, in light of the widespread diffusion of this understanding of spiritual communion; see chapter 2, pp. 41–48.

73. Karlstadt introduced the question of what Judas received in conjunction with a paraphrase of John 6:54 in *Exegesis*, fol. c4r–v; Burnett, *Pamphlets*, p. 156. The contrast between corporeal and spiritual eating is especially strong in the *Explanation*, where Karlstadt again denied that Judas received Christ's body and blood, fol. A3r–A4v, C4v–D1r, D2v–D3r; Burnett, *Pamphlets*, pp. 221–223, 233, 236. Weigelt saw any similarities with Karlstadt as parallels rather than as a direct influence; *Spiritualistische Tradition*, pp. 52–53. McLaughlin, "Genesis," pp. 12–13, also saw no evidence of Karlstadt's influence; he suggested that Schwenckfeld may have been influenced by Hoen's interpretation of John 6:48–57, but Karlstadt's position in the *Exegesis* was very close to Hoen's on this passage.

74. Schantz, *Crautwald*, pp. 13–25.

75. CS 14: 803–804. Crautwald recounted how he came to his new understanding of Christ's words in a letter to Schwenckfeld, CS 2: 194–209; synopses and analyses in Weigelt, *Spiritualistische Tradition*, pp. 53–65, and McLaughlin, "Genesis," pp. 110–114.

76. He cited the Decretum as well as Cyprian, Tertullian, Hilary, Ambrose, and Chrysostom, and he mentioned both Oecolampadius's *De genuina . . . expositione* and Zwingli's *Commentarius*, CS 2: 206–208. Crautwald told Schwenckfeld that he carried out this study with two friends; CS 2: 198–204.

77. In *Exegesis*, fol. b1v, Burnett, *Pamphlets*, p. 149, Karlstadt used John 6:51 ("the bread which I give is my flesh which I will give for the life of the world") to justify his equation of the two statements, "Christ gives you his body" and "Christ gives his body for you." If indeed Schwenckfeld had read Karlstadt's pamphlet, it is conceivable that he brought Karlstadt's argument to Crautwald's attention. It is perhaps more likely that Crautwald and Karlstadt both followed Erasmus here in making use of the figura prothysteron, the transposing of phrases in a sentence to change its meaning; Krodel, "Figura Prothysteron."

78. Although Schwenckfeld met with Luther at both the beginning and the end of his visit, he spent most of his time talking with Bugenhagen, and he spoke only briefly with Jonas. The editors describe the documents Schwenckfeld took to Wittenberg; CS 2: 223–234. Schwenckfeld wrote an account of these discussions fourteen years later, using notes taken while he was still in Wittenberg; CS 2: 240–282, esp. p. 273.

79. Caselius arrived in Wittenberg on 30 October 1525, WA Br 3: 593; Luther's response to the Strasbourgers is dated 5 November, BCorr 2: 55–58. The Strasbourgers' letters in BDS 3: 421–430 and Vogt, *Bugenhagens Briefwechsel*, pp. 32–50; summarized in Erika Rummel and

Milton Kooistra, eds., *The Correspondence of Wolfgang Capito* (Toronto: University of Toronto Press, 2005–), 1: 156–157, no. 248.

80. CS 2: 252, 256, 258, 260, 261, 275, 279.

81. CS 2: 253, 262 (Bugenhagen); 241–242 (Schwenckfeld).

82. CS 2: 279.

83. CS 2: 244–245, 261, 272.

84. CS 2: 280. McLaughlin misreads Schwenckfeld's words as a statement of uncertainty; "Genesis," pp. 118–119.

85. CS 2: 250–251, 253–257, 265–266, 268, 278. Because of this dissociation of sign and thing signified, Schwenckfeld's view cannot be seen as foreshadowing that of Calvin, contra McLaughlin, *Schwenckfeld*, p. 65. In fact, in his insistence that no external sign can strengthen faith, Schwenckfeld was closer to Zwingli than to Calvin.

86. CS 2: 244, 249, 258–259, 261, 271.

87. CS 2: 266–267, 270–272, citation at p. 272. The pamphlet was most likely the 1508 *Excusatio fratrum Valdensium*, which contained all the arguments Schwenckfeld introduced; see chapter 4, pp. 80–82. He and Bugenhagen also disputed the meaning of Matt. 24:23, but the association of this verse with the idea that priests could summon Christ's body down from heaven at will suggests that Bugenhagen was thinking of Karlstadt's *Dialogue*, fol. f4r, Burnett, *Pamphlets*, p. 197, where these points are discussed in close proximity; CS 2: 254, 268, 270.

88. CS 2: 222–224, 246, 248–249, 253, 274–275, 276, 277. Zwingli described his dream/revelation in the *Subsidium*, Z 4: 482–484; HZW 2: 209–210.

89. CS 2: 243, 278.

90. Surprisingly, one issue that apparently was not discussed was whether the godless received Christ's body and blood, although Schwenckfeld gave a copy of the "Twelve Questions" to Jonas; CS 2: 275.

91. Weigelt, *Spiritualistische Tradition*, p. 74.

92. WA Br 4: 52–53.

93. McLaughlin, *Schwenckfeld*, pp. 68–70.

94. WA 6: 358–359; LW 35: 86; Hartmut Hilgenfeld, *Mittelalterlich-traditionelle Elemente in Luthers Abendmahlsschriften*, Studien zur Dogmengeschichte und systematischen Theologie 29 (Zurich: Theologischer Verlag, 1971), p. 86.

95. Spruyt, *Hoen*, pp. 226, 232; Oberman, *Forerunners*, pp. 268, 275; cf. Spruyt's discussion, pp. 87–90, 121–125; Zwingli, *klare Vnterrichtung*, Z 4: 856, Geoffrey W. Bromiley, *Zwingli and Bullinger*, Library of Christian Classics 24 (Philadelphia: Westminster, 1953), p. 234; Oecolampadius, *De genuina . . . expositione*, fol. C1r; Bucer, *Grund und Ursach*, BDS 1: 248–249.

96. *Vßlegen der Schlussreden*, Z 2: 120–121, HZW 1: 98–99; *Commentarius*, Z 3: 758–759, *Commentary*, pp. 180–181.

97. Spruyt, *Hoen*, p. 233, Oberman, *Forerunners*, p. 276.

98. *Prove*, fol. A3r–v; Burnett, *Pamphlets*, pp. 117–118; *Abuse*, fol. A3v–B2r; Burnett, *Pamphlets*, pp. 208–211.

99. *Responsio ad epistolam Bugenhagii*, Z 4: 573–575; cf. the pastor's admonition and prayer before communion in the Zurich liturgy for the Lord's Supper, Z 4: 21–22.

100. There is a long historiographical debate concerning Rhegius's position in the eucharistic controversy, summarized in Zschoch, *Reformatorische Existenz*, pp. 165–169.

101. *Bilibaldi Birckheimheri de Vera Christi carne et vero eius sanguine, ad Ioan. Oecolampadius responsio* (Nuremberg: Petreius, 1526); *De Verbis Coenae Dominicae et opinionum uarietate. Theobaldi Billicani ad Vrbanum Regium Epistola. Responsio Vrbani Regij ad eundum* (Augsburg:

Ruff, 1526), esp. fol. A6r–C3v; German translation in Walch 17: 1547–70; brief summaries of both works in Köhler, *Zwingli und Luther* 1: 234–236, 251–253. Synopses and analyses of the *Syngramma* in Martin Brecht, *Die frühe Theologie des Johannes Brenz*, Beiträge zur historischen Theologie 36 (Tübingen: Mohr/Siebeck, 1966), pp. 73–87; Martin Honecker, "Die Abendmahlslehre des Syngramma," *Blätter für württembergische Kirchengeschichte* 65 (1965): 39–68; Friedrich Wilhelm Kantzenbach, "Johannes Brenz und der Kampf um das Abendmahl," *Theologische Literaturzeitung* 89 (1964): 561–580.

102. Wilhelm H. Neuser, *Die Abendmahlslehre Melanchthons in ihrer geschichtlichen Entwicklung (1519–1530)*, Beiträge zur Geschichte und Lehre der Reformierten Kirche 26 (Neukirchen-Vluyn: Neukirchener Verlag, 1968), pp. 265–291.

103. *Billiche Antwort Johan Ecolampadij auff D. Martin Luthers bericht des sacraments halb* (Basel: Wolf, 1526), reprinted in Walch 20: 582–635, here at p. 591.

104. *Dialogue*, fol. a4r–v; Burnett, *Pamphlets*, p. 169. This important point is obscured by Hertzsch's transposition of fol. A4r from *Schriften* 2: 11.34 to 40.33–41.25, an error followed in the English translations of Lindberg and Furcha.

APPENDIX

1. Grebel wrote to Joachim Vadian on 3 September 1524 that he had "written back" to Karlstadt; QGTS 1: 11–13. On 14 Oct., Grebel reported to Vadian on Westerburg's visit: he had showed Grebel "eight booklets, more or less," that he hoped to have printed, and Grebel promised to send copies of the pamphlets when they were available. Barge assumes that Westerburg left Saxony with Karlstadt; *Karlstadt*, 2: 141. Westerburg told the Swiss about the confrontation between Karlstadt and Luther in Jena but said nothing about Karlstadt's expulsion, and so he must have left Jena before 18 September, the date on which Karlstadt was ordered to leave Saxony; QGTS 1: 21–23.

2. The distance from Jena to Zurich is roughly 600 kilometers. For the sake of comparison, a month later it took the Strasbourg deacon Nicolaus Mersheimer three weeks to travel approximately the same distance from Strasbourg to Wittenberg bearing letters and copies of Karlstadt's pamphlets for Luther. The Strasbourg pastors' letter is dated 23 November 1524, BCorr 1: 288–297; on 14 December Luther reported to Spalatin that he had just received the letter; WA Br 3: 399. Most accounts assume that Grebel wrote to Vadian immediately after Westerburg's departure, but Westerburg could have left Zurich as much as two weeks earlier. On the role of Mantz and Castelberger, see Calvin Pater, *Karlstadt as Father of the Baptist Movements: The Emergence of Lay Protestantism* (Toronto: University of Toronto Press, 1984), pp. 159–160, as well as the testimony of the printer Johann Bebel, ABR 1: 174–176, English translation in Pater, *Karlstadt*, pp. 290–294, but with errors as noted below.

3. ABR 1: 174: "Acht tag oder 14 ongevorlich noch Frackfurter mesz." Pater translated this as "one or two weeks before the fair in Frankfurt" (rather than after) and then accused the printers of perjury; *Karlstadt*, p. 160; p. 290, n. 2. The dates he gives for the fair are also inaccurate. In the sixteenth century the book fair began on 8 September and lasted for two weeks; Leon Voet, *The Golden Compasses: A History and Evaluation of the Printing and Publishing Activities of the Officina Plantiniana at Antwerp in Two Volumes* (Amsterdam: Vangendt, 1972), 2: 396, n. 3. On the two Basel printers, Josef Benzing, *Die Buchdrucker des 16. und 17. Jahrhunderts im deutschen Sprachgebiet*, 2nd ed., Beiträge zur Buch- und Bibliothekswesen 12 (Wiesbaden: Harrassowitz, 1982), pp. 34–35.

4. Wolff told the authorities that the four pamphlets together used sixteen gatherings or sheets of paper, and that he had printed 1,000 copies of three of the pamphlets and 800 copies of the fourth, ABR 1: 176. It must therefore have taken a little more than two weeks to complete the printing of all four pamphlets. Pater, *Karlstadt*, p. 294, errs in interpreting Wolff's comments as "each [booklet] was printed on sixteen sheets"; the printer was referring to the total amount of paper used to produce one copy of all four pamphlets. Both *Ob man gemach faren* and *Wie sich der gelaub* had four gatherings; *Masses* had only one gathering, and *Prove* had seven gatherings.

5. *Ob man gemach faren, vnd des ergernüssen der schwachen verschonen soll* (Basel: Wolf, 1524); English translation in Furcha, *Carlstadt*, pp. 247–268; *Wie sich der gelaub vnd vnglaub gegen dem licht vnd finsternuß . . . halten* (Basel: Wolf, 1524).

6. This led Barge to identify Cratander, not Bebel, as the printer of these three pamphlets; "Zur Chronologie," 327–328. Cratander had also published Luther's New Testament, as well as biblical commentaries by both Luther and Oecolampadius. Oecolampadius had lived with Cratander during the year after his arrival in Basel at the end of 1522.

7. ABR 1: 174.

8. Barge, *Karlstadt*, 2: 138–151; Roy L. Vice, "Valentin Ickelsamer's Odyssey from Rebellion to Quietism," *Mennonite Quarterly Review* 69 (1995): 75–92. The frequently asserted view that Karlstadt was in Strasbourg in early October must therefore be revised.

9. The first to suggest this itinerary was Otto Albrecht, "Beiträge zum Verständnis des Briefwechsels Luthers im Jahre 1524," in *Beiträge zur Reformationsgeschichte: Herrn Oberkonsistorialrat Professor D. Köstlin bei der Feier seines siebzigsten Geburtstages ehrerbietigst gewidmet*, ed. P. Albrecht et al. (Gotha: Perthes, 1896), pp. 1–36, esp. p. 32ff. Albrecht suggested that Barge went from Strasbourg to Basel, then made a side trip to Zurich. Barge followed Otto's dating and said nothing about a stay in Basel before the trip to Zurich, although it might be assumed, since Basel lay on the direct route between Strasbourg and Zurich; *Karlstadt*, 2: 207, 215–218; see also "Chronologie," where Barge suggests that Karlstadt arrived in Basel after 23 October. More recent scholars have followed Barge; see the discussion in Thomas Kaufmann, *Die Abendmahlstheologie der Strassburger Reformatoren bis 1528*, Beiträge zur historischen Theologie 81 (Tübingen: Mohr, 1992), pp. 182–183.

10. See n. 2.

11. Barge, *Karlstadt*, 2: 206–207. The earliest mention I have found that places Karlstadt's visit to Strasbourg before his arrival in Zurich is Abraham Scultetus, *Annalium Evangelii Passim per Europam Decimo quinto salutis partae seculo renovati Decas Prima, ab Anno MDXVI ad Annum MDXXV* (Heidelberg: Lancellotus, 1618), p. 230, which reports that Karlstadt went from Franconia to Strasbourg, where he found a supporter in Otto Brunfels, and then to Basel, where his pamphlets were printed. Scultetus may simply have assumed that Karlstadt visited Strasbourg on his way to Basel. Since Brunfels traveled with Karlstadt to Heidelberg, however, it seems more probable that Karlstadt visited Strasbourg on his way north from Basel. The older works of Ludwig Lavater, *Historia de Origine et Progressv Controversiae Sacramentariae de Coena Domini* (Zurich: Froschauer, 1563), 2r–3r, and Rudolf Hospinian, *Historia Sacramentariae Pars altera: De origine et Progressv controversiae sacramentaria de coena Domini* (Zurich: Wolph, 1602), 31v–33r, do not mention Karlstadt's route.

12. Wilhelm Lang, "The Augsburg Travel Guide of 1563 and the Erlinger Road Map of 1524," *Imago Mundi* 7 (1950): 84–88, esp. the map on p. 85.

13. Zwingli, Z 4: 464; HZW 2: 195.

14. Karlstadt obviously had not arrived in Zurich by 14 October, the date of Grebel's letter to Vadian, QGTS 1: 21–23, but it is likely that he arrived soon after the letter was sent. The

distance between Rothenburg and Zurich is approximately 250 kilometers and so would have required at least a week of travel, without staying more than one night in any place en route.

15. ABR 1: 174–175. Alejandro Zorzin has argued that Karlstadt's dialogue on baptism was finally published in 1527, although Calvin Pater has challenged him on this point; on the debate, see Alejandro Zorzin, "Zur Wirkungsgeschichte einer Schrift aus Karlstadts Orlamünder Tätigkeit. Der 1527 in Worms gedruckte 'Dialog vom fremden Glauben, Glauben der Kirche, Taufe der Kinder.' Fortsetzung einer Diskussion," in *Andreas Bodenstein von Karlstadt (1486– 1541): Ein Theologe der frühen Reformation. Beiträge eines Arbeitsgesprächs vom 24–25. November 1995 in Wittenberg,* ed. Sigrid Looß and Markus Matthias (Wittenberg: Drei Kastanien Verlag, 1998), pp. 143–158.

16. Capito mentioned Karlstadt's four-day visit to Strasbourg in a letter to Zwingli, 6 February 1525, Z 8: 302, summarized in Erika Rummel and Milton Kooistra, eds., *The Correspondence of Wolfgang Capito* (Toronto: University of Toronto Press, 2005–), 2: 100–101, no. 236. It took two days of travel to go from Zurich to Basel. Travelers could reach Strasbourg from Basel by a 13-hour boat ride down the Rhine, but the trip took longer if made on horseback. On travel time between these three cities, see the account of Zwingli's trip to Marburg in 1529; Köhler, *Zwingli und Luther,* 2: 60. Karlstadt had with him copies of imprints from both printers when he arrived in Heidelberg in early November, according to the titles given in Frecht's letter, discussed below. Barge, "Chronologie," p. 329, believed that only the four pamphlets mentioned by Frecht had been printed, and the remaining pamphlets were printed before early December.

17. Barge, *Karlstadt,* 2: 217–218. The preface to the pamphlet is dated 6 November. Barge suggests that it was written on the way from Strasbourg to Heidelberg and that Brunfels took it back to Strasbourg with him. This suggestion is supported by Frecht's reference to the documents Karlstadt had with him in Heidelberg; see n. 18. The distance between Strasbourg and Heidelberg is approximately 150 kilometers; if the 80-kilometer trip from Zurich to Basel took two days, the direct trip from Strasbourg to Heidelberg probably required about four days.

18. The letter was published in Georg Veesenmeyer, *Sammlung von Aufsätzen zur Erläuterung der Kirchen-, Litteratur-, Münz- und Sittengeschichte besonders des 16. Jahrhunderts* (Ulm: Stettin, 1827), pp. 182–184; it is cited and short excerpts are quoted in every discussion of Karlstadt during this period. In view of its importance for the following discussion and the rarity of the book in which it was first published, the entire letter is reproduced here: Salvum te cupio in Christo Jesu, vir dignissime. Non potui tabellionem, et inopinato adeuntem et abeuntem, dimittere vacuum, quin Tuam dignitatem participem redderem novi cujusdam, proximo elapso die Lunae ad me delati. Advenit Heydelbergam die Lunae proximo sub horam primam Andreas Carolstadius una cum Doctore quodam Medico, divertitque ad Symonem Grynaeum, apud nos Graecarum Professorem, Carolstadii filii compatrem factum tum, quando Wittembergae olim vixit. Hi vix ad horulam familiariter collocuti sunt de Euangelii negotio tam graviter, quam qui maxime. Vtinam vero tam feliciter succedat Carolstadio, quam constanter contra eucharistiae abusus disserere conatus est. Nam reliquit post se Simoni aliquot libellos impressos, quamquam nondum passim evulgatos, nisi quod familiariter communicavit bonis quibusdam amicis, quos habet Argentinae et Rotenburgi ad Tauberum, unde ad nos venit. Tituli libellorum sunt uulgares, 1) wider die alte vnd newe papistische messe; 2) Außlegung diser wort christi: das ist mein leib; 3) ob man mit hailiger schrift erweysen möge das christus mit leib blut und sele im sacrament sey; 4) Dialogus oder ein gesprechbüchlein von dem mißbrauch des sacraments. Est autem libellorum unicus scopus, dicendo: Hoc est corpus meum. Pronomen hoc non ad panem referendum esse, sed ad corpus Christi: quo Moses, Prophetae, adeoque tota scriptura praedix-

erit, patiendum esse, et morte turpissima damnandum. Id enim Pronomen Graecum *touto* indicat, quod non ad *ho artos*, sed ad *to soma* referendum esse. Quare non sit Christus aut corpus eius in pane; neque in vino sanguis; idque probat meo iudicio christianissime. Nam tumultuarie perlegi argumentum, neque coram licuit cum Carolstadio loqui; etsi vocabar Simone, tamen tum infaustis avibus alio volaram, vixque horulam hic moratus est, statim etenim abiit, eductum familiam suam e Saxonia. Scripsit enim suppliciter Fridenricho, Saxonum Duci, ut coram sua illustri Dominatione et Luthero ea de re disputaret. At, (ut ipse auguratur) suasu et hortatu Lutheri Princeps rescripsit, ut, si hoc ulcus tangere velit: statim e ditione sua abeat, id quod fecit. Ob id parum aequus est in Lutherum, quem habet in eo negotio suspectissimum, quemque oblique perstringit ferme in his omnibus libellis. Totius acti negotii copias habet secum, quas dixit se evulgaturum typis. Tu ora mecum Christum, ut spiritum suum illis columinibus concordem impertiat, ne magno et scandalo et detrimento Euangelii male audiant. Vereor, ne id argumentum sit irritaturum exacebaturumque Principes eos quoque, qui hactenus abstinuere saevire in pios. Statim enim dicent: En nebulones discordantes, qui hactenus ferme totum mundum suis scriptis excitaverunt, nunc inter se dissident! Olim Petrus et Paulus, Barnabas et Paulus dissentiebant. Vtinam ad eum modum cum Luthero et Carlstadio res agatur! Haec quoque pro tua humanitate communicabis Apostolo uestrati, Chunrado Som. Caeterum de filio tuo nihil est, quod scribam propter festinantem tabellarium. Vale, et me commendatum habe. Raptim, Profesto Martini.

19. Frecht's mention of Karlstadt's visit to Rothenburg must refer to his stay in that city immediately after his expulsion from Saxony. It is possible that Karlstadt visited Rothenburg after leaving Strasbourg and before coming to Heidelberg, but this would have meant an extra day of travel each way. Since Karlstadt stayed in Heidelberg for only an hour, he was more likely on his way east, where he planned to rejoin his friends in Rothenburg.

20. Manfred Krebs and Hans Georg Rott, eds., *Elsass I*, Quellen zur Geschichte der Täufer 7 (Gütersloh: Mohn, 1959), pp. 21–22, no. 12.

21. On Reinhart, see Siegfried Hoyer, "Martin Reinhart und der erste Druck hussitischer Artikel in Deutschland," *Zeitschrift für Geschichtswissenschaft* 18 (1970): 1597–1615; Günter Vogler, *Nürnberg 1524–25: Studien zur Geschichte der reformatorischen und sozialen Bewegung in der Reichstadt* (Berlin: VEB, 1982), pp. 232–250.

22. *Wes sich doctor Andreas Bodenstein von Karlstadt mit doctor Martino Luther beredt zu Jhen*, also known as the *Acta Jenensis*, WA 15: 334–347, translation in Sider, *Battle*, pp. 38–48; Luther to Spalatin, 3 October 1524, WA Br 3: 354.

23. Variations in the Basel and Nuremberg imprints of *Abuse* demonstrate that the two versions were printed independently, since each contains a few phrases that are omitted from the other. The most telling of these occurs in the very last sentence of the pamphlet: the Basel imprint ends with a reference to "the use of all sacraments, which hasn't been preached rightly"; the Nuremberg imprint adds a final clause that improves the clarity of the sentence, "for several hundred years."

24. VD16 identifies a 1524 Erfurt imprint of the *Dialogue* (B 6142) but does not list any holding libraries. If this imprint existed, Reinhart's physical proximity to Erfurt in the fall of 1524, as well as his involvement in the printing of the Nuremberg/Bamberg edition, suggests that this was the first edition of the *Dialogue* and that Reinhart was the person responsible for its printing. On Reinhart's stay in Nuremberg, Vogler, *Nürnberg*, pp. 246–248.

25. Gerhard Pfeiffer, *Quellen zur Nürnberger Reformationsgeschichte*, Einzelarbeiten aus der Kirchengeschichte Bayerns 45 (Nuremberg: Verein für bayerische Kirchengeschichte, 1968), RV 228–230, 233, pp. 31–32.

26. Karl Schottenloher, *Die Buchdruckertätigkeit Georg Erlingers in Bamberg von 1522 bis 1541* (*1543*), Sammlung bibliothekswissenschaftlicher Arbeiten 21 (Leipzig: Haupt, 1907), pp. 91–92. Erlinger also printed the first edition of the *Acta Jenensis*, pp. 108–109.

27. Vogler, *Nürnberg*, pp. 249–293; Pfeiffer, *Quellen*, RV 196, p. 26, RV 243, 248–249, pp. 34–35, Greiffenberger's confession, pp. 295–299; Theodor Kolde, "Hans Denck und die gottlosen Maler von Nürnberg," *Beiträge zur bayerischen Kirchengeschichte* 8 (1902): 1–31, 49–72. The editors of Osiander, GA 1: 270–273, point to further parallels between Greiffenberg's confession and Karlstadt's *Dialogue*.

28. The early agitation associated with Karlstadt's supporters was attributed to the Zwinglians as well and helps account for Nuremberg's staunch Lutheranism; Heinrich R. Schmidt, "Die Häretisierung des Zwinglianismus im Reich seit 1525," in *Zugänge zur bäuerlichen Reformation*, ed. Peter Blickle (Zurich: Chronos, 1987), pp. 219–236.

29. He was in the area of Nördingen in early February; Barge, *Karlstadt*, 2: 250–251, 311–312; Roy L. Vice, "Ehrenfried Kumpf, Karlstadt's Patron and Peasants' War Rebel," *Archiv für Reformationsgeschichte* 85 (1996): 153–174; Vice, "Ickelsamer."

30. Vice, "Kumpf." Karlstadt stated at the beginning of *Explanation* that he received a copy of Luther's work on 26 February and began writing his response the next day; in an interrogation held in early July Götz reported that he had visited Rothenburg shortly after Easter (16 April) and sold copies of Karlstadt's pamphlets, including one published by Ulhart; Günther Franz, "Lienhart Götz von Schnelldorf: Ein Beitrag zur Geschichte Karlstadts und des Buchdruckers Philipp Ulhart," *Archiv für Reformationsgeschichte* 26 (1929): 265–269. On Ulhart, Karl Schottenloher, *Philipp Ulhart: Ein Augsburger Winkeldrucker und Helfershelfer der "Schwärmer" und" "Wiedertäufer" (1523–1529)*, Historische Forschungen 4 (Nieuwkoop: de Graaf, 1967), pp. 28–30.

31. Barge, *Karlstadt*, 2: 376–393; in a letter of 12 August 1528, Karlstadt told Elector Johann, "that I could accept Dr. Martin's opinion on the sacrament with good conscience and from the heart, as he has written it in all of his books, is as possible for me as it would be to fly through the air like a bird"; Barge, *Karlstadt*, 2: 584–585.

32. Hans-Peter Hasse, "Zum Aufenthalt Karlstadts in Zürich (1530–34)," *Zwingliana* 18 (1990/91): 366–389; Martin Anton Schmidt, "Karlstadt als Theologe und Prediger in Basel," *Theologische Zeitschrift* 35 (1979): 155–168.

33. Amy Nelson Burnett, "Basel and the Wittenberg Concord," *Archiv für Reformationsgeschichte* 96 (2005): 33–56; Burnett, "'Kilchen ist uff dem Radthus'? Conflicting Views of Magistrate and Ministry in Early Reformation Basel," in *Debatten über die Legitimation von Herrschaft: Politische Sprachen in der Frühen Neuzeit*, ed. Luise Schorn-Schütte and Sven Tode (Berlin: Akademie Verlag, 2006), pp. 49–65; Oswald Myconius to Heinrich Bullinger, 14 January 1542, HBBW 12: 27–29, no. 1596.

BIBLIOGRAPHY

PRIMARY SOURCES

Sixteenth-Century Imprints

Alveldt, Augustin. *Tractactus de communione Sub vtraque Specie.* . . . Leipzig: Stöckel, 1520.

Amsdorf, Nicolaus von. *Vermanung Nicolai von Amsdorf an die von Magdeburg widder den rotten secten geyst Doctor Cyclops.* Wittenberg: Weiß, 1525.

Artickel und Ursprung der Waldenser und der armen von Lugdun, auch Joannis Wicleffen, und Joannis Hussen. Nuremberg: Gutknecht, 1524.

Billican (Gerlacher), Theobald. *Von der Mess Gemayn Schlußred.* Augsburg: Ulhart 1524.

Billican (Gerlacher), Theobald, and Urbanus Rhegius. *De Verbis Coenae Dominicae et opinionum uarietate. Theobaldi Billicani ad Vrbanum Regium Epistola. Responsio Vrbani Regij ad eundum.* Augsburg: Ruff, 1526.

[Bracciolini, Poggio.] *Wie Hieronymus von Prag ain anhänger Johannis Huß durch das concilium zuo Costentz für ain Ketzer verurtailt vnd verpränt worden ist.* Augsburg: Oeglin, 1521.

Brunfels, Otto, ed. *Ioannes Hvss De Anatomia Antichristi, Liber Unus* . . . ; *Ioannis Huss Locorum aliquot ex Osee, & Ezechiele prophetis* . . . *Tomus Secundus; Sermonum Ioannis Huss ad Populum, Tomus Tertius.* Strasbourg: Schott, 1524.

———. *Vereum* [sic] *Dei multo magis expedit audire, quam missam.* Strasbourg: Schott, 1523.

Bryßgauer, Martin. *Wie man Christlicher weysz beychten: Sacrament emtpfahen: Messz halten/ vnd das Sacrament anbetten sol.* Strasbourg: Schwan, 1524.

Bugenhagen, Johann. *Contra novum errorem de Sacramento Corporis et sanguinis domini nostri Iesu Christi Epistola.* Wittenberg: Lotter, 1525.

———. *Eyn Sendbrieff widder den newen yrrthumb bey dem Sacrament des leybs vnd blutts vnsers Herrn Jhesu Christi.* Wittenberg: Klug, 1525.

———. *Von der Euangelischen Meß/ was die Meß sey . . . Auch wie man Meß soll hören/ vnd das hochwirdig Sacrament empfahen/ vnd warumb mann es empfachet.* Augsburg: Steiner, 1524.

———. *Wider den newen irsal vom Sacrament.* Augsburg: Ruff, 1525.

Capito, Wolfgang. *Was man halten/ vnnd antwurten soll/ von der spaltung zwischen Martin Luther vnd Andres Carolstadt.* Strasbourg: Köpfel, 1524.

Cyclops, Wolf. *Von dem aller hochwirdigsten Nachtmahl Jesu Christi.* Magdeburg: Oettinger, 1525.

Dialogus von Zweyen pfaffen Köchin/ Belangendt den abbruoch des opffers. . . . Erfurt: Buchfürer, 1523.

Diepold, Johann. *Ein nützlicher Sermon zu allen Christenmenschen von der rechten evangelischen Meß.* Augsburg: Steiner, 1522.

Eckart, Johann. *Ain Dialogus . . . das Höchst goldtrain opfer der heyligen Meß betreffent.* Ingolstadt: Lutz, 1521.

Engelbrecht, Anton. *Ein andechtige leer von dem hochwyrdigen sacrament vnsers herren/ gar nutzlich vnd fruchtbar zuo lesen.* Basel: Petri, 1518.

Epistola quinquagintaquattuor nobilium Moraviae, pro defensione Johannis Hussi, ad concilium Constantiense, commendata literis adulescentis cuiusdam, argumenti vice appositis. . . . Basel: Cratander, 1524.

Fener, Georg. *Sturm wider ain laymen thurn ains Römischen predigers/ der auß der hayligenn Meß gern ain opffer mächte.* Augsburg: Grimm & Wirsung, 1521.

Frey, Matthaeus. *Ain Schöne vnderweysung vnd leer/ zubetrachten das nachtmal vnsers lieben herren Jhesu Christ. . . .* Augsburg: Ramminger, 1525.

Herolt, Johann. *Sermones discipuli de tempore.* London, 1510.

Hohenlandenberg, Hugo von. *Christenlich vnderrichtung des Hochwirdigen Fürsten . . . Hugo Bischoffen zuo Constanz.* Freiburg/Br: Wörlin, 1524.

Hospinian, Rudolf. *Historia Sacramentariae Pars altera: De origine et Progressv controversiae sacramentaria de coena Domini.* Zurich: Wolph, 1602.

Hus, Jan. *De Causa Boemica.* Hagenau: Anshelm, 1520.

———. *Liber Egregius de unitate Ecclesiae, Cuius autor periit in concilio Constantiensi.* Basel: Petri, 1520.

Jud, Leo. *Ein Christenlich widerfechdung Leonis Jud/ wider Mathyß Kretzen zuo Ougspurg/ falsche/ Endchristliche Mäß.* Zurich: Hager, 1524.

———. *Ain Christenlich widerfechtung Leonis Jud/ wider Mathis Kretzen zuo Augspurg falsche Endchristische Meß.* Augsburg: Ulhart, 1525.

Karlstadt, Andreas. *Articuli super celebratione Missarum, Sacramenti Panis et Vini. . . .* Wittenberg: Schirlentz, 1521.

———. *Auszlegung dieser wort Christi. Das ist meyn leyb/ welcher für euch gegeben würt. Das ist mein bluoth/ welches für euch vergossen würt. Luce am 22.* Basel: Bebel, 1524.

———. *Dialogus oder ein gesprechbüchlin von dem grewlichen abgöttischen mißbrauch des hochwirdigsten sacraments Jesu Christ.* Basel: Bebel, 1524.

———. *Erklerung des x. Capitels Cor i. Das brot das wir brechen: Ist es nitt ein gemeinschaft des Leybs Christi.* Augsburg: Ulhart, 1525.

———. *Ob man mit heyliger schrifft erweysen müge/ das Christus mit leyb/ bluot vnd sele im Sacrament sey.* Basel: Wolff, 1524.

———. *Predig zu Wittenberg von Empfahung des Hailigen Sacraments.* Wittenberg: Schirlentz, 1522.

————. *Von anbettung und ererbietung der tzeychen des newen Testaments.* Wittenberg: Schirlentz, 1521.

————. *Von beiden gestaldten der heylige Messze. Von Czeichen in gemein was sie wirken vnd dewten. Sie seind nit Behemen oder ketzer, die beide gestaldt nhemen sonder Ewangelische Christen.* Wittenberg: Shirlentz, 1521.

————. *Von dem Newen vnd Alten Testament. Antwurt auff disen spruch: Der kelch das New Testament in meinem blut etc. Luce xxij .i. Corin. xj. . . . wie Carolstat widerrieft.* Augsburg: Ulhart, 1525.

————. *Von dem Priesterthum vnd opffer Christi.* Jena: Buchführer, 1523.

————. *Von dem widerchristlichen mißbrauch des hern brodt vnd kelch. Ob der glaub in das sacrament/ sünde vergäbe/ vnd ob das sacrament eyn arrabo/ oder pfand sey der sünde vergäbung. Außlegung deß xj. Capit. In der .j. Epistel Pauli zuo den Corinthiern von des hern abentmal.* Basel: Bebel, 1524.

———— *Von den Empfahern/ Zeychen/ vnd zusag des heyligenn Sacraments fleysch vnd bluts Christi.* Wittenberg: Schirlentz, 1521.

————. *Wider die alte vnd newe Papistische Messen.* Basel: Wolf, 1524.

Keller, Andreas. *Ein anzeygung was für gottzlesterung in der Papisten Messz ist/ vnd das sich alle fromen Christen daruor als vor der aller grösten gotzlesterung hyeten sollent.* Strasbourg: Schürer, 1524.

Keller, Michael. *Ettlich Sermones von dem nachtmal Christi.* Augsburg: Ulhart, 1525.

Kretz, Mathias. *Von der Mesz/ vnnd wer der recht priester sey.* Augsburg: Simprecht, 1524.

Krumpach, Nikolaus. *Eyn auszerwöllt Byechlin . . . mit schönen gebeten So eyn mensch dz Sacrament empfahen will. . . .* Augsburg: Ramminger, 1524.

Landsperger, Johann. *Ain nützlicher berücht von nyessung Des hochwirdigen Sacraments oder Testaments Christi in bayerlay zaichen das brots vnd wein/ Vnnd wa baide parthey (wider ainander streytend) filen bißher verborgen.* Augsburg: Ramminger, 1524.

Lavater, Ludwig. *Historia de Origine et Progressv Controversiae Sacramentariae de Coena Domini. . . .* Zurich: Froschauer, 1563.

Mansberger, Johannes. *Joannes Manberger Pfarrher ze Thun Costenzer bystumbs vff den Leimen thurn Gerg fenere von weil: das die meß ein opffer sy: Antwort.* Basel: Gengenbach, 1521.

Oechsner, Wolfgang. *Ein kurtzer vnterricht . . . von dem geplerre vnd mißbrauch der Seelmessen.* Nuremberg: Hergot, 1524.

Oecolampadius, Johann. *Ad Billibaldum Pyrkhaimerum de re Eucharistiae responsio.* Zurich: Froschauer, 1526.

————. *Apologetica . . . ad Theobaldvm Billicanvm quinam in uerbis Caenae alienum sensum inserant. . . .* Zurich: Froschauer, 1526.

————. *De genvina verborum domini, Hoc est corpus meum, iuxta uetutissimos authores expositione liber.* Strasbourg: Knoblauch, 1525.

————. *Ain Predig vnd ermanung . . . von wirdiger ereenbietung dem Sacrament des fronleichnam christi.* Augsburg: Grimm & Wirsung, 1521.

————. *De Sacramento Eucharistiae.* Augsburg: Grimm & Wirsung, 1521.

————. *Vom Nachtmal Beweisung ausz Euangelischen schrifften.* Augsburg: Ulhart, 1526.

————. *Vom Sacrament der Dancksagung. Von dem waren nateurlichen verstand der worten christi. . . .* Zurich: Froschauer, 1526.

Piccolomini, Aeneas Sylvius. *Commentariorum Aeneae Sylvii Piccolominei Senensis De Concilio Basileae celebrato libri duo, olim quidem scripti, nunc vero primum impressi.* Basel: Cratander, 1523.

Pirckheimer, Willibald. *Bilibaldi Birckheimheri de vera Christi carne et uero eius sanguine, ad Ioan. Oecolampadium responsio.* Nuremberg: Petreius, 1526.

Reinhart, Martin. *Antzeygung wie die gefallene Christenheit widerbracht mügen werden.* . . . Jena: Buchfürer, 1524.

———. *Vnderrichte wie sich ein frumer Christ bey den Papistischen Messen/ so yetz noch vil gehalten werden . . . halten sol.* Jena: Buchfürer, 1524.

Reuchlin, Johannes. *Principivm Libri II Ioannis Revchlin Phorcensis LL. Doc. ad Dionysivm fratrem svvm Germanvm de Rvdimentis Hebraicis.* . . . Pforzheim: Anshelm, 1506.

Rhegius, Urbanus. *Ain Sermon von dem hochwirdigen sacrament des Altars.* Augsburg: Otmar, 1521.

———. *Underricht wie sich ain Christen mensch halten sol das er frucht der Meß erlang und Christlich zu gotz tisch gangg.* Augsburg: Grimm & Wirsung, 1522.

———. *Vom hochwürdigen Sakrament des Altars vnderricht was man auß hayliger geschryfft wissen mag.* Augsburg: Ruff, 1523.

———. *Wider den newen irrsal Doctor Andres von Carlstadt/ des Sacraments halb/ warnung.* Augsburg: Ruff, 1524.

Ryss, Conrad. *Antwort dem Hochgeleerten Doctor Johann Bugenhage . . . das Sacrament betreffend.* Augsburg: Ulhart, 1525.

Scultetus, Abraham. *Annalium Evangelii Passim per Europam Decimo quinto salutis partae seculo renovati Decas Prima, ab Anno MDXVI ad Annum MDXXV.* Heidelberg: Lancellotus, 1618.

Strauss, Jakob. *Ain schöne liepliche Unndericht/ zuo bedencken vnnd enpfahenn/ der kostbarlichen hayligesten leib Christi/ vnd sein roßenfarbes pluot zuo nyessenn.* Augsburg: Steiner, 1524.

———. *Ein verstendige tröstlich Leer/ über das wort Sanct Paulus/ Der mensch sol sich selbs probieren.* . . . Strasbourg: Knoblauch, 1522.

———. *Wider den vnmilten Jrrthum Maister Vlrichs zwinglins so er verneünet die warhafftig gegenwirtigkait dess allerhailigsten leybs vnd bluets Christi im Sacrament.* . . . Augsburg: Ramminger, 1526.

Tectonus, Theophilus. *Compendiosa Boemice seu Hussitane Hereseos ortus & eiusdem damnatorum Articulorum descriptio.* Strasbourg: Grüninger, 1524.

Textus Biblie cum Glossa ordinaria, Nicolai de lyra Postilla, Moralitatibus eiusdem Pauli Burgensis . . . Sexta Pars. Basel: Petri and Froben, 1508.

Turnauer, Caspar. *Die Wort Pauli vom Nachtmal des Herren Cor. xi. Außgelegt.* Augsburg: Otmar, 1525.

Was schedlicher früchte der Bepstler Messz bracht hat. Strasbourg: Schwan, 1524.

Wyclif, John. *Io. Wiclefi viri vndiqvaque pijs. dialogorum libri quattuor.* . . . Hagenau: Schöffer, 1525.

Ziegler, Clemens. *Ein fast schon büchlin . . . von dem leib vnd bluot Christi.* Strasbourg: Schwan, 1525.

———. *Von der waren nyessung beyd leibs vnd bluots Christi . . . Vnd von dem Tauff.* . . . Strasbourg: Schott, 1524.

Ziegler, Jakob. *In hoc volumine haec continentur . . . Contra haeresim valdensium libri quinque.* Leipzig, 1512.

Zwingli, Ulrich. *Ein Antwurt Huldrychs Zuinglins vff die Epistel Joannis Pugenhag vss Pomeren das Nachtmal Christi betreffende.* Zurich: Froschauer, 1526.

———. *Von dem Nachtmal Christi widergedechtnus.* Zurich: Froschauer, 1525.

Modern Editions and Reference Works

Bartos, Franticek M. "Puer Bohemus. Dva projevy husitské propagandy." *Věstník Královské České Společnosti Nauk. Třída filosophicko-historicko-jazykozpytná. Ročník 1523, II* (Memoires de la Société Royale des Sciences de Bohême. Classe des lettres. Année 1923, II), no. II (1924): 1–58.

Baylor, Michael G., ed. *The Radical Reformation.* Cambridge Texts in the History of Political Thought. Cambridge: Cambridge University Press, 1991.

Benzing, Josef. *Die Buchdrucker des 16. und 17. Jahrhunderts im deutschen Sprachgebiet.* 2nd ed. Beiträge zur Buch- und Bibliothekswesen 12. Wiesbaden: Harrassowitz, 1982.

———, ed. *Lutherbibliographie. Verzeichnis der gedruckten Schriften Martin Luthers bis zu dessen Tod.* Baden-Baden: Heitz, 1966.

Bietenholz, Peter, ed. *Contemporaries of Erasmus: A Biographical Register of the Renaissance and Reformation.* 3 vols. Toronto: University of Toronto Press, 1985–1987.

Brenz, Johannes. *Werke. Eine Studienausgabe.* Vol. 1: *Frühschriften.* 2 vols. Edited by Martin Brecht et al. Tübingen: Mohr, 1970–1974.

Bromiley, Geoffrey W., ed. *Zwingli and Bullinger.* Library of Christian Classics 24. Philadelphia: Westminster, 1953.

Bucer, Martin. *Correspondance de Martin Bucer.* Martini Buceri Opera Omnia, Series III. Leiden: Brill, 1979–.

———. *Martin Bucers Deutsche Schriften.* Martini Buceri Opera Omnia, Series I. Gütersloh 1960–.

———. *Martini Buceri Opera Latina.* Martini Buceri Opera Omnia, Series II. Leiden: Brill, 1982–.

Bullinger, Heinrich. *Werke.* Abteilung 2: *Heinrich Bullingers Briefwechel.* Zurich: Theologischer Verlag, 1973–.

———. *Werke.* Abteilung 3: *Theologische Schriften.* Zurich: Theologischer Verlag, 1983–.

Calvin, John. *Treatises on the Sacraments: Catechism of the Church of Geneva, Forms of Prayer, and Confessions of Faith.* Translated by Henry Beveridge. Christian Heritage Society. Grand Rapids, Mich.: Reformation Heritage, 2002.

Dürr, Emil, and Paul Roth, eds. *Aktensammlung zur Geschichte der Basler Reformation in den Jahren 1519 bis Anfang 1534.* 6 vols. Basel: Historische und antiquarische Gesellschaft, 1921–1950.

Eckert, Alfred, ed. *Bekenntnisse der Böhmischen Brüder.* Nikolaus Ludwig von Zinzendorf Materialen und Dokumente Reihe 1, Quellen und Darstellung zur Geschichte der böhmischen Brüder-Unität 3. Hildesheim: Olms, 1979.

Erasmus, Desiderius. *Collected Works of Erasmus.* Toronto: University of Toronto Press, 1974–.

———. *Desiderii Erasmi Roterodami Opera Omnia,* ed. Jean Le Clerc. Leiden: Vander Aa, 1703–1706. Reprint, London: Gregg, 1962.

———. *Opera Omnia Desiderii Erasmi Roterodami.* Amsterdam: Elsevier, 1969–.

Friedberg, Emil, ed. *Corpus Iuris Canonici.* 2 vols. Leipzig: Tauchnitz, 1879–1881.

Furcha, Edward J. *The Essential Carlstadt. Fifteen Tracts by Andreas Bodenstein (Carlstadt) from Karlstadt.* Scottdale, Penn.: Herald, 1995.

Furcha, Edward J. and Wayne H. Pipkin,, eds. *Huldrych Zwingli: Writings.* 2 vols. Allison Park, Penn.: Pickwick Publications, 1984.

Grimm, Jacob, and Wilhelm Grimm. *Deutsches Wörterbuch.* Leipzig: Hirzel, 1962. Online at http://urts55.uni-trier.de:8080/Projekte/DWB/ (accessed 10 November 2010).

Hamm, Berndt, and Wolfgang Huber, eds. *Lazarus Spengler Schriften.* 2 vols. Quellen und Forschungen zur Reformationsgeschichte, 61, 70. Gütersloh: Gütersloher Verlagshaus, 1995–1999.

Herminjard, A.-L., ed. *Correspondance des Réformateurs dans les pays de langue Française*. 9 vols. Geneva: H. Georg, 1866–1897. Reprint, Nieuwkoop: De Graaf, 1966.

Hertzsch, Erich, ed. *Karlstadts Schriften aus den Jahren 1523–25*. 2 vols. Neudrucke deutscher Literaturewerke des 16. und 17. Jahrhunderts 325. Halle: Niemeyer, 1956–1957.

Höfler, Karl Adolf Constantin, ed. *Geschichtsschreiber der husitischen Bewegung in Böhmen*. 2 vols. Fontes Rerum Austriacarum. 1. Abt.: Scriptores, Bd. 6,2. New York: Johnson Reprint, 1969.

Hubmaier, Balthasar. *Schriften*. Edited by Gunnar Westin and Torsten Bergsten. Quellen zur Geschichte der Täufer 9. Gütersloh: Gütersloher Verlagshaus, 1962.

Iserloh, Erwin, and Peter Fabisch, eds. *Kaspar Schatzgeyer OFM Schriften zur Verteidigung der Messe*. Corpus Catholicorum 37. Münster: Aschendorff, 1984.

Kawerau, Gustav, ed. *Der Briefwechsel des Justus Jonas*. 2 vols. in 1. Hildesheim: Olms, 1964.

Köhler, Hans-Joachim, ed. *Bibliographie der Flugschriften des 16. Jahrhunderts*. Tübingen: Bibliotheca Academica, 1991–1996.

———. *Flugschriften des frühen 16. Jahrhunderts*. 1956 microfiches. Zug: IDC, 1978–1987.

Krebs, Manfred, and Hans Georg Rott, eds. *Elsass I*. Quellen zur Geschichte der Täufer 7. Gütersloh: Mohn, 1959.

Laube, Adolf, et al., eds. *Flugschriften vom Bauernkrig zum Täuferreich (1526–1535)*. 2 vols. Berlin: Akademie Verlag, 1992.

Lietzmann, Hans. *Die Wittenberger und Leisniger Kastenordnung*. Berlin: de Gruyter, 1935.

Lindberg, Carter. "Karlstadt's Dialogue on the Lord's Supper." *Mennonite Quarterly Review* 53 (1979): 35–77.

Luther, Martin. *Luther's Works*. St. Louis, Mo.: Concordia, 1955–1986.

———. *Werke. Kritische Gesamtausgabe*. Weimar: Böhlaus Nachfolger, 1883–1986.

Melanchthon, Philipp. *Melanchthons Briefwechsel: Kritische und kommentierte Gesamtausgabe*. Edited by Heinz Scheible et al. Stuttgart-Bad Cannstatt: Frommann-Holzboog, 1977–.

———. *Melanchthons Werke in Auswahl*. 7 vols. Edited by Robert Stupperich et al. Gütersloh: Bertelsmann, 1951–1983.

———. *Philippi Melanthonis Opera quae Supersunt Omnia*. Corpus Reformatorum 1–28. Halle: Schwetschke, 1834–1860.

Molnár, Amedeo, and Romolo Cegna, eds. *Confessio Taboritarum*. Fonti per la storia d'Italia 105. Rome: Istituto storico italiano per il medio evo, 1983.

Müller, Nicolaus. "Die Wittenberger Bewegung 1521 und 1522. Die Vorgänge in und um Wittenberg während Luthers Wartburgaufenthalt." *Archiv für Reformationsgeschichte* 6 (1909): 161–226, 261–325, 385–469; 7 (1909): 185–224, 233–293, 353–412; 8 (1910): 1–43.

Murner, Thomas. *Thomas Murners Deutsche Schriften*. Vol. 6, *Kleine Schriften, Pt. 1*. Berlin: de Gruyter, 1927.

Oberman, Heiko A., ed. *Forerunners of the Reformation: The Shape of Late Medieval Thought Illustrated by Key Documents*. Philadelphia: Fortress, 1981.

Osiander, Andreas. *Gesamtausgabe*. 10 vols. Gütersloh: Gütersloher Verlagshaus Mohn, 1975–1997.

Pegg, Michael A., ed. *A Catalogue of German Reformation Pamphlets (1516–1546) in Libraries of Great Britain and Ireland*. Bibliotheca Bibliographica Aureliana 45. Baden-Baden: Koerner, 1973.

———. *A Catalogue of German Reformation Pamphlets (1516–1550) in Libraries of Alsace*. Bibliotheca Bibliographica Aureliana 180, 200, 201, 206. Baden-Baden: Koerner, 2000–2004.

————. *A Catalogue of German Reformation Pamphlets (1516–1550) in Libraries of Belgium and the Netherlands*. Bibliotheca Bibliographica Aureliana 173. Baden-Baden: Koerner, 1999.

————. *A Catalogue of German Reformation Pamphlets (1516–1550) in Swiss Libraries*. Bibliotheca Bibliographica Aureliana 99. Baden-Baden: Koerner, 1983.

Peschke, Erhard. *Die Theologie der böhmischen Brüder in ihrer Frühzeit*. Vol. 1, *Das Abendmahl, Pt. 2: Texte aus alttschechischen Handschriften übersetzt*. Forschungen zur Kirchen- und Geistesgeschichte 20. Stuttgart: Kohlhammer, 1940.

Peter Lombard. *Sententiarum libri quatuor*. Edited by J.-P. Migne. Patrologiae Cursus Completus, Series Secunda, 192, 521–964. Paris, 1855.

Pfeiffer, Gerhard. *Quellen zur Nürnberger Reformationsgeschichte*. Einzelarbeiten aus der Kirchengeschichte Bayerns 45. Nuremberg: Verein für bayerische Kirchengeschichte, 1968.

Reichert, Franz Rudolf, ed. *Die älteste deutsche Gesamtauslegung der Messe*. Corpus Catholicorum 29. Münster: Aschendorff, 1967.

Rummel, Erika, and Milton Kooistra, eds. *The Correspondence of Wolfgang Capito*. Toronto: University of Toronto Press, 2005-.

Schiess, Traugott, ed. *Briefwechsel der Brüder Ambrosius und Thomas Blaurer 1509–1548*. 3 vols. Freiburg i.Br.: Fehsenfeld, 1908–1912.

Schwenckfeld, Kaspar. *Corpus Schwenckfeldianorum*. 19 vols. Leipzig: Breitkopf and Härtel, 1907–1961.

Sedlak, Jan, ed. *Táborské traktáty eucharistické*. Brno: Nákl. Papezské Knihtisk. Benedktinu Rajhradskych, 1918.

Sehling, Ernst, ed. *Die evangelischen Kirchenordnungen des XVI. Jahrhunderts*. Göttingen/Leipzig/Tübingen, 1902-.

Sider, Ronald J., ed. *Karlstadt's Battle with Luther: Documents in a Liberal-Radical Debate*. Philadelphia: Fortress, 1977.

Smend, Julius, ed. *Die evangelischen deutschen Messen bis zu Luthers deutscher Messe*. Reprint ed. Nieuwkoop: de Graaf, 1967.

Staehelin, Ernst, ed. *Briefe und Akten zum Leben Oekolampads, zum vierhundertjährigen Jubiläum der Basler Reformation*. 2 vols. Quellen und Forschungen zur Reformationsgeschichte 10, 19. Leipzig: Heinsius, 1927–1934.

Veesenmeyer, Georg. *Sammlung von Aufsätzen zur Erläuterung der Kirchen-, Litteratur- Münz- und Sittengeschichte besonders des 16. Jahrhunderts*. Ulm: Stettin, 1827.

Verzeichnis der im deutschen Sprachbereich erschienenen Drucke des 16. Jahrhunderts. http://www.vd16.de (accessed 10 November 2010).

Vogt, Otto, Eike Wolgast, and H. Volz, eds. *Dr. Johann Bugenhagens Briefwechsel*. Hildesheim: Olms, 1966.

Walch, Johann Georg, ed. *Dr. Martin Luthers Sämmtliche Schriften*. St. Louis, Mo.: Concordia, 1881–1910.

Wyclif, John. *Trialogus cum supplemento Trialogi*. Edited by Gotthard Lechler. Oxford: Clarendon, 1869.

Zwingli, Ulrich. *Commentary on True and False Religion*. Edited by Samuel Macauley Jackson. Durham, N.C.: Labyrinth, 1981.

————. *Huldreich Zwinglis sämtliche Werke*. Corpus Reformatorum 88–101. Leipzig/Zurich: Heinsius/TVZ, 1905–1991.

SECONDARY SOURCES

Albrecht, Otto. "Beiträge zum Verständnis des Briefwechsels Luthers im Jahre 1524." In *Beiträge zur Reformationsgeschichte: Herrn Oberkonsistorialrat Professor D. Köstlin bei der Feier seines siebzigsten Geburtstages ehrerbietigst gewidmet*, ed. P. Albrecht et al., 1–36. Gotha: Perthes, 1896.

Auerbach, Erich. "Figura." In Auerbach, *Scenes from the Drama of European Literature: Six Essays*, 11–76. Gloucester, Mass.: Peter Smith, 1973.

Barclay, Alexander. *The Protestant Doctrine of the Lord's Supper: A Study in the Eucharistic Teaching of Luther, Zwingli and Calvin.* Glasgow: Jackson, Wylie & Co., 1927.

Barge, Hermann. *Andreas Bodenstein von Karlstadt.* 2nd ed. 2 vols. Niewkoop: de Graff, 1968.

———. "Zur Chronologie und Drucklegung der Abendmahlsschriften Karlstadts." *Zentralblatt für Bibliothekswesen* 21 (1904): 323–331.

———. *Frühprotestantisches Gemeindechristentum in Wittenberg und Orlamünde: Zugleich eine Abwehr gegen Karl Müllers "Luther und Karlstadt."* Leipzig: Heinsius, 1909.

———. "Luther und Karlstadt in Wittenberg: Eine kritische Untersuchung." *Historische Zeitschrift* 99 (1907): 256–324.

Bartos, Frantisek M. "Erasmus und die böhmische Reformation." *Communio Viatorum* 1 (1958): 116–123, 246–257.

———. *The Hussite Revolution, 1424–1437.* Boulder, Colo.: East European Monographs, 1986.

———. "Picards et Pikarti." *Bulletin de la Société de l'histoire du Protestantisme Français* 80 (1931): 465–486; 81 (1932): 8–28.

Bauer, Karl. "Die Abendmahlslehre Zwinglis bis zum Beginn der Auseinandersetzung mit Luther." *Theologische Blätter* 5 (1926): 217–226.

———. "Symbolik und Realpräsenz in der Abendmahlsanschauung Zwinglis bis 1525." *Zeitschrift für Kirchengeschichte* 46 (1927): 97–105.

Berg, Cornelis H. W. "Anton Engelbrecht, un 'épicurien' strasbourgeois." In *Croyants et sceptiques au XVIe siècle: le dossier des "Epicuriens": actes du colloque organisé par le GRENEP, Strasbourg, 9–10 juin 1978*, ed. Marc Lienhard, 111–120. Strasbourg: Librairie ISTRA, 1981.

Beinert, Richard A. "Another Look at Luther's Battle with Karlstadt." *Concordia Theological Quarterly* 73 (2009): 155–170.

Bittner, Konrad. "Erasmus, Luther und die böhmischen Brüder." In *Rastloses Schaffen: Festschrift für Dr. Friedrich Lammert*, ed. Heinz Seehase, 107–129. Stuttgart: Kohlhammer, 1954.

Bizer, Ernst. *Studien zur Geschichte des Abendmahlsstreits im 16. Jahrhundert.* 2nd ed. Darmstadt: Wissenschaftliche Buchgesellschaft, 1962.

Brandy, Hans Christian. *Die späte Christologie des Johannes Brenz.* Beiträge zur historischen Theologie 80. Tübingen: Paul Siebeck, 1991.

Bransford, John, et al. *How People Learn: Brain, Mind, Experience, and School: Expanded Edition.* Washington, D.C.: National Academy Press, 2000.

Brecht, Martin. *Die frühe Theologie des Johannes Brenz.* Beiträge zur historischen Theologie 36. Tübingen: Mohr/Siebeck, 1966.

———. "Luther und Karlstadt. Der Beginn des Abendmahlsstreites 1524/25 und seine Bedeutung für Luthers Theologie." *Zeitschrift der Savigny-Stiftung für Rechtsgeschichte* 101, kanonistische Abteilung 70 (1984): 196–216.

———. *Martin Luther.* Vol. 2, *Shaping and Defining the Reformation, 1521–1532.* Translated by James Schaaf. Minneapolis: Fortress, 1990.

Browe, Peter, S.J. "Die Kommunionvorbereitung im Mittelalter." *Zeitschrift für katholische Theologie* 56 (1932): 375–415.

Bubenheimer, Ulrich. "Scandalum et ius divinum: Theologische und rechtstheologische Probleme der ersten reformatorischen Innovationen in Wittenberg 1521/1522." *Zeitschrift der Savigny-Stiftung für Rechtsgeschichte* 90, kanonistische Abteilung 59 (1973): 263–342.

Burnett, Amy Nelson. "Basel and the Wittenberg Concord." *Archiv für Reformationsgeschichte* 96 (2005): 33–56.

———. "'Kilchen ist uff dem Radthus'? Conflicting Views of Magistrate and Ministry in Early Reformation Basel." In *Debatten über die Legitimation von Herrschaft: Politische Sprachen in der Frühen Neuzeit*, ed. Luise Schorn-Schütte and Sven Tode, 49–65. Berlin: Akademie Verlag, 2006.

———. "The Social History of Communion and the Reformation of the Eucharist." *Past and Present*, forthcoming.

Bynum, Caroline Walker. *Wonderful Blood: Theology and Practice in Late Medieval Northern Germany and Beyond*. Philadelphia: University of Pennsylvania Press, 2007.

Caspers, Charles M. A. "The Western Church during the Late Middle Ages: Augenkommunion or Popular Mysticism?" In *Bread of Heaven: Customs and Practices Surrounding Holy Communion. Essays in the History of Liturgy and Culture*, ed. Charles M. A. Caspers and G. Lukken, 83–97. Kampen: Kok Pharos, 1995.

Chartier, Roger. "Texts, Printings, Readings." In *The New Cultural History*, ed. Lynn Hunt, 154–175. Berkeley: University of California Press, 1989.

Clemen, Otto. "Hinne Rode in Wittenberg, Basel, Zürich und die frühesten Ausgaben Wesselscher Schriften." In Clemen, *Kleine Schriften zur Reformationsgeschichte (1897–1944)*, 1: 24–52. Leipzig: Zentralantiquariat der DDR, 1982.

Cook, William R. "John Wyclif and Hussite Theology 1415–1436." *Church History* 42 (1973): 335–349.

Cross, Richard. "'Alloiosis' in the Christology of Zwingli." *Journal of Theological Studies* N.S. 47 (1996): 105–122.

Davis, Thomas J. *This Is My Body: The Presence of Christ in Reformation Thought*. Grand Rapids, Mich.: Baker Academic, 2008.

Dieckhoff, August Wilhelm. *Die evangelische Abendmahlslehre im Reformationszeitalter*. Göttingen: Vandenhoeck & Ruprecht, 1854.

Dix, Gregory. *The Shape of the Liturgy*. London: Dacre Press, 1945.

Douglas, Crerar. "The Coherence of Andreas Bodenstein von Karlstadt's Early Evangelical Doctrine of the Lord's Supper, 1521–1525." Ph.D. diss., Hartford Seminary Foundation, 1973.

Dufour, Alain. *Théodore de Bèze. Poète et théologien*. Cahiers d'Humanisme et Renaissance 78. Geneva: Droz, 2006.

Eberhard, Winfried. "Zur reformatorischen Qualität und Konfessionalisierung des nachrevolutionären Hussitismus." In *Häresie und vorzeitige Reformation im Spätmittelalter*, ed. Frantisek Smahel, 213–238. Munich: Oldenbourg, 1998.

Edwards, Mark U. *Luther and the False Brethren*. Stanford: Stanford University Press, 1975.

———. *Printing, Propaganda, and Martin Luther*. Berkeley: University of California Press, 1994.

Eire, Carlos M. N. *War against the Idols: The Reformation of Worship from Erasmus to Calvin*. Cambridge: Cambridge University Press, 1986.

Fischer, Robert H. "Luther's Stake in the Lord's Supper Controversy." *Dialogue* 2 (1963): 50–59.

Foucault, Michel. *The Archaeology of Knowledge and the Discourse on Language*. Translated by A. M. Sheridan Smith. New York: Pantheon, 1972.

——. "Nietzsche, Genealogy, History." In *Language, Counter-Memory, Practice: Selected Essays and Interviews*, ed. D. F. Bouchard, 139–164. Ithaca: Cornell University Press, 1977.

Franz, Günther. "Lienhart Götz von Schnelldorf: Ein Beitrag zur Geschichte Karlstadts und des Buchdruckers Philipp Ulhart." *Archiv für Reformationsgeschichte* 26 (1929): 265–269.

Friedrich, Reinhold. "'Eine Streit um Worte?' Bucers Position in der Abendmahlsfrage im Jahr 1530." In *Martin Bucer zwischen Luther und Zwingli*, ed. Matthieu Arnold and Berndt Hamm, 49–65. Tübingen: Mohr Siebeck, 2003.

——. *Martin Bucer—"Fanatiker der Einheit"? Seine Stellungnahme zu theologischen Fragen seiner Zeit (Abendmahls- und Kirchenverständnis) insbesondere nach seinem Briefwechsel der Jahre 1524–1541*. Biblia et symbiotica 20. Bonn: Verlag für Kultur und Wissenschaft, 2002.

——. "Martin Bucer—Ökumene im 16. Jahrhundert." In *Martin Bucer and Sixteenth Century Europe. Actes du colloque de Strasbourg, 28–31 août 1991*, ed. Christian Krieger and Marc Lienhard, 257–268. Studies in Medieval and Reformation Thought 52–53. Leiden: Brill, 1993.

Gecser, Otto. "The Social Significance of Communion: Eucharistic Preaching in the Fifteenth-Century Hungarian Sermon Collection *Sermones Dominicales*." *Annual of Medieval Studies at the CEU* 7 (2001): 113–134.

Ginzburg, Carlo. *The Cheese and the Worms: The Cosmos of a Sixteenth-Century Miller*. Translated by John and Anne Tedeschi. Baltimore: Johns Hopkins University Press, 1982.

Gollwitzer, Helmut. "Zur Auslegung von Joh. 6 bei Luther und Zwingli." In *In Memoriam Ernst Lohmeyer*, ed. Werner Schmauch, 143–168. Stuttgart: Evangelisches Verlagswerk, 1951.

Grass, Hans. *Die Abendmahlslehre bei Luther und Calvin. Eine kritische Untersuchung*. 2nd ed. Beiträge zur Förderung christlicher Theologie, 2. Reihe, 47. Band. Gütersloh: Bertelsmann, 1954.

Greschat, Martin. *Martin Bucer: A Reformer and His Times*. Translated by Stephen E. Buckwalter. Louisville, Ky.: Westminster John Knox Press, 2004.

Grötzinger, Eberhard. *Luther und Zwingli. Die Kritik an der mittelalterlichen Lehre von der Messe, als Wurzel des Abendmahlsstreites*. Ökumenische Theologie 5. Zurich: Benziger, 1980.

Gummelt, Volker. "Die Auseinandersetzung über das Abendmahl zwischen Johannes Bugenhagen und Huldrych Zwingli im Jahre 1525." In *Die Zürcher Reformation: Ausstrahlungen und Rückwirkungen. Wissenschaftlicher Tagung zum hundertjährigen Bestehen des Zwinglivereins (29. Oktober bis 2. November 1997 in Zürich)*, ed. Alfred Schindler and Hans Stickelberger, 189–201. Bern: Peter Lang, 2001.

Halmer, Notker M., O.P. "Der literarische Kampf Luthers und Melanchthons gegen das Opfer der Messe." *Divus Thomas* 21 (1943): 63–78.

Hasse, Hans-Peter. "Zum Aufenthalt Karlstadts in Zürich (1530–34)." *Zwingliana* 18 (1990/91): 366–389.

Hazlett, Ian. "Zur Auslegung von Johannes 6 bei Bucer während der Abendmahlskontroverse." In *Bucer und seine Zeit: Forschungebeiträge und Bibliographie*, ed. Marijn de Kroon and Friedhelm Krüger, 74–87. Wiesbaden: Steiner, 1976.

——. "The Development of Martin Bucer's Thinking on the Sacrament of the Lord's Supper in Its Historical and Theological Context, 1523–1534." Ph.D. diss., Universität Münster, 1977.

Heron, Alasdair I. C. *Table and Tradition*. Philadelphia: Westminster, 1983.

Heymann, Frederick G. "The Hussite Revolution and Reformation and Its Impact in Germany." In *Festschrift für Hermann Heimpel zum 70. Geburtstag am 19. September 1971*, 2: 610–626. Göttingen: Vandenhoeck & Ruprecht, 1971.

———. "The Hussite-Utraquist Church in the Fifteenth and Sixteenth Centuries." *Archiv für Reformationsgeschichte* 52 (1961): 1–16.

———. "John Rokycana—Church Reformer between Hus and Luther." *Church History* 28 (1959): 240–280.

Hilgenfeld, Hartmut. *Mittelalterlich-traditionelle Elemente in Luthers Abendmahlsschriften*. Studien zur Dogmengeschichte und systematischen Theologie 29. Zurich: Theologischer Verlag, 1971.

Hillerbrand, Hans J. "Andreas Bodenstein of Carlstadt, Prodigal Reformer." *Church History* 35 (1966): 379–398.

Hoffmann, Gottfried. "Sententiae Patrum. Das patristische Argument in der Abendmahlskontroverse zwischen Oekolampad, Zwingli, Luther und Melanchthon." Ph.D. diss., Universität Heidelberg, 1971.

Hohenberger, Thomas. *Lutherische Rechtfertigungslehre in den reformatorischen Flugschriften der Jahre 1521–22*. Spätmittelalter und Reformation Neue Reihe 6. Tübingen: Mohr Siebeck, 1996.

Holeton, David R. "The Bohemian Eucharistic Movement in Its European Context." In *The Bohemian Reformation and Religious Practice: Papers from the XVIIth World Congress of the Czechoslovak Society of Arts and Sciences, Prague 1994*, ed. David R. Holeton, 23–47. Prague: Academy of Sciences of the Czech Republic, 1996.

———. "The Communion of Infants and Hussitism." *Communio Viatorum* 27 (1984): 207–225.

Honecker, Martin. "Die Abendmahlslehre des Syngramma." *Blätter für württembergische Kirchengeschichte* 65 (1965): 39–68.

Hoyer, Siegfried. "Jan Hus und der Hussitismus in den Flugschriften des ersten Jahrzehnts der Reformation." In *Flugschriften als Massenmedium der Reformationszeit*, ed. Hans-Joachim Köhler, 291–307. Stuttgart: Klett-Cotta, 1981.

———. "Martin Reinhart und der erste Druck hussitischer Artikel in Deutschland." *Zeitschrift für Geschichtswissenschaft* 18 (1970): 1597–1615.

Hubert, Friedrich. *Die Straßburger liturgischen Ordnungen im Zeitalter der Reformation, nebst einer Bibliographie der Straßburger Gesangbücher*. Göttingen: Vandenhoeck & Ruprecht, 1900.

Hudson, Ann. "The Mouse in the Pyx: Popular Heresy and the Eucharist." *Trivium* 26 (1991): 40–53.

Iserloh, Erwin. *Der Kampf um die Messe in den ersten Jahren der Auseinandersetzung mit Luther*. Katholisches Leben und Kämpfen im Zeitalter der Glaubensspaltung 10. Münster: Aschendorff, 1952.

Joestel, Volkmar. "Auswirkungen der Wittenberger Bewegung 1521/22: Das Beispiel Eilenburg." In *700 Jahre Wittenberg. Stadt, Universität, Reformation*, ed. Stefan Oehmig, 131–142. Weimar: Herman Böhlaus Nachfolger, 1995.

———. "Neue Erkenntnisse zu Jenaer Karlstadtschriften 1524." In *Andreas Bodenstein von Karlstadt (1486–1541): Ein Theologe der frühen Reformation. Beiträge eines Arbeitsgesprächs vom 24.–25. November 1995 in Wittenberg*, ed. Sigrid Looß and Markus Matthias, 121–142. Wittenberg: Drei Kastanien Verlag, 1998.

————. *Ostthüringen und Karlstadt: soziale Bewegung und Reformation im mittleren Saaletal am Vorabend des Bauernkrieges (1522–1524)*. Berlin: Schelzky & Jeep, 1996.

Kähler, Ernst. *Karlstadt und Augustin: Der Kommentar des Andreas Bodenstein von Karlstadt zu Augustins Schrift De Spiritu et Litera*. Hallische Monographien 19. Halle: Niemeyer, 1952.

Kaminsky, Howard. *A History of the Hussite Revolution*. Berkeley: University of California Press, 1967.

————. "Peter Chelčický: Treatises on Christianity and the Social Order." *Studies in Medieval and Renaissance History* 1 (1964): 104–179.

Kantzenbach, Friedrich Wilhelm. "Johannes Brenz und der Kampf um das Abendmahl." *Theologische Literaturzeitung* 89 (1964): 561–580.

Kaufmann, Thomas. *Die Abendmahlstheologie der Strassburger Reformatoren bis 1528*. Beiträge zur historischen Theologie 81. Tübingen: Mohr, 1992.

————. "Jan Hus und die frühe Reformation." In *Biblische Theologie und historisches Denken. Wissenschaftsgeschichtliche Studien, aus anlass der 50. Wiederkehr der Basler Promotion von Rudolf Smend*, ed. Martin Kessler and Martin Wallraff, 62–109. Basel: Schwabe, 2008.

————. "Nouvelles sources de la controverse eucharistique à Strasbourg en automne 1524." *Revue d'histoire et de philosophie religieuses* 73 (1993): 137–153.

————. "Streittheologie und Friedensdiplomatie: Die Rolle Martin Bucers im frühen Abendmahlsstreit." In *Martin Bucer and Sixteenth Century Europe. Actes du colloque de Strasbourg, 28–31 août 1991*, ed. Christian Krieger and Marc Lienhard, 239–256. Studies in Medieval and Reformation Thought 52–53. Leiden: Brill, 1993.

————. "Zwei unerkannte Schriften Bucers und Capitos zur Abendmahlsfrage aus dem Herbst 1525." *Archiv für Reformationsgeschichte* 81 (1990): 158–188.

Kittelson, James M. "Martin Bucer and the Sacramentarian Controversy: The Origins of His Policy of Concord." *Archiv für Reformationsgeschichte* 64 (1973): 166–183.

————. *Wolfgang Capito, From Humanist to Reformer*. Studies in Medieval and Reformation Thought 17. Leiden: Brill, 1975.

Koch, Ernst. "Johannes Bugenhagens Anteil am Abendmahlsstreit zwischen 1525 und 1532." *Theologische Literaturzeitung* 111 (1986): 705–730.

————. "Das Sakramentsverständnis Thomas Müntzers." In *Der Theologe Thomas Müntzer. Untersuchungen zu seiner Entwicklung und Lehre*, ed. Siegfried Bräuer and Helmar Junghans, 129–155. Göttingen: Vandenhoeck & Ruprecht, 1989.

————. "Zwinglianer zwischen Ostsee und Harz in den Anfangsjahren der Reformation (1525–1532)." *Zwingliana* 16 (1983–1985): 517–545.

Köhler, Walther. [untitled review article]. *Göttingische gelehrte Anzeigen* 174 (1912): 515–550.

————. *Luther und die Kirchengeschichte nach seinen Schriften, zunächst bis 1521*. Beiträge zu den Anfängen protestantischer Kirchengeschichtsschreibung. Erlangen: Junge, 1900.

————. "Zu Zwinglis ältester Abendmahlsfassung." *Zeitschrift für Kirchengeschichte* 45 (1926): 399–408.

————. "Zur Abendmahlskontroverse in der Reformationszeit, insbesondere zur Entwicklung der Abendmahlslehre Zwinglis." *Zeitschrift für Kirchengeschichte* 47 (1928): 47–56.

————. *Zwingli und Luther: Ihre Streit über das Abendmahl nach seinen politischen und religiösen Beziehungen*. 2 vols. Quellen und Forschungen zur Reformationsgeschichte 6–7. Gütersloh: Bertelsmann, 1924–1953.

Kolář, Pavel. "Petr Chelčický's Defense of Sacramental Communion: Response to Mikuláš Biskupec of Tábor." In *The Bohemian Reformation and Religious Practice*. Vol. 6, *Papers from the Sixth*

International Symposium on the Bohemian Reformation and Religious Practice, ed. Zdenek V. David and David R. Holeton, 133–142. Prague: Academy of Sciences of the Czech Republic, 2007.

Kolde, Theodor. "Hans Denck und die gottlosen Maler von Nürnberg." *Beiträge zur bayerischen Kirchengeschichte* 8 (1902): 1–31, 49–72.

———. "Zum Prozess des Johann Denk und der 'drei gottlosen Maler' von Nürnberg." In Theodor Kolde et al., *Kirchengeschichtliche Studien, Hermann Reuter zum 70. Geburtstag gewidmet*, 228–250. Leipzig, 1888.

Kolesnyk, Alexander. "Hussens Eucharistiebegriff." In *Jan Hus. Zwischen Zeiten, Völkern, Konfessionen. Vorträge des internationalen Symposions in Bayreuth vom 22. bis 26. September 1993*, ed. Ferdinand Seibt, 193–202. Munich: Oldenbourg, 1997.

Krodel, Gottfried G. "Die Abendmahlslehre des Erasmus von Rotterdam und seine Stellung am Anfang des Abendmahlsstreites der Reformatoren." Ph.D. diss., Universität Erlangen, 1955.

———. "Figura Prothysteron and the Exegetical Basis of the Lord's Supper." *Lutheran Quarterly* 12 (1960): 152–158.

Kruse, Jens-Martin. "Karlstadt als Wittenberger Theologe. Überlegungen zu einer pluralen Darstellungsweise der frühen Reformation." *Mennonitische Geschichtsblätter* 57 (2000): 7–30.

———. *Universitätstheologie und Kirchenreform: die Anfänge der Reformation in Wittenberg, 1516–1522*. Munich: Philipp von Zabern, 2002.

Lang, Wilhelm. "The Augsburg Travel Guide of 1563 and the Erlinger Road Map of 1524." *Imago Mundi* 7 (1950): 84–88.

Lange, Albert de. "Friedrich Reiser und die 'waldensisch-hussitische Internationale.' Quellen und Literatur zu Person und Werk." In *Friedrich Reiser und die "waldensisch-hussitische Internationale" im 15. Jahrhundert. Akten der Tagung Ötisheim-Schönenberg, 2. bis 4. Oktober 2003*, ed. Albert de Lange and Kathrin Utz Tremp, 29–74. Waldenserstudien 3. Heidelberg: Verlag Regionalkultur, 2006.

Lange, Albert de, and Kathrin Utz Tremp, eds. *Friedrich Reiser und die "waldensisch-hussitische Internationale" im 15. Jahrhundert. Akten der Tagung Ötisheim-Schönenberg, 2. bis 4. Oktober 2003*. Waldenserstudien 3. Heidelberg: Verlag Regionalkultur, 2006.

Leroux, Neil R. "Karlstadt's 'Christag Predig': Prophetic Rhetoric in an 'Evangelical' Mass." *Church History* 72 (2003): 102–137.

Levy, Ian Christopher. *John Wyclif: Scriptural Logic, Real Presence, and the Parameters of Orthodoxy*. Marquette Studies in Theology 36. Milwaukee: Marquette University Press, 2003.

Lindberg, Carter. "The Conception of the Eucharist According to Erasmus and Karlstadt." In *Les Dissidents du XVIe siècle entre l'Humanisme et la Catholicisme*, ed. Marc Lienhard, 79–94. Baden-Baden: Koerner, 1983.

Locher, Gottfried W. "Zwingli's Theology Compared with Luther and Calvin." In Gottfried W. Locher, *Zwingli's Thought: New Perspectives*. Studies in Medieval and Reformation Thought 25, 142–234. Leiden: Brill, 1981.

———. *Die Zwinglische Reformation im Rahmen der europäischen Kirchengeschichte*. Göttingen: Vandenhoeck & Ruprecht, 1979.

Lohse, Bernhard. "Luther und Huß." *Luther. Zeitschrift der Luthergesellschaft* 36 (1965): 108–122.

Looß, Sigrid. "Andreas Bodenstein von Karlstadt (1486–1541) in der modernen Forschung." In *Andreas Bodenstein von Karlstadt (1486–1541): Ein Theologe der frühen Reformation. Beiträge eines Arbeitsgesprächs vom 24.–25. November 1995 in Wittenberg*, ed. Sigrid Looß and Markus Matthias, 9–23. Wittenberg: Drei Kastanien Verlag, 1998.

——— . "Zu einigen Aspekten des Verhältnisses zwischen Luther und Karlstadt, vorwiegend dargestellt an Karlstadts Straßburgaufenthalt im Oktober 1524." In *Martin Luther—Leistung und Erbe*, ed. H. Bartel, 142–147. Berlin: Akademie-Verlag, 1986.

Macy, Gary. *The Theologies of the Eucharist in the Early Scholastic Period: A Study of the Salvific Function of the Sacrament According to the Theologians, ca. 1080–ca. 1220.* Oxford: Clarendon, 1984.

Mann, Frido. *Das Abendmahl beim jungen Luther.* Beiträge zur ökumenischen Theologie 5. Munich: Hueber, 1971.

Martin, Max Wilhelm. *Johann Landtsperger: Die unter diesem Namen gehenden Schriften und ihre Verfasser.* Augsburg: Lampart, 1902.

Massa, Willi. *Die Eucharistiepredigt am Vorabend der Reformation. Eine material-kerygmatische Untersuchung zum Glaubensverständnis von Altarssakrament und Messe am Beginn des 16. Jahrhunderts als Beitrag zur Geschichte der Predigt.* Veröffentlichungen des Missionspriesterseminars St. Augustine, Siegburg 15. St. Augustin: Steyler Verlag, 1966.

Matous, Frantisek. "Johannes Hus in den Schweizer Chroniken des 15. und 16. Jahrhunderts." In *Jan Hus. Zwischen Zeiten, Völkern, Konfessionen. Vorträge des internationalen Symposions in Bayreuth vom 22. bis 26. September 1993*, ed. Ferdinand Seibt, 367–374. Munich: Oldenbourg, 1997.

McCue, James F. "The Doctrine of Transubstantiation from Berengar through Trent: The Point at Issue." *Harvard Theological Review* 61 (1968): 385–430.

McLaughlin, R. Emmet. *Caspar Schwenckfeld, Reluctant Radical: His Life to 1540.* Yale Historical Publications Miscellany, 134. New Haven, Conn.: Yale University Press, 1986.

——— . "The Genesis of Schwenckfeld's Eucharistic Doctrine." *Archiv für Reformationsgeschichte* 74 (1983): 94–121.

——— . "Reformation Spiritualism: Typology, Sources and Significance." In *Radikalität und Dissent im 16. Jahrhundert/Radicalism and Dissent in the Sixteenth Century*, ed. James M. Stayer and Hans-Jürgen Goertz. Berlin: Duncker & Humblot, 2002.

McNiel, William Wallace. "Andreas von Karlstadt and Thomas Muentzer: Relatives in Theology and Reformation." Ph.D. diss., Queen's University, 1999.

Menzel, Michael. "Predigt und Predigtorganisation im Mittelalter." *Historisches Jahrbuch* 111 (1991): 337–384.

Modestin, Georg. "'Dass sie unserer Stadt und diesem Land grosse Schmach und Unehre zugefügt haben.' Der Strassburger Waldenserprozess von 1400 und seine Vorgeschichte." In *Friedrich Reiser und die "waldensisch-hussitische Internationale" im 15. Jahrhundert. Akten der Tagung Ötisheim-Schönenberg, 2. bis 4. Oktober 2003*, ed. Albert de Lange and Kathrin Utz Tremp, 189–204. Heidelberg: Verlag Regionalkultur, 2006.

Moeller, Bernd. "Die Rezeption Luthers in der frühen Reformation." In *Reformationstheorien: Ein kirchenhistorischer Disput über Einheit und Vielfalt der Reformation*, ed. Bernd Moeller et al., 9–29. Göttingen: Vandenhoeck & Ruprecht, 1995.

——— . "Was Wurde in der Frühzeit der Reformation in den deutschen Städten Gepredigt?" *Archiv für Reformationsgeschichte* 75 (1984): 176–193.

Molnár, Amedeo. "Bekenntnisse der böhmischen Reformation." *Jahrbuch für die Geschichte des Protestantismus in Österreich* 96 (1980): 310–332.

——— . "L'évolution de la théologie hussite." *Revue d'histoire et de philosophie religieuses* 43 (1963): 133–171.

————. "Luthers Beziehungen zu den Böhmischen Brüdern." In *Leben und Werk Martin Luthers von 1526 bis 1546. Festgabe zu seinem 500. Geburtstag*, ed. Helmar Junghans, 1: 627–639. Göttingen: Vandenhoeck & Ruprecht, 1983.

————. *Die Waldenser. Geschichte und europäisches Ausmaß einer Ketzerbewegung*. Göttingen: Vandenhoeck & Ruprecht, 1980.

Mühlpfordt, Günter. "Luther und die 'Linken.' Eine Untersuchung seiner Schwärmerterminologie." In *Martin Luther. Leben—Werk—Wirkung*, ed. Günter Vogler, 325–345. Berlin: Akademie Verlag, 1986.

Müller, Joseph Th. "Die böhmische Brüderunität und Zwingli." *Zwingliana* 3 (1920): 514–524.

Müller, Karl. *Luther und Karlstadt: Stücke aus ihrem gegenseitigen Verhältnis*. Tübingen: Mohr, 1907.

Müsing, Hans-Werner. "Karlstadt und die Strasbourger Täufergemeinde." In *Origins and Characteristics of Anabaptism*, ed. Marc Lienhard, 169–195. The Hague: Martinus Nijhoff, 1977.

Neuser, Wilhelm H. *Die Abendmahlslehre Melanchthons in ihrer geschichtlichen Entwicklung (1519–1530)*. Beiträge zur Geschichte und Lehre der Reformierten Kirche 26. Neukirchen-Vluyn: Neukirchener Verlag, 1968.

————. "Bucers konfessionelle Position." In *Martin Bucer and Sixteenth Century Europe: Actes du colloque de Strasbourg, 28–31 août 1991*, ed. Christian Krieger and Marc Lienhard, 693–704. Studies in Medieval and Reformation Thought 52–53. Leiden: Brill, 1993.

————. "Martin Bucer als Mittler im Abendmahlsstreit (1530/31)." In *Kaum zu Glauben. Von der Häresie und dem Umgang mit ihr*, ed. Athina Lexutt and Vicco von Bülow, 140–161. Rheinbach: CMZ-Verlag, 1998.

Oehmig, Stefan. "Die Wittenberger Bewegung 1521/22 und ihre Folgen im Lichte alter und neuer Fragestellungen. Ein Beitrag zum Thema (Territorial-) Stadt und Reformation." In *700 Jahre Wittenberg. Stadt, Universität, Reformation*, ed. Stefan Oehmig, 97–130. Weimar: Herman Böhlaus Nachfolger, 1995.

Padberg, Rudolf. "Luther und der Canon Missae." *Catholica* 37 (1983): 288–305.

Pater, Calvin. *Karlstadt as Father of the Baptist Movements: The Emergence of Lay Protestantism*. Toronto: University of Toronto Press, 1984.

Payne, John B. *Erasmus: His Theology of the Sacraments*. Richmond, Va.: John Knox Press, 1970.

Penn, Stephen. "Wyclif and the Sacraments." In *A Companion to John Wyclif, Late Medieval Theologian*, ed. Ian Christopher Levy, 241–291. Leiden: Brill, 2006.

Peschke, Erhard. "Die Bedeutung Wiclefs für die Theologie der Böhmen." *Zeitschrift für Kirchengeschichte* 54 (1935): 462–483.

————. *Die Böhmischen Brüder im Urteil ihrer Zeit; Zieglers, Dungersheims und Luthers Kritik an der Brüderunität*. Arbeiten zur Theologie, 1. Reihe 17. Stuttgart: Calwer Verlag, 1964.

————. *Die Theologie der böhmischen Brüder in ihrer Frühzeit*. Vol. 1, *Das Abendmahl*. 2 vols. Forschungen zur Kirchen- und Geistesgeschichte 5. Stuttgart: Kohlhammer, 1935.

Peter, Rodolph. "Le Jardinier Clément Ziegler, l'homme et son oeuvre." *Revue d'histoire et de philosophie religieuses* 34 (1954): 255–282.

Peters, Christian. "Luthers Einfluß auf die frühreformatorische städtische Predigt: Das Beispiel des Ulmer Kaplans Johann Diepold (gest. vor 1539)." In *Luthers Wirkung: Festschrift für Martin Brecht zum 60. Geburtstag*, ed. W.-D. Hauschild et al., 111–133. Stuttgart: Calwer, 1992.

Pocock, J. G. A. *The Machiavellian Moment: Florentine Political Thought and the Atlantic Republican Tradition*. Princeton: Princeton University Press, 1975.

Pollet, J. V. *Huldrych Zwingli et le Zwinglianisme. Essai de synthèse historique et théologique mis à jour d'après les recherches récentes.* Paris: Vrin, 1988.

Ponader, Ralf. "Die Abendmahlslehre des Andreas Bodenstein von Karlstadt in den Jahren 1521–1524: die Kritik an der Realpräsenz durch Karlstadt untersucht vor dem Hintergrund der Chorismos-Problematik." Ph.D. diss., Universität Greifswald, 1993.

————. "'Caro nichil prodest. Joan. vi. Das fleisch ist nicht nutz/ sonder der geist.' Karlstadts Abendmahlsverständnis in der Auseinandersetzung mit Martin Luther." In *Andreas Bodenstein von Karlstadt (1486–1541): Ein Theologe der frühen Reformation. Beiträge eines Arbeitsgesprächs vom 24.–25. November 1995 in Wittenberg,* ed. Sigrid Looß and Markus Matthias, 223–245. Wittenberg: Drei Kastanien Verlag, 1998.

Preus, James S. *Carlstadt's "Ordinaciones" and Luther's Liberty: A Study of the Wittenberg Movement 1521–22.* Harvard Theological Studies 27. Cambridge, Mass.: Harvard University Press, 1974.

Rapp, Francis. "Notes sur l'eucharistie à la veille de la Réformation: ce que nous apprennent quelques documents sur la communion." *Revue d'histoire et de philosophie religieuses* 85 (2005): 5–16.

Roloff, Hans-Gert. "Die Funktion von Hus-Texten in der Reformations-Polemik (Erster Teil)." In *De captu lectoris. Wirkungen des Buches im 15. und 16. Jahrhundert, dargestellt an ausgewählten Handschriften und Drucken,* ed. Wolfgang Milde and Werner Schuder, 219–256. Berlin: de Gruyter, 1988.

Rüger, Hans Peter. "Karlstadt als Hebraist an der Universität Wittenberg." *Archiv für Reformationsgeschichte* 75 (1984): 297–308.

Rummel, Erika. *Erasmus' Annotations on the New Testament: From Philologist to Theologian.* Toronto: University of Toronto Press, 1986.

Rupp, E. Gordon. *Patterns of Reformation.* Philadelphia: Fortress, 1969.

Sanders, Paul. "Heinrich Bullinger et le 'zwinglianisme tardif' aux lendemains du 'Consensus Tigurinus.'" In *Reformiertes Erbe. Festschrift für Gottfried W. Locher zu seinem 80. Geburtstag,* ed. Heiko A. Oberman et al., 307–323. Zurich: Theologische Verlag, 1992.

Sasse, Hermann. *This Is My Body: Luther's Contention for the Real Presence in the Sacrament of the Altar.* Minneapolis, Minn.: Augsburg, 1959.

Schantz, Douglas H. *Crautwald and Erasmus: A Study in Humanism and Radical Reform in Sixteenth Century Silesia.* Bibliotheca Dissidentium Scripta et Studia 4. Baden-Baden: Koerner, 1992.

Scheible, Heinz. *Melanchthon. Eine Biographie.* Munich: Beck, 1997.

Schmidt, Heinrich R. "Die Häretisierung des Zwinglianismus im Reich seit 1525." In *Zugänge zur bäuerlichen Reformation,* ed. Peter Blickle, 219–236. Zurich: Chronos, 1987.

————. *Reichstädte, Reich und Reformation: Korporative Religionspolitik 1521–1529/30.* Veröffentlichungen des Instituts für europäische Geschichte Mainz 122. Stuttgart: Steiner, 1986.

Schmidt, Martin Anton. "Karlstadt als Theologe und Prediger in Basel." *Theologische Zeitschrift* 35 (1979): 155–168.

Schneider, Martin. "Friedrich Reiser—Herkunft, Berufung und Weg." In *Friedrich Reiser und die "waldensisch-hussitische Internationale" im 15. Jahrhundert. Akten der Tagung Ötisheim-Schönenberg, 2. bis 4. Oktober 2003,* ed. Albert de Lange and Kathrin Utz Tremp, 75–86. Heidelberg: Verlag Regionalkultur, 2006.

Schottenloher, Karl. *Die Buchdruckertätigkeit Georg Erlingers in Bamberg von 1522 bis 1541 (1543).* Sammlung bibliothekswissenschaftlicher Arbeiten 21. Leipzig: Haupt, 1907.

————. *Philipp Ulhart: ein Augsburger Winkeldrucker und Helfershelfer der "Schwärmer" und "Wiedertäufer" (1523–1529)*. Historische Forschungen 4. Nieuwkoop: de Graaf, 1967.

Schwab, Wolfgang. *Entwicklung und Gestalt der Sakramentstheologie bei Martin Luther*. Europäische Hochschulschriften: Reihe 23, Theologie 79. Frankfurt am Main: Lang, 1977.

Schwarz, Reinhard. "Abendmahlsgemeinschaft durch das Evangelium, obwohl der Tisch des Herrn 'durch menschliche Irrung versperrt ist.'" *Lutherjahrbuch* 59 (1992): 38–78.

————. "The Last Supper: The Testament of Jesus." *Lutheran Quarterly* 9 (1995): 391–403.

Scribner, Robert W. "Popular Piety and Modes of Visual Perception in Late Medieval and Reformation Germany." In Scribner, *Religion and Culture in Germany (1400–1800)*, ed. Lyndal Roper, 104–128. Studies in Medieval and Reformation Thought 81. Leiden: Brill, 2001.

Segl, Peter. "Die Auswirkungen der hussitischen Bewegung auf Europa." In *Reformer als Ketzer: Heterodoxe Bewegungen von Vorreformatoren*, ed. Günter Frank and Friedrich Niewöhner, 197–213. Stuttgart/Bad Cannstatt: Frommann-Holzboog, 2004.

Seibt, Ferdinand. *Hussitica. Zur Struktur einer Revolution*. Cologne: Böhlau, 1965.

Sider, Ronald J. *Andreas Bodenstein von Karlstadt: The Development of His Thought, 1517–1525*. Studies in Medieval and Reformation Thought 11. Leiden: Brill, 1974.

Simon, Wolfgang. "Karlstadt neben Luther. Ihre theologische Differenz im Kontext der 'Wittenberger Unruhen' 1521/22." In *Frömmigkeit, Theologie, Frömmigkeitstheologie: Contributions to European Church History. Festschrift für Berndt Hamm zum 60. Geburtstag*, ed. Gudrun Litz et al., 317–334. Studies in the History of Christian Traditions 124. Leiden: Brill, 2005.

————. *Die Messopfertheologie Martin Luthers. Voraussetzungen, Genese, Gestalt und Rezeption*. Spätmittelalter und Reformation, Neue Reihe 22. Tübingen: Mohr Siebeck, 2003.

Skinner, Quentin. *Visions of Politics*. Vol. 1. *Regarding Method*. Cambridge: Cambridge University Press, 2002.

Smahel, Frantisek. *Die Hussitische Revolution*. Translated by Thomas Krzenck. 3 vols. MGA Schriften 43. Hannover: Hahnsche Buchhandlung, 2002.

Spinka, Matthew. "Peter Chelčický: The Spiritual Father of the Unitas Fratrum." *Church History* 12 (1943): 271–291.

Spruyt, Bart Jan. *Cornelius Henrici Hoen (Honius) and His Epistle on the Eucharist (1525)*. Studies in Medieval and Reformation Traditions 119. Leiden: Brill, 2006.

————. "Das Echo des Jan Hus und der hussitischen Bewegung in den burgundischen Niederlanden, ca. 1420–ca. 1530." In *Jan Hus. Zwischen Zeiten, Völkern, Konfessionen. Vorträge des internationalen Symposions in Bayreuth vom 22. bis 26. September 1993*, ed. Ferdinand Seibt, 283–301. Munich: Oldenbourg, 1997.

Staedtke, Joachim. *Die Theologie des jungen Bullinger*. Studien zur Dogmengeschichte und systematischen Theologie 16. Zurich: Zwingli-Verlag, 1962.

————. "Voraussetzungen der Schweizer Abendmahlslehre." *Theologische Zeitschrift* 16 (1960): 19–32.

Staehelin, Ernst. *Das theologische Lebenswerk Johannes Oekolampads*. Quellen und Forschungen zur Reformationsgeschichte. Leipzig: Heinsius, 1939.

Steinmetz, David C. "Scripture and the Lord's Supper in Luther's Theology." In Steinmetz, *Luther in Context*, 72–84. Grand Rapids, Mich.: Baker Academic, 2002.

Stephens, W. Peter. *The Theology of Huldrych Zwingli*. Oxford: Clarendon, 1986.

Strupl, Milos. "The Confessional Theology of the Unitas Fratrum." *Church History* 33 (1964): 279–293.

Székely, György. "Das Erbe von Jan Hus in der Reformation Martin Luthers." *Annales Universitatis Scientiarum Budapestinensis, sectio historica* 24 (1985): 3–21.

Thayer, Anne T. "Learning to Worship in the Later Middle Ages: Enacting Symbolism, Fighting the Devil, and Receiving Grace." *Archiv für Reformationsgeschichte* 99 (2008): 36–65.

Trapman, J. "Le rôle des 'sacramentaires' des origines de la Réforme jusq'en 1530 aux Pays-Bas." *Nederlands archief voor kerkgeschiedenis* 63 (1983): 1–24.

Vice, Roy L. "Ehrenfried Kumpf, Karlstadt's Patron and Peasants' War Rebel." *Archiv für Reformationsgeschichte* 85 (1996): 153–174.

––––. "Valentin Ickelsamer's Odyssey from Rebellion to Quietism." *Mennonite Quarterly Review* 69 (1995): 75–92.

Voet, Leon. *The Golden Compasses: A History and Evaluation of the Printing and Publishing Activities of the Officina Plantiniana at Antwerp in Two Volumes.* Amsterdam: Vangendt, 1972.

Vogler, Günter. *Nürnberg 1524–25: Studien zur Geschichte der reformatorischen und sozialen Bewegung in der Reichstadt.* Berlin: VEB, 1982.

Wandel, Lee Palmer. "Envisioning God: Image and Liturgy in Reformation Zurich." *Sixteenth Century Journal* 24 (1993): 21–40.

––––. *The Eucharist in the Reformation: Incarnation and Liturgy.* Cambridge: Cambridge University Press, 2006.

Watkins, Oscar D. *A History of Penance, Being a Study of the Authorities.* 2 vols. New York: Franklin, 1961.

Weigelt, Horst. *Spiritualistische Tradition im Protestantismus: Die Geschichte des Schwenckfeldertums in Schlesien.* Berlin: de Gruyter, 1973.

Wendebourg, Dorothea. *Essen zum Gedächtnis: Der Gedächtnisbefehl in den Abendmahlstheologien der Reformation.* Beiträge zur historischen Theologie 148. Tübingen: Mohr Siebeck, 2009.

Wetzel, Richard. "Melanchthon und Karlstadt im Spiegel von Melanchthons Briefwechsel." In *Andreas Bodenstein von Karlstadt (1486–1541): Ein Theologe der frühen Reformation. Beiträge eines Arbeitsgesprächs vom 24.–25. November 1995 in Wittenberg,* ed. Sigrid Looß and Markus Matthias, 159–222. Wittenberg: Drei Kastanien Verlag, 1998.

Williams, George Huntston. *The Radical Reformation.* 3rd ed. Sixteenth Century Essays and Studies 15. Kirksville, Mo.: Sixteenth Century Journal Publishers, 1992.

Wislöff, Carl Fr. *Abendmahl und Messe: Die Kritik Luthers am Meßopfer.* Arbeiten zur Geschichte und Theologie des Luthertums 22. Berlin: Lutherisches Verlaghaus, 1969.

Zeman, Jarold K. *The Anabaptists and the Czech Brethren in Moravia 1526–1628: A Study of Origins and Contacts.* Studies in European History 20. The Hague: Mouton, 1969.

Zorzin, Alejandro. *Karlstadt als Flugschriftenautor.* Göttinger theologische Arbeiten 48. Göttingen: Vandenhoeck & Ruprecht, 1990.

––––. "Zur Wirkungsgeschichte einer Schrift aus Karlstadts Orlamünder Tätigkeit. Der 1527 in Worms gedruckte 'Dialog vom fremden Glauben, Glauben der Kirche, Taufe der Kinder.' Fortsetzung einer Diskussion." In *Andreas Bodenstein von Karlstadt (1486–1541): Ein Theologe der frühen Reformation. Beiträge eines Arbeitsgesprächs vom 24.–25. November 1995 in Wittenberg,* ed. Sigrid Looß and Markus Matthias, 143–158. Wittenberg: Drei Kastanien Verlag, 1998.

Zschoch, Hellmut. *Reformatorische Existenz und konfessionelle Identität. Urbanus Rhegius als evangelischer Theologe in den Jahren 1520 bis 1530.* Beiträge zur historische Theologie 88. Tübingen: Mohr, 1995.

INDEX OF NAMES, PLACES AND SUBJECTS

233